THE RELIGIOUS WORLD OF JESUS

THE
RELIGIOUS WORLD
OF
JESUS

AN INTRODUCTION TO SECOND
TEMPLE PALESTINIAN JUDAISM

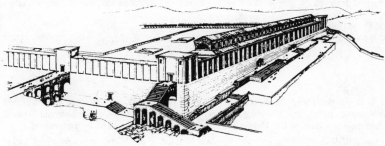

FREDERICK J.
MURPHY

ABINGDON PRESS
Nashville

THE RELIGIOUS WORLD OF JESUS: AN INTRODUCTION TO
SECOND TEMPLE PALESTINIAN JUDAISM

Copyright © 1991 by Abingdon Press

This book is printed on recycled, acid-free paper.

Library of Congress Cataloging-in-Publication Data

Murphy, Frederick James.
    The religious world of Jesus : an introduction to Second Temple Palestinian Judaism / Frederick
J. Murphy.
        p.   cm.
    Includes bibliographical references and index.
    ISBN 0-687-36049-8
    1. Jews—History—To 70 A.D. 2. Judaism—History—To 70 A.D. 3. Bible. O.T.—Criti-
cism, interpretation, etc. 4. Dead Sea scrolls—Criticism, interpretation, etc. 5. Jesus Christ.
I. Title.
DS117.M88   1991
296'.09'014—dc20   90-21922
                                                                                           CIP

Quotations from the Bible and the Apocrypha, except where noted, are from the New Revised
    Standard Version, copyright 1989 by the Division of Christian Education of the National Council
    of the Churches of Christ in the United States of America and are used by permission.

Quotations noted RSV are from the Revised Standard Version of the Bible, copyright 1946, 1952,
    1971 by the Division of Christian Education of the National Council of Churches of Christ in the
    U.S.A. Used by permission.

All quotations from *1 Enoch,* the *Testament of Moses (Assumption of Moses),* the *Psalms of
    Solomon,* and *2 Baruch* are from R. H. Charles, *The Apocrypha and Pseudepigrapha of the Old
    Testament,* vol. 2, Oxford: Clarendon Press, 1913. Quotations are adapted in places.

All quotations from the Qumran literature are taken from Geza Vermes, *The Dead Sea Scrolls in
    English,* 3rd ed., London: Penguin, 1987. Copyright © G. Vermes, 1962, 1965, 1968, 1975,
    1987; reproduced by permission of Penguin Books.

All quotations from Josephus are taken from the 9-volume edition of the Loeb Classical Library.
    Reprinted by permission of the publishers and the Loeb Classical Library from JOSEPHUS, vols.
    1-3 and 7-9; translators: H. St. J. Thackeray (vols. 1-3); Ralph Marcus (7); R. Marcus and Allen
    Wikgren (8); and L. H. Feldman (9). Cambridge, Mass.: Harvard University Press, 1926, 1927,
    1928, 1933, 1963, 1965.

The maps of Jerusalem and of Palestine are reprinted from *Israel in Revolution* by David Rhoads,
    copyright © 1976. Used by permission of Augsburg Fortress.

For my mother, Hazel Louise Murphy,
of blessed memory.
Through a long and cruel illness,
she showed us the meaning of courage.

CONTENTS

CONTENTS

CONTENTS

CONTENTS

PART II: SECOND TEMPLE JUDAISM IN PALESTINE

CONTENTS

CONTENTS

CONTENTS

CONTENTS

CONTENTS

PART III: CHRISTIAN INTERPRETATIONS, JEWISH ROOTS

PART IV: NOTES, GLOSSARY, INDEX

ABBREVIATIONS

AB: The Anchor Bible, Garden City, N.Y.: Doubleday

AI: John J. Collins, *The Apocalyptic Imagination: An Introduction to the Jewish Matrix of Christianity*, New York: Crossroad, 1984

AMW: David Hellhom, *Apocalypticism in the Mediterranean World and the Near East: Proceedings of the International Colloquium on Apocalypticism, Uppsala, August 12-17, 1979*, Tübingen: Mohr, 1983

ANRW: *Aufstieg und Niedergang der römischen Welt*, W. Haase and H. Temporini, eds., Berlin: de Gruyter

Ant.:   Josephus, *Jewish Antiquities*

APOT: R. H. Charles, ed., *The Apocrypha and Pseudepigrapha of the Old Testament*, vol. 2, Oxford: Clarendon Press, 1913

BASOR: *Bulletin of the American Schools of Oriental Research*

BBT: Donald Gowan, *Bridge Between the Testaments: A Reappraisal of Judaism from the Exile to the Birth of Christianity*, 3rd ed., rev., Allison Park, Pa.: Pickwick, 1986.

BCE: Before the Common Era

BJRL: *Bulletin of the John Rylands University Library of Manchester*

BR: *Biblical Research*

BTB: *Biblical Theology Bulletin*

CBA: Catholic Biblical Association of America

CBQ: *Catholic Biblical Quarterly*

CBQMS: Catholic Biblical Quarterly—Monograph Series

CD: *Damascus Document*

CE: Common Era

CH: *Chronicler's History*

ABBREVIATIONS

Compendia:	S. Safrai and M. Stern, eds., *The Jewish People in the First Century,* Compendia rerum iudaicarum ad Novum Testamentum, 2 vols., Assen: van Gorcum, 1974, 1975
DSSE:	Geza Vermes, *The Dead Sea Scrolls in English,* 3rd ed., London: Penguin Books, 1987
DtrH:	Deuteronomistic History
E:	The Elohist source of the Pentateuch
EJMI:	Robert A. Kraft and George W. E. Nickelsburg, eds., *Early Judaism and Its Modern Interpreters,* Atlanta: Scholars Press, 1986
HB:	Norman K. Gottwald, *The Hebrew Bible: A Socio-Literary Introduction,* Philadelphia: Fortress Press, 1985.
HBD:	*Harper's Bible Dictionary*
HeyJ:	*Heythrop Journal*
HI:	John Bright, *A History of Israel,* 3rd. ed., Philadelphia: Westminster Press, 1981.
HJPAJC:	Emil Schürer, *The History of the Jewish People in the Age of Jesus Christ (175 B.C.–A.D. 135),* 3 vols., G. Vermes, F. Millar, and M. Black, revisers and eds., Edinburgh: T. & T. Clark, 1973–87
HR:	*History of Religions*
HSM:	Harvard Semitic Monographs
HTR:	*Harvard Theological Review*
HUCA:	*Hebrew Union College Annual*
IB:	*The Interpreter's Bible,* Nashville/New York: Abingdon-Cokesbury Press, 1952
IDB:	G. A. Buttrick, ed., *The Interpreter's Dictionary of the Bible,* New York/Nashville: Abingdon Press, 1962
IDBSup:	Keith Crim, ed., *The Interpreter's Dictionary of the Bible: Supplementary Volume,* Nashville: Abingdon, 1976
IFAJ:	George W. E. Nickelsburg and John J. Collins, eds., *Ideal Figures in Ancient Judaism,* Chico, Calif.: Scholars Press, 1980
J:	The Yahwist source of the Pentateuch
JBL:	*Journal of Biblical Literature*
JHT:	Hans Jürgen Schultz, ed., *Jesus in His Time,* Philadelphia: Fortress Press, 1971
JLBBM:	George W. E. Nickelsburg, *Jewish Literature Between the Bible and the Mishnah: A Historical and Literary Introduction,* Philadelphia: Fortress Press, 1981
JR:	*Journal of Religion*

ABBREVIATIONS

JSJ:	*Journal for the Study of Judaism in the Persian, Hellenistic, and Roman Period*
JTS:	*Journal of Theological Studies*
JWSTP:	Michael Stone, ed. *Jewish Writings of the Second Temple Period,* Philadelphia: Fortress Press, 1984
NJBC:	Raymond E. Brown, Joseph A. Fitzmyer, Roland E. Murphy, eds., *The New Jerome Biblical Commentary,* Englewood Cliffs, N.J.: Prentice-Hall, 1990
NTS:	*New Testament Studies*
OTP:	James H. Charlesworth, ed., *The Old Testament Pseudepigrapha,* 2 vols., Garden City, N.Y.: Doubleday, 1983–85
OTT:	Gerhard von Rad, *Old Testament Theology,* London: S.C.M. Press, 1965
P:	The Priestly source of the Pentateuch
Pss. Sol.:	*Psalms of Solomon*
1QS:	*Community Rule*
4QTest:	(4Q175) *Messianic Anthology* or *Testimonia*
1QSa:	*Messianic Rule*
1QM and 4QM:	*War Rule*
4QpNah:	(4Q169) *Commentary on Nahum*
1QpHab:	*Commentary on Habakkuk*
1QpPs37:	*Commentary on Psalm 37*
1QH:	*Thanksgiving Hymns*
RB:	*Revue biblique*
RelSRev:	*Religious Studies Review*
RevQ:	*Revue de Qumran*
SBLDS:	Society of Biblical Literature Dissertation Series
SBT:	Studies in Biblical Theology
SSV:	Michael Stone, *Scriptures, Sects, and Visions: A Profile of Judaism from Ezra to the Jewish Revolts,* Philadelphia: Fortress Press, 1980
UOT:	Bernhard Anderson, *Understanding the Old Testament,* 4th ed. Englewood Cliffs, N.J.: Prentice-Hall, 1986
VT:	*Vetus Testamentum*
War:	Josephus, *Jewish War*

CHRONOLOGY

Some of these dates are approximate.

Before the Common Era

18th–17th centuries	Abraham and the patriarchs.
1280	Exodus.
13th century	Entry into the land.
1200–1020	Period of the judges.
1020–587	Period of the monarchy.
1000–961	Reign of David.
961–922	Reign of Solomon.
922	Split of the kingdom into Israel and Judah.
722	Fall of the northern kingdom to Assyria.
587	Fall of Jerusalem to the Babylonians; beginning of the Babylonian Exile.
538	Cyrus' edict allowing Jews to return to Judah.
520–515	Building of the Second Temple.
445	Nehemiah's first mission.
398	Ezra's mission.
333	Alexander the Great's first important victory over the Persians.
3rd century	Ptolemaic control of Palestine.
198	The Seleucid Antiochus III takes Palestine.
175	Hellenistic Reform in Jerusalem.
167	Antiochus IV persecutes the Jews; Maccabean Revolt.
164	Death of Antiochus IV.
161	Death of Judas Maccabeus.
152	Jonathan, brother of Judas, appointed high priest.
150	Founding of the Qumran community.

142	Jonathan killed; Simon succeeds him.
140	Simon named high priest by the Jews.
134–104	John Hyrcanus, son of Simon, rules as high priest and conquers much territory.
128	Destruction of the Samaritan temple by John Hyrcanus.
104–103	Aristobulus, son of Hyrcanus, rules; takes royal title.
103–76	Reign of Alexander Jannaeus.
76–67	Reign of Jannaeus' wife, Alexandra Salome.
67–40	Reign of Hyrcanus II, Alexandra's son.
63	Pompey takes Jerusalem.
48–47	Hezekiah the bandit operates in Galilee.
40	Parthians take Jerusalem and appoint a Hasmonean as high priest.
37–4	Reign of Herod the Great.

The Common Era

31 BCE–14 CE	Augustus reigns as Roman emperor.
4 BCE–6 CE	Archelaus reigns in Judea.
4 BCE	Revolts of Judas son of Hezekiah, Athronges, and Simon.
4 BCE–39 CE	Herod Antipas rules in Galilee and Perea.
4 BCE–34 CE	Philip rules in Gaulanitis, Trachonitis, etc.
6 CE	Tax Revolt of Judas the Galilean
6 CE–41	Roman procurators administer Judea.
14–37	Tiberius reigns as Roman emperor.
26–36	Pontius Pilate is procurator.
20s or 30s	Incident of the Samaritan prophet.
late 20s	Ministry of John the Baptist.
30–33	Ministry of Jesus of Nazareth.
37–41	Gaius (Caligula) reigns as Roman emperor.
37	Agrippa I becomes king of Philip's territory.
41	Agrippa I receives Judea as part of his kingdom.
41–54	Claudius reigns as Roman emperor.
44	Death of Agrippa I.
44–46	Fadus is procurator of Palestine.
45	Theudas' prophetic activity.
46–48	Tiberius Alexander is procurator of Palestine.
48–52	Cumanus is procurator of Palestine.
52–60	Felix is procurator of Palestine.
53–100	Agrippa II reigns.
54–68	Nero reigns as Roman emperor
56	Incident of the Egyptian Jewish prophet.
60–62	Festus is procurator of Palestine.
62–64	Albinus is procurator of Palestine.
62–69	Prophetic activity of Jesus son of Hananiah.

CHRONOLOGY

64–66	Florus is procurator of Palestine.
66	The Jewish revolt against Rome begins.
69–79	Vespasian reigns as Roman emperor.
70	The destruction of Jerusalem and the Second Temple.
74	The fall of Masada.
79–81	Titus reigns as Roman emperor.
81–96	Domitian reigns as Roman emperor.
96–98	Nerva reigns as Roman emperor.
98–117	Trajan reigns as Roman emperor.
117–138	Hadrian reigns as Roman emperor.
132–135	The second Jewish revolt against Rome.
200	Editing of the Mishnah.

PALESTINE

SYRIA

Berytus

Chalcis

COELE-SYRIA

6290

Abila

Sidon

ABILENE

9190

Damascus

Sarepta

PHOENICIA

Tyre

ITUREA

Caesarea Philippi

4190

GAULANITIS

TRACHONITIS

Gischala
3995

Ptolemais

GALILEE

Capernaum

Sea of Galilee

690

Carmaim

Jotapata

Gamala

Tiberias

Sepphoris

Cana?

Hippos

Abila

1840

Nazareth

1870

Gadara

Doro

Nain

DECAPOLIS

Caesarea

Scythopolis

Pella

SAMARIA

Salem

Aenon?

Sebaste

5030

Gerasa

3125

Shechem

Amata

2890

Alexandrium

Acrabatta

Phasaelis

Joppa

Antipatris

Gador

Thamna

Gophna

Ephraim

Philadelphia

Lydda

Modein

Archelais

JUDEA

Jericho

Jamnia

2725

Bethabara

Esbus

Emmaus

Jerusalem

Bethany

Livias

Ashdod

Qumran

2685

3310

Hyrcania

Ascalon

Bethlehem

Herodium

Bethsura

Machaerus

Dibon

Gaza

3420

Hebron

Engaddi

3520

IDUMEA

Masada

Aeropolis

800

Beersheba

Zoar

Nabateans

Mediterranean Sea

SHARON

Jordan

Dead Sea -1300

0   25 miles

Under Archelaus - 4 B. C. - 6 A. D.
and Procurators - 6 - 41 A. D.

Under Herod Antipas
4 B. C. - 39 A. D.

Under Philippus
4 B. C. - 34 A. D.

All under Agrippa I - 41 - 44 A. D.
and the Procurators - 44 - 66 A. D.

JERUSALEM

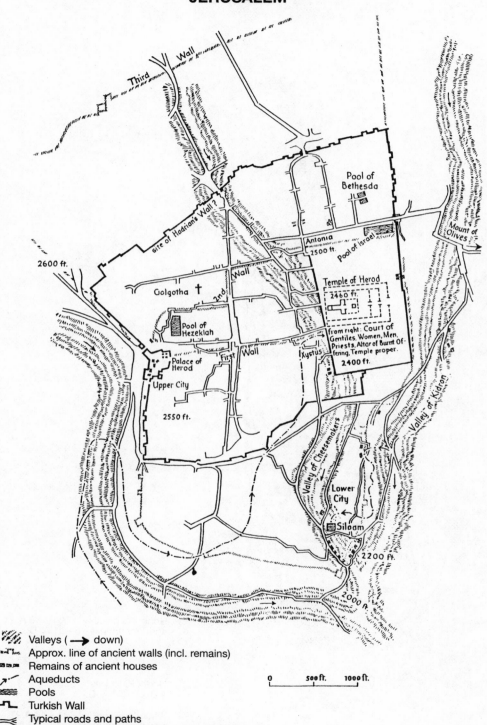

Valleys (→ down)

Approx. line of ancient walls (incl. remains)

Remains of ancient houses

Aqueducts

Pools

Turkish Wall

Typical roads and paths
(Access roads added in the modern period)

Labels within map:

Third Wall

site of Hadrian's Wall ?

Pool of Bethesda

Antonia 2500 ft.

Pool of Israel

Mount of Olives

2600 ft.

2nd Wall

Golgotha

Temple of Herod
2460 ft.

Pool of Hezekiah

from right: Court of Gentiles, Women, Men, Priests, Altar of Burnt Offering, Temple proper.
2400 ft.

Palace of Herod

First Wall

Kystus

Upper City

2550 ft.

Valley of Cheesemakers

Valley of Kidron

Lower City

Siloam

2200 ft.

2000 ft.

0   500 ft.   1000 ft.

26

THE JERUSALEM TEMPLE

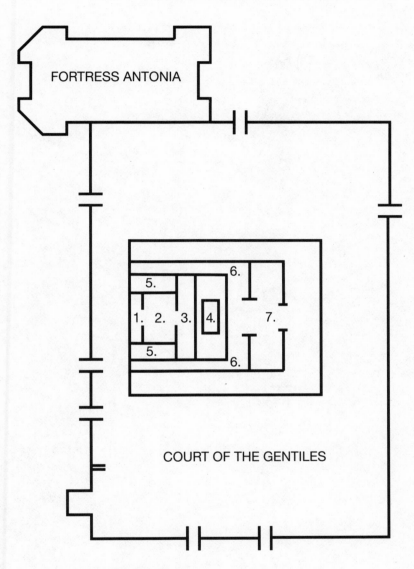

FORTRESS ANTONIA

COURT OF THE GENTILES

1. Holy of Holies
2. Holy Place
3. Porch
4. Altar
5. Court of Priests
6. Men's Court
7. Women's Court

PREFACE

One often hears that understanding the New Testament requires appreciation of the Hebrew Bible. True as that may be, it does not tell the whole story. In fact there is a considerable hiatus between the writing of the latest book included in the Hebrew Bible, Daniel (ca. 165 BCE), and the earliest book of the New Testament, 1 Thessalonians (ca. 50 CE). That interim period is crucial for comprehending a whole range of issues of great interest to Jews and Christians alike.

In my teaching of undergraduates at Holy Cross, I found that I needed to go beyond teaching the usual "Old Testament" and "New Testament" courses in order to give the students a wider view of Judaism in the late Second Temple period. Hebrew Bible courses stop the story of Israel before it really provides the social and theological matrix for early rabbinic Judaism and early Christianity. New Testament courses, even when they try to provide "Jewish background," can reinforce negative stereotypes of Jews and Jewish society that have deep roots in Christian traditions. They can also fail to give a balanced picture of Jesus the Jew, since the New Testament is primarily interested in his uniqueness.

To deal with these problems, I devised an introductory course on Second Temple Judaism in Palestine. The course examined Second Temple Judaism for its own sake, not concentrating exclusively on topics of special interest to Christians, but dealing with those topics as they occurred in the subject matter. ·At the end of the course, there was an investigation of the historical Jesus, and a look at Jewish elements in some important early Christian interpretations of Jesus, those of Matthew (Jesus as teacher of Torah), Hebrews (Jesus as High Priest), and Revelation (Jesus as eschatological warrior and judge). I found that this course was of great help in dealing with Christian denigration of Judaism and in appreciating Jesus as a Jew of his time.

No single text was satisfactory for the course. Students read a wide variety of primary and secondary sources, but there was no work that could tie everything together in a way appropriate for undergraduates. What was needed was a work combining analysis of primary sources, historical overview, treatment of special topics, and presentation of some of the more helpful aspects of recent research, all in a form accessible to introductory level students. I have written this book to fill that gap.

The book has been designed to be convenient for teachers and students. At the beginning of each chapter is a list of primary readings. In some cases, that list is too long to be read by students in its entirety. The chapters provide guidance to the primary works and analyses of some of their crucial passages, but teachers are encouraged to make the primary readings more specific, to accord with their needs and interests. A chief goal of the course is to foster familiarity with the primary texts, and work both in class and out of class should consist largely of reading those sources critically. Unlike standard fare in courses in Hebrew Bible and New Testament, a number of extracanonical works are given detailed attention. They include *1 Enoch,* many Qumran texts, Josephus, *The Psalms of Solomon, The Testament of Moses,* 4 Ezra, and *2 Baruch.* Deuterocanonical texts treated are 1 and 2 Maccabees, and Sirach. Teachers are encouraged to add other texts as appropriate, such as *The Book of Jubilees* and *The Biblical Antiquities* of Pseudo-Philo. I regret that there was not more space to treat additional extracanonical texts here.

Each chapter contains a select bibliography that is more suggestive than exhaustive. Many of the entries in the bibliographies are very influential in the body of the chapter, as one familiar with them will observe, but extensive footnoting is avoided as unhelpful in an introductory work. References within the chapters to entries in the bibliographies are made by author's last name, and short title of the work if necessary. At the beginning of the book are a chronology and a list of abbreviations, and at the end are a glossary and a general index. The table of Contents is very detailed, and in combination with the Index it should enable readers to find their way around.

I have found that there is little background knowledge that can be taken for granted when teaching a course of this type. Chapters 1 and 3, "Preexilic Israel" and "The Exile," give the student a basic familiarity with key persons, events, and issues in preexilic and exilic Israel that are of special importance for Second Temple Judaism in Palestine. Students who have had a course in Hebrew Bible may find those chapters unnecessary, or they might use them for a quick review. Chapter 2, "Priestly Religion," spans preexilic, exilic, and postexilic Israel. It is placed before chapter 3 because the treatment of Ezekiel in the latter chapter presupposes the discussion of priestly religion.

Because I believe that language both reflects and influences thought, I have tried to use gender inclusive language consistently. Furthermore, except for instances in quotations, I have avoided the use of the male pronoun in referring to God, although that made for some awkwardness at times.

I am grateful for the constant support of my colleagues in the Department of Religious Studies at Holy Cross. Grants through Holy Cross's Committee on Professional Standards and the Committee for Research and Publication helped me substantially. I am thankful for frequent advice on computer-related matters by Joel Villa and Ken Scott of Holy Cross, and for the willing assistance of the college library staff. I owe profound thanks to Alice Laffey of Holy Cross, who read the entire manuscript. She spent countless hours making detailed comments on content, presentation, style, organization, and other matters. No one who knows Alice will be surprised at her unfailing and enthusiastic generosity. Other scholars also were very generous with their time and expertise. John J. Collins of Notre Dame read chapters 5, 6, and 7. John Esposito of Holy Cross read chapter 14. Bruce Malina of Creighton University read chapter 2. Gary Phillips of Holy Cross read chapters 1, 2, and 9. Anthony J. Saldarini of Boston College read chapter 8. The insightful comments of these scholars were invaluable, and the book is far better for their help. I also want to thank the Spencers, the O'Connells, the Ryans, the Tromblys, Jeffrey Trencher and Ruth Garvey, and Dennis Osborn and Elaine Bafaro for their support and friendship. They truly helped me keep a balanced view of the world as the work progressed. Special thanks go to my good friend Tom Spencer for the music. I cannot fail to mention my children, Rebecca and Jeremy. I did not always welcome their frequent interruptions during the researching and writing of this book. Now that the task is completed, I can see how their often delightful presence helped me to keep the important things in perspective. My wife, Leslie, has shown me a loving and constant support that I fear I take too much for granted. I hope that this public acknowledgment of her help makes up in some small degree for all that she has had to endure during this project. I thank my father, "James F.," and my sisters, Patricia and Debbie, who continue to support me in the strange roads I have taken. With love I dedicate this book to my mother, Hazel, whose loss we feel so deeply. Her example has always been and continues to be one of the guiding forces in my life.

INTRODUCTION

GOING BEYOND THE CANON

Most students interested in studying ancient Israel, Jesus Christ, Christian origins, or Scripture will choose a course named something like "Introduction to the Old Testament" or "Introduction to the New Testament." That would be a logical choice, because those courses examine foundational documents of Christianity and Judaism. "Foundational" means that the Hebrew Bible and the New Testament are the bases for the two religions.[1] But because those two collections of writings occupy such a privileged place in the two religions, it is problematic to study them in isolation from other evidence. One can too easily assume that the Bible supplies complete and accurate portrayals of the people, groups, institutions, and events of the ancient world. Historical study is necessary for developing a balanced understanding of the people behind the biblical texts and of the world they inhabited.

Texts contained in the New Testament and Hebrew Bible belong to the "canon." "Canon" comes from the Greek word *kanōn* meaning a reed of fixed length used for measuring. The canon of Judaism or Christianity is that body of writings accepted as authoritative and normative. Belief and practice are measured and judged by those writings. By choosing to include some writings in the canon and to exclude others from it, each religion has defined its own contours. The normativity of the included texts is expressed through the notion that they are "inspired," that is, that God is responsible for them in some way. There is a range of ways in which inspiration can be defined, from the idea that the writers of Scripture were inspired much as poets are, to the literalistic conviction that God dictated every word and letter. Belief in inspiration does not necessarily deny a substantial human role in the composition of Scripture.

Because it seeks appreciation of the world in which the Bible was written, this

33

book does not confine itself to the canon. The decision to include certain books in the canon meant the exclusion of others. Those other works offer evidence for what people did, thought, and felt in the ancient world, as well as for what their cultural, social, political, and economic institutions were like. Fortunately, there is a large body of extracanonical Jewish literature from the first century CE and preceding centuries.[2]

The original impetus for this book came from an interest in teaching about the world in which Jesus Christ lived, first-century Jewish Palestine. But that world cannot be fully appreciated by plunging directly into it. Singling out the first century without examining the events and persons that led up to it builds certain distortions into the study, especially if what is desired is a sympathetic understanding of the groups and people who made up first-century Jewish society in Palestine. The period of the Second Temple (520 BCE to 70 CE) has a clear beginning and end, and its character, although it changes over time, is somewhat consistent. The building of the Second Temple was a new beginning in Israel's history, society, and religion. In crucial ways, Israel in Palestine was very different at the beginning of the Second Temple period from what it was just before that. Likewise, the destruction of the Second Temple by the Romans in 70 CE marked a radical change in Israel. The change went beyond the loss of a physical temple. It had profound implications for every aspect of Jewish life and society.

Chapters 1 through 3 on the one hand, and chapters 12 and 13 on the other, supply a frame within which Second Temple Judaism can be viewed. Chapters 1–3 lay the groundwork for the rest of the book by discussing Israel prior to the Second Temple period. They introduce persons, groups, events, and issues in preexilic and exilic Israel that are central to understanding Second Temple Judaism. Chapter 12, after discussing the war against the Romans and the fall of Jerusalem, indicates the direction Judaism took in subsequent years, and then analyzes two Jewish texts written after the war. Chapter 13 looks at three Christian interpretations of Jesus written after the destruction of Jerusalem.

THE STUDY OF HISTORY

Since the scriptural texts were composed in social and historical settings quite different from those of modern readers, part of the task of interpretation must be to try to appreciate how the writings made meaning in their own circumstances. "Historical criticism" is a mode of analysis that aims to discover through historical methods—critical examination of textual and material evidence—what the authors of texts meant, and how those texts would have been interpreted by their original audiences. The study takes place in dialogue with what is known of the ancient world in which the documents were produced. There are potential problems with the method: (a) It at times assumes that one can get back to the bare, uninterpreted "facts" of a situation; (b) it sometimes identifies truth with the original meaning of the text, so that historical knowledge is privileged almost to the exclusion of other ways of making sense of the text; (c) it may not critically examine its own presuppositions—philosophical, social, and political. These problems must be addressed by all who engage in historical criticism. However, it would be a mistake simply to reject the quest for historical knowledge. To suggest why this is so, a few observations are appropriate.

People from post-Enlightenment Western cultures, even religious people, tend to prize history highly. With respect to Jesus Christ, Christians often think that the picture they have of Jesus is identical to the historical Jesus, the Palestinian Jew of two thousand years ago. They feel secure in their interpretation of Jesus because it corresponds with their reading of the gospels, which to them are pure history. Further, it is often assumed that first-century Palestinian Jewish society is accurately portrayed in the gospels. To neglect historical study is to leave such assumptions unchallenged.

It is also important to ask historical questions since failing to do so would make it impossible to have even tentative answers to what brought us to where we are. The nature of society and religion today is a result of decisions made, thoughts developed, and institutions constructed in the past. If one ignores those decisions, thoughts, and institutions, one neglects an essential key to understanding the present.

For both Christians and Jews, there are theological reasons for taking history seriously. Each tradition teaches that God is encountered in history, in the real-life interactions of people in their everyday world. Whether the subject be ancient Israel grappling with world empires, or Jesus Christ in conflict with the religious authorities of his day, both traditions seek not to escape from history but to understand it. The rereading and rewriting of sacred stories and history evident in the Bible itself attests to a basic drive in each of these religions to find meaning in past events.

The writing of history is no easy matter. One problem is that one's presuppositions color the way one reads historical evidence. An example would be the debate about miracles among Christian scholars over the past few centuries. Those who believe that God operates through miracles judge Jesus' miracles to have actually happened. Rationalistic critics explain them away as products of a nonscientific world view, of psychosomatic phenomena, or of explicable events of nature. Historical research will not resolve the difficulty. There are basic differences of world view that result in varying readings of the same evidence.

To write history is not simply to chronicle events. Even if historians could agree on a set of events as actually having happened, one would have only a chronicle, a list of events. Historical analysis does not just list facts, but tries to connect them, analyze them, discover their causes and effects, and investigate their meaning within their historical, economic, political, cultural, social surroundings. But how one brings discrete facts into a coherent whole is not simply a matter of scientific investigation. One's explanation of events will be determined by one's belief about what causes what, what people are like, and how the universe works.

An everyday example of talking about the past shows how problematic is the view that description of the past can be unfettered by personal opinion or bias. Suppose thirty students take the same course and meet a year later to discuss what happened. They are all eyewitnesses, but their experiences of the class can differ substantially. Was the professor organized or chaotic, clear or confusing, interesting or boring? Was the workload easy, hard, or moderate? Were the exams fair or unfair? Were the professor's comments on the paper helpful or not? It is the rare class that will not elicit the full range of possible comments. A student's experience of a class will depend on what the student's interests are, what sort of background she or he has, how much work the student does, and who the student is, as well as on what actually happens in the classroom. It is hoped that all thirty students will be able to agree on some basic facts about the course a year later—course title, required books, professor's name—but as soon as the conversation shifts to more significant questions such as how good or fair or insightful the course was, there is plenty of room for disagreement.

As eyewitnesses give different descriptions of a common experience a short time after it occurs, there is still more room for disagreement when it comes to events in the distant past. If one has studied American history, one knows who George Washington is. One knows when he was born, when he died, where he lived, what offices he held, and so on. But does one know what he had for breakfast before an important battle? Probably not. Historians do not find his breakfast significant. But if one thinks that diet determines behavior, Washington's eating habits are crucial. This is an extreme example, since few historians think that Washington's food is worthy of such attention. Conflicts of interpretation become quite real, however, when a conservative capitalist historian compares analyses with those of a Marxist. The way that one looks at the world, the way one thinks things work, will affect what one chooses to tell and how one tells it.

There is no such thing as uninterpreted history. History is interpretation. Interpretation implies a world view, a conceptual framework, a philosophical stance on the part of the interpreter, whether acknowledged or not. When one writes history for an audience with which one shares a broad base of common assumptions, the assumptions appear self-evident and do not seem to need examination. In a pluralistic society, such history becomes problematic. In the history of a religion, the matter becomes more acute, since one's attitude toward religion colors what questions are asked and how they are answered. If one thinks that religion is primarily a psychological phenomenon, then psychology will explain it; if it is a political phenomenon, political analysis will explain it.

History as interpretation comes into play on two levels in this book. One level is that of modern scholarship. The same evidence can be interpreted in varying ways by different scholars. Sometimes disagreement is due to scarcity or ambiguity of evidence. At other times, different conclusions come from different assumptions and convictions. On another level, the primary sources offer interpretation of their own world or a past world, as will become clear in our analysis. Part of the task of the historian is to analyze the viewpoints of the sources, so that their world views and biases can be taken into account when they are used to write history.

THE APPROACH OF THIS BOOK

This book draws on various methodologies. The historical method furnishes a basic framework in which all questions are asked. Because this study deals with texts, it also uses literary criticism, attending to the literary genre of the works studied and trying to appreciate them as literature. Literary study has a historical dimension because biblical and related texts employ genres, languages, and thought patterns from the ancient world. Because of the importance of social setting, questions proper to anthropology and sociology are asked, disciplines particularly appropriate for the study of groups. Anthropology in particular holds much promise for the study of ancient Israel and Christianity because it is accustomed to studying diverse cultures. Because the social sciences raise issues of societal structure, symbol systems and culture, the relationships of politics, economics, kinship, and religion, and related matters, they can help to flesh out historical studies, so as to provide a fuller picture of the world in which the ancient documents were produced. The study of language is relevant, since the texts studied here were originally written primarily in Hebrew, Aramaic, and Greek, and survive in an even greater variety of languages. English translations are already interpretations of the texts, since it is impossible to translate a text without interpreting it.

This study covers an immense stretch of Israel's history. Choices must be made about what to treat in detail, what to summarize, which issues to raise, and so on. The choices make for a particular reading of the period that should be challenged and supplemented by other readings. This book makes accessible some of the best recent research on Second Temple Judaism. By bringing together old and well-tested interpretations with newer approaches, a new view of the evidence is presented.

PRIMARY SOURCES

Primary sources are those that date from the period being studied. It is crucial to read the primary sources listed at the beginning of each chapter and referred to in the body of the chapter. This study aims to foster familiarity with the primary evidence, which consists mainly of textual sources. Throughout the book, extensive portions of primary sources are reproduced to ensure that the reader will examine them and not be content with generalizations arising from another's analysis. But even reading such passages is not sufficient. The documents discussed should be seen as wholes. The primary texts should be read in their entirety to achieve familiarity with them, to place the passages discussed into a fuller context, and even to challenge readings defended in this book by attending to contradictory passages or by reading the same ones in a different light.

Because of the importance of primary documents, much of this book consists of description and analysis of those documents. When possible, the history is written through analysis of documents. Such an approach results in greater familiarity with the sources, and supplies a firsthand view of how sources must be treated critically, by taking into account their genre, world view, and biases, if they are to yield historical evidence. It also gives full weight to the sources as *part* of the history being studied. For example, the gospels say something about the historical Jesus, but they are also historically important for what they say about the early Christians who wrote them.

STEREOTYPES OF JUDAISM

When one limits one's study to the canon of the Hebrew Bible or the New Testament, certain viewpoints and prejudices are reinforced that are supported by the principles of selection that led to the formation of the canon in the first place. That is especially true with respect to the New Testament. The New Testament's treatment of Judaism is, on the whole, biased. As long as New Testament texts are the only ones studied in detail, it is very difficult to break down negative stereotypes of Jews and Judaism contained in the texts that continue to influence Christian perception. Just to analyze the apostle Paul or the Gospel of Mark can reinforce stereotypes, unless one simultaneously maintains a running commentary demonstrating that what they say is a one-sided view of Judaism.

In a course on Second Temple Judaism, it is possible to present a fairer and more balanced portrait of Jewish society and of groups such as priests, Sadducees, Pharisees, Roman procurators, city crowds, Jewish rebels, and others. Then when New Testament texts are read, they are already prepared for by a broader and deeper appreciation of first-century Judaism than can be achieved by presenting such information along the way in the study of the

INTRODUCTION

New Testament, or by short chapters at the beginnings of New Testament introductions. It is also more likely that students will take the Jewishness of Jesus seriously, because they will recognize countless ways in which an understanding of Second Temple Judaism provides necessary knowledge for comprehending what Jesus does and says, and perhaps even how he thinks. One can see Jesus *within* Judaism, which is crucial for appreciating him as a historical figure.

Criticism of stereotypes of Judaism is not systematic or direct throughout most of this book. Rather, it is accomplished by trying to present fairly and in a historical framework the Judaism of Jesus' day. A sympathetic understanding of another group, even if it does not lead to acceptance of its world view, makes it more difficult to operate on the basis of stereotypes. One cannot see all Jews as legalists if one reads their texts and observes their actions. One cannot listen with equanimity to the Gospel of John saying that the Jews cried out, "We have no king but Caesar," when one knows that a few years later many Jews of Palestine lost their lives opposing Roman injustice. One will be far less apt to set Jesus over against Judaism, or blindly blame the Jews for the death of Jesus or for rejecting him as Messiah, if one learns to see Jesus as *part* of Second Temple Judaism.

An important goal here is to challenge a view that sees Judaism as monolithic. The variety of ways of being Jewish in the Second Temple period is stressed and illustrated throughout. One might even say that the subject is Judaisms of the Second Temple era.

SELECT BIBLIOGRAPHY

Gager, John G. *The Origins of Anti-Semitism: Attitudes Toward Judaism in Pagan and Christian Antiquity*. New York: Oxford University Press, 1983.

Ruether, Rosemary. *Faith and Fratricide: The Theological Roots of Anti-Semitism*. New York: Seabury Press, 1974.

Saldarini, Anthony J. "Judaism and the New Testament," in Eldon J. Epp and George MacRae, eds., *The New Testament and Its Modern Interpreters*. Atlanta: Scholars Press, 1989, 27-53.

Stone, Michael. "The Sources and Our View of Reality," and "Hidden Streams in Judaism: Essene Scrolls and Pseudepigrapha," in *SSV*, 49-70.

PART I

Preexilic and Exilic Israel:
Foundations of Second Temple
Judaism

CHAPTER ONE

Preexilic Israel

Primary Readings: Genesis, Exodus, Leviticus, Numbers, Deuteronomy

This book is about Second Temple Judaism. The Second Temple was built from 520-515 BCE and lasted until the Romans destroyed it in 70 CE. But this study must begin earlier than 520 BCE, because by then Israel already had a long history, developed institutions, complex legal, historical, and theological traditions, and a diversified social structure. The purpose of the present chapter is to ensure a basic familiarity with persons, events and ideas from preexilic Israel that are of particular importance to Second Temple Judaism. The chapter is in four parts. The first briefly sketches some of the story line of the Hebrew Bible from creation to the destruction of Solomon's Temple (587 BCE). The second examines some of the sources for the Hebrew Bible. The third discusses specific topics concerning preexilic Israel. The last part examines the structure of ancient Jewish society.

THE STORY OF ISRAEL

The primary source here is Genesis through 2 Kings. Regardless of its historical accuracy, the biblical narrative reflects the self-understanding of a great portion of Israel. This section is not a substitute for reading the Bible, but it can serve to focus that reading.

The Time Before Abraham

Genesis 1–11 covers the period from the creation to the time of Abraham. A general theme is that prior to Abraham, humanity repeatedly fails to obey God. A second theme is that God always gives humanity another chance. Genesis takes up myths common to many cultures in the ancient Near East (the Flood, for example), whose original purpose was to explain certain features of human existence such as the diversity of languages, women's subordination to men, the repulsiveness of snakes, the pain of childbearing, the difficulty of farming, and human mortality. Genesis adapts the myths, transforming them into vehicles for its own themes.

The God of Israel is Creator of the entire world (Genesis 1–2). The crowning work of creation is the making of the first humans, Adam and Eve, whom God places in the Garden of Eden. In Genesis 3 God gives them one command, not to eat of the tree of the knowledge of good and evil. Tricked by the serpent, they eat the forbidden fruit, thinking they will thereby attain equality with God. They are expelled from the garden lest they eat also of the tree of life and so live forever. God curses the ground, saying that cultivation will be difficult. God curses the snake, stating that it will be most hated of all creatures. Eve is told that her childbirth will be painful and that she must be subject to her husband. Adam learns that he must eventually die. God intends a harmonious creation with humans at its apex, but humans ruin that plan through disobedience. Humanity's ills are due to that disobedience. Human evil increases until God resolves to destroy humanity through a flood (6:7).

Noah and his family are saved from the flood because of Noah's righteousness. This is an example of God's mercy tempering his anger. Noah builds a large boat called an ark, and fills it with his family and with every kind of animal. The flood comes and kills every animal and human on earth except those in the ark. Then the waters abate and the inhabitants of the ark emerge to begin God's creation anew. Noah is promised that God will not destroy the world by water again. This promise is called a "covenant" (Hebrew: bĕrîth), meaning "agreement," "alliance," "compact," or "treaty." As a sign of the covenant, God creates the rainbow. As part of the Noachic covenant, God allows humans to eat animals, but forbids the eating of blood because it contains the life of the animal, which belongs only to God. This is a change from Genesis 1:29-30, where God gives humanity only plants for food. In Genesis 9 God also forbids murder, on the grounds that humans are made in the image of God.

God grants humanity a second chance through Noah, but humans immediately revert to their old ways. In Genesis 11 the earth's inhabitants decide to build a tower reaching into heaven. This recalls the sin of Adam and Eve in Genesis 3 that sprang from their desire to be equal to God. Sin is revolt against God and desire to usurp God's power and authority. God spoils the plans for the tower by confusing human language. Before the building of the tower all humans speak a single language. God now causes them to speak many languages, making cooperation on the tower impossible.

The Mothers and Fathers of Israel

Genesis 12–50 deals with Israel's patriarchs (Abraham, Isaac, Jacob, Jacob's twelve sons), and matriarchs (Sarah, Rebekah, Rachel, Leah). A theme connecting the stories is that the fulfillment of the promise to Abraham encounters multiple obstacles that God must overcome. A common expression of the theme is that women through whom the promise is transmitted are barren, and God cures their barrenness. Sarah is barren (Gen 11:30), as are Rebekah (Gen 25:21), Rachel (29:31; 30:1-2), and perhaps Leah (Gen 29:31, 35; 30:9).

Against the background of the failure of humanity to live up to God's demands, God says to Abraham,

> Go from your country and your kindred and your father's house to the land that I will show you. I will make of you a great nation, and I will bless you, and make your name great, so that you will be a blessing. I will bless those who bless you, and the one who curses you I will curse; and in you all the families of the earth shall be blessed. (Gen 12:1-3)

God's promise to Abraham is in three parts: (a) land; (b) numerous progeny that will become a great nation; (c) blessings so great that all nations will look to Abraham as the model of being blessed. The promise is called a covenant in Genesis 15 and 17. Genesis 17 makes circumcision (cutting off of the male foreskin) a sign of the covenant between God and Abraham's descendants. Abraham believes God's promise and leaves his home in Mesopotamia to go to Canaan (the biblical name for Palestine). Abraham, Isaac, Jacob, and Jacob's offspring live there as "sojourners," that is, as resident aliens, people on the margins of the societies that control the land.

In Genesis 32:24-28 Jacob spends a night wrestling with an angel from whom he exacts a blessing. The angel changes Jacob's name to Israel because, as the angel says, "You have striven with God and with humans, and have prevailed" (Gen 32:28). The angel interprets the word "Israel" to mean "he who strives with God," probably an inaccurate etymology. Jacob's descendants collectively receive this new name, and so Jacob is the "eponym" of Israel; he is the ancestor for whom they are named.

Genesis 37 and 39–50 tells the story of Joseph, the eleventh son of Jacob, much favored by his father. His jealous brothers sell him into slavery in Egypt. Later a famine occurs in Palestine, forcing Jacob and his sons to look to Egypt for food. On a trip to Egypt the brothers encounter Joseph, who has since become a trusted deputy of Pharaoh (the generic name for an Egyptian king). There is a reconciliation between the brothers, and Jacob and his sons come to Egypt. The stage is set for the Exodus of the Israelites.

The Exodus from Egypt (ca. 1280 BCE)

Hundreds of years pass, and a Pharaoh comes to the throne who is threatened by Israel's rapid growth. He decrees that Israel's male babies must be put to death and reduces Israel to slavery. Now Moses is born. His mother hides her son for three months. She then sets him adrift on the Nile in a basket. The basket is discovered by the daughter of Pharaoh, who raises Moses as her own. When Moses reaches adulthood he kills an Egyptian who is mistreating an Israelite

(Exod 2:11-12). Moses then flees to the desert and comes to a tribe called the Midianites. He marries the daughter of a Midianite priest (Exod 2:15-22). Exodus 3 tells of Moses meeting God in a burning bush on Mount Sinai. God commissions Moses to go to Pharaoh to demand the Israelites' release. God says, "When you have brought the people out of Egypt, you shall worship God on this mountain" (Exod 3:12).

Pharaoh resists the liberation of Israel, so God sends ten plagues upon Egypt. The first nine fail to convince Pharaoh, so God sends a tenth consisting of the killing of the firstborn of the Egyptians and their animals. Israel is told to prepare for the plague by killing lambs and smearing the blood on their doorposts. When the angel of death kills the firstborn of the land the houses with blood are passed over, an event later commemorated by blood rites at Passover. The tenth plague persuades Pharaoh to let the people go. As Israel leaves Egypt Pharaoh changes his mind and pursues them. The Israelites are pinned between the Egyptian army and the Sea of Reeds.[1] God rescues them by splitting the sea and allowing them to pass through. The Egyptians are drowned by the returning waters when they attempt to follow. The Israelites then travel through the desert to God's mountain, led by a pillar of cloud during the day and a pillar of fire at night. The pillars symbolize God's guiding and protective presence.

Mount Sinai

The people arrive at Sinai in Exodus 19:1. Their stay is said to last eleven months. The Sinai material occupies the rest of Exodus, all of Leviticus, and just over ten chapters of Numbers. Much of it consists of laws. The sheer bulk of material indicates the importance of Sinai to those who constructed the Hebrew Bible. The significance of the Sinai events is explained in God's words to Moses when they first meet on the mountain.

> Thus you shall say to the house of Jacob, and tell the Israelites: You have seen what I did to the Egyptians, and how I bore you on eagles' wings and brought you to myself. Now therefore, if you obey my voice and keep my covenant, you shall be my treasured possession out of all the peoples. Indeed, the whole earth is mine, but you shall be for me a priestly kingdom and a holy nation. (Exod 19:3-6)

God makes a covenant with the entire "house of Jacob," all Israel, reminding them of what has already been done for them. If they obey God's laws, they will be God's own possession and will continue to receive divine help.

God's holiness, might, and majesty are portrayed dramatically in the Sinai episode. The divine presence is marked by smoke and fire and the quaking of the mountain (Exod 19:18). No one but approved intermediaries may even touch the mountain (Exod 19:10-13, 23-25). The people and priests must purify themselves before encountering God lest they perish (Exod 19:10-15, 22).

Exodus 24 narrates a covenant ceremony. The day before the ceremony, "Moses came and told the people all the words of the LORD and all the ordinances; and all the people answered with one voice, and said, 'All the words that the LORD has spoken we will do'" (24:3). Moses then writes down God's commands. The next day animals are sacrificed and Moses takes the blood and throws half against an altar he has built. "Then he took the book of the covenant, and read it in the hearing of the people; and they said, 'All that the LORD has spoken we will do, and we will be obedient'" (24:7). Moses then throws the remaining blood on the people and says, "See the blood of the covenant that the LORD has made with you in accordance with all these words" (24:8). Whatever the precise meaning of this ritual, it establishes a close connection between God and the people, even a "blood" relation.

God tells the Israelites to construct an ark, a box containing the stone tablets on which the covenantal commands are written. The Ark symbolizes God's throne or footstool, the divine presence in the community. God instructs Israel on how to build the sanctuary, a tent where God appears to Moses, often called the "Tent of Meeting." The Ark and sanctuary accompany the Israelites when they leave Sinai and set out across the desert. God chooses the tribe of Levi to serve in the sanctuary. They carry the sacred objects (Ark, tent, etc.). Aaron, the brother of Moses and a member of the tribe of Levi, becomes the first priest, and his descendants are named legitimate priests, who offer the prescribed sacrifices. Other members of the tribe are referred to as "Levites." Levites are often portrayed as lower clergy, whose purpose is to aid the sons of Aaron in their cultic tasks.

Leviticus 8 describes the consecration of Aaron and his sons. An important part of the ceremony is their being anointed with oil by Moses. Anointing, or the pouring of oil on their heads, is a symbol of their being set aside for a special task. The Hebrew word for "anointed one" is *māšîah,* from which "Messiah" comes. In the Greek the word is translated *christos* from which "Christ" comes.

Entrance into the Land (ca. 1300–1200 BCE)

In Numbers 13–14 the people refuse God's order to enter Canaan because they fear the inhabitants. God condemns the people to wander in the desert for forty years, the length of a generation. Israel may not enter the promised land until the rebellious generation has died. In Deuteronomy 34 Moses is about to die. He passes on his authority to Joshua, who will lead the people into the promised land. Deuteronomy highlights the importance of Moses for Israelite tradition: "Never since has there arisen a prophet in Israel like Moses, whom the LORD knew face to face. He was unequaled for all the signs and wonders that the LORD sent him to perform in the land of Egypt" (Deut 34:10-11).

The book of Joshua claims that Israel conquers most of Canaan in three great campaigns. It portrays the people as obedient to God during the conquest. The book ends with a farewell speech by Joshua to the people enjoining exclusive worship of God (Joshua 23), and a covenant ceremony in which the people pledge service to God alone (Joshua 24). Joshua's speech reminds the people of what God has done for them, and predicts that God will conquer the Canaanites so that the Israelites can possess Canaan. It warns the people, however, that failure to obey God will be punished with loss of the land. The chief pitfall the Israelites are to avoid is contact with the Canaanites, especially through marriage, because that would bring temptations to idolatry.

The Judges (ca. 1200–1020 BCE)

When Israel first settles in the promised land, it is led by "judges." The institution of judgeship lasts until the rise of the monarchy. Under the judges, Israel consists of twelve loosely allied tribes named for the twelve sons of Jacob from whom they are thought to descend, united for worship of God and for mutual defense. The book of Judges portrays the judges as charismatic (spirit-filled) leaders raised up by God. They do not pass on their authority to their posterity. In some cases they may have judicial functions.

The Monarchy (ca. 1020–587 BCE)

The first book of Samuel tells of the miraculous birth of Samuel, who is portrayed as judge, prophet, and priest. He is a transitional figure, presiding over the transformation of Israel from a loose confederation of tribes to a monarchy. During Samuel's lifetime Israel faces the problem of the Philistines, new arrivals in Palestine who threaten the highland territory of the Israelite tribes. As Samuel nears the end of his life the Israelites approach him with a demand for a king. God instructs him to appoint Saul as king (ca. 1020 BCE). Saul fights the Philistines and other enemies of Israel. Because he disobeys God, God decides that Saul will not found a dynasty. God chooses David as the new king of Israel. To that end, Samuel anoints David in 1 Samuel 16.

David originally belongs to Saul's entourage, but they part company because of Saul's jealousy over David's military victories. After splitting with Saul, David becomes leader of a group of bandits. After Saul's death in battle (ca. 1000 BCE), David is anointed king of Judah (the main tribe occupying the southern part of Palestine; 2 Sam 2:4, 11). He is king of the south for seven years before he manages to incorporate the northern tribes into his kingdom (2 Sam 5:1-5). The early chapters of 2 Samuel tell of David's struggle to overcome the resistance to his rule in the north, a resistance led by Saul's successors. Eventually David establishes a united kingdom. David then conquers the Philistines. He also conquers the Jebusite city of Jerusalem and makes it his capital, bringing to it the sacred Ark to symbolize God's protection of David, Jerusalem, and the monarchy.

In 2 Samuel 7 David wants to build a temple for God. Through the prophet Nathan, God tells David that Solomon, David's son and successor, will build the Temple. The books of 1 and 2 Kings tell the story of Israel from Solomon (ruled ca. 961–922 BCE) to the Babylonian Exile. The books begin with Solomon's ambitious building programs. Solomon alienates the northern tribes through heavy demands on their resources, and at his death they successfully revolt under the leadership of Jeroboam (922 BCE). From this time on there are two kingdoms that worship Yahweh. The north is called Israel, and the south Judah. There is some ambiguity about the name "Israel," however, because it can still be used either for the northern kingdom or for all who worship Yahweh, north and south. Jeroboam builds two great shrines as national and royal sanctuaries, Bethel in the south and Dan in the north.

Nathan's importance in the David story illustrates the key role prophets played in bringing God's word to the kings and their subjects. Elijah is another such prophet. Elijah spends most of his career prophesying God's anger about Baal worship in the northern kingdom. Pursued by Jezebel, King Ahab's Baal-worshiping wife, Elijah journeys to Mount Sinai. God gives him three tasks: to anoint a certain Hazael to be the Syrian king, to anoint Jehu king of Israel, and to anoint Elisha to continue his prophetic work after he is gone (1 Kgs 19:15-16). At the end of his career, Elijah is taken to heaven in a fiery chariot.

In 722 BCE the kingdom of Israel falls to the expanding Assyrian empire. The Assyrians deport the prominent members of society and resettle the northern kingdom with foreigners. In the south, Hezekiah takes the throne (ruled ca. 715–687 BCE). Hezekiah reforms Judah by abolishing places of worship outside Jerusalem, a step that brings the cult under closer control by Hezekiah and Jerusalem's priests. It also makes easier the effort to enforce Hezekiah's desire to purify the cult from foreign influences.

Hezekiah's son, Manasseh (ruled 687–642 BCE), undoes the reforms of his father and rebuilds cultic places outside Jerusalem (2 Kgs 21:1-18). The next king, Josiah (ruled 640–609 BCE), follows the political and religious policies of Hezekiah. The history of the kingdom of Judah comes to an end when the Babylonians conquer Judah, destroy Jerusalem and its Temple, and lead most of the upper-class members of Judahite society into exile (587 BCE).

SOURCES OF THE HEBREW BIBLE

The Bible and History

The Bible is a complex collection of sources from many different times and places, developed and combined. Each of the sources that went into the making of the Bible has its own perspective. So there are many voices in the Bible representing a variety of vantage points. But even when all voices recorded in the

Bible are attended to, not all segments of society get a fair hearing. For example, kings often have their version of history recorded, but peasants seldom do.

Because the sources do not present "objective" history so much as argue for particular interpretations, and because many segments of society do not receive adequate representation in the sources, reconstruction of Israel's history is difficult. That the sources are not objective does not mean that they are worthless for reconstructing history. It simply means that their points of view must be taken into account when using them. There are at least two levels in the sources that must be kept in mind. First, the historical writers in the Bible tell of what is in their past. Thus, one may learn something of the history that is the object of their attention. Second, the concerns and world views of the biblical writers constantly affect the way they tell of those past events, so their works reveal something about their own time. The writings not only interpret Israel's history, they are themselves part of history.

Sustained examination of Genesis through Kings has shown that these books are the result of a long process of formation. Written sources are discernible behind the text. Genesis, Exodus, Leviticus, and Numbers represent a combination of three important sources, J, E, and P. "J" stands for the Yahwist, a source especially fond of the proper name "Yahweh" for Israel's God. ("J" is used because the German spelling is *Jahwist,* and German scholars first identified the source.) "E" stands for the Elohist, so named because it calls God *Elohim* (Hebrew for "god" or "gods"), until it reaches the time of Moses. "P" refers to the Priestly source.

The Southern Source, J

When J and E are disentangled, they each have a distinctive vocabulary. J and E use different terms for the same things. For example, their use of different names for God is mentioned above. J calls the mountain of the Law Sinai, and E calls it Horeb. J calls the father-in-law of Moses Hobab or Reuel, and E calls him Jethro. J refers to the inhabitants of Palestine as Canaanites, and E refers to them as Amorites.

J makes Judah central among the twelve tribes, so scholars think that it was written in the southern kingdom of Judah. The Yahwist tells of God's judging and saving action in history, beginning at creation. For J, human action and resourcefulness is always potentially problematic because of human pride. To J belong such narratives as the eating of the forbidden fruit in the Garden of Eden and the building of the Tower of Babel. Social division, violence, and sexual misconduct are seen as hallmarks of the human condition. God punishes such transgressions, but always has mercy on humanity and allows it a new start (with Adam and Eve, Noah, and Abraham, for instance). Some recent studies see J as supporting the Davidic monarchy in that it portrays the promises to the ancestors so that they can be seen as fulfilled in the Davidic dynasty, and see J at the same time warning against monarchical power because it speaks of the subservience of all human beings to God and of the dangers of human pride.

The Northern Source, E

E probably arose in nonroyal circles in the north in the ninth century BCE. Judah is not at the center of its concern, nor is the state. It has a stronger interest in cult than does J, suggesting a connection with cultic circles in the north. Many think that the body of law called the Covenant Code (Exod 20:22–23:19) was preserved in E. If so, it shows E's commitment to a pure cult, undefiled by foreign elements. It also shows a concern for social justice and the protection of the poor (22:25-27), women (21:7-11), and slaves (21:1-6).

The Priestly Source, P

It is unclear whether "P," the Priestly source, was ever a connected narrative. It may date from the fifth, or at the earliest the sixth century BCE. P accounts for more verses in the Pentateuch than any other source. (The "Pentateuch" is the first five books of the Hebrew Bible. The word comes from the Greek, and means "five scrolls.") Most of P consists of legislation, much of it cultic. The final redaction of the Pentateuch was a priestly one. But P also contains earlier materials. The redaction of Israel's traditions by P was part of priestly consolidation of power over the whole of Israel during and after the Babylonian Exile.

There are two versions of the creation of the world in Genesis 1–2. The first (Gen 1:1–2:4a) is from P. In the priestly world view of P, the world is created in six days. On the seventh day God rests. The seven-day schema manifests P's concept of creation as ordered by God. It also shows P's interest in the sabbath. That God rested on the seventh day is used as the rationale for the sabbath in the version of the ten commandments found in Exodus 20:2-17. The prominence of the priestly outlook in postexilic times makes sense because after the Exile Israel had to define itself anew, to create order out of chaos, so to speak.

In the ancient Near East, creation was frequently thought of as God conquering chaos. The symbol for chaos (that which opposes God's order) is often the sea, a powerful, mysterious, and uncontrollable force. The creation story in Genesis 1 conceives of the inhabitable world not as a sphere, but as a disk of dry land surrounded above, below, and all around with threatening waters. Genesis opens with God's Spirit hovering over the face of the waters, the world being "a formless void" (Gen 1:2). On the second day God creates the "firmament," a bowl-shaped barrier that holds the waters above away from the earth. On the third day God confines the waters under the firmament to one place, thus creating dry land.

51

Like other ancient Near Eastern cultures, Israel believed that God's order was not just for the natural world, but was also reflected in society and maintained by the cult (public worship). For P, social order is hierarchical and must not change. Priestly legislation safeguards divine order: Only priests may minister in the sanctuary; only the high priest may enter the holiest part of the sanctuary; women are controlled by men; Israelites are not to marry non-Israelites. P's program was not simply "religious" but was a comprehensive definition of the Jewish community, complete with a strategy for keeping that identity intact.

Essential to P's view of God's ordering of the world are a series of unconditional covenants that structure human history. Covenants are made with Noah (Genesis 9), Abraham (Genesis 17), and the people under the leadership of Moses (Exod 31:12-18). Another way P structures history is through the use of "completion formulas," which mark the end of important actions. For example, Genesis 2:1-2 says, "Thus the heavens and the earth were finished, and all their multitude . . . God finished the work that he had done." When the tabernacle is completed at Sinai the narrative summarizes, "In this way all the work of the tabernacle of the tent of meeting was finished . . . so Moses finished the work" (Exod 39:32; 40:33). When Palestine is divided up among the tribes, the text says, "So they finished dividing the land" (Josh 19:51). The completion formulas suggest that the three most important events in history are creation, the institution of the Israelite cult, and Israel's division of the land. Genealogies are yet another way that P structures history (Genesis 5, for example). They are an ordering device both because they divide time into generations and because they categorize humanity according to descent.

Chapter 2 investigates priestly religion in detail.

The Deuteronomistic History (DtrH)

Deuteronomy 12–26 is a collection of laws with a number of characteristics, among which are a critical acceptance of the monarchy, concern for social justice in Israel, and centralization of the cult. The Deuteronomistic History (Deuteronomy to 2 Kings) applies the viewpoint of Deuteronomy 12–26 to the period from Moses to the Exile. Israelites are evaluated according to their conformity to the Deuteronomistic interpretation of Mosaic traditions. Faithfulness to covenant obligations is thought to bring blessing, and violation brings curses.

The collection of laws in Deuteronomy 12–26 probably got its original impetus from a reform movement that started in the north in the eighth century BCE. The legal material may have been preserved by northern Levites, perhaps in the course of covenant renewal. When the north fell to Assyria in 722 BCE, the reformers may have fled south bringing their convictions with them. Hezekiah's reform in Judah may have been connected with the reformers. Hezekiah's centralization of the cult was compatible with the program of cultic centralization found in Deuteronomy 12. King Josiah followed Hezekiah's example of religious reform. There is a fascinating story about Josiah's reform in 2 Kings 22. While repairing the Temple the priests find "the book of the law," which has been lost or neglected. The prophetess Huldah assures Josiah that it is indeed God's word. On the basis of this book Josiah pursues his reforms. Many scholars see the book as Deuteronomy 12–26. This is the first known instance in Israel of an authoritative and normative book. Because of the status accorded this writing, it is a significant step in the formation of the Hebrew Bible.

Prophets play an important role in DtrH. God often predicts events through the prophets, and the predictions always prove true, showing God's control of history. Prophets are often central players in the action as well. In Deuteronomy 34:10, it is said that Moses was the greatest of Israel's prophets (*see* Deut 18:15-22; Num 12:6-8). Samuel was considered a prophet by DtrH (1 Sam 9:6-9). Prophets are prominent in the stories of the kings and challenge royal abuses.

DtrH is not "scientific" history but attempts to trace a theological pattern in human events. For example, northern kings are pronounced bad simply because they do not worship at Jerusalem, but that view conflicts with sources used by DtrH in which God appoints and supports northern kings. The prophet Ahijah tells Jeroboam about God's plans to found the northern kingdom, and Elisha anoints Jehu king of Israel. Actions of northern kings are at times praiseworthy. Favorable stories are preserved even about Ahab (1 Kgs 20:1-34). The originally independent traditions about Ahab, Elijah, Elisha, and others are from the sources used by DtrH. The core of the book of Deuteronomy, chapters 12–26, is another source, because scholars think that it predates DtrH as a whole. The DtrH also makes frequent reference to sources such as the "Book of the Acts of Solomon" (1 Kgs 11:41), the "Book of the Annals of the Kings of Israel" (1 Kgs 14:19), and the "Book of the Annals of the Kings of Judah" (14:29). Thus DtrH is a reinterpretation of the varied traditions of Israel and Judah.

SELECTED TOPICS

Covenant

"Covenant" denotes a formal agreement between two parties. Covenants can also be established between superiors and inferiors. In Israel, the latter kind of covenant is a model for the relationship between God and humans. The covenant at Sinai is like a conditional covenant between an emperor and a vassal king, or a suzerainty treaty. A suzerain is an over-lord who allows his subjects some degree of autonomy. There are models of such covenants in Hittite treaties of the fourteenth and thirteenth centuries BCE and in Assyrian treaties of the seventh and sixth centuries BCE. They follow a pattern present to some degree in several biblical texts. The pattern consists of the following elements:

a) an identification of the suzerain (God, in the Israelite covenant);
b) historical preamble in which the acts of the suzerain on behalf of the vassal are enumerated (for example, Israel's liberation from Egypt);
c) stipulations of the treaty that must be kept by the vassal (all of God's commands to Israel);
d) a list of witnesses (heaven and earth, in Deut 30:19);
e) blessings and curses (blessings such as a numerous progeny and curses such as the loss of the land; Deuteronomy 27–28).

The last element specifies the good that will happen to the vassal if the stipulations are obeyed and the bad if they are not. The covenant form may be responsible for the frequency of such phrases as "I am Yahweh who brought you up out of the land of Egypt" as introductions to God's words. The covenant is a prominent way for modeling Israel's relation to God throughout its history.

Torah

The Hebrew word *tôrāh* is usually translated "law," but it really has a broader meaning. Before the Exile and probably for some time afterward, *tôrāh* meant "instruction" by God on some cultic or legal matter, usually through a priest. Deuteronomy 12–26 represents a narrowing of the term *tôrāh* when it refers to itself as the definitive *book* of law. Even the king is subject to this book: "He [the king] shall have a copy of this law *[tôrāh]* written for him in the presence of the levitical priests" (Deut 17:18). Deuteronomy is meant to be definitive: "You must diligently observe everything that I command you; do not add to it or take anything from it" (Deut 12:32). This is an early step toward the formation of a "canon," a body of authoritative literature that cannot be changed.

In the Hebrew Bible *tôrāh* most often refers to the commands given to Moses on Sinai. After the Pentateuch came together in the postexilic period, the five-scroll collection became known as "the Torah," and Deuteronomy became part of the larger collection. Although the Pentateuch contains much legal material, it is not simply a collection of laws. It tells the story of creation, of the patriarchs and matriarchs, of Israel's election, of the Exodus and desert wanderings, and so on. It is the story of the relationship between God and Israel that is paradigmatic for all time.

Torah's significance as a symbol continued to expand. Although it is still used today to mean the Pentateuch, it can also have a wider meaning, including rabbinic tradition as presented in the Jerusalem and Babylonian Talmuds. It can also be used widely to denote the entire Jewish way of life.

The God(s) of the Fathers

Exodus 3 tells of Moses meeting God in the burning bush on Mount Sinai. God tells Moses to go to Egypt and tell Pharaoh to let the Israelites leave their slavery in Egypt. Then the following interchange takes place.

But Moses said to God, "If I come to the Israelites and say to them, 'The God of your ancestors has sent me to you,' and they ask me, 'What is his name?' what shall I say to them?" God said to Moses, "I AM WHO I AM." He said further, "Thus you shall say to the Israelites, 'I AM has sent me to you.'" God also said to Moses, "Thus you shall say to the Israelites, 'The LORD, the God of your ancestors, the God of Abraham, the God of Isaac, and the God of Jacob, has sent me to you':
  This is my name forever,
  and this my title for all generations.
Go and assemble the elders of Israel, and say to them, 'The LORD, the God of your ancestors, the God of Abraham, of Isaac, and of Jacob, has appeared to me.'"

(Exod 3:13-16)

The NRSV uses "LORD" to render the proper name of Israel's God, "Yahweh." Beginning in the last centuries BCE and continuing into the present time Jews have had such respect for the name of God that they pronounce it only under special circumstances. When they encounter the sacred name in the Hebrew text, they substitute 'ădōnāy meaning "LORD." The NRSV respects this usage by rendering "Yahweh" as "LORD," in capital and small capital letters.

This passage has undergone some development, as is indicated by the three beginnings to God's response ("God said . . . ," "He said further . . . ," "God also said . . ."), and by its repetitiveness. One reason that the passage has been reworked is that the mysterious name "Yahweh" needed explanation. Exodus 3 tries to explain it, but even the explanation is unclear. What is most striking about this passage is that it implies that Israel will not know whom Moses means when he says, "The God of your ancestors has sent me to you." The God who interacts with the patriarchs does so under different names, such as El-Shaddai and El-Elyon. That suggests that the patriarchs each had their own clan gods, and that it was after the patriarchal period that each of the clan gods was considered a manifestation of the one God Yahweh. It was according to this later recognition that originally independent stories of patriarchs were rewritten to form a connected narrative of one God in continuous interaction with the patriarchs, now seen as a single family in successive generations.

A passage in Exodus supports the suggestion just made: "And God said to Moses, 'I am the LORD. I appeared to Abraham, Isaac, and Jacob as God Almighty [Hebrew: El-Šaddāy], but by my name "the LORD [Yahweh]" I did not make myself known to them'" (Exod 6:2-3). This is P's explanation of the fact that only at the time of Moses did Israel come to know Yahweh. Before that they

55

worshiped other gods, later interpreted as being Yahweh under another name.

The Yahwist claims that Yahweh was recognized and worshiped in the time of Enosh, grandson of Adam (Gen 4:26), and implies that the patriarchs knew Yahweh by name (*see* Gen 12:1), a view contrary to that of P as discussed here. It is more likely that P is a more accurate account of what happened, since it is improbable that it would invent the idea that the patriarchs did not know God by name. Israel's idea of God developed over time and in response to its experiences. As a community worshiping Yahweh, Israel's history probably really began at Sinai. As it redefined itself it read its own history differently. As its self-understanding grew, it rewrote its own story. The process of rewriting traditions is typical of the Bible and continues into the postbiblical period and into Christianity.

The Israelite Confederacy

Before the establishment of the monarchy, Israel existed as a confederation of tribes living in the highlands of Canaan. The tribal confederacy called "Israel" had the egalitarian social structure of tribal and peasant culture. No single tribe ruled the others. Consensus was the only way to achieve concerted action. Such egalitarianism contrasted with the stratified social structure of the Canaanite city-states.

Gottwald furnishes an account of the economic, social, and political consequences of Israel's egalitarianism.

> The socioeconomic relations of Israelites were egalitarian in the sense that the entire populace was assured of approximately equal access to resources by means of their organization into extended families, protective associations of families (sometimes called "clans," but not to be construed as exogamous clans that mandate marriage outside the group), and tribes, federated as an intertribal community called "Israel," "Israelites," or "tribes/people of Israel/Yahweh." . . . The defining feature of politics in old Israel was that the political functions were diffused throughout the social structure or focused in temporary ad hoc assignments. (285-86)

> Land was to be held continuously within extended families and never sold for speculation. It was obligatory to extend aid to other Israelites in need and no interest was charged on such emergency loans. Strict limits were placed on contract servitude. Special provisions for the socially vulnerable (widows, orphans, strangers) were insisted on. An even-handed judicial system was highly prized. (287)

Holy War

Most wars were to some degree religious in the ancient world. People consulted and depended on gods to help them against their enemies. Israel was no exception. God was conceived of as a mighty warrior who would fight for the people. The song celebrating Israel's escape from Egypt (Exodus 15) sings of that escape as a military victory of God over the Egyptians: "The LORD is a warrior" (Exod 15:3). In the battle of Jericho, God delivers the city to the Israelites when the priests blow the ceremonial trumpets (Joshua 6–7). Since God is in the midst of the people as they fight, soldiers must be ritually pure, as if for participation in a liturgy (Josh 3:5; Deut 23:15; Num 5:3). Because God wins the victory, to God belong the spoils of war (Hebrew: *herem*). No one else may touch them. If they do, they incur the Lord's anger. God often demands that the spoils be destroyed. In 1 Samuel 15, Saul does not destroy all of the plunder that falls into his hands when he conquers the Amalekites. Saul's disobedience renders him unworthy to found a dynasty.

Monarchy

During the eleventh century BCE the tribal confederacy was threatened by the expansion of the newly arrived Philistines. The Philistines occupied city-states on the Mediterranean plain west of Judah's highlands. The story of the crisis appears in the books of Samuel. Samuel appointed Saul to confront the challenge (ca. 1020 BCE). Theoretically, Saul was to be leader of all Israel, although his power base was primarily among the northern tribes, the tribe of Benjamin in particular. It is not certain that Saul was actually even called king. The oldest traditions call him *nāgîd*, "prince." In any case, later tradition saw him as the first king of Israel. Saul's rule did not resemble other Near Eastern monarchies of the time. His headquarters was more like a military camp than a royal capital, his army was raised according to traditional tribal methods, not according to royal conscription, and he did not have a court as such.

Jerusalem had not been conquered by the Israelite tribes in Saul's time. The city lay on the central mountain range near the border between the northern and southern tribes. David was a shrewd politician and saw the advantage in choosing for his capital a city that lay between the two principal tribal divisions and did not belong to any one of them. His choice of Jerusalem as his capital was comparable to the choice of Washington, D.C., as capital of the United States. David conquered Jerusalem, made it his capital, and moved the Ark of the Covenant there. He appointed two professional priests, Abiathar and Zadok, as priests of his royal sanctuary.

David successfully subdued the Philistine threat. He extended Israelite hegemony over most of Palestine and into the territory across the Jordan (Ammon, Moab, and Edom) and northward to the Euphrates River. He now ruled people who were not part of the original tribal confederacy. Troops continued to be recruited through tribal processes, and revenue was raised not by taxes on the tribes but through tribute imposed on the areas he conquered. Thus

David's kingship did not destroy all tribal institutions and ideals. But the very institution of monarchy was bound to bring radical changes in Israel over time. The system of monarchy was inherently nonegalitarian. David exhibited the danger of royal abuse when he used his power and influence to seduce Bathsheba and eliminate her husband, Uriah (2 Samuel 11).

Solomon (ruled ca. 961–922 BCE) transformed Israel into a typical ancient Near Eastern monarchy. Shortly after he took the throne he ordered the death of his older brother Adonijah. Since the priest Abiathar had supported Adonijah, Solomon deposed him, leaving Zadok sole priest. He engaged in large building programs both inside Jerusalem and throughout Palestine. The Temple was one of his most enduring building accomplishments, but his palace was even more impressive than the Temple. He built fortifications throughout his kingdom, and raised a standing army with a strong chariot contingent. He also contracted many foreign alliances. Such alliances were often sealed through political marriages. In 1 Kings 11 it is said that Solomon "loved many foreign women," and had 700 wives and 300 concubines. The women brought their foreign gods with them to Jerusalem, and Solomon allowed them to build idolatrous shrines. The Deuteronomist blames Solomon's laxity with respect to idolatry for the split between the northern and southern kingdoms. Solomon also established an elaborate and expensive court. One way he got the revenue necessary for such expenditures was through taxes. Since Palestine was agricultural, he had to expropriate peasant "surpluses." As his expenses grew, so must his taxes have grown, supplemented by tolls exacted from those who had to pass through his kingdom and by trade. Solomon also required labor for his projects. To control his empire and to gain access to its resources Solomon drew up twelve administrative districts. Significantly, the boundaries of the twelve districts did not match those of the twelve tribes. The districts not only helped in the management of the empire, they also hastened the breakdown of old tribal divisions and weakened old institutions and social structures that embodied different values based on tribal autonomy and social and economic egalitarianism.

Palestine was located on a corridor of land between Egypt and the other great world powers. Much of Israel's history must be read in that context. When Israel's more powerful neighbors were in decline, its strategic location could work in its favor. David and Solomon could maintain a strong kingdom during the tenth century BCE because the states that traditionally exercised hegemony over Palestine were in decline (Egypt, Assyria, Babylonia). At other times Israel was besieged by foreign nations because of its strategic significance. Assyrians, Egyptians, Babylonians, Persians, Greeks, and Romans took turns controlling the small strip of land.

Given the originally loose organization of the tribes and the fact that the

Davidic dynasty belonged to the southern tribe of Judah, it is not surprising that resistance to the new order arose first in the north under Jeroboam. Although the northern kingdom emerged in reaction to the harsh demands of Solomon, its kings soon followed Solomon's example in establishing an empire that aspired to a role in international politics and had a court, standing army, temples, and forced labor. King Omri built Samaria as his capital. The implications of foreign alliances were evident in the north in that foreign religious and social practices gained influence there.

Israel's adoption of monarchy was a step that endangered Israel's values and institutions. It is hardly surprising that it was controversial, probably from the beginning, but it became more so as royal abuses mounted and Israelites found themselves oppressed by their own kinsmen. Ambivalence toward monarchy is observable in the sources that DtrH uses. Behind the stories of the establishment of the monarchy there are at least two sources, one of which is pro-monarchy (usually considered an early source: 1 Sam 9:1–10:16; 11:1-15; 13:1-7a; 13:15b–14:52; etc.) and the other anti-monarchy (a late source: 8:1-22; 10:17-27; 12:1-25). In the pro-monarchy source, God decides to found the monarchy as a way to rescue his people from the Philistines.

> Now the day before Saul came, the LORD had revealed to Samuel: "Tomorrow about this time I will send to you a man from the land of Benjamin, and you shall anoint him to be ruler over my people Israel. He shall save my people from the hand of the Philistines; for I have seen the suffering of my people, because their outcry has come to me." (1 Sam 9:15-16)

The anti-monarchy source presents a different picture.

> Then all the elders of Israel gathered together and came to Samuel at Ramah, and said to him, "You are old and your sons do not follow in your ways; appoint for us, then, a king to govern us, like other nations." But the thing displeased Samuel when they said, "Give us a king to govern us." Samuel prayed to the LORD, and the LORD said to Samuel, "Listen to the voice of the people in all that they say to you; for they have not rejected you, but they have rejected me from being king over them. Just as they have done to me, from the day I brought them up out of Egypt to this day, forsaking me and serving other gods, so also they are doing to you. Now then, listen to their voice; only—you shall solemnly warn them, and show them the ways of the king who shall reign over them." (1 Sam 8:4-9)

The passage goes on to list practices that were in fact adopted by kings north and south—military conscription, forced labor, confiscation of land, taxes.

One resolution of the problem of kingship can be seen in Deuteronomy 17:14-20.

When you have come into the land that the LORD your God is giving you, and have taken possession of it and settled in it, and you say, "I will set a king over me, like all the nations that are around me," you may indeed set over you a king whom the LORD your God will choose. One of your own community you may set as king over you; you are not permitted to put a foreigner over you, who is not of your own community. Even so, he must not acquire many horses for himself, or return the people to Egypt in order to acquire more horses, since the LORD has said to you, "You must never return that way again." And he must not acquire many wives for himself, or else his heart will turn away; also silver and gold he must not acquire in great quantity for himself. When he has taken the throne of his kingdom, he shall have a copy of this law written for him in the presence of the levitical priests. It shall remain with him and he shall read in it all the days of his life, so that he may learn to fear the LORD his God, diligently observing all the words of this law and these statutes, neither exalting himself above other members of the community nor turning aside from the commandment, either to the right or the left, so that he and his descendants may reign long over his kingdom in Israel.

The Deuteronomist asserts that God has accepted Israel's desire for a king and has in fact chosen the king. But the king is to be subject to many restrictions. He must be an Israelite and not a foreigner. The king is not to be "exalting himself above other members of the community," nor is he to amass riches, multiply wives, become too strong militarily, or pursue foreign alliances. All this is summed up in the idea that the king is subject to God's Law, now conceived of as contained in a book (notice the language, "*this* Law [*tôrāh*]" and "*these* statutes"). If he obeys God's Law, in which social justice figures prominently, God will permit him to continue his rule. Royal propaganda found in the Bible depicts the king's true function as enforcing proper worship of Yahweh and adherence to the divine ideal of justice for all Israelites.

A key passage encapsulating the Davidic royal ideal that much later becomes the basis of messianic hope is 2 Samuel 7. David offers to build God a house (a temple), and the prophet Nathan responds by using the word "house" in the sense of a dynasty.

Moreover the LORD declares to you that the LORD will make you a house. When your days are fulfilled and you lie down with your ancestors, I will raise up your offspring after you, who shall come forth from your body, and I will establish his kingdom. He shall build a house for my name, and I will establish the throne of his kingdom forever. I will be a father to him, and he shall be a son to me. When he commits iniquity, I will punish him with a rod such as mortals use, with blows inflicted by human beings. But I will not take my steadfast love from him, as I took it from Saul, whom I put away from before you. Your house and your kingdom shall be made sure forever before me; your throne shall be established forever.

(2 Sam 7:11*b*-16)

The legitimate Davidic king is both Son of David and Son of God. He is God's anointed (Hebrew: *māšîaḥ*; Greek: *christos*). He is the one who acts for God on earth and through whom God exercises his rule. God's rule is characterized by a concern for the poor, the marginal, the oppressed, and so the rule of God's anointed must conform to this. The king being God's representative means that God is the power behind the Israelite empire.

Psalm 2 was probably recited in the Temple at the coronation of a new Israelite king after the old one had died. The ideal time for subject peoples to revolt against an overlord was at a change of command owing to the death of the emperor. That is the situation envisaged by the psalm. Israel's vassals see their chance for independence in the death of the king. Before they can accomplish their aim of revolt, God anoints the new king and puts him on Mount Zion to rule from Jerusalem.

> Why do the nations conspire, and the peoples plot in vain? The kings of the earth set themselves, and the rulers take counsel together, against the LORD and his anointed, saying,
> "Let us burst their bonds asunder, and cast their cords from us."
> He who sits in the heavens laughs; the LORD has them in derision.
> Then he will speak to them in his wrath, and terrify them in his fury, saying,
> "I have set my king on Zion, my holy hill."

The next words of the psalm are probably recited by the new king.

> I will tell of the decree of the LORD:
> He said to me, "You are my son, today I have begotten you.
> Ask of me, and I will make the nations your heritage, and the ends of the earth your possession.
> You shall break them with a rod of iron, and dash them in pieces like a potter's vessel."
> Now therefore, O kings, be wise; be warned O rulers of the earth.
> Serve the LORD with fear, with trembling kiss his feet, or he will be angry, and you will perish in the way; for his wrath is quickly kindled.
> Happy are all who will take refuge in him.

"You are my son, today I have begotten you" seems to be an adoption formula. In some other Near Eastern nations, the king was considered actually a son of the god. Israel does not see the king as divine, but nonetheless speaks of him as son of God.

Gottwald summarizes the characteristics ideally expected of the Davidic kings and relates them to later messianic hopes.

> In one way or other the Judahite kings were judged to be (1) in a distinctive filial relation to Yahweh; (2) intermediaries between Yahweh and his people; (3)

exemplars of piety and obedience to Yahweh; and (4) executors of Yahweh's justice domestically and among the nations. From these roots sprang the later "messianism" associated with the Davidic dynasty. (336)

Four and a half centuries of monarchy changed Israel forever. Gottwald finds four "enduring structural effects" of the Israelite monarchy (323-25). The first was political centralization. Israel now had a state with powers of taxation and conscription, a monopoly on force within Israel, standing armies, and a large bureaucracy. The second effect was social stratification with its attendant inequities. The third was that the possession of land shifted from families and clans and tribes to the hands of a rich upper class. The final change was that the state was now fully involved in international trade, diplomacy, and war, which was expensive. The chief source of wealth was agriculture, so the peasants bore the brunt of the new expenses.

Prophecy

Prophecy was prevalent primarily during the time of the monarchy, but existed before that time and continued into the Second Temple period. Some prophets worked for the royal or cultic establishment, and others were outside it. For some, prophesying was a full-time job, but others were also priests or shepherds or had some other occupation. Some had disciples and others did not. Some wrote their words down, others had their words written down by their followers, and the words of yet others were never recorded at all. Some were considered true prophets, and others false. The common denominator among all the prophets is that each claimed to speak for God. They were intermediaries between God and the people. They claimed to be able to tell the king and people what God wanted of them.

There is a basic theology implied in the acts and messages of the prophets. They all assumed that Israel was chosen to be God's people, and that God maintained a unique relationship with Israel throughout history. The prophets were acutely aware that the people had obligations in that relationship and that they frequently failed to live up to those obligations. Their message often criticized the people, king, or whoever violated the covenant. Oracles of judgment threatened transgressors with punishment. Most seemed to expect God's forgiveness and the restoration of Israel after punishment had been inflicted. The prophets spoke to their own times. They told Israel what God would do to them if they did not act a certain way in their specific situation. Understanding the prophets involves appreciating their historical circumstances and the particular problems they addressed in their own times.

The most famous prophets are those whose words were collected in books. It is clear that the words of the prophets underwent a process of transmission in which they were applied to new situations, supplemented with later oracles, rewritten, edited, arranged in larger works. This process is evident in the book of Isaiah. Isaiah 1–39 contains oracles assigned to a prophet living in Jerusalem in the eighth century BCE. It also contains later additions. Isaiah 40–55 is from a prophet living in the Babylonian Exile sometime around 538 BCE. Isaiah 56–66 consists of oracles uttered during the early postexilic period. All 66 chapters are collected under the name of Isaiah. The assumption is that since prophets speak the word of God, that word is valid for all generations, and should be preserved and reapplied to new circumstances. Those who attributed later oracles to the earlier Isaiah were saying that the newer oracles were in the tradition of Isaiah and were a valid and authoritative application of his message to a new situation. This is not forgery, because forgery implies personal authorship and intellectual ownership of ideas, which are concepts foreign to Israel at the time the Hebrew Bible was being recorded.

The prophets were fully engaged in Israel's life—economic, political, and religious. Samuel presided over the transition of Israel from tribal federation to monarchy by anointing the first two kings, Saul and David. Ahab came in for sharp attack from Elijah and Elisha. Those prophets also anointed Jehu to overthrow Ahab's line and create a new dynasty. Amos condemned the social injustices of the northern kingdom. Hosea condemned Israel's devotion to the Canaanite god Baal. Isaiah of Jerusalem warned kings Ahaz and Hezekiah against foreign alliances. Jeremiah condemned Judah for failing to realize religious reform. The prophets did not distinguish between politics, economics, culture, and religion. God's will embraced all aspects of Israelite life, and the covenant covered all categories of human action. The idea that there was a specific sphere of life that could be labeled ''religion'' was foreign to their world view. They stood ready to attack any abuses of God's will—cultic, political, economic, or ethical. But there was much room for disagreement between prophets. A claim to speak for God was no guarantee that one did so. One prophet might attack the message of another, and society might reject a given prophet as a lunatic or a schemer.

The Wisdom Tradition

The roots of Israel's wisdom tradition lie partly in its own patriarchal-matriarchal past. Wisdom consisted of reflections about and prescriptions for life and how it should be lived. The clan passed down its accumulated wisdom to the younger generation. That wisdom was the fruit of countless generations of lived experience. Certain members of a clan or a tribe attained a reputation for greater wisdom than others. Wisdom need not be limited to male members of a tribe, as is suggested by the episode in which the wise woman of Tekoa influences David in an important political decision (2 Samuel 14).

Israel's wisdom entered a new stage with the advent of monarchy. The bureaucracy created by Solomon's kingdom required professional scribes who could read and write. Not many people were literate in the ancient world. Scribes were educated men who served as recordkeepers, advisors, diplomats, teachers, and in other capacities. Kingdoms needed a battery of scribes to keep records, read correspondence, write decrees, read and write laws, and more. Scribes became an integral part of Israelite government and society. Among the scribes were the intellectuals of ancient Israel, called "the wise" or "sages." Since literacy was limited to royal circles and urban elites, the social location of the wise was to be found there. Contact with other kingdoms and empires was common in the Solomonic court, and sages were open to outside influences. There was an international wisdom tradition in the ancient Near East that shared literary genres, themes, ways of teaching, and so on.

Solomon is portrayed in the Bible as an extremely wise man. Whether this is historically accurate or not cannot be known for sure. Solomon's support of the sapiential (from the Latin *sapiens*, "wise") establishment is remembered through the attribution to him of three canonical or deuterocanonical works—Proverbs, Qoheleth, and Wisdom. Few would maintain that these books are actually by Solomon. But in the portrayal of Solomon one can learn something about Israelite wisdom. In 1 Kings 3, God invites Solomon to ask for whatever he wants. Solomon says that since he has been given the task of ruling God's people, he needs wisdom and understanding. In this instance wisdom means skill in ruling. Solomon's ability to rule is shown in the famous story of the two women claiming the same child in 1 Kings 3:16-28. When Solomon commands that the child be split in two so that the women can share it, the true mother withdraws her claim so that the child will not be slain. In this way Solomon cleverly discovers who is the real mother, and commands that the child be given to her. He renders a just judgment.

In 1 Kings 4:32-33 there are further instances of Solomon's alleged wisdom: "He composed three thousand proverbs; and his songs numbered a thousand and five. He would speak of trees, from the cedar that is in the Lebanon to the hyssop that grows in the wall; he would speak of animals, and birds, and reptiles, and fish." The proverb is the form most characteristic of wisdom. Proverbs are short sayings containing general reflections on life. They are the product of human reason acting on everyday experience to discern the "way things work." "A stitch in time saves nine," "You can't win 'em all," and "The early bird gets the worm" are all proverbs in use today. That many proverbs carry the conviction of "common sense" attests to their origin in the cumulative experience of a group, not just an individual.

Ancient sages were interested in the way everything worked—nature, family life, the court, politics, and so on. Solomon's wisdom is shown in 1 Kings 4:33 by his knowledge of trees, animals, and fish, showing that the wisdom tradition conceived of the universe as an organic whole and prized knowledge in all spheres of experience. Knowledge about nature was knowledge that affected humans. Proverbs aimed at discovering the sense behind things. They assumed that there was a discoverable order in the universe. Primary evidence for the way things worked was not so much a sacred text or even Israel's sacred covenantal traditions, but was human experience in the world, although as the Second Temple period progressed, wisdom became more explicitly interested in Israel's sacred traditions. To learn how the world worked was also to learn how one should fit into it, how one should act. The ultimate aim of the wisdom tradition was practical and successful living.

Biblical books considered to be from the wisdom tradition are the Proverbs of Solomon, Job, and Ecclesiastes (otherwise known as Qoheleth, which is Hebrew for "Preacher"). Two other wisdom books are deuterocanonical, meaning that they are accepted as canonical by Catholics but not by Jews or Protestants. They are Ecclesiasticus (also known as the Wisdom of Jesus ben Sirach, or just Sirach), and the Wisdom of Solomon.

ANCIENT JEWISH SOCIETY

Society

The word "society" is used broadly in this book to denote the full communal life of a given group, including its religious, cultural, political, kinship, economic, and ideological aspects.[2] "Culture" refers to an array of interconnected symbols, values, and goals shared by a group of people. "Politics" means the set of mechanisms and interactions, formal and informal, by which society is governed. "Kinship" means family relationships. "Economics" means the arrangements determining the production, distribution, and consumption of goods and services. "Ideology" is used broadly to indicate the system of beliefs and theories that is the theoretical underpinning for a particular sociopolitical outlook espoused by a group within a larger society. Within a given religion there may be many possible ideologies.

Religion

There was no word for "religion" in ancient Jewish society because religion was not conceived of as an entity independent of other aspects of society. Religion was a set of symbols, beliefs, practices, and social structures thought to be of divine origin, embedded in politics and kinship. Jews thought of themselves as descended from a common ancestor, Abraham, and so every Jew was ultimately related to every other Jew. The distinction between church and state, common in post-Enlightenment thought, was unknown to ancient Jews. God's will, expressed in divine oracles mediated by prophets and priests, touched every aspect of Israelite and Jewish life. Israel's sacred law dealt not just with liturgy and morality, but with civil and criminal law, too. It also governed political structures, military preparations, and the prosecution of warfare. Political institutions were thought of as expressions of the will of God. Any political structure that could not make that claim was illegitimate. Israel's life as a whole was determined by God. In this, Israel was not much different from cultures contemporary with it.

The interrelatedness of all aspects of ancient Jewish society must be emphasized for readers within twentieth-century Western culture. For such readers, religion means something quite different from what it did for Israel. Today religion is frequently thought of as having little to do with politics, and even less to do with economics. Modern American society is pluralistic, including a multitude of religious groups. The basic attitude is that everyone is entitled to his or her own opinion, and everyone should leave everyone else alone. Religion is a matter of personal choice. Such an attitude would be incomprehensible to the ancient world, Israel in particular. The following statement in a recent study makes the point well.

> Religious belief and practice were part of the family, ethnic and territorial groups into which people were born. People did not choose their religion, nor did most social units or groups have members with different religions. Religion was integral to everything else and inseparable from it. People might worship new gods in addition to the old ones and engage in additional cultic practices, but they remained what they were culturally and socially. Radical conversion to another religion and rejection of one's inherited beliefs and behavior meant (and still mean today in such societies) separation and alienation from family and hereditary social group. Thus, involvement with religion is in itself political and social involvement in the broad sense of those terms.[3]

Agrarian Empires

Throughout the Second Temple period, Israel was an agrarian society. During most of the period, it was also part of large empires that also were primarily agrarian. Peasants working the land accounted for at least 90 percent of the population. Given certain technological implements, especially the plow, the peasants were capable of producing more than they consumed. But ancient agrarian societies were not free-market economies. The peasants' surplus was usually taken over by rich landowners, priests, and central governments, which made up a very small percentage of the population. Taxes could be a substantial burden. Peasants usually lived at little better than subsistence levels, and their surplus went to support the aristocracy, the military, and those involved in building projects.

Social structure in agrarian empires was hierarchical, and there was little social mobility. Belonging to a social class usually entailed having a certain amount of material wealth, but it was not always true in the ancient world that a certain amount of wealth guaranteed membership in a certain class. The possession of a certain degree of power or privilege might also be important in determining who belonged to a specific class, but even more might be involved. The following is a definition of social class that does justice to the complexity of the phenomenon in ancient societies. A class is

> a large body of persons who occupy a position in a social hierarchy by reason of their manifesting similarity of valued objective criteria. These latter include kinship affiliation, power and authority, achievements, possessions, and personal attributes. Achievements involve a person's occupational and educational attainments; possessions refer to material evidences of wealth; moral attributes include one's religious and ethical beliefs and actions; and personal attributes involve speech, dress and personal mannerisms.[4]

This definition of social class shows that many variables went into defining a class. Therefore, there was some overlap between groups and classes.

Since ancient Jewish society was highly stratified, it is necessary to have some appreciation of the criteria of stratification and of how it affected the way society operated. The following nine-class schema fits ancient Jewish society fairly well.[5] The classes fall into two categories, upper and lower. There is no real middle class. Groups that would be considered middle class in a modern setting are so dependent upon the ruling class in ancient society that they do not constitute a middle class in the usual meaning of that term.

The upper classes consisted of five groups. The ruler was in a class by himself because of the extent of his power and wealth. The ruler of Jewish society possessed varying degrees of power and wealth during the Second Temple period. Since Israel was for the most part under foreign domination, the foreign overlords affected the situation of Israel's rulers. The second class was the ruling class, which controlled all of society. It was composed of 2 percent or less of the population. Because of its control of society, it was usually wealthy. In ancient societies, wealth usually flowed from social position, rather than the converse as is true in modern Western societies.

The third class of the upper classes was the retainer class. Retainers existed to fulfill the needs of the ruling class. They may have composed about 5 percent of the population. They performed many functions, military, bureaucratic, educational, financial, and religious. Scribes belonged to this class. This class contained all sorts of people, some of whom were close to the ruling class and others of whom were lower on the social scale. There was probably some overlap between the ruling class and the retainer class. For example, the foremost scribes were members of the ruling class. The merchant class, the fourth class, probably overlapped the upper and lower classes. Because of their commercial relation with the rulers, the foremost merchants may have had some degree of independence from them.

Priests formed the fifth class. There was some overlap between the priestly class and the ruling class. At times the high priest, along with other prominent priests and rich landowners, ruled Judah. At other times they were subordinate to other authorities, such as the Herodian rulers of the first century BCE and the first century CE. Even when they were subject to other authorities, they maintained an independent influence and power owing to their relation to central religious institutions of Israel, the Temple, and the Torah. Priesthood was hereditary, and not all who were of priestly lineage belonged to the central families that were of the upper classes. There were poor priests who lived as artisans or peasants, just as there were priests among some members of the retainer classes, such as scribes.

There were four lower classes. The peasants formed the bulk of the population because of the agrarian nature of ancient Jewish society. The artisan class was probably quite small, 3 to 7 percent of the population. Like the peasants, they probably earned just about enough to survive, although it is possible that some, if their skills were rare enough, commanded high wages. The other two classes of the lower classes consisted of the unclean class and the expendable class. The former was composed of workers who did tasks extraordinarily distasteful to the rest of the population, such as mining and tanning. The expendable class, estimated to be about 5 to 10 percent of the population in ancient societies, probably consisted primarily of peasants driven off their land through economic pressures. Some of them banded together and lived by raiding villages and caravans. They may have been fertile ground for recruiting by messianic movements.

The Ancient City

It would be misleading to assume that ancient cities were essentially similar to modern cities. Ancient cities existed to serve the needs of the ruling class. The cities were where the ruling class lived, along with their retainers. Activities related to the control of society—the political, economic, religious, educational, and military functions—took place in the cities. Jewish Palestine's principal cities were Jerusalem, the only real city in Judah, Caesarea on the coast, which served as the Roman administrative center in the first centuries BCE and CE, and Sepphoris and Tiberias in Galilee. Most residents of the cities were probably not actively engaged in working the land, and conversely most peasants did not live in the cities. The result was often some urban-rural tension. Members of the lower classes who lived in the cities, such as artisans, served the upper classes for the most part. The Temple in Jerusalem required craftsmen and workers for its rebuilding under Herod and for its maintenance.

Dyadic Personality

Individualism is so much a part of the way modern Western societies look at the world that it must be mentioned here.[6] Today, phrases with the word "self" in them proliferate. One must strive for self-fulfillment, self-determination, self-satisfaction, for a healthy self-image. One must stand on one's own two feet. Dependency is considered negative. Inhabitants of the ancient world did not share this emphasis on individuality. They thought far more in terms of groups than do moderns. Being a good and loyal member of a group was a more dominant value to them than it is to us. This way of being has been called "dyadic personality." That means that a person defines himself or herself primarily in relation to one or more groups. One could not define oneself apart from significant groups.

A good example of this difference between moderns and ancients occurs with respect to religion. Modern Western societies tend to think that an individual stands back and decides freely what religion to belong to, and how to live out that commitment. The ancients seldom thought in terms of such free choice with regard to religion, and they were more interested in being faithful to the tradition passed down through the ages than in deciding for themselves what aspects of the tradition were good and which were undesirable.

CONCLUSION

What precedes provides a basis for the rest of this book. Israel of the Second Temple period was heir to stories, symbols, concepts, customs, and institutions that evolved during the preexilic period. To some degree, the following study investigates how Israel changed and how it remained the same as it faced new circumstances in its history. This examination of preexilic Israel supplies some of the materials necessary for the pursuit of that investigation.

SELECT BIBLIOGRAPHY

Norman Gottwald's *Introduction* has been very influential in this chapter.

Alt, Albrecht. "The God of the Fathers," in *Essays on Old Testament History and Religion*. Garden City, N.Y.: Doubleday, 1968.

Anderson, Bernhard. *UOT*.

Bright, John. *HI*.

Crenshaw, James L. *Old Testament Wisdom: An Introduction*. Atlanta: John Knox Press, 1981.

Eisenstadt, S. N. *The Political Systems of Empires: The Rise and Fall of Historical Societies.* New York: Collier-Macmillan, 1963.

Gottwald, Norman K. *HB.*

Hayes, John H., and J. Maxwell Miller. *Israelite and Judaean History.* Philadelphia: Westminster Press, 1977.

Hillers, D. R. *Covenant: The History of a Biblical Idea.* Baltimore: Johns Hopkins, 1969.

Laffey, Alice. *An Introduction to the Old Testament: A Feminist Perspective.* Philadelphia: Fortress Press, 1988.

Lenski, Gerhard E. *Power and Privilege: A Theory of Social Stratification.* New York: McGraw-Hill, 1966.

Malina, Bruce. *The New Testament World: Insights from Cultural Anthropology.* Atlanta: John Knox Press, 1981.

Murphy, Roland. *Wisdom Literature.* Grand Rapids: Wm. B. Eerdmans Publishing Co., 1981.

Neusner, Jacob. *Torah: From Scroll to Symbol in Formative Judaism.* Philadelphia: Fortress Press, 1985.

Noth, Martin. *The History of Israel,* rev. ed. New York: Harper and Brothers, 1960.

Rad, Gerhard von. *Wisdom in Israel.* Nashville/New York: Abingdon Press, 1972.

Saldarini, Anthony J. *Sadducees, Scribes, and Pharisees in Palestinian Society,* Wilmington, Del.: Michael Glazier, 1988.

Sjoberg, Gideon. *The Preindustrial City: Past and Present.* New York: Free Press, 1960.

DeVaux, Roland. *Ancient Israel: Its Life and Institutions.* New York: McGraw-Hill, 1965.

Wilson, Robert R. *Prophecy and Society in Ancient Israel.* Philadelphia: Fortress Press, 1980.

Priestly Religion

Primary Readings: Leviticus

PRIESTLY RELIGION AS A SYSTEM

By priestly religion is meant the Jewish religion insofar as it is focused upon the Temple, its personnel and activities. Priestly religion is a system whose parts fit together into a coherent and functional whole. The system has an implied world view, and rituals and structures expressing that world view. But religion goes beyond belief in a world view and performance of rituals. World view, ritual, and religious structures are replicated in the political, economic, social, and cultural realities of ancient Israel. The religion of Israel is a *symbolic* system. It is symbolic not just of supernatural entities, but of Israelite society as a whole.

Any analysis of a system involves abstraction and idealization. Actual situations conform to the ideal system to varying degrees. Nonetheless, one is justified in speaking of the existence of a religious system if it is implied by certain societal structures, enunciated in particular documents and traditions, embodied in specific institutions, and so on. Priestly religion was an important factor in Israel's life in the preexilic, exilic, and postexilic periods. Thus this chapter builds on insights into the priestly world view enunciated in chapter 1, prepares for the discussion of the Exile in chapter 3, and describes institutions essential to Second Temple Judaism.

THE HUMAN ACTIVITY OF DRAWING BOUNDARIES

Religions always look strange to outsiders who do not share their cultural assumptions. One way to understand other religions is to see them as particular instances of common human activities. This section investigates some human activities that are transcultural and that underlie both ancient priestly religion and modern religions.

The world in which humans live is not just physical but is also conceptual. "Conceptual" is used here in a broad sense, meaning ideas and symbols in the scope of their full import for human life, including their emotional import. Humans need to make sense of experience. To make sense of the world is to know where things and people belong. To decide where things belong is to classify them, put them into categories. Categories imply distinctions, and distinctions mean drawing boundaries or lines. Boundaries can be drawn between one place and another, between one time and another, between one person or group and another. To be aware of boundaries is to know where one is, what belongs to one, what belongs to one's group, and what does not. The clearer the boundaries, the clearer the categories. Categories are invested with feeling values. People learn to feel one way about one category and another way about another. They also learn how categories are arrayed with respect to one another. One category is better, wiser, more powerful than another, one category depends on another, and so on. The sum of such classifications forms a symbolic system or "map." If the system is coherent, then it is replicated throughout society, reinforcing the system. The system often goes unchallenged, appearing self-evident to those who live in it. It is often thought to be God-given.

People and things often cross from one category into another. In many such crossings, some sort of ritual presided over by a professional is needed to affirm that the boundary has indeed been crossed. When persons or things first belong to one category and then enter another, a change of status and definition is involved. Ritual draws attention to the change of status and validates it. There are also rituals that put something or someone back in the proper place when dislocation occurs. Further, no map can be completely inclusive. There will be persons, things, and experiences that simply do not fit the system.

Place

Boundaries between places can be physical, such as rivers or oceans. They can also be purely conventional, such as national boundaries. A United States citizen who steps over the Canadian border will find himself or herself only a few feet farther north. Nonetheless, that person is now in a different nation, with different traditions, leaders, laws, and institutions. Understanding that there is a boundary and what it signifies is crucial to the well-being of the person and systems involved. Boundaries may exist primarily in human minds, but they are real. The legal crossing of a national boundary is often accompanied by some sort of ritual presided over by an official of the political system—the offering of the passport, the inspection of papers and baggage, and a stamping of the passport to indicate official approval and legitimation of entrance.

There are also less formal rituals for crossings of boundaries. To cross into someone else's yard, one needs to be invited, and to respond with a "thank you." That is even more true when passing into another's house. If one can cross such boundaries without rituals, that implies a "closeness" between people equivalent to saying that there are no boundaries between them. The people belong to the same category. They are relatives, perhaps, or close friends.

Time

As with physical categories, some temporal ones are provided by nature. The seasons and day and night are natural temporal categories. But natural categories are inadequate for complex human needs. For example, "company time" and "your own time" are essential categories for most people. People resent being asked to do something for the company on their own time, and the company often forbids doing something personal on company time. It is perhaps in this kind of division of time that one can become most fully aware that categorization involves feeling. One certainly feels different about vacation time from how one feels about work time.

Rituals often accompany the passing from one time to another. This is evident in the stages of a person's life. A ritual called a "birthday party" marks the passage from one year to the next. Confirmation or Bar Mitzvah ceremonies mark passing from childhood to young adulthood. Graduation from college often marks the beginning of full adulthood.

Things

Most people feel different about what belongs to them from how they feel about what belongs to others. Two identical pairs of jeans can arouse quite different feelings. To take possession of a pair of jeans from a pile belonging to the store, one goes through a ritual called "buying," which involves taking the jeans to a salesperson, giving that person some paper or metal called "money," and getting a receipt. Once this is done, the status of that same pair of jeans, which in no way are physically changed by the procedure, is altered in one's eyes and in the eyes of society. If they were to get ripped, one would certainly feel different about it than if one saw a ripped pair of jeans on a store shelf.

People

Boundaries between countries are boundaries between places and between people as well. A citizen of the United States is different from a Canadian citizen. The words "us" and "them" are used to indicate that distinction. To change from one group to another, one must undergo a ritual or series of rituals such as naturalization. There are many ways to belong to one or another group within a country. Belonging to one religion is different from belonging to another. Passing from one religion to another requires a ritual to mark the passage. Social boundaries are crossed at marriage, graduation, entering a profession, buying a house, having a first child, and so on. Each crossing is marked by a ritual. Relatives form a very special category. Although sympathy might be felt for a nonrelative who is sick, for example, the feeling will probably be deeper if the sick person is one's wife or husband, mother, father, or child. Culture teaches that feelings are supposed to be different in such cases, and socialization consists partly in learning such differences.

Values and Feelings

Societal and individual values are expressed in the boundaries people draw and the feelings associated with those boundaries. Because cultures are different, their stake in certain kinds of lines may be different. In the United States, private property is a prominent cultural value. Lines drawn around property are important and are frequently expressed physically by fences or hedges. Violations of those lines produce anxiety. Suppose one is sitting in one's backyard and a stranger walks through it without permission. Again, suppose the stranger walks through the house. To take an extreme example, suppose the stranger decides to enter the bedroom. In each case lines have been crossed. The lines around yard, house, and bedroom form a system of concentric circles. As the stranger crosses each line he or she gets closer to the center, the symbol of what is most personal (and therefore sacred) and so needs most to be protected. The owner's anxiety mounts as each line is crossed.

Because individualism is such a strong value in American culture, boundaries defining the individual are well marked. Body odors that blur bodily boundaries by letting one's body impinge on another's space are suppressed. Likewise, many do not like to be touched by anyone not within a certain range of close friends and family. If one is very concerned to keep the home and what is outside the home separate and well defined, then rituals such as taking off shoes before entering, or changing clothes as soon as one arrives home may be followed. When they are not, anxiety ensues.

Society is full of examples of strong feelings aroused when categories are mixed. A child might hate it if different foods even touch each other on his or her plate, or if someone else drinks from his or her glass. Even if one were convinced that dog food were the most nutritious food available, one would probably still be repulsed by the idea of eating it because of the feeling that dog food is for dogs. A germ-conscious culture frequently rationalizes this by claiming that such feelings arise from a desire to avoid what is unhealthful. That is to miss the implied symbolic system.

A society's categories change over time. Civil rights laws enacted in the United States over the past several decades are a dramatic example of such change. When boundaries change, anxiety rises because one feels, and rightly so, that one's world is passing out of existence.

PRIESTLY CATEGORIES

Dirt

"Clean" and "unclean" are terms central to priestly religion. "Dirt" is matter out of place. After working in the garden all day, it is not a good idea to tramp over the living room rug and sprawl out on the best couch. One is "dirty" and should wash and change clothes first. Garden dirt does not belong on the couch. On the other hand, if one sees a freshly tilled garden, one is unlikely to say, "What a dirty place." Although there is soil everywhere in the garden, that is precisely where it belongs, so in a sense it is not really "dirt." If dirt gets into the home, one will try to get rid of it. That is a process of purification, of putting it back in its place, of taking it to where it no longer makes things "dirty." The very fact that soil can be thought of as dirt, as matter out of place, implies that things have their place, which implies a system, which in turn implies categories that in turn imply lines and relationships between categories. Thus clean-dirty, pure-impure are appropriate metaphors for speaking of systems and violations of those systems.

Holiness and Purity

Two concepts crucial to priestly religion are "holiness" and "purity" ("cleanness"). Today, holiness is often identified with morality. If one is morally upright, then one is holy. This definition can be misleading regarding ancient priestly religion. There holiness means that which belongs to God, in short, that which does not belong to humanity or to the "natural" realm. Since God is always by definition holy, anything that belongs to God is also holy. Another word for "holy" is "sacred." The word "sanctuary" denotes the place where God is to be found. It is derived from the Latin word *sanctus,* which means "holy." There are also degrees of holiness. The closer one comes to God, the holier one must be. Purity is related to holiness. To be pure (or clean) means to be free of anything offensive to God, and therefore to be able to approach God as closely as one's position in society allows. It is to be able to pass from natural to divine space. Since the category of the natural depends on that of the divine for its welfare and very existence, crossing the boundary in order to make contact with the divine is essential. To become pure when one is not, one undergoes a ritual that effects the passage from the state of impurity to that of purity. This is often conceived of as "washing." The analogy at work is that what offends God is like dirt and must be washed off. To be ritually pure is to have undergone the process of purification, so that one can participate in rituals that are meant to accomplish other things, such as securing God's help for the community.

Rules about who can and who cannot approach God in the sanctuary are thought to have been given by God. They protect God's holiness. They protect the people as well, for to approach God in an inappropriate manner is dangerous. God is powerful, and may react to the approach of an impure person. Purity rules delineate clearly what is holy and what is "profane" (not holy). To cross such boundaries without proper rituals or without being in the proper state is to be out of place in the system, and to invite disaster. An example is found in the story of David bringing the Ark to Jerusalem.

> When they came to the threshing floor of Nacon, Uzzah reached out his hand to the
> ark of God and took hold of it, for the oxen shook it. The anger of the LORD was
> kindled against Uzzah; and God struck him there because he reached out his hand to
> the ark; and he died there beside the ark of God. (2 Sam 6:6-7)

Uzzah was only trying to keep the Ark from falling. But he was not of the class
authorized to touch the Ark, and he paid the price for his presumption.

THE TEMPLE: ISRAEL'S SACRED PLACE

The Temple Building

The Jerusalem Temple was built early in the reign of Solomon (961–922 BCE),
and was destroyed by the Babylonians in 587 BCE. The exiles returning from
Babylonia rebuilt it between 520 and 515 BCE. It was partially destroyed in the
first half of the second century BCE, but was soon repaired. Herod the Great (37–4
BCE) undertook a great expansion of the Temple and its surrounding precincts.
The Temple's architecture symbolized God's presence and the necessity of firm
boundaries between the sacred and the natural worlds. It consisted of three rooms
in a row. It was oriented on an east-west axis, with the entrance to the Temple on
the east. As the outline of the Temple on page 27 illustrates, the innermost room
was the *qōdeš haqqŏdāšîm,* the "Holy of Holies" or the "Most Holy Place."
The name "Holy of Holies" is appropriate for the place of God's presence in the
Temple in view of the definition of holiness discussed above. The priests
deposited the Ark, symbol of God's presence, in the Holy of Holies. The room
was a perfect cube, twenty cubits to a side (1 royal cubit equals 20.9 inches). It
had no windows or lamps, so Solomon says that God "said that he would dwell
in thick darkness" (1 Kgs 8:12). The cherubim over the Ark (1 Kgs 8:6) were
large carvings of strange and frightening winged creatures there to protect the
Ark, and so to protect God. Access to the Holy of Holies was strictly limited.
Only the high priest could enter, and only once a year on the Day of Atonement.

The middle room of the Temple was the largest. It was forty cubits long,
twenty wide, and thirty high. It was called the *qōdeš,* the "Holy Place," and was
the site of most of the activity inside the Temple. It contained the small altar on
which incense was offered, ten golden lampstands arranged five on a side, and a
golden table for the "bread of the Presence" (bread continually offered to God).
Access to this room was granted to priests. The Holy Place was more accessible
than the Holy of Holies, and less so than the parts of the Temple where those who
were not priests could go. It represented a high state of holiness, but was less holy
than the inner sanctuary.

The third room, through which one entered the Holy Place, was the porch. It was only ten cubits deep, twenty cubits wide, and thirty cubits high. It was an antechamber to the Holy Place corresponding to the entry of a dwelling. The door to the vestibule was flanked by two very large bronze pillars, corresponding to the gate posts of a residence, their grand scale and ornate work indicating the power and grandeur of the house's inhabitant.

Steps led down from the vestibule's entrance to the area in front of the Temple. As one looked down the steps there was a large altar for burnt offerings to the left (north) with a ramp leading up to it, and on the right (south) was a large "sea of bronze," presumably for ritual washings. The area immediately surrounding the Temple was enclosed by a wall, and formed a courtyard to which the priests had access. The Temple building was surrounded on three sides by three stories of side chambers that seem to have been used for a variety of purposes, among which was storage.

Temple and Dynasty

When David undertook to unite the loose confederation of autonomous tribes he used the Ark, symbol of God's presence among and covenant relationship with the people. God's agreeing to enter Jerusalem and live there signified divine approval of the new Davidic dynasty. It also made Jerusalem the focus of God's protective presence, a holy city. Solomon's first priority on becoming king was to build a Temple for God. Dynasties of the ancient Near East proved their legitimacy by demonstrating the support of the national gods for their rule. There was no better way to demonstrate that approval than the willingness of the highest god to live beside the king. Therefore the founding of dynasties was accompanied by the building of temples. Solomon built the Temple on Zion, a hill in Jerusalem. Thus the word "Zion" is used in the Bible to speak of the Temple, the hill on which it was built, or Jerusalem as a whole, which owes its significance to God's presence.

Temple as the Presence of God

At the completion of the Temple, a lavish fourteen-day feast was held. It began with the bringing of the Ark to the Temple.

> Then the priests brought the ark of the covenant of the LORD to its place, in the inner sanctuary of the house, in the most holy place, underneath the wings of the cherubim. . . . And when the priests came out of the holy place, a cloud filled the house of the LORD, so that the priests could not stand to minister because of the cloud; for the glory of the LORD filled the house of the LORD. Then Solomon said, "The LORD has said that he would dwell in thick darkness. I have built you an exalted house, a place for you to dwell in forever." (1 Kgs 8:6, 10-13)

The Hebrew terms denoting the Temple, *bayit* and *hêkāl,* mean "house" and "palace" respectively. The basic definition of the Temple is that it was God's dwelling place. Solomon's dedicatory prayer shows that the Israelites could have a sophisticated appreciation of what that meant.

> But will God indeed dwell on the earth? Even heaven and the highest heaven cannot contain you, much less this house that I have built! Regard your servant's prayer and his plea, O LORD my God, heeding the cry and the prayer that your servant prays to you today; that your eyes may be open night and day toward this house, the place of which you said, "My name shall be there," that you may heed the prayer that your servant prays toward this place. Hear the plea of your servant and of your people Israel when they pray toward this place; O hear in heaven your dwelling place; heed and forgive. (1 Kgs 8:27-30)

Some Israelites were aware of the problems in thinking that God could live on earth, much less in a specific temple. Nonetheless, they needed to designate a particular locale as a place where they could encounter God. They knew that God could not be limited or restricted to that place, but the divine presence there had to be real and reliable. In 1 Kings 8, two verbal devices for conveying this tension appear. It is said that God's "glory" is present in the Temple, and that the divine "name" dwells there. Both phrases are circumlocutions for God, expressing the idea that God is present but cannot be contained.

In 1 Kings 8, the priests bring the Ark to the holiest part of the Temple. As soon as they leave the Holy Place, the middle room of the Temple, "a cloud filled the house of the LORD, so that the priests could not stand to minister because of the cloud; for the glory of the LORD filled the house of the LORD" (1 Kgs 8:10-11). Whatever the ultimate origin of the symbol of a cloud for God (a volcano has been suggested—see the appearance of God at Sinai, Exodus 19), God used that form to lead the Israelites out of Egypt, through the Reed Sea, and through the desert to the promised land. That the priests cannot remain in the Temple while the cloud is there shows that God's presence is too much for humans to endure. The category of the divine is one to which humans do not belong. Their presence in sacred space is risky and can be accomplished successfully only in strict accordance with God's rules.

God was the source of life, fertility, prosperity, and strength. God's presence in the Temple was necessary for these things to be realized. The Temple ideology rooted in this basic presupposition is evident in the book of Psalms. The psalms were the hymnbook of the Temple. As such, they affected not just priests, but influenced people who participated in the cult.

Psalm 48 was probably written for pilgrims to Jerusalem.

Great is the Lord and greatly to be praised in the city of our God.
His holy mountain, beautiful in elevation, is the joy of all the earth,
Mount Zion, in the far north, the city of the great King.
Within its citadels God has shown himself a sure defense.
Then the kings assembled, they came on together.
As soon as they saw it, they were astounded; they were in panic, they took to flight;
trembling took hold of them there, pains as of a woman in labor,
as when an east wind shatters the ships of Tarshish.
As we have heard, so we have seen in the city of the Lord of hosts,
in the city of our God, which God establishes forever.
We ponder your steadfast love, O God, in the midst of your temple.
Your name, O God, like your praise, reaches to the ends of the earth.
Your right hand is filled with victory. Let Mount Zion be glad,
let the towns of Judah rejoice because of your judgments.
Walk about Zion, go all around it, count its towers,
consider well its ramparts; go through its citadels,
that you may tell the next generation that this is God,
our God forever and ever. He will be our guide forever.

The psalm lauds God's strength. Because of the divine presence, Mount Zion is invincible. Foreign kings tremble at the very sight of it. Particularly interesting is that what the pilgrims had *heard* of before, the mighty acts of God, they now *see*. The very buildings of Jerusalem are concrete expressions and symbols of God's strength. The "city of our God" will last "forever." The psalmist goes so far as to tell the pilgrims to tour the city looking at its ramparts and citadels so that they might tell their posterity that "this is God." God's "steadfast love," a translation of the Hebrew word *hesed,* means what God has graciously done for his people. The people recall those gracious deeds in the Temple because God is available there and can be thanked. Other elements often associated with the Temple appear in this psalm. Zion is beautiful and lofty. All the world delights in it. It is the place where God speaks, delivering divine judgments.

Similar thoughts are found throughout the psalter and beyond. One reads in Psalm 46:4-5, "There is a river whose streams make glad the city of God, the holy habitation of the Most High. God is in the midst of the city; it shall not be moved; God will help it when the morning dawns." The river signifies fertility, and God's presence in the city ensures its invincibility. Prayers should be directed toward the Temple, as is seen in Psalm 28:2: "Hear the voice of my supplication, as I cry to you for help, as I lift up my hands toward your most holy sanctuary" (*see* 1 Kings 8). The Temple sums up and embodies everything that is of worth to Israel. It is no wonder, then, that its sanctity was guarded by an elaborate set of purity rules concerning who could enter and under what circumstances.

TEMPLE PERSONNEL: ISRAEL'S SACRED PERSONS

Priests and Levites

To be a priest in Israel was not a vocation in the modern sense. One was born into the priesthood. It was hereditary. God chose one tribe, Levi, to serve in the sanctuary. Of that one tribe, God chose Aaron and his descendants to be the higher clergy, those who carried out the sacrifices and entered the Temple to minister to God. The Levites, the portion of the tribe of Levi who were not sons of Aaron, seem to have had different functions at different times. They frequently appear as servants in the Temple, doing much of the menial work. They also served as gatekeepers. In the postexilic period they had a prominent role in the worship of the Temple as singers, and were teachers of Torah.

There is a story in Numbers 16 that suggests that the establishment of a professional priesthood did not come without a struggle. Korah, a Levite, led a rebellion against Moses and Aaron in the desert. Protesting against the authority of Moses and Aaron, those rebelling said, "You have gone too far! All the congregation are holy, everyone of them, and the LORD is among them. So why then do you exalt yourselves above the assembly of the LORD?" (Num 16:3). Holiness was an attribute of all the people. The challenge, then, was to legitimate a special class who could be holier than the people, and as such could get closer to God. The story presumes a transitional period from a society with no priestly class to one with such a class. Moses' answer to Korah includes the following.

> "The man whom the LORD chooses shall be the holy one. You Levites have gone too far!" Then Moses said to Korah, "Hear now, you Levites. Is it too little for you that the God of Israel has separated you from the congregation of Israel, to allow you to approach him in order to perform the duties of the LORD's tabernacle, and to stand before the congregation and serve them? He has allowed you to approach him, and all your brother Levites with you; yet you seek the priesthood as well! Therefore you and all your company have gathered together against the LORD. What is Aaron that you rail against him?" (Num 16:7-10)

"To approach him" is a cultic term meaning to approach God in the sanctuary. Different divisions of the clergy were allowed different degrees of closeness to God. God decided who could approach. Aaron is called "the holy one" because he could come closest to God. The Levites were also allowed to approach God closely, though less closely, and this meant that they were "separated from the congregation of Israel" and stood "before the congregation" to minister to them. But there was a divinely ordained hierarchy within the clergy. To challenge that hierarchy was to challenge God. Degrees of holiness of parts of the Temple were replicated in degrees of holiness of segments of the community.

Ordination

The ordination ceremony for Aaron and his sons narrated in Leviticus 8–9 illustrates many of the features of the priesthood. First, the priest was washed, a symbol for washing away impurities (8:6). Next he was dressed in priestly robes (8:7-9). To take off one's clothing and put on clothing of special significance is a familiar act both in religious settings and outside them. Special clothing distinguishes a person from the rest of society and puts him or her into a special category. The priest was anointed with oil (8:10-12). To anoint someone or something with oil meant that the person or thing was set apart for a special task. In the Bible there are examples of priests, kings, and prophets being anointed. "Messiah" is from the Hebrew for "anointed one."

Law

As cultic mediators between Israel and God, priests could speak for God, whose house they attended. Moses says of them: "They teach Jacob your ordinances, and Israel your law [Hebrew: *tôrāh*]" (Deut 33:10). An important part of priestly teaching of the Law included instruction on the cult. It was up to priests to decide who and what was pure, that is, able to enter into God's presence or be presented to God as a fitting sacrifice. God says to Aaron, "You are to distinguish between the holy and the common, and between the unclean and the clean; and you are to teach the people of Israel all the statutes that the LORD has spoken to them through Moses" (Lev 10:10-11). Israel depended on access to God in the cult for its well-being, and the priests were powerful as those who controlled that access. In effect they exercised control over society. That control was balanced by the might of the king and later of foreign kings, but it was not entirely dependent on them.

Cult and Society

Through its purity rules Israel classified all humanity in terms of degree of access to the cult. One's position with respect to the cult corresponded to one's position in society. This is an example of replication of structure in various spheres of life. The structure of Temple and cult corresponds to the structure of the community. In descending order of degree of access to the cult were pure priests, pure Levites, and pure laypersons. Laywomen could not be priests or Levites, nor did they participate in the activities of the Temple as much as did the men. Their position in the cult reflected their position in a patriarchal society where they belonged to men and their status was defined primarily through marriage and childbearing. Gentiles were denied access to the cult and so were definitively outside the covenant community. Between Gentiles and pure Israelites were various classes of persons, some of whom never had access to the cult, such as eunuchs (Deut 23:1; probably because they were not "whole" or were unable to pass on their covenantal status through procreation) and bastards (Deut 23:2; because their lineage and so their covenantal status was questionable). Temporary hindrances to participation in the cult included what the Bible calls leprosy (any skin disorder), nocturnal emissions by males, and contact with a corpse. For temporary impurities purifications were decreed. Marriage strategy was defensive, that is, designed to keep intact the divisions of society by discouraging marriage between Jews and Gentiles or between members of different social classes.

Herod's Temple symbolized the structure of society because it included a court for the men of Israel, located outside that of the priests, and another for the women of Israel, placed outside that of the men. It also had a court for Gentiles, which was still farther from the Temple. Thus, degrees of access to the cult by priests, Jewish men, Jewish women, and Gentiles, were symbolized in the architecture of the Temple precincts.

Economic Support

Although the entire people belonged to God and was therefore holy (Exod 19:3), the priests belonged to God in a special way, and so were especially holy. Each of the tribes was to inherit a specific part of the land of Israel, but Levi's portion was God. That means that the priests and Levites lived off the cult. Rules for sacrifice gave much of the animal or grain sacrificed to the priests as their "portion."

Tithing was the practice of giving a tenth of agricultural products to the priests. Besides the proceeds from tithes and sacrifices, the priests received the first fruits of the land and the herds, as well as a ransom for the firstborn of Israel. The symbolism is that the land and Israel belong to God, and therefore their produce does too. Offering the first fruits to God frees the rest for Israel's use. Giving offerings to the priests is giving them to God because the priests belong to God. In addition to priestly dues, there was a Temple tax on Jews during the Second Temple period. Besides money belonging directly to the Temple, there were also private deposits there for safekeeping. Thus the Temple functioned as a bank. The considerable riches within its walls attracted the attention of various foreign rulers, who tried and sometimes succeeded in gaining access to them.

SACRIFICES: MAKING THINGS SACRED

Sacrifice as Gift

The word "sacrifice" comes from the Latin *facere,* "to make," and *sacer,* "holy" or "sacred." To sacrifice something was to make it holy, to give it to God. It was to transfer it from the realm of the profane into the category of things that belong to God, the sacred. A ritual had to be performed to make the transfer, and that ritual was the sacrifice that God prescribed. A sacrifice would be useless if God were not there to receive it. For this reason, sacrifices were performed in the Temple. The Temple symbolized the three realms: the divine, the human, and the place of interaction between the two. There was a court before the Temple where Israel could assemble; God lived or appeared in the Holy of Holies; and the space between (the altar and the Holy Place) was a place of interaction where the priests gave God his animal sacrifices, grain, and incense.

Acceptable Offerings

One could offer to God only what was acceptable. There was a correspondence between what was acceptable to the Israelites and what was acceptable to God. Israel, like most peoples, saw its own likes and dislikes, taboos and categories, as self-evident and God-given, and so societal features were replicated in the cult. Surely God would not want anything that the Israelites would not want. The rules in Leviticus and elsewhere in the Bible specify what was an appropriate sacrifice. Since in sacrifice the people gave something of its own to God, Israel's offerings came only from its domestic animals. Wild animals would not do. Further, the purity rules that governed what Israel could eat were replicated in rules that said what was permissible to sacrifice to God. Animals forbidden to Israel were also unfit for God. Israel's taboos concerning animals have been the subject of much discussion. The most familiar taboo is pork because it is observed to this day among many Jews. But pigs get no special attention in Israel's literature until the second century BCE, and then only because pigs were the sacrificial animals of those with whom the Jews were in conflict. Before that, pigs were just one instance of a forbidden category of land animal.

One popular explanation of such taboos involves hygiene, suggesting that purity rules exclude animals that are risky to eat because of disease. But this could explain only a very small number of cases. A glance at Leviticus 11 shows that the hygiene theory cannot fully explain Israel's categorization of animals. Another theory is that of historical survivals. This theory sees the purity laws as quaint survivals from an earlier and more primitive time in Israel's past. Assumed by the theory is an evolution of Israelite religion toward a more spiritual and ethical religion embodied in the prophets. There are several problems with such a theory. First, it does not explain the specifics of the purity rules. Second, it has a very narrow concept of religion. Purity rules continued to be central throughout Israel's history, and indeed play a key role in Judaism today. To relegate them to a "primitive" state of religion is to misunderstand their role in the world-making function of religion. Third, the theory forces an evolutionary scheme on the history of Israel's religion. Fourth, although the prophets attacked the idea of sacrifice within accompanying ethical behavior, they did not attack the cult or sacrifice as an institution.

The best explanation of the animal purity rules comes from anthropologist Mary Douglas. She sees purity rules as a *symbolic* system. Purity rules exist to define categories of things, people, and times, to draw firm boundaries between those categories, and to relate the categories in an integrated system. Leviticus 11 organizes the animal world. It divides it into three principal divisions: air, water, and land. It sees as clean (edible by Israel) animals that belong clearly to one category or another. A proper land animal "has divided hoofs and is cleft-footed and chews the cud." Proper water animals are those that have fins and scales. Proper air animals do not eat blood or other dead animals, can achieve true flight, and hop on two legs (so insects are not pure, for example). Animals that "swarm" on the land (those that travel in large close groups pushing and jostling one another) are "abominations," and do not fit the categories. Swarming is a type of movement that should belong to sea animals—schools of fish, for example. Some things seem "right" to the Israelites and others do not. Something that does not fit into existing categories is repulsive. Today there are similar repulsions. Part of the reason for unease toward bats may be that "mice" are not supposed to fly. The repulsiveness of snakes may be partly because they do not move like other land animals, because they have no feet or legs and crawl on their belly.

Just as one could classify all humanity in terms of its degree of access to the Temple, so also could the animal kingdom be classified. At one end of the scale, animals defined as unclean in Leviticus 11 were not brought into the Temple. At the other end were acceptable sacrifices, unblemished clean animals of a specific age or quality. Just as members of different human categories were not supposed to marry, so also was it forbidden to cross-breed different kinds of animals (Lev 19:19). Everything had a place and everything was kept in its place.

Sacrifice as Food

If sacrifice meant giving something to God, and if that something was usually food, then the question arises whether Israel thought God actually needed to be fed. The conception of sacrifice as food lies behind Leviticus 3:11: "Then the priest shall turn these into smoke on the altar as a food offering by fire to the LORD." Such a conception was probably the origin of the phrase "sweet-smelling" as applied to sacrifices. Nonetheless, the Hebrew Bible seldom speaks of sacrifices as food. A protest against a more literal understanding of sacrifice as food appears in Psalm 50:12-13: "If I were hungry, I would not tell you; for the world and all that is in it is mine. Do I eat the flesh of bulls, or drink the blood of goats?" The psalm may be protesting a popular understanding of sacrifice. But the idea of feeding God is rare in the Hebrew Bible. Similarly there is little or no evidence for seeing the sacrificial feasts as attempts at mystical union with God or endeavors to assimilate the life-force of the animal.

Blood

The Hebrew Bible gives two main reasons for sacrifice—gift (in petition or thanksgiving) and purification (expiation). In both cases the efficacy of sacrifice may have come from the nature of the blood shed.

> If anyone of the house of Israel or of the aliens who reside among them eats any blood, I will set my face against that person who eats blood, and I will cut that person off from the people. For the life of the flesh is in the blood; and I have given it to you for making atonement for your lives on the altar; for, as life, it is the blood that makes atonement. (Lev 17:10-11)

The offering that was entirely burned on the altar was relatively rare. Usually the blood was poured out at the foot of the altar, and so the life of the animal was returned to God. Parts of the animal were burned on the altar, some (all of the rest, if it was a sin offering) was eaten by the priests as their portion, and some (if it was a peace offering) was eaten by those who brought the sacrifice. God always got the blood. The symbolism seems to be that the life of the animal belonged only to God. Humans were strictly forbidden to consume the blood, because then they would be consuming something belonging to God. This recalls Genesis. Before the flood, humans were vegetarians (Gen 1:29). After the flood, God gave permission to eat animals, provided that the blood was not eaten (Gen 9:2-5). This is one of the principles behind dietary laws (kosher laws) still followed by many Jews. To be kosher an animal must be killed in a way that ensures that there is no blood in the meat.

Atonement

The word translated "atone" or "expiate" in most texts is the Hebrew word *kipper*. In those contexts it means "to wipe off" or "to purge." Its object was not usually a person but a thing—the sanctuary, for example. This is clear in the case of the *ḥaṭṭā't*, usually translated "sin offering." It was not a gift to appease an angry God but a means of purging (cleansing) the sanctuary. A better translation for *ḥaṭṭā't* than "sin offering" would be "purification offering." The root idea is that sin defiled the sanctuary. The sanctuary was like a magnet that attracted the "dirt" caused by the sins of the people. The degree of seriousness of the sin determined the extent to which the defilement penetrated the sanctuary. The sanctuary could be purged of lesser sins by "washing off" the outer altar with the blood of the sin offering. Once a year the high priests entered the Holy of Holies to cleanse it of the defilement caused by sins. That occurred on the Day of Atonement, *Yôm Kippûr,* the holiest day of the Jewish year. It was necessary to purge God's dwelling of the defilement caused by the sin of the people because eventually the buildup of defilement would make it impossible for God to remain there. Purification made it possible for God to remain among the people, and God's presence among the people was necessary for the covenant to remain in effect. Thus, an important priestly function was maintenance of the covenant.

It would be wrong to think that Israel had a mechanistic system whereby one's inner disposition did not matter for forgiveness of sin. That is belied by the numerous expressions of sorrow for and confession of sin throughout the Hebrew Bible, expressions found in the sacrificial laws themselves (Lev 5:5; 16:21). Furthermore, the sins to be atoned for were both ethical and ritual. Rather, the sacrificial system was a symbolic system. It assumed that the presence of the divine with the human is a necessary but somewhat unstable circumstance. Human acts that do not belong in the presence of God were made palpable by being thought of as producing a kind of dirt that must be washed away. Sacrificial activity accomplished this washing in ways dictated by God and so guaranteed to be successful if done correctly and with the right intent.

The ritual for the Day of Atonement (Leviticus 16) illustrates the process of cleansing on that day. The Ark of the Covenant was in the Holy of Holies. On top of it was a cover, which was the holiest part of the Ark. It was called the "mercy seat" (in Hebrew, *kappōreth,* from the same root as *kipper*). It was this part of the Ark that had to be cleansed. The high priest took a bull with which to make atonement for himself. He also took two goats, one of which was a "scape-goat." The guilt of the people would be placed upon the scape-goat and it would be driven into the desert. The other goat would make atonement for the sins of the people. First the high priest killed the bull. He then took its blood, along with some burning incense, and entered the Holy of Holies.

The high priest "put the incense on the fire before the LORD, that the cloud of the incense may cover the mercy seat that is upon the covenant, or he will die" (Lev 16:13). The mercy seat was so holy that the high priest endangered himself by looking at it, so the incense hid it.

> He shall take some of the blood of the bull, and sprinkle it with his finger on the front of the mercy seat, and before the mercy seat he shall sprinkle the blood with his finger seven times. He shall slaughter the goat of the sin offering that is for the people and bring its blood inside the curtain, and do with its blood as he did with the blood of the bull, sprinkling it upon the mercy seat and before the mercy seat. Thus he shall make atonement for the sanctuary, because of the uncleannesses of the people of Israel, and because of their transgressions, all their sins; and so he shall do for the tent of meeting, which remains with them in the midst of their uncleannesses. (Lev 16:14-16)

After the cleansing of the inner sanctuary, the altar of sacrifice had to be cleansed as well.

> Then he shall go out to the altar that is before the LORD and make atonement on its behalf, and shall take some of the blood of the bull and of the blood of the goat, and put it on each of the horns of the altar. He shall sprinkle some of the blood on it with his finger seven times, and cleanse it and hallow it from the uncleannesses of the people of Israel. (Lev 16:18-19)

The blood of the sacrificial animals was like a ritual detergent that washed away the defilement caused by transgression of the Torah.

FEASTS: ISRAEL'S SACRED TIMES

Sabbath

Every seventh day was a sabbath on which no work could be done and special sacrifices were offered. This was the way that Israel obeyed God's command, "Remember the sabbath day, and keep it holy" (Exod 20:8). It set aside a portion of every week for God. It reminded the people constantly of their special relationship to God, and so reinforced Israel's identity. When Israel later lost the sacred Temple and holy land, Sabbath observance became still more crucial for the maintenance of their identity as a people.

Day of Atonement

The Day of Atonement occurred once a year in the fall. It was the only feast on which fasting was prescribed, because it was (and is) a time of sorrow for sins.

Pilgrimage Feasts

There were three pilgrimage feasts, feasts on which Jewish men were supposed to make their way to Jerusalem. They were Passover-Unleavened Bread, Weeks, and Booths. Each feast was agricultural. When the Israelites turned from a nomadic to a farming life-style, they adopted the agricultural feasts of the land, but adapted them so that the feasts became reminders of Israel's history.

Passover-Unleavened Bread

Passover-Unleavened Bread combined two feasts. Unleavened Bread was in the spring during the barley harvest. It was customary to make unleavened barley loaves during that celebration. The feast lasted seven days. A sheaf of the first fruits of the barley was brought to the Temple and became a "wave offering" to God. That meant that it was not burned, but merely shown to God in recognition that it was God's. Then the rest of the crop of barley was released for use by the people. When Israel entered the land, they added their own pastoral feast of Passover to the beginning of the agricultural feast of Unleavened Bread and celebrated them together. Today the word "Passover" refers to the entire eight-day festival. The origin and history of Passover is complex. The origin of the word "Passover" (Hebrew: *pesaḥ*) may be the Hebrew verb *psḥ*, "to limp." This may be explained by a limping dance performed early in the history of the rite. The Israelite feast was probably originally a spring lambing festival, meant to ward off evil spirits at the beginning of a new nomadic year. The Bible takes the word to mean a "passing over."

During the Second Temple period the ritual consisted of two parts. The first part of the ritual involved the Temple and the priesthood. The second part was a domestic ritual. If possible, one traveled to Jerusalem and procured a room and a lamb with which to celebrate Passover. At 3:00 PM on the eve of Passover (the Jewish day goes from sunset to sunset), the lambs were slaughtered in the Temple by the Levites and the blood thrown against the altar by the priests who thereby returned the life of the animal to God. The fatty portions were burned on the altar, and the rest returned to the offerer. In the second part of the ritual, the lamb was brought back to the room to be roasted and eaten by the offerer and others belonging to his group.

Exodus 12–13 is the longest biblical description of Passover. It associates the rites of both Passover and Unleavened Bread with the Exodus of the Israelites from Egypt. Unleavened bread is explained by the fact that the Israelites had to bake loaves without leaven because of the haste with which they fled Egypt. The blood ritual is a reminder that when the angel of death killed the firstborn of the Egyptians he passed over the Israelite dwellings that had blood smeared on the doorposts. For Exodus 12, Passover was a private domestic ritual. No mention is made of the Temple or of pilgrimage. The later command to celebrate Passover in Jerusalem and the role the Temple assumed in the Passover rite indicate how the priestly establishment of the Temple took control of the feast.

Weeks

The feast of Weeks (also known as the feast of Harvest, Pentecost, Day of First Fruits, Assembly) marked the wheat harvest. It was held fifty days after the feast of Unleavened Bread. Because of the fifty days it was known among Greek-speaking Jews as Pentecost (from the Greek *pentēkostos* meaning "fiftieth"). The feast was a thanksgiving to God for the harvest. God was presented with a wave offering of two loaves of bread from the new wheat.

Booths

The feast of Booths (Tabernacles, Succoth, Ingathering) was a seven-day feast to mark the autumn harvest of olives and fruits. It was marked by water libations, probably to ensure adequate rainfall during the winter rainy season, nightly dancing in the Temple precincts under the light of menorahs, processions with the "lulab" or palm branches, to which were attached twigs of myrtle, willow, and a citron, and the building of booths in which to live. The building of the booths may go back to the custom of guarding olive trees during harvesting by living among them in makeshift shelters. Leviticus' rationale for the booths is: "That your generations may know that I made the people of Israel live in booths when I brought them out of the land of Egypt" (Lev 23:43).

CONCLUSION

It is easy to judge priestly religion as ritualistic, as politics or self-interest posing as religion, or as primitive. Such judgments rest on various misunderstandings. The first misunderstanding concerns ritual. Ritual is often denigrated and seen as unimportant to the essence of religion. Such a view misconstrues the nature of ritual. Most present-day religions have a ritual component that is taken very seriously. That is because ritual symbolizes things that people take seriously, such as service to God, maintenance of social structure, and stages of life. Although people are seldom fully conscious of their own rituals, rituals maintain social structures and personal identity. When one becomes conscious of one's own rituals, one can appreciate priestly rituals as expressing ideas and serving functions that make sense. Sacrifice is out of style today, but one must look at it as a language expressing human longings, needs, and viewpoints that are comprehensible.

The second misunderstanding is due to a modern view of religion as devoted entirely to morality and "spiritual" values. Modern people often emphasize religion as personal belief and consider it purely a matter of private, individual choice. The privatization and spiritualization of religion is more characteristic of some cultures than others, but such a view is really an anomaly in the sweep of human history. During most of history, people have not seen ethics, prayer, public liturgy, politics, economics, and other affairs as easily separable from one another. There is no doubt that such divisions would be strange to Second Temple Jews and most of their contemporaries.

The third misunderstanding is closely related to the second. It is the idea that religion, politics, and economics do not mix. Temple priests were deeply involved in politics, economics, civil law, and so forth. They believed that God had decreed it so. That might seem strange to those who prize the separation between church and state. But it is difficult even today to completely separate religion from political, economic, and cultural realities—that is, from society in general. In Second Temple Judaism, religion had no autonomous existence apart from other aspects of society, but was deeply embedded in politics, economics, kinship, and culture.

The fourth misunderstanding is the assumption that attention to matters of ritual and purity means neglect of other aspects of religion. It is not true that priestly religion attended only to the surface of things and ignored spiritual and ethical values. Sins that sacrifices were meant to eradicate were ethical as well as ritual. The very division between ritual and ethical would be puzzling to an ancient Jew. The bottom line was obedience to God. When Jesus was asked which was the greatest commandment in the Torah he replied, ''The first is, 'Hear, O Israel: The Lord our God, the Lord is one; you shall love the Lord your God with all your heart, and with all your soul, and with all your mind, and with all your strength.' The second is this, 'You shall love your neighbor as yourself.' '' Jesus did not invent these commandments; he quoted them from Torah. The first commandment comes from Deuteronomy 6:4, a book concerned with the status of the Levites, the location of sacrifice in Jerusalem, and other ''ritual'' matters, as well as with the care of the poor and afflicted in society. The second commandment is taken from the heart of priestly legislation, the book named after the priestly tribe of Levi, Leviticus (19:18).

SELECT BIBLIOGRAPHY

This chapter owes much to Malina, Douglas, and Milgrom.

Büchler, A. *Studies in Sin and Atonement in the Rabbinic Literature of the First Century.* New York: Ktav, 1967.

Clements, R. E. *God and Temple.* Philadelphia: Fortress Press, 1965.

Douglas, Mary. *Purity and Danger: An Analysis of the Concepts of Pollution and Taboo.* London: Routledge and Kegan Paul, 1966.

Gammie, John G. *Holiness in Israel.* Minneapolis: Fortress Press, 1989.

Leach, Edmund. *Culture and Communication: The Logic by Which Symbols Are Connected.* Cambridge: Cambridge University, 1976.

Levenson, Jon D. *Sinai and Zion: An Entry into the Jewish Bible.* Minneapolis: Winston, 1985.

Malina, Bruce. *Christian Origins and Cultural Anthropology: Practical Models for Biblical Interpretation.* Atlanta: John Knox Press, 1986.

_____. *The New Testament World: Insights from Cultural Anthropology.* Atlanta: John Knox Press, 1981.

Meyers, Carol L. ''The Temple,'' in *HBD*, 1021-29.

Milgrom, Jacob. ''Atonement in the OT,'' in *IDBSup*, 78-82.

_____. *Studies in Cultic Theology and Terminology.* Leiden: Brill, 1983.

Neusner, Jacob. *The Idea of Purity in Ancient Judaism.* Leiden: Brill, 1973.

————. *The Religious Study of Judaism: Description, Analysis, Interpretation,* vol. 2: *The Centrality of Context.* Lanham, Md.: University Press of America, 1986.

Patai, Raphael. *Man and Temple in Ancient Jewish Myth and Ritual.* New York: Ktav, 1967.

Rylaarsdam, J. C. "Passover and Feast of Unleavened Bread," in *IDB* 3, 663-68.

Smith, Jonathan Z. *To Take Place: Toward Theory in Ritual.* Chicago: University of Chicago Press, 1987.

Sweeney, Marvin A. "Tithe," in *HBD,* 1078-79.

De Vaux, Roland. *Ancient Israel: Its Life and Institutions.* New York: McGraw-Hill, 1965.

CHAPTER THREE

The Exile

Primary Readings: Jeremiah, Ezekiel, Isaiah 40–55

THE SOURCES

There is no extant history of the exilic period in the Bible or other ancient literature. There are prophetic sources dating from the exilic period in parts of Jeremiah, Ezekiel, and Isaiah. This chapter looks at a few passages from those writings. The use of prophetic books for historical purposes is always problematic. Many oracles attributed to a given prophet may in fact have been uttered by that prophet, but there are usually later additions to and revisions of the original oracles. In general, the procedure followed here will be to treat prophetic books as ''voices'' from a particular historical period, authentic witnesses to what someone who lived during the period in question felt and thought.

THE END OF THE KINGDOM OF JUDAH

The Deuteronomistic History pronounces King Josiah of Judah (ruled 640–609 BCE) good because he pursued a religious reform that had purification and centralization of the cult at its core. In 609 BCE Josiah died fighting Egypt. The Egyptians put Josiah's son Jehoiakim on the throne as their vassal. When the Babylonians drove the Egyptians out of Palestine, they retained him as their own vassal. He soon revolted against his Babylonian lord, Nebuchadnezzar, and in 597 BCE the Babylonian ruler marched against Jerusalem. Jehoiakim died before the city was taken. His son Jehoiachin surrendered almost immediately, and was deported to Babylonia along with others: ''The king of Babylon brought captive to Babylon all the men of valor [soldiers], seven thousand, and the artisans and the smiths, one thousand, all of them strong and fit for war'' (2 Kgs 24:16). Clearly the purpose was to make Judah less capable of revolution.

The Babylonians placed another of Josiah's sons, Mattaniah, on the throne of Judah, changing his name to Zedekiah as a sign of vassalage. Zedekiah ruled for about a decade, but allied himself with Egypt against Babylonia and paid the price. In 587 BCE Jerusalem again fell to the Babylonians. The king was captured, blinded, and deported to Babylonia. The following verses describe what happened next.

93

He [Nebuchadnezzar's general] burned the house of the LORD, the king's house, and all the houses of Jerusalem; every great house he burned down. All the army of the Chaldeans who were with the captain of the guard broke down the walls around Jerusalem.[1] Nebuzaradan the captain of the guard carried into exile the rest of the people who were left in the city and the deserters who had defected to the king of Babylon—all the rest of the population. But the captain of the guard left some of the poorest people of the land to be vinedressers and tillers of the soil.

(2 Kgs 25:9-12)

With Jerusalem destroyed, the Babylonians transferred the capital of the region to Mizpah, just north of Jerusalem. They gave up on the monarchy as a way of ruling Judah and appointed Gedaliah governor. He was a prominent citizen of a courtly family and a friend of the prophet Jeremiah. In 582 BCE Gedaliah was killed by Ishmael, a member of the royal family. Many fled to Egypt to escape reprisal. The events of 597, 587, and 582 BCE resulted in a Judah deprived of most of its leaders, craftsmen, smiths, courtiers, and others. Judah entered the third decade of the sixth century with a capital destroyed, its upper classes and skilled workmen exiled, its leadership decimated, and its population severely depleted. But this is only one side of the issue.

The sources in the Hebrew Bible were preserved primarily by the part of Israel that went into exile and returned, and the story is told from their perspective. One hears little about those left in the land, who must have continued to till the land, for that was the principal source of livelihood there. Politically they were subservient to the officials appointed first by the Babylonians and then by the Persians who conquered the Babylonians and took their empire. At the beginning of Persian rule, Judah was administered from Samaria. Yahweh worshipers may have continued to worship at the sacred site of the ruins of the Temple in Jerusalem.

The Exile brought not just material devastation to Israel but a challenge to its entire world view. It must have seemed clear to many that the gods of Babylonia were far stronger than the Lord of Israel. God no longer even had a Temple on earth to call home. God's land was desolate, God's people depleted and dispersed. It was the end of an era. It was one of the greatest watersheds in Israel's history. The time of the First Temple was at an end. The monarchy was no more. For some, Israel had no future. It is against this backdrop that Second Temple Judaism takes shape.

THE EXILE: TERMINOLOGY

It is conventional usage to speak of "the Exile" and to use the adjectives "preexilic" and "postexilic." The terminology is useful and accurate to the extent that an important segment of Israel was exiled to Babylonia and then returned to Judah in various stages over the next two centuries. Nonetheless, the terminology is misleading if it is taken to mean that all of Israel went to Babylonia and then returned. Many, probably a majority, of the people of Israel were left in Palestine by the Babylonians. They regain the attention of the Hebrew Bible when some of the exiles return and have to deal with them. Furthermore, not all the exiles returned to Judah. Many stayed in Babylonia and established a community that was to be important well into the common era. In addition, many Jews went to neighboring lands such as Syria, Egypt, Phoenicia, and the lands across the Jordan, some of which were to grow into important centers of Judaism. Israel now consisted of a homeland and a dispersion. The term "Dispersion," or "Diaspora" (the Greek word for "dispersion"), denotes Jews living outside Palestine.

The Exile created a new situation. There was no longer a kingdom of Yahweh-worshipers; rather, there were Yahweh-worshipers living in Babylonia, Egypt, Palestine, and elsewhere. Since all were descendants of those who had lived in the kingdom of Judah, they were all in some sense "Judeans." (The term "Jews" comes from the term "Judeans.") A "Jew" was now a Yahweh-worshiper wherever he or she might live. The shift in terminology signals a shift in self-understanding. It defines the covenant in such a way that it can be lived out anywhere in the world, even in the absence of a Temple and independent nation.

JEREMIAH

Jeremiah preaches a message of social justice similar to that found in the DtrH. It is thought that he supported Josiah's reforms, and was disenchanted with Josiah's son Jehoiakim who was more interested in pursuing a reckless foreign policy and in increasing his own wealth than in reform. Jeremiah addresses the following words to Jehoiakim.

> Are you a king because you compete in cedar? Did not your father eat and drink and do justice and righteousness? Then it was well with him. He judged the case of the poor and needy; then it was well. Is not this to know me? says the LORD. But your eyes and heart are only on your dishonest gain, for shedding innocent blood, and for practicing oppression and violence. (Jer 22:15-17)

Jeremiah follows Deuteronomistic theology when he considers Josiah's success a result of his justice and righteousness. Jeremiah predicts disaster for Jehoiakim and Judah because of their abandonment of Josiah's reforms.

The prophet Jeremiah counseled submission to the rule of Babylonia and the institution of reform. In this he was supported by a minority of the upper classes. Those whom he opposed, who actually held the reins of power, were pursuing a policy of independence from Babylonia and consolidation of their own power. Gottwald characterizes the position of Jeremiah's opponents as "autonomist," for they wanted to win autonomy for Judah. He calls the supporters of Jeremiah "coexisters" because they thought that Judah's objective should be to pursue societal reforms that were not incompatible with coexistence with Babylonia.

> The "autonomists" saw the ruling class as faithful representatives of the people's interests and, therefore, its overthrow would mean the downfall of the people. The "coexisters," by contrast, viewed the internal socioeconomic policies of the ruling class as disastrous to the interests of the people, and saw any strengthening of that ruling class against Babylonia as an indefensible promotion of social injustice that would only further harm the common people. (403)

The Temple was built by Solomon as a sign of divine approval of his kingdom and empire. God's presence in the Temple was seen as an assurance of the invincibility of Jerusalem and the Davidic monarchy. Further proof that Jerusalem and Mount Zion would stand forever was found in the fact that Judah survived Assyrian attacks in the eighth century whereas the northern kingdom of Israel perished. But Jeremiah, as spokesman for an earlier covenantal ideology, attacked what he judged as unfounded confidence in Yahweh's unconditional support of the people and protection of the Temple. Jeremiah's attack is preserved in his famous "Temple Sermon."

> The word that came to Jeremiah from the LORD: Stand in the gate of the LORD's house, and proclaim there this word, and say, Hear the word of the LORD, all you people of Judah, you that enter these gates to worship the LORD. Thus says the LORD of hosts, the God of Israel: Amend your ways and your doings, and let me dwell with you in this place. Do not trust in these deceptive words: "This is the temple of the LORD, the temple of the LORD, the temple of the LORD." For if you truly amend your doings, if you truly act justly with one another, if you do not oppress the alien, the orphan, and the widow, or shed innocent blood in this place, and if you do not go after other gods to your own hurt, then I will dwell with you in this place, in the land that I gave of old to your ancestors forever and ever. (Jer 7:1-7)

To undermine confidence in the Temple was to challenge the priestly and royal establishment that it symbolized, and to call its policies into question.

Jeremiah 24 contains a vision in which Jeremiah sees two baskets of figs, one good and one rotten. The vision refers to the time between the first deportation (597 BCE) and the second (587 BCE), a period during which there was a substantial group of exiles in Babylonia, and Zedekiah was in Judah plotting revolt. The rotten figs are symbolic of the rebels in Judah. The good figs are explained as follows.

> Thus says the LORD, the God of Israel: Like these good figs, so I will regard as good the exiles from Judah, whom I have sent away from this place to the land of the Chaldeans. I will set my eyes upon them for good, and I will bring them back to this

land. . . . I will give them a heart to know that I am the Lord; and they shall be my
people and I will be their God, for they shall return to me with their whole heart.

(Jer 24:5-6*a*, 7)

Jeremiah says that Israel's hope lies with the exiles. Jeremiah 29 contains a letter
allegedly sent by Jeremiah to the exiles in Babylonia telling them that their exile
would last for seventy years, and that in the meantime they were to settle down in
Babylonia. He urges them not to listen to the prophets who preach rebellion.

The book of Jeremiah contains one of the most famous prophecies of
restoration in the Bible, one that was later utilized by both Jews and Christians.

The days are surely coming, says the Lord, when I will make a new covenant with
the house of Israel and the house of Judah. It will not be like the covenant that I
made with their ancestors when I took them by the hand to bring them out of the
land of Egypt—a covenant that they broke, though I was their husband, says the
Lord. But this is the covenant that I will make with the house of Israel after those
days, says the Lord: I will put my law within them, and I will write it on their hearts;
and I will be their God, and they shall be my people. No longer shall they teach one
another, or say to each other, "Know the Lord," for they shall all know me, from
the least of them to the greatest, says the Lord; for I will forgive their iniquity, and
remember their sin no more. (Jer 31:31-34)

Jeremiah sees Israel's misfortunes at the hands of Babylonia as punishment for
its unfaithfulness. When God reestablishes God's covenant with Israel, the Law
will be implanted in the hearts of all Israelites. The prophecy foresees the day
when Israel will again be united, north and south (Israel and Judah). The Law
will be equally accessible to all, small and great.

EZEKIEL

Ezekiel was a priest and a prophet living among the exiles. He prophesied
from 593 to 571 BCE. Ezekiel 1–24 comes from before the catastrophe of 587 BCE,
and the rest of the book comes from after that date. Ezekiel 1–24 criticizes Israel
and looks to God's punishment, Ezekiel 25–32 contains oracles against foreign
nations, and Ezekiel 33–48 predicts Israel's restoration. The book of Ezekiel is
of special interest for a number of reasons. First, it originates among the exiled
members of Israel. Second, it represents a priestly analysis of the destruction of
Jerusalem and the Temple. Third, it affords a glimpse into a priestly power
struggle.

Ezekiel opens with a vision of God. It combines aspects of theophanies
(appearances of God, such as at Sinai) and mythological elements (elements
deriving from the sacred stories of the ancient Near East) to create a powerful and
mysterious description of God. The description validates the book's message

97

because it shows that the prophet has encountered God. God appears with the conventional elements of stormy wind, cloud, and fire. God rides something that is a combination of throne and chariot, like the Canaanite storm god Baal, who rides the clouds as his chariot. God is accompanied by four "living creatures" who are cherubim guarding God, as cherubim guarded the Ark of the Covenant. The summation of the theophany is important: "Such was the appearance . . . of the likeness of the glory of the LORD. When I saw it, I fell on my face, and I heard the voice of someone speaking (Ezek 1:28*b*). The phrase "the appearance . . . of the likeness of" shows a reluctance to claim too much for the vision lest it imply that God can be captured in a description. The "glory of the LORD" is a priestly way of speaking of the presence of God without limiting God in any way. Ezekiel's falling on his face expresses fear and reverence appropriate to an appearance of God. It is a conventional element in a theophany. God's response is also conventional; that is, it pulls Ezekiel out of his attitude of fear into one of attention to the revelation about to take place.

God's appearance to Ezekiel in Babylonia signifies that God is present with the exiles, even though they no longer inhabit God's land, Judah. God's presence with the exiles is made explicit in 11:16: "Thus says the Lord GOD: Though I removed them far away among the nations, and though I scattered them among the countries, yet I have been a sanctuary to them for a little while in the countries where they have gone." Ezekiel is told to bring the message to Israel that they are soon to be punished for their sins. Jerusalem is soon to be destroyed: "As I live, says the Lord GOD,[2] surely, because you have defiled my sanctuary with all your detestable things and with all your abominations—therefore I will cut you down; my eye will not spare, and I will have no pity" (5:11).

The verse uses priestly terms and concepts that appear throughout Ezekiel. Israel's sins, especially idolatry, have "defiled" God's sanctuary, and God must respond. Behind this is the idea that God remains in the sanctuary only so long as those things which are repugnant, "abominations," are kept out of it.

An example of Ezekiel's priestly outlook occurs in chapter 36. The chapter looks forward to Israel's restoration and explains why Israel was exiled.

Mortal, when the house of Israel lived on their own soil, they defiled it with their ways and their deeds; their conduct in my sight was like the uncleanness of a woman in her menstrual period.[3] So I poured out my wrath upon them for the blood that they had shed upon the land, and for the idols with which they had defiled it. I scattered them among the nations, and they were dispersed through the countries; in accordance with their conduct and their deeds I judged them. But when they came to the nations, wherever they came, they profaned my holy name, in that it was said of them, "These are the people of the LORD, and yet they had to go out of his land." But I had concern for my holy name, which the house of Israel had profaned among the nations to which they came. Therefore say to the house of

Israel, Thus says the Lord God: It is not for your sake, O house of Israel, that I am about to act, but for the sake of my holy name, which you have profaned among the nations to which you came. (36:17-22)

God accuses Israel of bloodshed and idolatry. Since blood symbolizes life, and life belongs only to God, to take the life of human beings without God's approval is to usurp God's authority. It is an indirect attack on God because humans are in God's image. The prolific shedding of blood at the end of the seventh and the beginning of the sixth centuries BCE defiled God's land. Further, the defiling influence of foreign religion in Judah is clear in that Hezekiah and Josiah needed reforms to remove it.

When Israel is exiled, the entire world learns of their disgrace, and that reflects negatively on God. If the situation is to be rectified, God must demonstrate power and faithfulness by restoring the people to their land and prosperity. God says that will happen, but not because the people deserve it. "I will sanctify my great name, which has been profaned among the nations, and which you have profaned among them; and the nations shall know that I am the LORD, says the Lord God, when through you I display my holiness before their eyes" (36:23). The nations know that God is almighty only through God's actions. That the nations "shall know that I am the LORD" is a refrain in Ezekiel that is a frequent motivation for divine action. Implied by all this is the assumption that political events and theological conclusions go hand in hand. They cannot be separated. The exile of Israel will lead to certain conclusions by the nations about Israel's God, and God knows that political action, the restoration of Israel and the punishment of its enemies, is necessary to set the record straight.

God cannot simply put the people back in the holy land without first purifying them. "I will sprinkle clean water upon you, and you shall be clean from all your uncleannesses, and from all your idols I will cleanse you" (36:25). But the following verses give the lie to those who would see the priestly way of looking at things as superficial or merely external, based on quasi-magical assumptions.[4]

A new heart I will give you, and a new spirit I will put within you; and I will remove from your body the heart of stone and give you a heart of flesh. I will put my spirit within you, and make you follow my statutes and be careful to observe my ordinances. Then you shall live in the land that I gave to your ancestors; and you shall be my people, and I will be your God. (36:26-28)

These words recall the "new covenant" in Jeremiah 31. They speak of an internal change in the people that brings them into harmony with God's will. Then they will be fit to dwell in God's land.

The ideal situation for priestly religion is God present in his Temple, accepting the gifts of his people, offering them protection and prosperity. It is an entirely this-worldly goal, with everything in harmony and in accord with God's ordering of the universe. The connection of a pure people in a pure land with prosperity is explicit in 36:29-30: "I will save you from all your uncleannesses; and I will summon the grain and make it abundant and lay no famine upon you. I will make the fruit of the tree and the produce of the field abundant, so that you may never again suffer the disgrace of famine among the nations." Famine indicates God's disfavor. God is the source of rain and fertility. When the people are cleansed from their sin, there will be no reason for God to deny them rain and plentiful harvests. God's plan is to bring Israel back into conformity with the divine will, making them pure and obedient. Then the world will operate as originally intended. The image of the Garden of Eden conveys the rightness of this state of affairs. It corresponds to what God wanted for the world in the beginning: "And they will say, 'This land that was desolate has become like the garden of Eden; and the waste and desolate and ruined towns are now inhabited and fortified'" (36:35). Priestly religion sees proper observance of God's regulations, rituals, and ethical standards as the way to ensure that the world will work properly.

True to a priestly orientation, Ezekiel 36 concludes by comparing future human fertility to the feasts held in Jerusalem: "I will also let the house of Israel ask me to do this for them: to increase their population like a flock. Like the flock for sacrifices, like the flock at Jerusalem during her appointed festivals, so shall the ruined towns be filled with flocks of people" (36:37-38).

Dissatisfaction with the kings of Judah is evident in several places in Ezekiel. One of the clearest instances is chapter 34. The people are compared to a flock, a common image, and the kings are their shepherds. The chapter begins with a sharp accusation: "Mortal, prophesy against the shepherds of Israel: prophesy, and say to them—to the shepherds: Thus says the Lord GOD: Ah, you shepherds of Israel who have been feeding yourselves! Should not shepherds feed the sheep?" (34:2). According to Davidic royal ideology the main function of the king was to execute justice in the land, to make sure that God's will was carried out. Since one of God's central characteristics was to protect the powerless and poor, the king was supposed to do the same. The passage uses this ideology to accuse the kings: "You have not strengthened the weak, you have not healed the sick, you have not bound up the injured, you have not brought back the strayed, you have not sought the lost, but with force and harshness you have ruled them" (34:4). The chapter holds the kings responsible for the Exile. If the people sin, it is because they do not have adequate leadership. The people become a prey for the wild beasts because there is no shepherd (34:8).

Since God's royal representatives have failed in their responsibilities, God will take over their work. "I myself will search for my sheep, and will seek them out" (34:11). Since the people have been scattered to Babylon, Egypt, and elsewhere, God must now "bring them out from the peoples and gather them from the countries, and . . . bring them into their own land" (34:13).

I myself will be the shepherd of my sheep, and I will make them lie down, says the Lord God. I will seek the lost, and I will bring back the strayed, and I will bind up the injured, and I will strengthen the weak, but the fat and the strong I will destroy. I will feed them with justice. (34:15-16)

The people do not escape unscathed. "As for you, my flock, thus says the Lord God: I shall judge between sheep and sheep, between rams and goats" (34:17).[5]

Ezekiel does not renounce the monarchy. The picture of restoration in 34:20-31 sees Israel resettled prosperously under David. The reference to the rule of David is probably not to be taken literally, but as a symbol of a restored Davidic monarchy. Restoration of king and Temple appears also in 37:24-28.

My servant David shall be king over them; and they shall all have one shepherd. They shall follow my ordinances and be careful to observe my statutes. They shall live in the land that I gave to my servant Jacob, in which your ancestors lived; they and their children and their children's children shall live there forever; and my servant David shall be their prince forever. I will make a covenant of peace with them; it shall be an everlasting covenant with them; and I will bless them and multiply them, and will set my sanctuary among them forevermore. My dwelling place shall be with them; and I will be their God, and they shall be my people. Then the nations shall know that I the Lord sanctify Israel, when my sanctuary is among them forevermore.

One could hardly expect a fuller statement of the priestly ideal of restoration.

In 593 BCE, Ezekiel prophesies against those who had not been exiled in 597 BCE. God is angry at Judah's continued idolatry. In chapter 8 Ezekiel is transported "in visions of God" to Jerusalem to view the idolatry. The religions of foreign deities have been brought into Jerusalem and even into the Temple itself. The next few chapters are structured partially by descriptions of God's departure from the Temple, which has become so repulsive that God must leave it. The worst possible scenario for a priest, the abandonment of the Temple by God, must become reality.

In 9:3 God leaves the place over the Ark and goes to the doorway of the Holy Place: "Now the glory of the God of Israel had gone up from the cherubim on which it rested to the threshold of the house." The next step occurs in 10:3-5:

Now the cherubim were standing on the south side of the house when the man went in, and a cloud filled the inner court. Then the glory of the Lord rose up from the cherub to the threshold of the house; the house was filled with the cloud, and the court was full of the brightness of the glory of the Lord. The sound of the wings of the cherubim was heard as far as the outer court, like the voice of God Almighty when he speaks.

101

The cloud symbolizes the presence of God such as when God appeared on Sinai, and when God originally took possession of the sanctuary in 1 Kings 8. God is now present in the Holy Place (the main room of the Temple) and in the courtyard just outside the front door of the Temple where the altar is located. Those in the court beyond the inner court are now able to hear the commotion.

"The cherubim rose up. These were the living creatures that I saw by the river Chebar" (10:15). The verse refers to Ezekiel's original vision in Babylon. He recognizes the cherubim who guard God in the Temple as the ones he saw guarding God in Babylonia where God spoke to Ezekiel.

> Then the glory of the LORD went out from the threshold of the house and stopped above the cherubim. The cherubim lifted up their wings and rose up from the earth in my sight as they went out with the wheels beside them. They stopped at the entrance of the east gate of the house of the LORD; and the glory of the God of Israel was above them. (10:18-19)

God rides the cherubim to the east gate of the Temple. The east gate leads from the courtyard surrounding the Temple to the outside. God is thus continuing along the path from the Holy of Holies, through the Holy Place, the inner court, and is now about to leave the Temple precincts altogether.

The final stage of God's departure from the Temple and the city is depicted in 11:22-23: "Then the cherubim lifted up their wings, with the wheels beside them; and the glory of the God of Israel was above them. And the glory of the LORD ascended from the middle of the city, and stopped on the mountain east of the city."[6] Since God has now left the Temple and Jerusalem, they can be taken by the Babylonians. God heads east, the direction of Babylonia.

The fullest statement of Ezekiel's program for restoration is Ezekiel 40–48. Most of the section is devoted to detailed plans for the restored Temple. It is basically the Solomonic Temple rebuilt, but with some idealizing features. The form this section takes is a vision given to Ezekiel by God, meant to be taken as authoritative. After a description of the Temple and its precincts, God returns to the rebuilt Temple.

> Then he [an angel] brought me to the gate, the gate facing east. And there, the glory of the God of Israel was coming from the east; the sound was like the sound of mighty waters; and the earth shone with his glory. The vision was like the vision that I had seen when he came to destroy the city, and like the vision that I had seen by the river Chebar; and I fell upon my face. As the glory of the LORD entered the temple by the gate facing east, the spirit lifted me up, and brought me into the inner court; and the glory of the LORD filled the temple. (43:1-5)

The path God takes to reenter the Temple is the reverse of the one God followed out of it. God is now back in the Temple. The effect of the Exile and of the destruction of Jerusalem has been to purge the city and the people so that God can dwell among them again.

The plan of restoration in Ezekiel involves keeping the Temple and its precincts holy in every respect. It is a concern one would expect from a priest. Atonement must be made for the new altar; it must be purified with blood (43:20-22). Foreigners are strictly banned from the Temple precincts (44:9). Purity now means even tighter definitions of who is a true Israelite and the enforcement of those definitions in the cult, which is a symbol for the structure of society itself.

Chapter 44 tells of a distinction between priest and Levite that Ezekiel presents as new.

> But the Levites who went far from me, going astray from me after their idols when Israel went astray, shall bear their punishment. They shall be ministers in my sanctuary, having oversight at the gates of the temple, and serving in the temple; they shall slaughter the burnt offering and the sacrifice for the people, and they shall attend on them and serve them. . . . They shall not come near to me, to serve me as priest, nor come near any of my sacred offerings, the things that are most sacred; but they shall bear their shame; and the consequences of the abominations that they have committed. Yet I will appoint them to keep charge of the temple, to do all its chores, all that is to be done in it. But the levitical priests, the descendants of Zadok, who kept the charge of my sanctuary when the people of Israel went astray from me, shall come near to me to minister to me; and they shall attend me to offer me the fat and the blood, says the Lord GOD. It is they who shall enter my sanctuary, it is they who shall approach my table, to minister to me, and they shall keep my charge. (44:10-11, 13-16)

Ezekiel believes that some segments of the priesthood should be kept from altar duty as a punishment for their lax attitude to foreign influences in the cult. Ezekiel refers to these sinning ministers as "Levites." They are to be restricted to less sacred duties such as the slaying of sacrifices and the watching of the gates. They are not allowed to bring the fat and the blood to the altar itself, a function reserved to the "descendants of Zadok," who are seen as the only true "levitical priests." That the Levites are being denied altar duty implies that this is a demotion for them and that they had been allowed closer approach to the altar in the preexilic period.

Such desires for restructuring the priesthood were not carried out in the actual restoration. Priests other than those who claimed descent from Zadok served at the altar along with the Zadokites in the postexilic period. But Ezekiel reveals that there were factions in the priesthood, and that there were power struggles between those factions. The history of Second Temple Judaism shows that conflicts within the priesthood did not end with Ezekiel.

According to the priestly symbolic system, priests were at the apex of society,

103

being allowed closest approach to God. They were also powerful in the structuring of the rest of society because it was they who declared clean and unclean, and so interpreted purity rules guarding society's structure. Both of these aspects, that of the holiness of the priests and of their authority to declare clean and unclean, appear in chapter 44 where the functions of the sons of Zadok are elucidated. "When they [the priests] go out into the outer court to the people, they shall remove the vestments in which they have been ministering, and lay them in the holy chambers; and they shall put on other garments, so that they may not communicate holiness to the people with their vestments" (44:19). This verse expresses the privileged access the priests have to the most holy places, the lack of access of the people to those places, and the role of the priests as middlemen, inhabitants of both the world of the sacred and the world of the profane. They belong to the people, but are separate from them ("holy").

> They shall teach my people the difference between the holy and the common, and show them how to distinguish between the unclean and the clean. In a controversy they shall act as judges, and they shall decide it according to my judgments. They shall keep my laws and my statutes regarding all my appointed festivals, and they shall keep my sabbaths holy. (44:23-24)

SECOND ISAIAH

In 539 BCE the Babylonian empire was taken over by Cyrus, the first Persian emperor. One of Cyrus' policies was to allow local states to rebuild and establish a ruling structure loyal to the empire. Palestine was in a strategic location, controlling access to Egypt. Cyrus decreed that the Jews would be allowed to return to Judah, rebuild their Temple and capital city, and reestablish their society. A prophet arose at this time to explain to the exiles that the great international shifts that were taking place were due to God's plan for Israel. His oracles were preserved in what are now chapters 40–55 of the book of Isaiah. The chapters assembled in his name are referred to as "Second Isaiah." Second Isaiah saw the despair that many of his fellow Jews felt at God's inaction in the face of their misery:

> Why do you say, O Jacob, and speak, O Israel, "My way is hidden from the LORD, and my right is disregarded by my God"? Have you not known? Have you not heard? The LORD is the everlasting God, the Creator of the ends of the earth. He does not faint or grow weary; his understanding is unsearchable. (40:27-28)

For Second Isaiah, those who question God are unjustified. God's might and faithfulness are a source of hope. If God is faithful to the people, and if God is the almighty God responsible for creation, then God's apparent inaction must be part of the divine plan, a plan mere humans could not hope to understand. The interweaving of the images of God as Creator and God as the one who chose Israel and led them out of Egypt is characteristic of Second Isaiah. The Yahwist had already shown the relation of Israel's history to creation by putting Genesis 2–11 at the beginning of his version of the Israelite epic. Second Isaiah now plays out the implications of that.

Second Isaiah counsels patience. "Those who wait for the LORD shall renew their strength" (40:31a). As Isaiah sees the successive victories of Cyrus, he realizes that the exiles do not have long to wait.

It is a fairly universal theme in Jewish writing that the Babylonian Exile was a punishment for Israel's sins. Second Isaiah is no exception. The book begins, "Comfort, O comfort my people, says your God. Speak tenderly to Jerusalem, and cry to her that she has served her term, that her penalty is paid, that she has received from the LORD's hand double for all her sins" (40:1-2). The Exile is indeed punishment for sin, but Israel has paid the price and more. Jerusalem is told that its time of misery is finished.

The next verses recall Ezekiel's vision of God's return to Jerusalem.

A voice cries out:
"In the wilderness prepare the way of the LORD, make straight in the desert a
  highway for our God.
Every valley shall be lifted up, and every mountain and hill be made low;
the uneven ground shall become level, and the rough places a plain.
Then the glory of the LORD shall be revealed, and all people shall see it together, for
  the mouth of the LORD has spoken." (40:3-5)

Babylon is east of Jerusalem. Between the two cities stretches a desert, full of obstacles to anyone daring to cross it. It is through this wilderness that God will come back to Jerusalem. A heavenly voice orders preparation of God's way by making the wilderness easy to traverse. The entire world will witness God's journey back to Jerusalem: "All people shall see it together." This sounds the note of universalism audible throughout Second Isaiah. God is the creator of all. But God chose Israel to be a special people. It is through Israel and God's interaction with it that the world will come to know God as its Creator and its only hope of well-being. All other gods are but idols with no real existence.

God's triumphant march to Jerusalem is further described in 40:9-11.

Get you up to a high mountain, O Zion, herald of good tidings;
Lift up your voice with strength, O Jerusalem, herald of good tidings, lift it up, do not
  fear;
say to the cities of Judah, "Here is your God!"
See, the Lord GOD comes with might, and his arm rules for him; his reward is with
  him, and his recompense before him.
He will feed his flock like a shepherd; he will gather the lambs in his arms.
and carry them in his bosom, and gently lead the mother sheep.

Zion is the mountain on which the Temple was built, Jerusalem the city in which God dwells. Jerusalem itself is told to announce to all the cities of Judah that God is coming back. God's return is described in joyous terms. He comes both as a powerful king ("His arm rules for him") and as tender shepherd, images that recall Ezekiel 34.

The rest of Isaiah 40 emphasizes God's might. To hear the following verses must have been especially surprising for the exiles: "Even the nations are like a drop from a bucket, and are accounted as dust on the scales; see, he takes up the isles like fine dust" (40:15). "All the nations are as nothing before him; they are accounted by him as less than nothing and emptiness" (40:17). "Who [God] brings princes to naught, and makes the rulers of the earth as nothing" (40:23). Those who had experienced the destruction of Jerusalem and the Exile might have pointed out that recent political events seemed to cast doubt on this view. The God of Israel had a strange way of showing power.

Second Isaiah claimed that a true interpretation of the rise of Cyrus king of Persia would reveal what God was really doing now. It made the astounding claim that Cyrus' earth-shaking and meteoric rise to power was all for the benefit of Israel! God brought him to power for the purpose of letting the Israelites return to Judah to rebuild.

> Thus says the LORD to his anointed, to Cyrus, whose right hand I have grasped
> to subdue nations before him and strip kings of their robes,
> to open doors before him—and the gates shall not be closed:
> I will go before you and level the mountains,
> I will break in pieces the doors of bronze and cut through the bars of iron,
> I will give you the treasures of darkness and riches hidden in secret places,
> so that you may know that it is I, the LORD, the God of Israel, who call you by your name.
> For the sake of my servant Jacob, and Israel my chosen,
> I call you by your name, I surname you, though you do not know me.
> I am the LORD, and there is no other; besides me there is no god. I arm you, though you do not know me,
> so that they may know, from the rising of the sun and from the west, that there is no one besides me; I am the LORD, and there is no other.
> I form light and create darkness, I make weal and create woe; I the LORD do all these things. (45:1-7)

Second Isaiah admits that Cyrus is not aware of being an instrument of God, but it is the God of Israel who has made the victories of Cyrus possible. God has opened city gates and given him the treasures of kingdoms, and it is all for the sake of Israel. Cyrus is so important in God's plans that Second Isaiah goes so far as to call him God's anointed (messiah). This is the only passage in the Hebrew Bible where a non-Israelite is called God's messiah.

Second Isaiah's picture of restoration is more general than the priestly picture painted by Ezekiel. Second Isaiah looks forward to the freeing of the exiles, the rebuilding of Jerusalem, and the recognition of the God of Israel as the only true God. All of this is to happen soon: "Listen to me, you stubborn of heart, you who are far from deliverance: I bring near my deliverance, it is not far off, and my salvation will not tarry; I will put salvation in Zion, for Israel my glory" (46:12-13). God's deliverance and salvation do not consist of some other-worldly reward to be given after death. It is the very concrete reestablishment of Israel in the land. Hope of an afterlife is not in question.

Universalism is an important element of Second Isaiah. The oracles were uttered amidst a group that had its own history and religion, but not its own land or state. In spite of that, the oracles see great international events as focused on the Jews, and as brought about by their God. Second Isaiah claims not only that Israel's God is greater and stronger than those of other nations, but also that Israel's God is the only real God. This is a step beyond what is attested by earlier parts of the Hebrew Bible where worship of Yahweh did not necessarily mean disbelief in the existence of other gods. In earlier texts it could mean that although other gods might exist, Yahweh demanded exclusive worship. The first commandment can be read as implying the existence of other gods but prohibiting their worship: "You shall have no other gods before me" (Deut 5:7).

Second Isaiah is uncompromising in its denial of any reality to foreign deities. In the end, even the nations will recognize the truth of Second Isaiah's position.

Thus says the LORD:
The wealth of Egypt and the merchandise of Ethiopia, and the Sabeans, tall of stature,
    shall come over to you and be yours, they shall follow you; they shall come over in
    chains and bow down to you.
They will make supplication to you, saying, "God is with you alone, and there is no
    other; there is no god besides him."
Truly, you are a God who hides himself, O God of Israel, the Savior.
All of them are put to shame and confounded, the makers of idols go in confusion
    together.
But Israel is saved by the LORD with everlasting salvation;
you shall not be put to shame or confounded to all eternity. (45:14-17)

The theme of universalism reemerges in one of four poems referred to as the "Servant Songs," so named because they feature a figure called "servant" (42:1-4; 49:1-6; 50:4-11; 52:13–53:12). "Servant" is a word common in Second Isaiah, but its precise referent shifts from context to context. Sometimes it means the prophet himself, sometimes Israel, and sometimes the meaning is unclear.

Such is the case for the identity of the servant in the four songs. In the following passage the servant is the prophet himself.

> And now the Lord says, who formed me in the womb to be his servant,
> to bring Jacob back to him, and that Israel might be gathered to him,
> for I am honored in the sight of the Lord, and my God has become my strength—
> he says, "It is too light a thing that you should be my servant to raise up the tribes of Jacob and to restore the survivors of Israel;
> I will give you as a light to the nations, that my salvation may reach to the end of the earth." (49:5-6)

The prophet is not to confine his mission to Israel. God sends him to proclaim salvation to all nations. All nations will find salvation by recognizing the Creator, the God of Israel. God says in 45:22-23, "Turn to me and be saved, all the ends of the earth! For I am God, and there is no other."

To recognize God is to obey the Law. The nations must understand that God's Law, revealed at Sinai and proclaimed from Jerusalem, is binding on them, too. God says, "Listen to me, my people, and give heed to me, my nation; for a teaching will go out from me, and my justice for a light to the peoples" (51:4). Zion is the symbol for the unity of the entire human race in worship of the God of Israel, in obedience to the Law, and in benefiting from God's protection and salvation. These elements in one form or another became part of the Zion theology inherited and interpreted by later Jews and Christians.

An important embodiment of the servant figure in Second Isaiah is the suffering servant found in the final song, 52:13–53:12. The song begins (52:12-15) by saying that the servant suffered tremendously, but would be "exalted and lifted up." "So he shall startle many nations; kings shall shut their mouths because of him" (52:15), because of the reversal of his fortune. The kings themselves then take up the song.

> Who has believed what we have heard? And to whom has the arm of the Lord been revealed?
> For he grew up before him like a young plant, and like a root out of dry ground;
> he had no form or majesty that we should look at him, nothing in his appearance that we should desire him.
> He was despised and rejected by others; a man of suffering and acquainted with infirmity;
> and as one from whom others hide their faces he was despised, and we held him of no account.
> Surely he has borne our infirmities and carried our diseases;
> yet we accounted him stricken, struck down by God, and afflicted.
> But he was wounded for our transgressions, crushed for our iniquities;

upon him was the punishment that made us whole, and by his bruises we are healed.
All we like sheep have gone astray; we have all turned to our own way,
and the LORD has laid on him the iniquity of us all.
He was oppressed, and he was afflicted, yet he did not open his mouth;
like a lamb that is led to the slaughter, and like a sheep that before its shearers is silent,
    so he did not open his mouth.
By a perversion of justice he was taken away. Who could have imagined his future?
For he was cut off from the land of the living, stricken for the transgression of my
    people.
They made his grave with the wicked and his tomb with the rich,
although he had done no violence, and there was no deceit in his mouth.
Yet it was the will of the LORD to crush him with pain.
When you make his life an offering for sin, he shall see his offspring, and shall
    prolong his days;
through him the will of the LORD shall prosper. Out of his anguish he shall see light;
he shall find satisfaction through his knowledge. The righteous one, my servant, shall
    make many righteous, and he shall bear their iniquities.
Therefore I will allot him a portion with the great, and he shall divide the spoil with the
    strong;
because he poured out himself to death, and was numbered with the transgressors;
yet he bore the sin of many, and made intercession for the transgressors. (53:1-12)

The passage has been used to interpret the sufferings of Jesus, but its original meaning is unclear. One interpretation sees the suffering servant as Israel, whose suffering in the Exile and subsequent rescue by God is a sign to the nations that Israel's God is the true God. Israel's sufferings bring the world to a recognition of its God, and so the sufferings are salvific.

Second Isaiah reinterpreted Israel's traditions. It brings together covenant, creation, Exodus, servanthood, the call of Abraham, and other traditional elements to form a new work that speaks to a situation:

"I am the LORD, your Holy One, the Creator of Israel, your King."
Thus says the LORD, who makes a way in the sea, a path in the mighty waters,
who brings out chariot and horse, army and warrior;
they lie down, they cannot rise, they are extinguished, quenched like a wick:
"Do not remember the former things, or consider the things of old.
I am about to do a new thing; now it springs forth, do you not perceive it?
I will make a way in the wilderness and rivers in the desert.
The wild animals will honor me, the jackals and the ostriches;
for I give water in the wilderness, rivers in the desert,
to give drink to my chosen people, the people whom I formed for myself
so that they might declare my praise." (Isa 43:15-21)

The passage reminds the people of what God has done for them by alluding to the Exodus, but it tells them to forget past events because what is happening now is so much greater.

CONCLUSION

The Babylonian Exile marks the transitional period between monarchical Israel and Israel of the Second Temple. Since so little is known about the history of the Exile, this chapter has concentrated on three voices from the period, those of Jeremiah, Ezekiel, and Second Isaiah. Each of these three prophets had to confront the disaster of the destruction of Jerusalem and its Temple, and the loss of the land. Each prophet explained Israel's misfortune as punishment for its sins, and each looked forward to a restoration of God's people in the future.

SELECT BIBLIOGRAPHY

Ackroyd, Peter R. *Exile and Restoration: A Study of Hebrew Thought of the Sixth Century B.C.* Philadelphia: Westminster Press, 1968.

_____. *Israel Under Babylon and Persia.* Oxford: Oxford University Press, 1970.

Anderson, Bernhard. *UOT,* chaps. 13 and 14.

Bright, John. *HI,* 341-464.

_____. *Jeremiah,* AB 9, Garden City, N.Y.: Doubleday, 1965.

Gottwald, Norman. *HB,* 390-438, 482-502.

Gowan, Donald. *BBT,* chap. 2.

Klein, Ralph W. *Israel in Exile: A Theological Interpretation.* Philadelphia: Fortress Press, 1979.

Levenson, Jon. *Theology of the Program of Restoration of Ezekiel 40-48.* Missoula, Mont.: Scholars Press, 1976.

Muilenburg, James. "Introduction and Exegesis to Isaiah 40–66," in *IB* 5, 381-773.

Smith, Morton. *Palestinian Parties and Politics That Shaped the Old Testament.* New York: Columbia University Press, 1971.

Westermann, Claus. *Isaiah 40–66.* Philadelphia: Westminster Press, 1969.

Zimmerli, Walther. *Ezekiel,* 2 vols. Philadelphia: Fortress Press, 1979.

PART II

Second Temple Judaism
in Palestine

CHAPTER FOUR

The Restoration

Primary Readings: Haggai, Zechariah 1–8, Isaiah 56–66, Malachi, Ezra, Nehemiah

THE SOURCES

This chapter covers the period from the rebuilding of the Temple in 520–515 BCE to the conquest of Palestine by Alexander the Great in 332 BCE. The main source for the period is the Chronicler's History (CH) comprising 1 and 2 Chronicles, Ezra, and Nehemiah. To provide eyewitness reflections on the period, four prophetic writings are examined: Haggai, Zechariah 1–8, Isaiah 56–66, and Malachi.

The Chronicler's History tells the story of Israel from the creation to the missions of Ezra and Nehemiah (late fifth to early fourth centuries BCE). The CH rewrites DtrH extensively, and then continues the story into the postexilic period. It shares DtrH's view that obedience to God brings reward and disobedience brings punishment. The Chronicler is unique, however, in its extreme emphasis on Temple, cult, and Torah as the center of Israel's existence and the goal of history. David and Solomon are prominent in the history, but their importance is due to their founding the cult in Jerusalem. Kings of the northern kingdom are not deemed worthy to be included in the history, most likely for the same reason they are judged bad by the DtrH—they worship at their own shrines, not at Jerusalem. Each of the kings of Judah is judged according to his faithfulness to a pure cult.

Because the last events narrated by the Chronicler probably take place in 398 BCE, the work should be dated sometime in the fourth century BCE. It assumed its final shape when Israel was well established in the land and its restored cultic institutions had been in operation for some time. The CH remembers the restoration of the cult and community as what gave rise to its own situation. It sees the establishment of the cult by David and Solomon and its maintenance by successive Davidic kings as the goal of Israelite history. Unfaithfulness to the Temple led to the Exile, but God's mercy allowed the cultic community to be reestablished. In the Chronicler's estimation, all of Israel was exiled to Babylonia. As the exiles return, it is they who represent the true Israel. The claim of any others still resident in the land to be part of Israel is suspect, and can be accepted only if they conform to the kind of Judaism that had developed in the exiled community.

THE RETURN TO JUDAH

Israel was ruled by Persia from 539 to 332 BCE. Cyrus allowed the Jewish exiles in Babylonia to return home in 538 BCE. He thought that the best way to rule an extended empire was to establish local governments loyal to him. It was especially important for Persia to strengthen Palestine because of its strategic location. There were several large-scale returns of exiles over the next century and a half, and all were led by Jews who had become prominent in the Persian government. The first was led by a Jewish court official named Sheshbazzar in 538 BCE (Ezra 1:5-11; 5:13-16). He may be the same as the Davidic Shenazzar of 1 Chronicles 3:17-18. Some identify him with the Zerubbabel who was prominent during the building of the Temple. The book of Ezra tells us that Cyrus gave Sheshbazzar the Temple's sacred vessels to bring back to Jerusalem. Ezra 5:16 asserts that Sheshbazzar laid the foundations of a new temple. It is unclear just how much he accomplished, but when the building of the Temple was taken up in 520 BCE it does not seem that much had yet been done. The return of 538 BCE either was of quite limited scope or was not very successful.

In 520 BCE a large group of exiles returned to Judah under the leadership of Zerubbabel and Joshua (not to be confused with the Joshua who succeeded Moses and who led the Israelites into Canaan). Zerubbabel was appointed governor of the province by the Persians (Hag 1:1; 2:2), and Joshua was the head priest. Ezra 3–6 describes the rebuilding of the Temple under the leadership of these two men.[1] Some inhabitants of Palestine opposed the new building program. When Nebuchadnezzar destroyed Jerusalem, some of the neighboring peoples took advantage of the situation to expand into Judah's territory. They would have resisted the reestablishment of Jerusalem and its ruling class. It is also possible that Israelite peasants left in the land were not eager to submit to the authority of returning exiles, most of whom had been born in Babylonia (it was now sixty-seven years after the fall of Jerusalem).

There were some inhabitants of Palestine who wanted to join in the rebuilding:

> When the adversaries of Judah and Benjamin heard that the returned exiles were building a temple to the LORD, the God of Israel, they approached Zerubbabel and the heads of families and said to them, "Let us build with you, for we worship your God as you do, and we have been sacrificing to him ever since the days of King Esarhaddon of Assyria who brought us here." But Zerubbabel, Jeshua [Joshua], and the rest of the heads of families in Israel said to them, "You shall have no part with us in building a house to our God; but we alone will build to the LORD, the God of Israel, as King Cyrus of Persia has commanded us." (4:1-3)

The returned exiles confront a group that traces its origins to the colonization of the northern kingdom by the Assyrians. After the Assyrians exiled members of

114

the northern kingdom of Israel in 721 BCE, they brought in foreigners to resettle Samaria. According to the view of DtrH repeated here, the new settlers in the north, the Samaritans, adopted the religion of Yahweh, the God of the land (2 Kgs 17:25-28). The returned exiles did not recognize these Samaritans as legitimate Yahweh worshipers, and declined their involvement in rebuilding the Temple. The Samaritans, scorned by the returned exiles, tried to stop the building by sending word to the Persian emperor (now Darius I) that if he allowed the Jews to settle Jerusalem, the restored community would rebel against him. Darius ultimately overruled the protesters. The builders finished their work, and Israel celebrated the dedication of the Temple and resumed the liturgical life of the Temple ''as it is written in the book of Moses'' (6:18). Here is another of the themes of the CH. The restored cult is seen as a fulfillment of Mosaic Law.

The returned people celebrated their first Passover in Palestine.

> On the fourteenth day of the first month the returned exiles kept the passover. For both the priests and the Levites had purified themselves; all of them were clean. So they killed the passover lamb for all the returned exiles, for their fellow priests, and for themselves. It was eaten by the people of Israel who had returned from exile, and also by all who had joined them and separated themselves from the pollutions of the nations of the land to worship the LORD, the God of Israel. (6:19-21)

Noteworthy in this passage is the repetition of the phrase ''returned exiles.'' It is they who celebrate Passover. The others who may join them are only those who separate themselves from the ''pollutions of the nations of the land.''

Joining the returned exiles implied separation from those who already lived in the land. Some of the latter were Yahweh worshipers, so the need to remain apart from others meant avoidance not just of idolatry, but also of others who believed themselves to be Israelites. The returned exiles emphasized communal boundaries. The boundaries were expressed by way of ritual purity—who might and who might not legitimately celebrate the Passover. Defining the community properly was a matter of survival, a survival that can be looked at sociologically (failing to maintain clear boundaries would result in assimilation into a larger culture where self-identity would be lost) or religiously (God demanded pure worship and would punish anyone who defiled it).

HAGGAI

The return to Judah under Zerubbabel involved a large group, but many Jews remained in Mesopotamia. Jeremiah had encouraged them to settle in and do well there, and they had done so. In 520 BCE Jerusalem lay in ruins; the land was either untended or cultivated by those indifferent or hostile to the exiles. For many, returning to Judah may have seemed like starting from scratch. Furthermore, the majority of Jews living in Babylonia had never seen Judah.

115

It is easy to understand why they would be unenthusiastic about going there.

In 520 BCE it must have seemed to many of the returned exiles that there were more important things to be done than to rebuild the Temple. The construction of houses, the tending of fields, and self-defense may have seemed more urgent. Haggai and Zechariah arose at this time.

> Now the prophets, Haggai and Zechariah son of Iddo, prophesied to the Jews who were in Judah and Jerusalem, in the name of the God of Israel who was over them. Then Zerubbabel son of Shealtiel and Jeshua [Joshua] son of Jozadak set out to rebuild the house of God in Jerusalem; and with them were the prophets of God, helping them. (Ezra 5:1-2)

The four oracles in the book of Haggai are precisely dated. The first (1:1-15) is dated mid-August to mid-September, 520 BCE, and is directed to Zerubbabel and Joshua.

> Thus says the LORD of hosts: These people say the time has not yet come to rebuild the LORD's house. Then the word of the LORD came by the prophet Haggai, saying: Is it a time for you yourselves to live in your paneled houses, while this house lies in ruins? Now therefore thus says the LORD of hosts: Consider how you have fared. You have sown much, and harvested little; you eat, but you never have enough; you drink, but you never have your fill; you clothe yourselves, but no one is warm; and you that earn wages earn wages to put them into a bag with holes. (1:2-6)

The returned exiles were too busy with survival to build the Temple. Harvests were not good, and there was a shortage of food, drink, clothing, and housing. The oracle claims that there was a connection between the sad state of the people and the fact that they were neglecting the Temple.

> You have looked for much, and, lo, it came to little; and when you brought it home, I blew it away. Why? says the LORD of hosts. Because my house lies in ruins, while all of you hurry off to your own houses. Therefore the heavens above you have withheld the dew, and earth has withheld the produce. And I have called for a drought on the land and the hills, on the grain, the new wine, the oil, on what the soil produces, on human beings and animals, and on all their labors. (1:9-11)

Haggai assumes the Temple ideology examined in chapter 2. He condemns the "practical" point of view that care of physical needs is more crucial than the cult. A truly practical view of the world takes account of the fact that God controls rain and crops. Unless the people stay on God's right side, God brings famine and drought. To build the Temple and institute proper liturgy will be more effective in ensuring the well-being of the settlers than the allegedly more "useful" things they are doing. A narrative section (Hag 1:12-15) indicates that Zerubbabel, Joshua, and the people heed the word of God, and begin to build. Accordingly, God assures them that God is with them (1:13).

The next oracle (2:1-9) is dated almost two months after the first. The people have been working on God's house, but are discouraged because it is such an uninspiring edifice. God tells them to take heart, for this house will eventually be even greater than Solomon's Temple: "Once again, in a little while, I will shake the heavens and the earth and the sea and the dry land; and I will shake all the nations, so that the treasure of all nations shall come, and I will fill this house with splendor, says the LORD of hosts" (2:6-7). The book of Haggai expects all the nations to pay tribute to God in Jerusalem. From this small beginning by the returned exiles, God will bring earth-shaking results.

The third oracle (2:10-19) comes two months after the second. God invites the people to contrast how they fared before beginning the Temple and how they have fared afterward. Harvests have improved, and God says that it is because the people are now paying attention to the Temple.

God sends Haggai a fourth oracle (2:20-23) on the same day as the third:

Speak to Zerubbabel, governor of Judah, saying, I am about to shake the heavens and the earth, and to overthrow the throne of kingdoms; I am about to destroy the strength of the kingdoms and of the nations, and overthrow the chariots and their riders; and the horses and their riders shall fall, every one by the sword of a comrade. On that day, says the LORD of hosts, I will take you, O Zerubbabel my servant, son of Shealtiel, says the LORD, and make you like a signet ring; for I have chosen you, says the LORD of hosts. (2:21-23)

God appears as the heavenly warrior battling the nations of the earth. The very title "Lord of hosts" means "leader of armies," for "hosts" (multitudes) was used in this sense. God will attack and overthrow the foreign nations. The language echoes that of Exodus 15, which describes the crossing of the Reed Sea in terms of holy war: "Horse and rider he has thrown into the sea. . . . Pharaoh's chariots and his army he cast into the sea" (Exod 15:1c, 4a). The oracle expects God to go to war for Israel as he did at the Exodus.

At that time God will "choose" Zerubbabel, descendant of David, to be the divine "signet ring"—which was a ring bearing the official seal of the king. With this seal one could sign decrees and run the kingdom. For God to give the signet ring to Zerubbabel meant that Zerubbabel would be God's representative. The rule of Zerubbabel would replace the rule of those whom God was about to defeat. The political implications of this are clear. From the Persian point of view, what is being suggested would be seditious in the extreme. Whether there actually was a revolt under Zerubbabel is not known. What is clear is that for

Haggai the building of the Temple raised hopes of a complete restoration, including not just the reestablishment of the cult, but also the independence of Judah.

ZECHARIAH 1–8

Zechariah addresses the same situation as Haggai.[2] The book repeatedly presents a picture of an ideal restored Jerusalem. Zechariah agrees with Haggai that, before the building of the Temple began, conditions in Judah were grim, but that since then harvests have been good and peace has reigned (7:9-13). The full return of all Jewish exiles to Judah and restoration of the city are expected. The city will be protected by God: "For I will be a wall of fire all around it, says the LORD, and I will be the glory within it" (2:5).

Like Isaiah 40–55 and Haggai, Zechariah 1–8 portrays the restoration of Zion as affecting the whole world. The foreign nations who oppressed Israel acted as instruments of God, but they overstepped their bounds and punished Israel too harshly. Therefore, God will punish them (1:15).

> See now, I am going to raise my hand against them, and they shall become plunder for their own slaves. Then you will know that the LORD of hosts has sent me. Sing and rejoice, O daughter of Zion! For lo, I will come and dwell in your midst, says the LORD. Many nations shall join themselves to the LORD on that day, and shall be my people; and I will dwell in your midst. And you shall know that the LORD of hosts has sent me to you. The LORD will inherit Judah as his portion in the holy land, and will again choose Jerusalem. (2:9-12)

When God finally raises Jerusalem to its intended status, all nations will recognize it as the capital of the only true God. The entire population of the earth then will become God's people.

Zechariah makes extensive use of visions. There is a repeated pattern of the prophet receiving a vision, asking what it means, and having it interpreted for him by God. The fourth vision is in chapter 3. It begins, "Then he showed me the high priest Joshua standing before the angel of the LORD, and Satan standing at his right hand to accuse him" (3:1). The term "high priest" is not used before the Exile. Although there was a chief priest in the preexilic period, the use of the new title corresponds to the increased influence and power of the head priest in the postexilic period owing to the absence of a monarch. The scene is heaven, portrayed as a courtroom. Joshua is accused by Satan. This is Satan's first appearance in the pages of the Hebrew Bible. The Hebrew text translated literally says "*the* satan," meaning "the accuser."[3] As the accuser, Satan is the prosecuting attorney in God's court. He is not God's enemy, but is a heavenly figure, perhaps an angel. When Satan accuses Joshua, however, God objects: "And the LORD said to Satan, 'The LORD rebuke you, O Satan! The LORD who has chosen Jerusalem rebuke you! Is not this man a brand plucked from the fire?' '' (3:2). God does not say that Joshua deserves no criticism, but the high priest is like a survivor of a fire, probably meaning the Exile, and is part of a restored Jerusalem. Given the extraordinary circumstances, it is not right to hold Joshua accountable for his unworthiness, symbolized in the next verse by the filthy clothes Joshua wears. Accordingly, God commands that Joshua be stripped of his dirty clothes and dressed in pure, clean priestly vestments. He is now fit to be God's high priest.

Joshua now receives a promise expressing priestly ideology. "Thus says the LORD of hosts: If you will walk in my ways and keep my requirements, then you shall rule my house and have charge of my courts, and I will give you the right of access among those who are standing here" (3:7). The "here" God speaks of is the heavenly court. If Joshua follows God's Law, he will have charge of the Temple (God's "house") and its precincts, and will have access to God in heaven. This recalls the discussion of priestly religion in chapter 2 where the Holy of Holies represents where God is, the outer courts are where the people are, and the places in between are a zone of interaction between humans and God. Only the priests are authorized to be in this in-between space of interaction, and only the high priest is allowed to enter the Holy of Holies. Contact with the most holy places means intimate access to God.

Zechariah 3 ends with another promise: "I am going to bring my servant the Branch" (3:8b). "The Branch" is a title that occurs elsewhere (Isa 4:2; 11:1; Jer 23:5; 33:15). In Isaiah 11:1, the phrase appears in a prophecy of salvation in which Isaiah promises that there will be a Davidic king who will truly fulfill God's will and bring righteousness to the land. Peace will reign on earth, and Jerusalem will be the center of a world restored to the state God has always intended. The two occurrences of "branch" in Jeremiah also refer to the perfect Davidic king. The most plausible referent for "branch" in Zechariah 3:8 is Zerubbabel, who was a descendant of David. Zechariah may imply the same kind of hope as did Haggai 2:20-23 about a future Jewish state with a Davidic descendant at its head. In 3:8-10, the rule of the branch is associated with God's removal of guilt from the land and with fertility for the land.

Chapter 4 contains a vision whose principal thrust is that Zerubbabel is to build the Second Temple through God's strength. The vision is of a golden lampstand, recalling the lampstand in the sanctuary (Exod 25:31-40). Two olive trees flank the lampstand, supplying it with oil. Zechariah asks, "What are these two olive trees on the right and the left of the lampstand?" (4:11). An angel explains, "These are the two anointed [messiahs] who stand by the Lord of the whole earth" (4:14). To be anointed means that oil is poured over one's head. Zechariah sees two anointed ones (messiahs) supplying the lamp with oil, thus keeping the cult in operation. The vision graphically portrays the dual nature of leadership in the postexilic community. Aaron and his sons were anointed at

Sinai for the task of ministering to God in God's sanctuary, and Saul and David were later anointed kings over Israel. Zechariah's vision brings the two kinds of leaders (priestly and royal) together and balances them. This represents a theologizing of the politico-religious structure of the restored community, established under Persian authority.

In the eighth vision Zechariah receives instructions from God.

> Collect silver and gold from the exiles—from Heldai, Tobijah, and Jedaiah—who have arrived from Babylon; and go the same day to the house of Josiah son of Zephaniah. Take the silver and gold and make a crown, and set it on the head of the high priest Joshua son of Jehozadak; say to him: Thus says the Lord of hosts: Here is a man whose name is Branch: for he shall branch out in his place, and he shall build the temple of the Lord. It is he that shall build the temple of the Lord; he shall bear royal honor, and shall sit and rule on his throne. There shall be a priest by his throne, with peaceful understanding between the two of them. (6:10-13)

This passage is confusing. As it reads, it is Joshua who is to be crowned, called "branch," to build the Temple, bear royal honor, sit on a throne, and have a priest by his side. All of these things would be more suitable for a king, a Davidic descendant. Joshua cannot be of Davidic descent and also be a priest, because priests come from the tribe of Levi while David was of the tribe of Judah. Zechariah 3 records that Zerubbabel builds the Temple. When the passage reports that the royal figure has a priest by his throne, it seems as if the royal figure is not himself a priest. These considerations make it plausible that the passage originally referred to Zerubbabel, but that at some point in the editing of the book of Zechariah it was altered to refer to Joshua. In its present form the oracle combines priestly and royal elements. The high priest has become civil ruler also.

It has been suggested that the prophecy about the signet ring in Haggai 2:23 and the one about the branch in Zechariah 3:8 both reflect a time when Judah attempted a revolution to take advantage of the unrest in the Persian empire early in the reign of Darius I. In this interpretation, the attempt failed, and the oracle originally referring to Zerubbabel was amended to refer to Joshua. This hypothesis is conjectural. In any case, the combination of royal and priestly elements in the figure of Joshua in Zechariah 6 reflects a period when leadership roles in Judah were changing and the high priesthood was gaining power.

THIRD ISAIAH (ISAIAH 56–66)

Second Isaiah was written during the Exile. Its oracles presume a situation in which the people have not been restored to Judah, but liberation is near. Such is not the case for Third Isaiah. Whoever uttered these oracles was in Judah. In fact, the oracles reflect several different situations in postexilic Judah. The oracles were uttered over time, perhaps by different people. They are in the tradition of Second Isaiah, as can be seen by their inclusion in the book of Isaiah, and by their language, imagery, and hopes. They seem to hope for the kind of restoration Second Isaiah envisaged and to reflect disappointment that such a restoration is not what actually occurs. Precise dating of the oracles is not possible, but a plausible relative dating based on form and content has been established.[4] According to this relative dating, the group that produced the oracles, perhaps followers of Second Isaiah, returned to Judah with the exiles, either in 538 or 520 BCE. At first they were optimistic about the fulfillment of Second Isaiah's predictions, but that optimism turned to pessimism and bitterness. Their change of attitude was caused by two things: (a) the priestly faction that took over the Temple edged them out of active participation in the running of the cult; (b) the group in power and the people as a whole did not fulfill the covenant.

Oracles proclaiming the glorious restoration of Zion are found in Isaiah 60–62 as well as 57:14-20, 63:1-3, 65:17-25, and 66:10-14. Much in the manner of Second Isaiah, chapters 60–62 begin with the prophet addressing Zion itself. All nations will be in darkness, but God will personally shine on Zion. Therefore, the nations who once oppressed Jerusalem will come to its light and praise God, bringing treasures to offer God in Jerusalem. The gates of Jerusalem will not be able to be shut because of the endless stream of Gentiles bringing gifts (60:11).

> The descendants of those who oppressed you shall come bending low to you,
> and all who despised you shall bow down at your feet;
> they shall call you the City of the LORD, the Zion of the Holy One of Israel.
> Whereas you have been forsaken and hated, with no one passing through,
> I will make you majestic forever, a joy from age to age.
> You shall suck the milk of nations, you shall suck the breasts of kings;
> and you shall know that I, the LORD, am your Savior, and your Redeemer, the
> Mighty One of Jacob. (60:14-16)

God is Savior because he brings rescue from exile. As Redeemer he "buys back" the people from slavery.

Isaiah 61 is a picture of the glorious restoration.

> The spirit of the Lord GOD is upon me, because the LORD has anointed me;
> he has sent me to bring good news to the oppressed, to bind up the brokenhearted,
> to proclaim liberty to the captives, and release to the prisoners;
> to proclaim the year of the LORD's favor, and the day of vengeance of our God; to
> comfort all who mourn.
> to provide for those who mourn in Zion—to give them a garland instead of ashes,
> the oil of gladness instead of mourning, the mantle of praise instead of a faint spirit.

They will be called oaks of righteousness, the planting of the LORD, to display his
glory.
They shall build up the ancient ruins, they shall raise up the former devastations;
they shall repair the ruined cities, the devastations of many generations. (61:1-4)

In the Hebrew Bible the ''spirit of God'' is not an entity separate from God, but is a way of speaking about the activity of God. By claiming that he has the spirit of God the prophet claims to be God's agent. He says the same thing when he claims that God has anointed him. Third Isaiah's task is to proclaim the good news to those who are unhappy in Zion. The good news is that Jerusalem will be restored and the renewed community will be ''planted'' there. The ancient ruins will be rebuilt.

In 61:6 there is a new element: ''But you shall be called priests of the LORD, you shall be named ministers of our God.'' Third Isaiah addresses not just the priestly class, but all Israel. The priesthood has been extended to the entire people because they are all holy to the LORD, living in Jerusalem and serving God there (Exod 19:6). Israel has become priest to the nations, for humanity now recognizes its special status in God's eyes. It is this ''democratized'' vision of the restored community that may have caused the clash between the group behind Third Isaiah and the priestly class installed by the Persians.

In addition to considering the entire people as priests, and therefore challenging cultic classes in Jewish society, Third Isaiah has a universalistic vision of God's restored cult. All Gentiles who keep God's covenant, especially the Sabbath, can be part of God's people.

And the foreigners who join themselves to the LORD, to minister to him, to love the
name of the LORD, and to be his servants,
all who keep the sabbath, and do not profane it, and hold fast my covenant—
these I will bring to my holy mountain, and make them joyful in my house of
prayer;
their burnt offerings and their sacrifices will be accepted on my altar;
for my house shall be called a house of prayer for all peoples. (56:6-7)

Chapter 62 assumes that Jerusalem has not yet been rebuilt, but Third Isaiah has not lost hope. He promises to continue to petition God for salvation. The prophet says, ''For Zion's sake I will not keep silent, and for Jerusalem's sake I will not rest, until her vindication shines out like the dawn, and her salvation like a burning torch'' (62:1). The prophet promises not to cease appealing to God until the people's hope is fulfilled: ''Upon your walls, O Jerusalem, I have posted sentinels; all day and all night they shall never be silent. You who remind the LORD, take no rest, and give him no rest until he establishes Jerusalem and makes it renowned throughout the earth'' (62:6-7). The central section of Third Isaiah (chaps. 60–62) ends on a note of hope:

> The LORD has proclaimed to the end of the earth:
> Say to daughter Zion, "See, your salvation comes;
> his reward is with him, and his recompense before him."
> They shall be called, "The Holy People, The Redeemed of the LORD"; and you
> shall be called, "Sought Out, A City Not Forsaken." (62:11-12)

Another oracle from this early optimistic period recalls Second Isaiah's claim that what God now does surpasses anything God has done before (43:18-19). "For I am about to create new heavens and a new earth; the former things shall not be remembered or come to mind. But be glad and rejoice forever in what I am creating; for I am about to create Jerusalem as a joy, and its people as a delight" (65:17-18).

There are oracles in Third Isaiah that reveal that its hopes did not come true. A strong complaint seems to be that the class supported by the Persian crown was exclusive with respect to cult, power, and social status. This ruling class does not include the visionaries of the Third Isaiah group. Their anguish is contained in these verses: "For you are our father, though Abraham does not know us and Israel does not acknowledge us; you, O LORD, are our father; our Redeemer from of old is your name" (63:16). Pushed to a marginal status in the community, the group turns to God, "our father." The beginnings of the restoration were promising, but the results were disappointing: "Your holy people took possession for a little while; but now our adversaries have trampled down your sanctuary" (63:18).

Third Isaiah draws the line between those whom God accepts and those God does not accept within Israel itself. The prophet takes up the word "servant," a favorite word of Second Isaiah to designate one who serves God, and claims it as a title for one group within Israel. He seems to be saying that even the name "Israel" must be changed to underline a future rejection of the majority of the old community and the foundation of the new.

> Therefore thus says the Lord GOD:
> My servants shall eat, but you shall be hungry;
> my servants shall drink, but you shall be thirsty;
> my servants shall rejoice, but you shall be put to shame;
> my servants shall sing for gladness of heart, but you shall cry out for pain of heart,
>   and shall wail for anguish of spirit.
> You shall leave your name to my chosen to use as a curse, and the Lord GOD will put
>   you to death; but to his servants he will give a different name. (65:13-15)

Chapter 58 addresses those who, like Haggai, expected that once the cult was back in operation all would be well for Israel. Third Isaiah proclaims that cult is useless without social justice. To serve God in the Temple but to ignore the needs of one's fellow humans is purposeless. God says,

> Yet day after day they seek me and delight to know my ways,
> as if they were a nation that practices righteousness and did not forsake the ordinance of their God;
> they ask of me righteous judgments, they delight to draw near to God.[5]
> "Why do we fast, but you do not see? Why humble ourselves, but you do not notice?"
> Look, you serve your own interest on your fast day, and oppress all your workers.
> Look, you fast only to quarrel and to fight and to strike with a wicked fist.
> Such fasting as you do today will not make your voice heard on high.
> Is such the fast that I choose, a day to humble oneself?
> Is it to bow down the head like a bulrush, and to lie in sackcloth and ashes?
> Will you call this a fast, a day acceptable to the LORD?
> Is not this the fast that I choose: to loose the bonds of injustice, to undo the thongs of the yoke?
> Is it not to share your bread with the hungry, and bring the homeless poor into your house;
> when you see the naked, to cover them, and not to hide yourself from your own kin? (58:2-7)

In the place of cult as that thing which God demands in return for blessing, as in Haggai, Isaiah puts care for the poor, the hungry, the oppressed workers, the homeless. The ruins of Jerusalem will not be rebuilt until God is satisfied with Israel's record of social justice (58:12).

MALACHI (ca. 500–450 BCE)

Malachi's prophecies are directed primarily against the priests of his day. He sees them as lax in their practice and teaching.

> For the lips of a priest should guard knowledge, and people should seek instruction [Hebrew: *tôrāh*] from his mouth, for he is the messenger of the LORD of hosts. But you have turned aside from the way; you have caused many to stumble by your instruction; you have corrupted the covenant of Levi, says the LORD of hosts, and so I make you despised and abased before all the people, inasmuch as you have not kept my ways but have shown partiality in your instruction. (2:7-9)

Malachi puts his indictment into the context of his perception that all the world recognizes Israel's God as the true God: "For from the rising of the sun to its setting my name is great among the nations, and in every place incense is offered to my name, and a pure offering; for my name is great among the nations, says the LORD of hosts'' (1:11). ''For I am a great King, says the LORD of hosts, and my name is reverenced among the nations'' (1:14).

The specific issues that concern Malachi are the offering of improper sacrifices (blemished animals), marriages with Gentiles, divorce, and laxity of the community with respect to tithes. A more general list of Israel's shortcomings includes issues of social justice:

> Then I will draw near to you for judgment; I will be swift to bear witness against the sorcerers, against the adulterers, against those who swear falsely, against those who oppress the hired workers in their wages, the widow and the orphan, against those who thrust aside the alien, and do not fear me, says the LORD of hosts. (3:5)

Malachi predicts the coming of God for judgment. Before judgment God sends a forerunner.

> See, I am sending my messenger [Hebrew: *mal'ākî;* the same as the Hebrew name of the prophet] to prepare the way before me, and the Lord whom you seek will suddenly come to his temple. The messenger of the covenant in whom you delight—indeed, he is coming, says the LORD of hosts. But who can endure the day of his coming, and who can stand when he appears? For he is like a refiner's fire and like fullers' soap; he will sit as a refiner and purifier of silver, and he will purify the descendants of Levi and refine them like gold and silver, until they present offerings to the LORD in righteousness. Then the offering of Judah and Jerusalem will be pleasing to the LORD as in the days of old and as in former years. (3:1-4)

The Temple service is interpreted as ''seeking'' God, but Malachi says that when the one who is sought suddenly comes to the Temple, what happens will be a surprise for the worshipers. God will purify the cult and priesthood as with fire.

Malachi 4:5 may be a later addition identifying the coming messenger with Elijah: ''Lo, I will send you the prophet Elijah before the great and terrible day of the LORD comes. He will turn the hearts of parents to their children and the hearts of children to their parents, so that I will not come and strike the land with a curse.'' Elijah is the ninth-century prophet who did not die but was taken into heaven in a fiery chariot. Here Elijah is expected to come to reform Israel to save it from punishment.

Malachi, like Third Isaiah, does not question the priestly system or the validity of the covenant, but sees the Jewish community as failing to live up to God's demands. Both are critical of the establishment, although their criticisms are quite different. Both expect God to punish the people for their transgressions, but neither expects that to be the end of the story. As in the past, God will preserve a refined Israel.

THE MISSION OF NEHEMIAH

Ezra and Nehemiah were two Jews of the Babylonian exilic community who returned to Judah at different times with royal authority to perform certain tasks. The Chronicler's History says that Ezra came to Judah first (458 BCE), and then Nehemiah came while Ezra was still there (445 BCE). There are problems with this chronology. Both Ezra and Nehemiah were important emissaries of the Persian crown, but they hardly seem to interact with each other, even though their tasks are closely related. Their connection in the text is quite superficial. There seem to be two blocks of material, one dealing with Ezra and the other with Nehemiah, that are dovetailed but not fully integrated in the Chronicler's History.

There is evidence that Ezra came to Judah after Nehemiah. Nehemiah lists the exiles who returned to Judah, but does not mention the return under Ezra. Nehemiah comes to a Jerusalem without walls and almost deserted. When Ezra arrives the city is rebuilt and has walls. Nehemiah holds office in Judah while Eliashib is high priest, whereas Ezra is contemporary with Eliashib's grandson Jehohanan. If the Persian emperor Ahasuerus with whom Ezra is associated is really Artaxerxes II (ruled ca. 404–358 BCE), then Ezra would have arrived in Judah ca. 398 BCE. The solution adopted as a working hypothesis here is that Ezra came to Jerusalem in 398 BCE.

The Chronicler's History incorporates a writing often called "Nehemiah's memoirs" (Neh 1:1–7:73a; 11:1-2; 12:27-43; 13:4-31). The memoirs seem to be Nehemiah's genuine reminiscences of his time as governor of Judah. Nehemiah was a Jew prominent in the court of the Persian emperor, Artaxerxes I (ruled ca. 465–424 BCE). In the year 445 BCE, Nehemiah heard that the Jewish community in Judah was not doing well, and that Jerusalem was in a poor state and had no fortifications. Nehemiah requested permission to go to Judah to rebuild Jerusalem's walls. The king sent him on his way with letters to the other governors of the area telling them not to hinder his work. When the rulers of Samaria and Ammon across the Jordan heard of Nehemiah's mission, they were displeased. A strong and defensible Judah would not be good news for them, even if Jerusalem were under the control of the Persians. When Nehemiah arrived in Jerusalem, he inspected the walls by night for fear of resistance. When work began he stationed a guard around the working parties and the workers were armed for fear of attack. The work was completed despite harassment by those opposed to the building. Because Jerusalem was still not a comfortable place to live, lots were cast (a move similar to throwing dice) to choose 10 percent of the population of Judah to live there (Neh 11:1-2). "And the people blessed all those who willingly offered to live in Jerusalem" (11:2).

What Nehemiah found on his arrival in Jerusalem was worse than broken walls. He found a society in violation of Mosaic Law. The people complained.

> For there were those who said, "With our sons and our daughters, we are many; we must get grain, so that we may eat and stay alive." There were also those who said, "We are having to pledge our fields, our vineyards, and our houses in order to get grain during the famine." And there were those who said, "We are having to borrow money on our fields and vineyards to pay the king's tax. Now our flesh is the same as that of our kindred; our children are the same as their children; and yet we are forcing our sons and daughters to be slaves, and some of our daughters have been ravished; we are powerless, and our fields and vineyards now belong to others." (Neh 5:2-5)

Jewish peasants were being squeezed between famine and taxes. Unscrupulous persons were taking advantage of the unfavorable conditions to get the peasants into debt and then take over their fields. Land was passing out of the control of peasants into the hands of the upper class. Nehemiah said,

> I was very angry when I heard their outcry and these complaints. After thinking it over, I brought charges against the nobles and the officials; I said to them, "You are all taking interest from your own people." And I called a great assembly to deal with them, and said to them, "As far as we were able, we have bought back our Jewish kindred who had been sold to other nations; but now you are selling your own kin, who must then be bought back by us!" (Neh 5:6-8)

Nehemiah did not try to decrease the Persian tax, being himself an agent of the Persian crown. He did attack the upper class, which did not live according to the Mosaic covenant. Deuteronomy is permeated with the principle that Israelites are brothers and sisters and are to be treated as such. One does not charge interest to a fellow Israelite, one never refuses help to the poor, one is not harsh with respect to loans, even those that may not be paid back. Nehemiah saw the opposite attitude on the part of the upper class, and said, "The thing that you are doing is not good. Should you not walk in the fear of our God, to prevent the taunts of the nations our enemies?" (Neh 5:9). The nobles relented, and returned the land they had seized and the interest they had charged. Nehemiah set an example by forgoing his food allowance as governor "because of the heavy burden of labor on the people" (Neh 5:18).

Nehemiah 8–10 describes a covenant ceremony that supposedly took place when Nehemiah and Ezra were in Jerusalem together. Such a scenario is unlikely. It is likely that Nehemiah 8–9 belongs to the Ezra story, and Nehemiah 10 belongs to that of Nehemiah. In Nehemiah 10 the people promise a number of things. The first is that they will refuse intermarriage with those who do not belong to the covenant. There is always a close correspondence between family structure, marriage strategy, and ideology. For the Jews to adopt a defensive marriage strategy meant that they were trying to create a group with a strong self-identity and well-defined borders. Such a concern lies behind the long lists of those who returned from the Exile in the CH (Ezra 2:1-70; Neh 7:6-73), those who had helped in building the Temple (Nehemiah 3), those who signed the covenant (Neh 10:1-27), and those who were living in Jerusalem under Nehemiah (Neh 11:3-26). Nehemiah introduces his list saying, "Then my God put it into my mind to assemble the nobles and the officials and the people to be enrolled by genealogy. And I found the book of the genealogy of those who were the first to come back" (Neh 7:5).

The second promise made by the people is that they will observe the sabbath. Sabbath observance was especially important to Jews in the Exile because it distinguished them from the people around them. Since they no longer had their sacred space, the Jerusalem Temple, and since their sacred times could not be celebrated properly in the absence of their sacred space, a proportionately greater weight fell on the sacred time, the sabbath, that could be celebrated in a strange land.

The rest of the promises made by the people had to do with their maintenance of the cult. They promised financial support in the amount of one-third of a shekel (the contribution later became an obligatory tax and was increased to half a shekel). They promised to supply the Temple with the wood needed for sacrifices and to bring offerings of first fruits. Finally, they agreed to pay to the Levites the tithes due them. There follows the decision to have a tenth of the people live in Jerusalem, and the list of those who did so. Then there was a reading of the Law (13:1). "When the people heard the law, they separated from Israel all those of foreign descent" (13:3).

Nehemiah was governor for twelve years. Then he returned to the Persian court for a time. After a while he returned to Judah. The rest of the book of Nehemiah deals with his return to Judah and his handling of the problems there. The first problem involved a certain Tobiah from the land of Ammon across the Jordan. Tobiah was Jewish and a worshiper of Yahweh, as his name indicates. The ending "-iah" at the end of a name is short for "Yahweh." The Hebrew for "good" is *ṭôb*. Thus "Tobiah" means "Yahweh is good." Tobiah had opposed Nehemiah on his first mission. At that time he used his alliances and marriage connection among the upper class in Judah to work against Nehemiah (Neh 6:17-19). Tobiah's business interests were probably jeopardized by the land reform and financial policies of Nehemiah.

During Nehemiah's second stay in Judah he discovered that Eliashib the priest had given Tobiah a room in the Temple previously reserved for cultic materials. Eliashib did so because he "was related to Tobiah" (Neh 13:4). Tobiah undoubtedly had much business in Jerusalem, and a room in the well-fortified Temple would have served as a place for the safe-keeping of his property. Nehemiah threw Tobiah out of the Temple because he considered his presence a desecration of the sacred precincts. He gave orders to cleanse the defiled rooms and to bring back the cultic materials previously stored there (13:4-9).

Nehemiah also found that the promise made by the people to support the Levites through their tithes had not been kept. The Levites who should have served the Temple had been forced to leave their posts and take jobs in the fields to support themselves. Nehemiah reversed this situation, restoring the Levites to their proper roles. Nehemiah further discovered that the sabbath was not being observed by Jerusalem's inhabitants. Trade was carried out on every sabbath. Nehemiah forbade this practice, and when traders persisted in coming to the city on the sabbath, he commanded that the city gates be closed during the sabbath. That put an end to the violation (13:10-22).

Finally, Nehemiah saw that mixed marriages had not been ended by his earlier measures. He saw Jewish children growing up speaking the languages of the surrounding peoples and unable to speak the language of Judah (13:23-24).

> And I contended with them and cursed them and beat some of them and pulled out their hair; and I made them take an oath in the name of God, saying, "You shall not give your daughters to their sons, or take their daughters for your sons or for yourselves. Did not Solomon king of Israel sin on account of such women? Among the many nations there was no king like him, and he was beloved by his God, and God made him king over all Israel; nevertheless, foreign women made even him to sin. Shall we then listen to you and do all this great evil and act treacherously against our God by marrying foreign women?" (13:25-27)

Nehemiah singled out the case of the family of the high priest who married into the family of Sanballat, governor of Samaria.

> And one of the sons of Johoiada, son of the high priest Eliashib, was the son-in-law of Sanballat the Horonite; I chased him away from me. Remember them, O my God, because they have defiled the priesthood, the covenant of the priests and Levites. (Neh 13:28-29)

Defilement here is something out of place, as defined in chapter 2 on priestly religion. By marrying a foreign woman, a Samaritan, the priest had brought her into intimate contact with God's Temple. Such a mixing of things that did not belong together was defilement of the Temple.

THE MISSION OF EZRA (398 BCE)

Ezra is introduced in Ezra 7. Ezra 7–10 and Nehemiah 8–10 contain his story. Ezra's lineage went back to "the chief priest Aaron." He thus had impeccable priestly credentials. Two other elements in his credentials are mentioned in 7:6: "He was a scribe skilled in the law of Moses that the Lord the God of Israel had given; and the king granted him all that he asked, for the hand of the Lord his God was upon him.'' In this passage, being a scribe means more than merely being able to read and write. It also means being knowledgeable regarding the content and application of the Torah of Moses. Further, Ezra was sent by the king of Persia. He therefore was a priest, a scribe, and one empowered by the government of Persia.

Ezra came to Judah with a group of exiles, laypersons, priests, and Levites (7:7-10). He was enabled to do so because God favored him, according to the Chronicler. The reason that God favored him is given in verse 10: ''For Ezra had set his heart to study the law of the LORD, and to do it, and to teach the statutes and ordinances in Israel.'' The king of Persia sent him to Judah with royal contributions to the Temple, with the news that the Temple and its staff would be tax-free, and this commission: ''For you are sent by the king and his seven counselors to make inquiries about Judah and Jerusalem according to the law of your God, which is in your hand'' (7:14).

Ezra's commission is explained in what the Chronicler presents as a decree by the king himself in 7:12-26, which may well be genuine.

> And you, Ezra, according to the God-given wisdom you possess, appoint magistrates and judges who may judge all the people in the province Beyond the River who know the laws of your God; and you shall teach those who do not know them. All who will not obey the law of your God and the law of the king, let judgment be strictly executed on them, whether for death or for banishment or for confiscation of their goods or for imprisonment. (7:25-26)

This passage states the rules under which Judah now existed. All of Judah was to be ruled by the law of God in Ezra's hand, the law book brought back from Babylonia. That law was to be enforced as the law of the land by the power of the Persian government. Some may already have known the Law, but others would need to learn it. In other words, Ezra, a prominent Babylonian Jew, expert in the Law that seems to have been assembled among the Babylonian Jewish community, came to Judah with that law in the form of a book. He was to teach the Law to the inhabitants of Judah, to appoint judges who understood and could apply that Law, and to punish harshly those who did not accept this version of the Mosaic commands. In the process, he was also to enforce the king's law insofar as it covered areas not covered by Mosaic Law. He was an agent of the Persian crown and derived his power from that source.

Israel had lived for four and a half centuries under the rule of independent or at least semi-independent Israelite monarchs. A royal ideology had developed in which the kings were the guarantors of the Mosaic laws and covenant, and in return were granted, at least in the case of the Davidic dynasty, the assurance that their rule would last forever. Now it was a crown of a different sort that guaranteed the Mosaic laws. Judah had to obey the Law as interpreted by the

130

exilic community, and the Persians authorized Ezra and his judges to punish those who disobeyed. Restored Judah thus differed in two critical ways from the Judah of the preexilic period. First, there was no Jewish monarchy. Second, Judah was now governed by a law that to some degree was fixed in writing.

A major aspect of Nehemiah's reform was the abolition of mixed marriages so that the returned community could remain pure. Ezra found that the reforms had still not taken root.

> The officials approached me and said, ''The people of Israel, the priests, and the Levites have not separated themselves from the peoples of the lands with their abominations, from the Canaanites, the Hittites, the Perizzites, the Jebusites, the Ammonites, the Moabites, the Egyptians, and the Amorites. For they have taken some of their daughters as wives for themselves and for their sons. Thus the holy seed has mixed itself with the peoples of the lands, and in this faithlessness the officials and leaders have led the way.'' When I heard this, I tore my garment and my mantle, and pulled hair from my head and beard, and sat appalled. (Ezra 9:1-3)

The priestly view of the Chronicler (and perhaps of Ezra himself) is apparent here. Israel was a ''holy seed'' that must be kept ''separated'' from other nations and not ''mix'' with them, lest God be dissatisfied with it and no longer live in it. Ezra's next step shows his authority.

> They made a proclamation throughout Judah and Jerusalem to all the returned exiles that they should assemble at Jerusalem, and that if any did not come within three days, by order of the officials and the elders all their property should be forfeited, and they themselves banned from the congregation of the exiles.
> (Ezra 10:7-8)

The text expresses again the Chronicler's view that the returned exiles were the true Israel. When they arrived in Jerusalem, all Jews were ordered to divorce their non-Jewish wives. There follows a list of those who did so. A substantial number of priests, Levites, and laypersons are in that list.

Nehemiah 8 and 9 narrate the covenant ceremony by which the people of Judah pledged to obey the version of the Law that Ezra brought to them. The process took many days. What follows is a condensed version of the first day.

> All the people gathered together into the square before the Water Gate. They told the scribe Ezra to bring the book of the law of Moses, which the LORD had given to Israel. Accordingly, the priest Ezra brought the law before the assembly, both men and women and all who could hear with understanding. This was on the first day of the seventh month. He read from it facing the square before the Water Gate from early morning until midday, in the presence of the men and the women and those who could understand; and the ears of all the people were attentive to the book of

the law. The scribe Ezra stood on a wooden platform that had been made for the purpose. . . . And Ezra opened the book in the sight of all the people, for he was standing above all the people; and when he opened it, all the people stood up. . . . The Levites helped the people to understand the law, while the people remained in their places. So they read from the book, from the law of God, with interpretation. They gave the sense, so that the people understood the reading.

(8:1-4a, 5, 7b-8)

The entire community was allegedly present to hear and understand the Law. Ezra's qualifications as scribe (expert in the Law), and priest (an intermediary between God and the community) are stressed. The Law was in the form of a book. Ezra stood above the crowd in full view of all, emphasizing that the words were not his own but came directly from the book. The people stood, in respect for the word of God. In the reverence that Ezra, the Levites, and the people showed for the Law, one can sense the power the book was to have in the community, and the way in which it would evolve into a source of religious authority rivaling even the priesthood and the Temple establishment.

The role of the Levites in this passage is not entirely clear. Although Ezra read the Law, so did they. Whereas Ezra simply read the Law through, the Levites helped the people understand it. Precisely how they did this is disputed. In particular, the precise meaning of the word translated here as "with interpretation" is uncertain. The fact that the Levites made it possible for the people to understand and not merely to hear the Law is foremost in Nehemiah 8:8-9. Some have read the Hebrew to mean that the Levites had to translate the Law from Hebrew into Aramaic, since later in Jewish history the main language of the Jews in Judah and Babylonia was Aramaic, the official language of the Persian empire. An alternative view is that the Levites interpreted the Law for the people. The Law's application might not have been obvious, and the people would have needed skilled teachers to specify what the Law demanded.

On the second day Ezra and the people came together to study the Law. They found the prescriptions for the celebration of the feast of Booths (8:13-18). The commandments for the feast seemed new to the people, and since it was the time for the feast they set about celebrating it properly. The text makes the surprising statement "for from the days of Jeshua [Joshua] son of Nun to that day the people of Israel had not done so" (Neh 8:17). The Law as read by Ezra was not known to the inhabitants of Judah, nor was it practiced in that way even in the period of the monarchy or of the judges. The feast was supposedly celebrated in the generation after Moses, that of Moses' successor Joshua, but fell into disuse after that. Exactly what this means historically is a matter for discussion, but it is clear that the Chronicler considers Ezra's version of the Law something new. Yet despite its being the introduction of something fairly novel to Israel, the Chronicler claims that Ezra's Law derives from Moses himself. The redaction of the Law accomplished in the Babylonian Exile and brought to Judah by Ezra was considered to be the Law given to Moses on Sinai.

Ezra was the perfect transitional figure between the preexilic and postexilic periods. He was a priest, a direct descendant of Aaron, although the text never shows him serving at the altar. He was a scribe, which meant he was skilled in God's Torah. He was an agent of the Persian government. In the preexilic period there was no fixed law book until toward the end of the monarchy under Josiah (2 Kings 22). Israelite kings reigned over Israel, and the priests gave legal instructions (Hebrew: *tôrāh*). In the postexilic period the Israelite monarchy had been replaced in some of its functions by Persian rule, the Law was becoming a book with a status potentially independent of the Temple establishment, and any scribe could in theory pick up the law book and read and interpret it in a way unfavorable to the priests in power. At the very time that the internal power of the Temple was increased because of the absence of the Israelite monarchy, another power center based on interpretation of Torah was made possible. This new situation helped pave the way for such later movements as the Pharisees and the Jesus movement.

CONCLUSION

This chapter has examined the reestablishment of Israel in Palestine after the Babylonian Exile. The loss of Temple and land caused certain shifts of emphasis in the religion of the exilic community. Circumcision and sabbath observance came to have increased significance for Israel's identity. The exilic community gathered and rewrote the sacred narratives and legal rulings and forged them into a new written form that became the written Torah.

When Cyrus, the Persian emperor, allowed the exilic community to return to Jerusalem and rebuild the city and the Temple, the monarchy was not reestablished. The returned exiles initially had a dual leadership consisting of Zerubbabel, perhaps a Davidic descendant, and Joshua, the high priest. Soon the high priest emerged as sole leader of the nation. Not all were happy with the nature of the restored community. The community behind Third Isaiah felt excluded from power, and disagreed with the outlook of the new priestly establishment in the Temple. Malachi criticized the priesthood for its practices and teachings. Nehemiah came to Jerusalem with authority from the Persian crown to rebuild the city walls and institute social reforms. Later, the priestly scribe Ezra came to Palestine with a written Torah, and with Persian authority to enforce it as the law of the land. The Torah, whose final redaction was a priestly one, reinforced priestly hegemony in the restored community, but the very fact of a written Torah was to make possible other centers of authority in Israel that were based not on hereditary priesthood, but on knowledge and interpretation of Torah.

SELECT BIBLIOGRAPHY

Ackroyd, Peter R. *Exile and Restoration: A Study of Hebrew Thought of the Sixth Century B.C.* Philadelphia: Westminster Press, 1968.

————. *1 and 2 Chronicles, Ezra, Nehemiah.* London: SCM, 1973.

————. *Israel Under Babylon and Persia.* Oxford: Oxford University Press, 1970.

Anderson, Bernhard, *UOT,* chap. 15.

Bickermann, Elias. *From Ezra to the Last of the Maccabees: Foundations of Post-biblical Judaism.* New York: Schocken Books, 1962.

Bright, John. *HI.*

Gottwald, Norman K. *HB,* chaps. 9, 10, 12.

Hanson, Paul. *The Dawn of Apocalyptic: The Historical and Sociological Roots of Jewish Apocalyptic Eschatology,* rev. ed. Philadelphia: Fortress Press, 1979.

Peterson, David L. *Haggai and Zechariah 1–8.* Philadelphia: Westminster Press, 1984.

Smith, Morton. *Palestinian Parties and Politics That Shaped the Old Testament.* New York: Columbia, 1971.

Stone, Michael. "Exile, Restoration, and the Bible," in *SSV,* 19-25.

CHAPTER FIVE

Hellenism and the Maccabees

Primary Readings: 1 and 2 Maccabees, book of Sirach

HISTORICAL OVERVIEW

The period known as the Hellenistic era extends from the time of Alexander the Great (lived 356–323 BCE) to the conquest of Judah by the Romans in 63 BCE. "Hellenistic" comes from the Greek word for Greece, *Hellas*. During the Hellenistic period, Greek culture, political forms, and language spread widely throughout the eastern Mediterranean region and the Near East and interacted with native cultures, including that of Judah.

The Greek mainland was organized according to a system of city-states, the most famous of which are Athens and Sparta. The city was the basic political unit and controlled the surrounding countryside. The cities were independent of one another, although at times alliances (leagues) were formed for mutual defense. Closer political unity between the cities was hindered by the mountainous terrain of Greece, which tended to keep the cities separate. The Greeks were known for their military prowess and were even hired by the Persians as mercenaries. Owing to a combination of their military abilities and their rugged land they escaped being made part of the Persian empire, although they lost their colonies in Asia Minor (present-day Asian Turkey) to Persia. When not fighting against Persia, the cities often fought one another.

To the north of Greece lay Macedonia, a land that had long been under Greek influence. By the time of Alexander, its language was Greek and its culture was heavily influenced by Greece. Alexander himself was tutored by the philosopher Aristotle. Alexander's father, King Philip of Macedonia, tried to unite the Greek cities under his hegemony, but was assassinated before accomplishing his goal (336 BCE). Alexander, only twenty years of age when his father died, quickly completed the task of unification his father had begun. Having finished his work in Greece, Alexander turned toward the Persian empire. Alexander recaptured the Greek cities in western Asia Minor controlled by the Persians. He then proceeded to a series of decisive victories over the Persian emperor Darius III. Many areas capitulated without a fight, even welcoming a change in imperial administration. Judah surrendered to Alexander peacefully. In 326 BCE Alexander reached India. In 323 he died of illness at the age of thirty-two. When

135

Alexander died, he left the new empire in the hands of his generals, often called the "successors" (Greek: *diadochoi*). Each general took responsibility for a different part of the empire, but they soon turned those territories into independent kingdoms warring with one another for the largest share of the imperial pie. After about two decades of bitter and destructive warfare the kingdoms reached an uneasy equilibrium. By 301 BCE Ptolemy reigned in Egypt (including Palestine and Phoenicia), and Seleucus ruled in Syria and Mesopotamia. Each founded dynasties, the Seleucids in Syria and the Ptolemies in Egypt.

Judah was ruled by the Ptolemies until 198 BCE when it came under Seleucid rule. In 175 BCE, the Seleucid king Antiochus IV Epiphanes came to the throne. For reasons discussed below he decided in 167 BCE to try to force Greek culture on Judah to the extent of outlawing essential elements of Jewish religion. The Jews revolted under the leadership of a priestly family from the countryside (the "Maccabees"). In the decades that followed the Jews gradually won first religious freedom, then political independence, and then an empire. Independence came to an end when the Romans conquered Jerusalem in 63 BCE.

HELLENISM

The Greek City

There was some interaction between Greece and Persian lands before Alexander, but after Alexander's conquests that interaction increased dramatically. Alexander believed in the superiority of Greek culture, but was at the same time somewhat open to other cultures. He actively promoted contact between his soldiers and the conquered peoples. He himself married a foreign princess, and he encouraged ten thousand troops to wed foreign women. Persians became leaders in his army, bodyguards, and members of his court. Alexander wanted to put into practice the idea that all the world was a single city and all people inhabitants of that city. Alexander was pursuing a cosmopolitan ideal (from the Greek *kosmos* meaning "world" and *polis* meaning "city"), but it was an ideal based on the conviction of the superiority of Greek views of the world and Greek institutions. When the world was taken over by Alexander's successors, the Hellenistic empires were potentially more onerous than any previous empire, since their imperialism was cultural as well as political.

Greek culture was based on the *polis,* the city. Even before Alexander, the Greeks had formed colonies in western Asia Minor and elsewhere, and had patterned cities there according to the model of Greek city-states. Ideally the Greek city, wherever located, would be autonomous, though when it was part of an empire its independence was often compromised. The city was ruled by its citizens, citizenship usually being restricted to land-owning males. From time to time the citizenry would assemble in a meeting called the *ekklēsia,* the word for "church" in the New Testament. Since such a large body could not run the city on a daily basis, a city council (Greek: *boulē*) did so.

Greek cities contained institutions that carried on Greek tradition and culture. One of these was the marketplace, the *agora*. The agora was a large open square, often surrounded by porticoes (Greek: *stoa*), porches with open sides and a roof held up by rows of columns. The agora also served as a marketplace for ideas where philosophers could get a hearing. Religious missionaries could do likewise. Theaters and gymnasia were important fixtures of the Greek city. In the theater, plays immortalized Greek mythology and society was both praised and satirized. The gymnasium was much more than a place for sports, although sports were an important medium of social interaction and helped to substantiate the Greek idea of a sound mind in a strong body. Gymnasia also served varied social functions, from meeting places for political clubs, to a kind of high school for Greek boys. The high school taught the classics and trained the boys militarily. The gymnasium was a key vehicle for preserving, spreading, and transmitting Greek culture. A Greek city also contained temples to its gods. Worship of the city's deities was a civic duty. Since there was no division between civic and religious life, shrines were found in gymnasia, theaters, and elsewhere.

Since Greek culture was centered on the city, Alexander and his successors used cities to spread that culture. They did so by building new cities, restructuring and chartering old cities on the Greek model, and organizing clusters of towns as a city. The most enduring and influential city founded by Alexander was named after him, Alexandria in Egypt, which still exists today. The Ptolemies made it a showplace of Hellenistic culture. During the Hellenistic period it was the world's most important intellectual center.

Syncretism

The Hellenistic age was characterized by "syncretism." Syncretism is the mixing of cultural elements to create a new cultural entity. For example, one might see the present Christian concept of God as a combination of Israelite and Greek elements. The idea that God is intimately involved with a specific group of people whose history constitutes "salvation history" is a way of thinking that Christians inherited from Jews. The idea that God is unchanging and impassive, the unmoved mover, is inherited from the Greek philosophers. The Christian concept of God is not identical with either the Greek philosophical or the Israelite concepts, but combines the two.

The implantation of Greek institutions in foreign soil resulted in cultures that combined Greek and native elements in a new synthesis. Thus Hellenism looked somewhat different in Egypt from how it looked in Palestine, different in Palestine from its appearance in Asia Minor. Greek culture was most influential in cities, but even in cities there were degrees of influence. Hellenism was less apparent among the lower than the upper classes. It was strongest where trade and other sorts of interaction were greatest, and was less influential in isolated mountain towns in Asia Minor and parts of the highlands of Palestine.

The essential precondition for communication is a common language. The official language in the vast area ruled by Macedonians and Greeks was Greek, so native peoples had a powerful incentive to learn the language. An added motive to learn Greek was the fact that one could advance socially through education. It would be an exaggeration to say that anyone born in the Hellenistic world could advance to the highest levels of society. Ancient society was marked by stability, and social mobility was rare. However, avenues to higher levels of society were more open in the Hellenistic period than previously. Since strong cultural similarities were now found throughout the Hellenistic empires, culture was to some degree international. "Greek" no longer necessarily referred to nationality, but to culture. A "Greek" was now one who spoke Greek and was immersed in Hellenistic culture. Geographical and social mobility for "Greeks" was great because of the large number of places where Greek was spoken and Greek culture understood.

Alienation

Peoples previously ruled by their own kings or by a Persian government with no interest in cultural hegemony now found themselves confronted by cultural imperialism. Greek-style cities were springing up in people's backyards. Greek began to be heard everywhere. Emigration became more common. The Greek religion and world view clashed with other religions and world views, and so people's world views were challenged. The reaction of many was apprehension. Such changes were not perceived as good by everyone.

As life became more complex, and as politics were determined by enormous empires often at war with one another, it seemed to many that control of one's individual or national life was not in one's own hands. Economic pressure increased as native peoples financed the Hellenistic wars through taxes. Wars periodically disrupted economic activity. Fate became more important as a force in people's lives. Astrology was popular, because if one could not control one's fate, one might as well know what one's fate was. Some religions evolved elaborate systems in which superhuman evil forces were seen at work in historical events. Hope was generated through apocalyptic and messianic expectations. Philosophy and religion changed to meet the new challenges and furnished ways for people to survive the overturning of their worlds.

Hellenistic Philosophy

There were schools in the ancient world devoted to the teachings of each of the great philosophers, Plato (Platonism), Aristotle (Aristotelianism or Peripateticism), Zeno (Stoicism), and Diogenes (Cynicism), but in the spirit of the Hellenistic age they influenced one another. Each school contributed to Hellenistic culture, especially since they were devoted not just to metaphysical speculation but to discerning how to live the good life. They spent much time on what might be called "ethics." Their discussions influenced religious groups as well, and one can trace Stoic and Platonic influence among Hellenized Jews and then among Christians. A few illustrations of Hellenistic philosophy's influence on groups, world views, and individuals relevant to this study will be helpful.

Plato (427–347 BCE) thought of the human person as divided into body and soul, the soul being trapped in the body as in a prison. The task of humans was to escape the body. This was possible to some extent even in this life by looking beyond the world of appearance and change, and meditating on what is good, true, and beautiful. At death, the soul was released from the body, and ascended to pure spiritual realms above. Plato also spoke of the existence of spiritual beings called *demons*. At the minimum, Plato contributed to Hellenistic conceptions of the dualistic nature of the universe (divided into the material and the spiritual), the body-soul dichotomy, mystical meditation, and the belief in spirits.

Stoicism was perhaps the single most influential philosophy of the Hellenistic period. To it is attributed the idea of the cosmopolis, the "global village" so to speak, where all people are brothers and sisters. This ideal was somewhat imperfectly fulfilled in Hellenistic culture itself. Stoics conceived of the universe on the analogy of a human person, with body and soul, but they thought of the soul as material of a finer sort than that of the body. What others might call God they called the world-soul or *logos* (Greek for "word," "mind," "reason"). It was the rational element of the universe by which all was ordered and held together. Thus the Stoics were pantheists, believing in the ultimate unity and divinity of the universe. They saw conventional religion as an allegorical expression of the relation of humanity to the one logos, and so were in favor of religious practices and mythologies but interpreted them allegorically. Each human mind was a particular instance of that world-soul coming to consciousness, and when a human died his or her soul would return to the world-soul. Since all humans were related in this way, they were all equal and were all brothers and sisters, and love was an appropriate way for them to relate. For the Stoic, a happy life was possible only if one lived in conformity with one's nature. Alignment with the rationality of the universe, the logos, was the goal. Stoics felt that one should not make one's happiness depend upon what one could not have, and so they aimed at not desiring what they could not have. Being content with oneself and with what one had was the rational way to live.

Hellenistic Religion

Luther Martin looks at Hellenistic religions from the point of view of three "strategies of existence." The first is "piety." "Piety, then, designates the traditional system of conventional practices concerning the home and family and, by extension, those practices which surround and are part of being at home in one's world under the rule of a family of gods" (11). This strategy undergirds public social order and expresses the world view of a specific people. It is public, and accessible to all in the community. Such would be a fair characterization of the religion of Ezra and Nehemiah, for example, or the civic religion of the Greek cities. The second strategy is "mystery." For those engaged in this strategy, the order of the world was not apparent, and one needed to establish a special relationship with some god or goddess for protection from a hostile world. The third strategy is "gnosis." In this view, one needed special esoteric knowledge in order to be saved from a world that was evil. A given religion such as Judaism could have various expressions that fit into each of these strategies.

Most Hellenistic religions had roots in the past, so one can speak of how they remained the same and how they changed with the coming of Hellenism. Judaism was no exception. Judaism of the Hellenistic era was not identical with the religion of the patriarchs, the Israelite religion of the confederated tribes, the state religion of the monarchy, or even the restored Temple religion under the Persians. Hellenistic influence on Judaism is one example of something happening throughout the Hellenistic world, and much of Hellenistic Judaism's world view was shared by other religions. Thus there was a Hellenistic "spirit of the times" (German: *Zeitgeist*).

Many Hellenistic religions existed both in their lands of origin and in foreign lands. The Jews had important communities in Babylonia, Egypt, Asia Minor, Greece, and even Rome. They were a sizable and influential community in Alexandria. The communities of Jews living outside Palestine are collectively referred to as the "Diaspora." A common characteristic of religions in their land of origin was resistance to Hellenism through nationalistic or messianic movements. Native cultures also emphasized their ancient pasts, sometimes reviving old forms, languages, texts, and practices in an effort to maintain their identities in face of Hellenism. But at the same time, native religions were influenced by Hellenism. In the diasporic expressions of these religions, Hellenization was sometimes deeper than in the homeland. The diasporic centers welcomed outsiders as full proselytes to their religion or as sympathizers. Ancient religions translated their traditions into Greek and interpreted them for Hellenistic audiences. Sacred texts were reinterpreted allegorically to build bridges between the texts and Hellenistic ideas and modes of thought.

Before the Hellenistic period, many religions of the ancient world were ones in which humanity's task was to fit into the cosmic order. In the Hellenistic period, traditional ways of looking at the world were shaken, and the order of the universe was no longer so apparent to many. The world was experienced by many as threatening, and its order was not necessarily benevolent. Religions of individual salvation became more popular, and gods and goddesses were looked to for liberation from the evil world. Divinities sometimes seemed remote and had to be reached by mystical means. Religious associations devoted to the worship of a specific deity became popular. Such associations were voluntary and involved paying dues, following rules of behavior, and submitting to some authority. They created a sense of security in an unsure world, and members often met for meals to enhance a sense of community.

There was a special type of religious association called a "mystery." Mysteries were supposed to be kept in secrecy, so not as much is known about them as one would like. They were voluntary and focused on the individual. Each mystery originated in a specific locale, but true to the international outlook of the Hellenistic world they were not restricted to that locale. Through an initiation ceremony one was granted close association with a god or goddess, which resulted in a close relationship between the person and that deity. Access to the divine was thus guaranteed, as well as divine protection in this life and the next.

The Hellenistic world was not for the most part monotheistic. True, Stoics could allegorically interpret the variety of divinities as expressions of the one logos, and some philosophers questioned the plurality of gods. There were identifications of different divinities, so that Syrian deities could be seen as manifestations of Greek ones, for example. Nonetheless, most people were polytheists. They believed that there were many divine beings, and that one would do well to stay on the right side of as many deities as might affect one's well-being. It is not surprising that the Jewish insistence on the worship of Yahweh alone was perceived at times as strange and perhaps even anti-social. Service to the gods was a civic duty, and Jewish refusal to participate could be interpreted as hostile to the political order. Although this was not always the case, such an interpretation sometimes surfaced when there were other conflicts between Jews and non-Jews.

DIASPORA JUDAISM

It was once conventional wisdom to make an absolute distinction between Diaspora and Palestinian Judaism. Diaspora Jews were allegedly completely Hellenized, whereas Palestinian Jews were not Hellenized at all. That view has been disproved by recent study, which shows that the Jews of Palestine were indeed exposed to Hellenism, and that the influence of Hellenism is apparent in their writings, inscriptions, institutions, and so on. But there were still differences between Palestinian Jewish communities and those in the Diaspora.

141

A full discussion of the similarities and differences between these Judaisms would be out of place here, but it will be helpful to say a few words about Diaspora Judaism.

In the Diaspora, Jews were in the minority. In Judah they were the majority. In the Diaspora, Jews spoke Greek as their native tongue. In Judah the language was primarily Aramaic, or perhaps in some cases Hebrew. Greek was spoken by some in Judah, most of them probably members of the upper class. These two contrasts alone suggest that even if both Diaspora and Palestinian Jews were Hellenized, the Hellenization was more widespread and deeper among Diaspora Jews than among Jews of Judah, with some exceptions, depending on position in society. The bulk of the Jewish literature presenting Judaism in Hellenistic literary forms and philosophical concepts comes from the Diaspora.

JUDAISM IN THE HOMELAND

The Sources

There are several literary sources for second-century BCE Judea. (From now on the area governed by Jerusalem will be called "Judea," the name by which the Romans called it.) One of these sources is the book of Daniel, an apocalypse written in 165 BCE. Daniel will be discussed in the next chapter. The first-century CE Jewish historian Josephus discusses the period, but much of what he says derives from 1 and 2 Maccabees. Both 1 and 2 Maccabees are histories. A date of about 100 BCE is assigned to 1 Maccabees. It begins its story with Alexander the Great, but within ten verses arrives at the reign of Antiochus IV of Syria in 175 BCE. The bulk of the book deals with three of the Maccabee brothers, Judas, Jonathan, and Simon, as well as Simon's son, John Hyrcanus. It was probably written in Hebrew, but it survives in Greek and Latin. It is strongly pro-Hasmonean and was written to prove that Hasmonean leadership was legitimate and divinely ordained. Although the book is biased, its history is fairly straightforward, not referring frequently to supernatural events. Since 1 Maccabees treats events leading up to the Maccabean revolt in a very brief and somewhat tendentious manner, its usefulness as a source for those events is limited. Because of its interest in the Hasmoneans it supplies valuable information about them.

The other source for this period, 2 Maccabees, tells of events from the high priesthood of Onias III to the Jews' defeat of the Syrian general Nicanor in 161 BCE. The book claims to be a condensation of a five-volume work by a certain Jason of Cyrene in North Africa. Both the original work and the condensation were written in Greek. Jason did his work toward the end of the second century, so that the condensation of it belongs somewhere in the first century BCE. The purpose of 2 Maccabees is to interpret history theologically. In so doing the author narrates supernatural events such as the appearance of angels who fight

God's enemies. The book must be examined with caution, but it does contain valuable historical information. It is more detailed and probably more accurate than 1 Maccabees regarding the events that lead to the Jewish revolt against Antiochus IV.

Israel Under Greek Rule

During the third century BCE, Judea was part of the Ptolemaic empire. The Ptolemies inherited a centralized system in which everything belonged to the Pharaoh and everything was controlled from the capital. The Ptolemies made bureaucratic control even tighter. They taxed their subjects heavily. Papyri that date from the middle of the third century tell of a visit to Palestine by Zenon, a Ptolemaic financial official. He had dealings with Tobiah of Ammon across the Jordan River from Judea, an officer in the Ptolemaic army. His name is the same as Tobiah of Ammon of the time of Nehemiah. The earlier Tobiah was a well-to-do Yahweh worshiper from Transjordan with connections in Jerusalem. The later Tobiah was probably a member of the same family, two centuries later.

Josephus also mentions Joseph, the son of Tobiah of Ammon. He says that the high priest Onias II refused to pay the Ptolemies money owed (probably sometime in 242–240 BCE; *Ant*. 12.4.1-5 §§ 156–85). It is possible that Onias II looked to the Seleucids as potentially more congenial overlords than the Ptolemies. In any case, Joseph the son of Tobiah of Ammon journeyed to Egypt and worked out a deal with the king in which Joseph would be the tax collector for Palestine. Some of the elements that would figure in events in the next centuries are evident in this episode. First, the actions of the high priest affected the entire nation, for he was its leader. Second, politics in Judea were played out under the circumstances of struggles between leaders of the world empires. Third, some Jews stood to gain or to lose much depending on their relationships to the world powers, the examples in this case being Onias, who seems to have favored the Seleucids, and Joseph, who worked for the Ptolemies.

The Seleucid king Antiochus III was called Antiochus the Great because he regained much of the territory his predecessors had lost over the years. He conquered Judea and added it to his empire in 198 BCE, a move that may have been favored by some Jewish leaders who shared pro-Seleucid sympathies with people like Onias II. Thus the Jews in Palestine passed from Ptolemaic to Seleucid control. That turned out to be a fateful event, as will be seen. Despite his successes, Antiochus III was defeated by Rome in the battle of Magnesia in Asia Minor in 190 BCE, and so lost Asia Minor. The defeat points to the growing power of the Romans and to the limitation of Seleucid power.

When Antiochus III captured Jerusalem, he granted its inhabitants the right to live "according to their ancestral laws." His grant continued what had probably been the case under the Ptolemies as well—the Jews were allowed to live by

Torah insofar as that did not interfere with foreign policy or taxation. In 175 BCE, a new king came to the Syrian throne, Antiochus IV Epiphanes. At the same time, a Jewish party favoring Hellenization was influential in Jerusalem, consisting of some priests and members of the upper class. Tensions began to rise between the Hellenizers and more traditional Jews. Antiochus IV finally tried to resolve the conflict by outlawing the practice of Judaism. That led to open revolt, led by Mattathias, a priest from the countryside, and his five sons. Mattathias died early in the revolt, and his son Judas took over. Judas was called "Maccabeus" meaning "hammer," probably because of his military successes. During the next decades the "Maccabees," the name by which scholars call all the brothers, won first religious and then political independence from the Seleucids and established an independent Jewish kingdom. The Maccabees, once established as the rulers of Judea, were called the "Hasmoneans" after one of their ancestors.

THE EVIDENCE OF 2 MACCABEES

Social Conflict and Temple Ideology

Chapter 3 of 2 Maccabees is informative for what it reveals about social relations within Jerusalem, and about 2 Maccabees' attitude toward the Temple. In 3:1, it paints a picture of harmony: "While the holy city was inhabited in unbroken peace and the laws were strictly observed because of the piety of the high priest Onias and his hatred of wickedness. . ." Here is the ideal. The high priest is devoted to the Torah, and the result is peace. Then comes trouble: "But a man named Simon, of the tribe of Benjamin, who had been made captain of the temple, had a disagreement with the high priest about the administration of the city market" (3:4). It is not clear what the precise duties of "captain of the temple" were, but the Greek word implies an oversight role. Simon's disagreement with Onias had to do with financial matters.

Because Simon does not prevail he goes to the Seleucids and tells them that there are large sums of money in the Temple. The Temple was, among other things, a financial institution. Because of the wealth that flowed to it from tithes, contributions, and the Temple tax begun by Nehemiah, it had substantial funds of its own. It also served as a secure deposit for the upper class. The Seleucids were in desperate need of money and had begun confiscating temple funds throughout the empire. Simon knows that his information will cause Onias trouble, and he hopes it will ingratiate himself to the Seleucids. The king sends his representative Heliodorus to get the money. Onias pleads with Heliodorus not to confiscate the funds: "And he [Onias] said that it was utterly impossible that wrong should be done to those people who had trusted in the holiness of the place and in the sanctity and inviolability of the temple which is honored throughout the whole world" (3:12).

According to the narrator, the entire city and its priests are alarmed and mourn the impending desecration of the Temple. When the king's emissary arrives at the Temple to take its money, superhuman figures appear who give him a sound thrashing. But then Onias offers a sacrifice of atonement, and Heliodorus is cured. Heliodorus' report to the king is an expression of the Temple ideology espoused by 2 Maccabees: "There is certainly some power of God about the place. For he who has his dwelling in heaven watches over that place himself and brings it aid, and he strikes and destroys those who come to do it injury" (3:38-39). These verses balance an acknowledgment of the close association between God and the Temple, and a reservation about saying that God actually lives there (*see* 1 Kings 8).

The Hellenistic Reform

In 175 BCE, Antiochus IV Epiphanes came to the throne.

When Seleucus died and Antiochus, who was called Epiphanes, succeeded to the kingdom, Jason the brother of Onias obtained the high priesthood by corruption, promising the king at an interview three hundred sixty talents of silver, and from another source of revenue eighty talents. In addition to this he promised to pay one hundred fifty more if permission were given to establish by his authority a gymnasium and a body of youth for it, and to enroll the people of Jerusalem as citizens of Antioch. When the king assented and Jason came to office, he at once shifted his compatriots over to the Greek way of life. He set aside the existing royal concessions to the Jews, secured through John the father of Eupolemus, who went on the mission to establish friendship and alliance with the Romans; and he destroyed the lawful ways of living and introduced new customs contrary to the law. He took delight in establishing a gymnasium right under the citadel, and he induced the noblest of the young men to wear the Greek hat. There was such an extreme of Hellenization and increase in the adoption of foreign ways because of the surpassing wickedness of Jason, who was ungodly and no true high priest, that the priests were no longer intent upon their service at the altar. Despising the sanctuary and neglecting the sacrifices, they hurried to take part in the unlawful proceedings in the wrestling arena after the signal for the discus-throwing, disdaining the honors prized by their ancestors and putting the highest value upon Greek forms of prestige. For this reason heavy disaster overtook them, and those whose ways of living they admired and wished to imitate completely became their enemies and punished them. It is no light thing to show irreverence to the divine laws—a fact that later events will make clear. (4:7-17)

Israel's high priesthood was hereditary. In this passage there is a departure from that practice. Jason (a Greek name, perhaps indicating Jason's Greek sympathies) ousts his brother Onias III by paying Antiochus for the office. In other Hellenistic religions it was not uncommon for there to be periodic changes of priests. Wealthy persons payed for the honor of being priest for a year. Although Antiochus must be aware that he violates Jewish custom by the transaction, he does what was normal in other Hellenistic centers. Jason and other members of the upper class want to turn Jerusalem into a Greek city. As is true in any Greek city, not all inhabitants are citizens. Land-owning males compose the body of citizens, so the citizen body of the projected Greek city of Jerusalem would be only a small proportion of the local population.

The gymnasium was an integral part of Greek life. One of its functions was to serve as a kind of high school in which young men would be trained physically, mentally, and spiritually to assume the duties and privileges of citizenship. Accordingly, Jason applies for permission to establish "a gymnasium and a body of youth for it" (4:9). Jerusalem's establishment as a full-fledged Greek city means that it is making a new beginning and so needs a new name. Since Antiochus is its official founder, the city is named after him, and the new citizens are enrolled as "citizens of Antioch." Every Greek city needed a city council. Jerusalem already had an institution termed "elders," which consisted of the heads of the leading families. It was probably those men who become the city council.

With Antiochus' permission, the stage is set for the shifting of Jason's countrymen over to the "Greek way of life." "He set aside the existing royal concessions to the Jews" means that the permission given to the Jews by Antiochus III to live by their ancestral laws (Torah) is abrogated so that Jason can modify that Law where necessary to accommodate Hellenistic elements, or as the text has it, to introduce "new customs contrary to the law."

Jason immediately proceeds to transform Jerusalem. He founds a gymnasium in the city, and to add insult to injury he locates it "right under the citadel," in proximity to the Temple itself. Since Greek religious rites would be part of gymnasium activity, one can imagine the horror of many Jews at this new development. An additional source of scandal is that young men compete in the games of the gymnasium naked (the word "gymnasium" comes from the Greek word for "naked," *gymnos*). Nakedness contravened Jewish practice. The passage reports that many youth of the upper class wear the "Greek hat," representing Greek culture as a whole. The priests who live and serve at Jerusalem are members of Judea's upper classes. Those classes have most contact with the larger world. Young priests accept Hellenization happily and join the Greek games in the gymnasium.

The Motives of the Hellenistic Reformers

The Hellenizers probably did not think that they were overthrowing their ancestral way of life. The text does not say that they stopped worshiping God, or introduced Greek rites into the Temple, or ceased sacrificing altogether. They did change some customs, but Judaism had always adapted to new situations in its history, and the Hellenizers may have considered this to be just one more such instance. One might imagine their making arguments to their fellows about the need to "modernize" and "keep up with the times." The Hellenizers knew that they were changing Judaism, but probably they felt they were preserving its essence. In their eyes the financial and political advantages of Hellenization outweighed the consequences of losing a few outmoded customs: "In those days certain renegades came out from Israel and misled many, saying, 'Let us go and make a covenant with the Gentiles around us, for since we separated from them many disasters have come upon us'" (1 Macc 1:11). That these people were "renegades" is a judgment made by the text. One cannot assume that they themselves thought that they were lawless, or that they intended to be so. As far as 2 Maccabees is concerned, however, the Hellenizers violate Torah. Writing after the events, the author knows that civil war, persecution by Antiochus, and war against the Greeks resulted from the Hellenistic reform. In 2 Maccabees 4:16-17, those tragedies are seen as punishment for disobeying Torah. But there is no reason to suppose that the Hellenistic reformers themselves saw things this way.

In twentieth-century America, many tend to see religion as something that should be separate from politics, economics, and social life. Such separations were not part of the world view of these ancient people. The divinely given Torah, the first five books of what we now call the Hebrew Bible, was the law of the land, instituted as such by the Persian government and confirmed by the Ptolemies and then the Seleucids. Its regulations involved cult and personal piety, but they also governed social relations, economics, and even foreign policy. All of this formed a unity in the Torah itself. In practice, Torah needed to be interpreted and applied and even changed. But if one Jewish group perceived another to be compromising Torah or even abrogating it, then that was seen as an act against God. To attack Torah was to attack the divinely ordained order of political, economic, social, and religious life. All were connected. Given the interconnectedness of these spheres of Israel's life, it is not surprising to find that different social classes could have different interpretations of how Torah should be implemented in society. The upper class was most prone to Hellenization, and they were the ones most likely to benefit from it. One's social location affected how one saw society and how one interpreted Torah.

An example of the kind of compromises Hellenizers were willing to make, but also of the kind of lines they drew, is supplied in 2 Maccabees 4:18-21.

When the quadrennial games were being held at Tyre and the king was present, the vile Jason sent envoys, chosen as being Antiochian citizens from Jerusalem, to carry three hundred silver drachmas for the sacrifice to Hercules. Those who carried the money, however, thought best not to use it for sacrifice, because that was inappropriate, but to expend it for another purpose. So this money was intended by the sender for the sacrifice to Hercules, but by the decision of its carriers it was applied to the construction of triremes.

The games held every four years were a symbol of the Greek way of life. Included in the ceremonies were rites honoring the Greek gods. Jason is willing to donate money toward the sacrifices to be offered to the Greek god Hercules. His envoys are "citizens of Antioch" (Jerusalem), but they have no intention of going as far as Jason in Hellenization. Deeming it wrong for Jewish money to be contributed to a foreign cult, they foil Jason's intentions by contributing the money toward the construction of ships.

The Role of Antiochus IV

Three years after Jason's accession to the high priesthood, Menelaus, brother of the Simon who was captain of the Temple, outbids Jason for the high priesthood. Jason retires to Transjordan. Meanwhile Antiochus IV marches to Egypt as part of his long-term plan to bring it under his control (2 Macc 5:1). When a rumor circulates that Antiochus has been killed on the Egyptian campaign, Jason sees an opportunity (5:5). He attacks Jerusalem and besieges Menelaus in the fortifications called "the citadel" in the neighborhood of the Temple. Meanwhile Antiochus, who is still alive, is confronted by the Romans in Egypt. His expansion into Egypt is contrary to Roman interests because the Romans do not want the Seleucid empire to get too powerful. The Romans insist that Antiochus leave Egypt. He comes to Jerusalem, enters the Temple, and steals its treasures, intending both to subdue Judea and obtain spoils to finance his expenditures (5:11-16).

The text explains how Antiochus can defile the Temple with impunity, whereas Heliodorus pays so dearly for the same act.

> Antiochus was elated in spirit, and did not perceive that the Lord was angered for a little while because of the sins of those who lived in the city, and that this was the reason he was disregarding the holy place. But if it had not happened that they were involved in many sins, this man would have been flogged and turned back from his rash act as soon as he came forward, just as Heliodorus had been, whom King Seleucus sent to inspect the treasury. But the Lord did not choose the nation for the sake of the holy place, but the place for the sake of the nation. Therefore the place itself shared in the misfortunes that befell the nation and afterward participated in its benefits; and what was forsaken in the wrath of the Almighty was restored again in all its glory when the great Lord became reconciled. (5:17-20)

This explanation is in the Deuteronomistic tradition, which claims that evil-doing brings punishment and doing good brings reward. God allows the

Temple to be dishonored as punishment for Israel's sins. The passage reconciles Temple ideology, in which God protects the Temple, with historical events, which seem to contradict that ideology.

Antiochus leaves Judea, but the unrest continues. The king sends another army to Jerusalem and establishes a permanent garrison there in a fortification (Greek: *akra*) in what was called the "city of David," a hill just to the south of the Temple.

> Then they fortified the city of David with a great strong wall and strong towers, and it became their citadel. They stationed there a sinful people, men who were renegades. These strengthened their position; they stored up arms and food, and collecting the spoils of Jerusalem they stored them there, and became a great menace. (1 Macc 1:33-35)

The foreign troops stationed in Jerusalem affect the city adversely. Their demands for food and other supplies are heavy. They bring with them their own gods and religions, abhorrent to strict observers of Torah. Their presence defiles the sanctuary (1:36-40).

Religious Persecution

Now Antiochus IV outlaws Judaism altogether. Exactly why he does so is debated among scholars. Some depict him as mentally unstable, others as a champion of Hellenization, others as desperate to unite his diverse empire. If full weight is given to the fact that the Hellenization of Jerusalem was a plan of the Jewish upper classes, then a plausible interpretation of his action is that he decides to throw his weight entirely behind the indigenous Hellenizing party in an effort to carry Hellenization through to its logical conclusion. In so doing he would strengthen the hand of those most likely to support him. But his next acts go far beyond anything anticipated or desired by the Jewish Hellenizers. Antiochus forbids Judaism and persecutes anyone who violates his prohibitions. His far-reaching orders are described in 2 Maccabees 6:1-11 and 1 Maccabees 1:41-64. Copies of the Torah are destroyed, possessors of the Torah are put to death, circumcision is outlawed, Jewish sacrifices and rites are prohibited, altars are built to foreign gods and Jews are forced to participate in the sacrifices, and Jews are compelled to eat pigs, forbidden by the Torah. An altar to Olympian Zeus is set up in the Temple and sacrifices are performed on it. According to 1 Maccabees, some few Jews are in favor of the proceedings, some capitulate unwillingly, and many resist and either flee to the wilderness or suffer the consequences of their resistance.

Chapters 6 and 7 of 2 Maccabees contain the stories of martyrs to the cause of Torah. In chapter 7 a mother and her seven sons are martyred before Antiochus. The sons make speeches before they die. They attribute Israel's suffering to its own sins. Nonetheless, they say that if they die loyal to Torah, God will raise them to new life. The mention of resurrection is something not encountered so far in the Hebrew Bible. The context of this story is the persecution of the righteous (the sons) by the wicked (Antiochus). The concept of resurrection emerges as a solution to the age-old problem of why the wicked prosper, while the righteous suffer. Explaining such apparent injustice by positing an afterlife where all get their just deserts becomes more prevalent as time goes on, especially in apocalyptic literature.

In 2 Maccabees 7, the seventh son predicts that God will punish Antiochus, and asks God to have mercy on Israel, "and through me and my brothers to bring to an end the wrath of the Almighty that has justly fallen on our whole nation" (7:38). He is saying that the brothers' suffering might be instrumental in causing God to be merciful. The efficacy of the sufferings of one or a few for the whole people first appeared in Second Isaiah. Here the context is different, but the idea of vicarious suffering is similar.

THE EVIDENCE OF 1 MACCABEES

A basic theme of 1 Maccabees is that God chose the Hasmoneans to liberate Jerusalem from the tyranny of Antiochus IV and then to rule the Jews until God should take more decisive steps to restore Jerusalem and Israel to their rightful place in the world. When the people and their leaders confirm the Hasmonean Simon as high priest in 1 Maccabees 14:27-45, they recognize God's will.

Mattathias Begins the Revolt

After telling of Antiochus' persecution, 1 Maccabees introduces the Maccabees in chapter 2. The text declares that they leave Jerusalem to escape persecution and go to a small town north of Jerusalem named Modein. The family consists of an elderly priest, Mattathias, and his five sons. The narrator emphasizes their grief at the desecration of Jerusalem and the Torah, thus presenting them as the perfect choice to resist the evil plans of Antiochus IV. When the king's agents arrive at Modein to enforce the king's decree requiring all Jews to offer idolatrous sacrifice, Mattathias refuses and kills a Jew who complies with the demand of the royal agents. Mattathias, the sons, and their sympathizers then flee to the wilderness. Chapter 2 then describes some pious Jews who flee to the wilderness and are trapped by the king's men. The king's troops attack them on the sabbath day. The Jews are too pious to break the sabbath by fighting, and so they are slaughtered. Mattathias and his followers take it upon themselves to suspend Torah's sabbath regulations so as to be able to fight the enemy (2:39-41).

Chapter 2 summarizes the Maccabees' activity.

> And Mattathias and his friends went around and tore down the altars; they forcibly circumcised all the uncircumcised boys that they found within the borders of Israel. They hunted down the arrogant, and the work prospered in their hands. They rescued the law out of the hands of the Gentiles and kings, and they never let the sinner gain the upper hand. (2:45-48)

Forced circumcision was not just a religious symbol; it was a statement about how Israel should live, and about the limits of Hellenization. Circumcision was an important sign by which Jews distinguished themselves from the rest of the world. Some adult Jews Hellenized themselves so far as to remove the marks of circumcision (1:15). This meant that they underwent an operation to undo their circumcision. Such a step was especially desirable for those who participated naked in the Greek games. When the Maccabees forcibly circumcised babies, they reemphasized the boundaries between Jew and Gentile that other Jews wished to eradicate or at least to blur.

Mattathias delivers a speech as he is about to die. In the speech he briefly lists some of Israel's heroes as examples of those who put their trust in God and were rewarded for it. One figure is of particular significance for the Hasmoneans: "Phinehas our ancestor, because he was deeply zealous, received the covenant of everlasting priesthood" (2:54). Phinehas killed an Israelite who had married a foreigner contrary to God's command (Num 25:6-15). As a reward for his action, God said, "Therefore say, 'I hereby grant him my covenant of peace. It shall be for him and for his descendants after him a covenant of perpetual priesthood, because he was zealous for his God, and made atonement for the Israelites'" (Num 25:12-13). In 1 Maccabees 2:26, Mattathias' killing of the Jew who was to sacrifice to the foreign god is compared to what Phinehas did: "Thus he [Mattathias] burned with zeal for the law, just as Phinehas did against Zimri son of Salu." The Hasmoneans' claim to the high priesthood is their zeal for the Law. The comparison with Phinehas connects this claim with a precedent in Israel's history of a special covenant of priesthood being awarded for acting because of zeal for God's Law.

Judas Maccabeus Rededicates the Sanctuary

Leadership of the revolution now passes to Mattathias' son Judas. His tactics are those of guerrilla warfare. His exploits are painted in the colors of holy war. Judas' victories are associated with those of Israel in the past (e.g., 3:16-22; 3:43-60; 4:6-11). Eventually Judas enters Jerusalem in 164 BCE and takes control of most of it. He is not able, however, to penetrate the Akra, the Seleucid citadel in the city of David. Judas' first act in Jerusalem is to purify and rededicate the sanctuary.

He chose blameless priests devoted to the law, and they cleansed the sanctuary and removed the defiled stones to an unclean place. They deliberated what to do about the altar of burnt offering, which had been profaned. And they thought it best to tear it down, so that it would not be a lasting shame to them that the Gentiles had defiled it. So they tore down the altar, and stored the stones in a convenient place on the temple hill until a prophet should come to tell what to do with them. Then they took unhewn stones, as the law directs, and built a new altar like the former one.

(4:42-47)

The passage features cultic language. The use of the Temple precincts for the unholy rites of the foreigners makes it unfit for the worship of God. Purification is necessary. The very stones are contaminated and must be replaced. The altar was used for unclean sacrifices, so it also must be replaced, but stones that had been dedicated to so holy a use must not be simply discarded. At a loss about what to do with the old altar, they decide to wait for instructions from God through a future prophet on that matter. That no prophet is available to the Hasmoneans reflects a belief that prophecy had ceased sometime shortly after the Exile. Chapter 9 makes this belief explicit: "So there was great distress in Israel, such as had not been since the time that prophets ceased to appear among them" (9:27). The Jewish historian Josephus expresses the same belief two centuries later. The Hasmoneans put the stones aside until a prophet should arise, showing that at least as far as 1 Maccabees is concerned, prophecy will be renewed at some unspecified future date.

"Then Judas and his brothers and all the assembly of Israel determined that every year at that season the days of dedication of the altar should be observed with joy and gladness for eight days, beginning with the twenty-fifth day of the month of Chislev" (4:59). The Hebrew word for "dedication" is *ḥănukkāh*. The feast instituted by the Maccabees is indeed still celebrated by Jews today.

"When the Gentiles all around heard that the altar had been rebuilt and the sanctuary dedicated as it was before, they became very angry, and they determined to destroy the descendants of Jacob who lived among them" (5:1-2). Jews in Palestine lived not only in Judea, but also throughout Palestine and Transjordan. They sometimes lived in the same cities and areas as Gentiles. When the Seleucid empire decided to stamp out Judaism, some of the Jews' Gentile neighbors may have rejoiced, perhaps hoping to profit in some way. When Judas rededicated the sanctuary, the neighbors reacted negatively.

Seleucid Power Struggles and the Maccabees

Sometime around the time of the dedication of the altar Antiochus IV dies (6:8-16; 164 BCE), and the Seleucids face what is to be a common situation, rival claimants to the throne. A pattern emerges over the next decades in which royal claimants use the Hasmoneans in their maneuvers against one another. The Jews in turn use the warring Seleucids to their own advantage by striking deals with one and then another of them (chaps. 6–15). When Antochus IV dies, his nine-year-old son is next in line for the throne. Antiochus' general Lysias is his regent and besieges Jerusalem (6:18-54). Hearing, however, that Antiochus IV had appointed another regent, Philip (6:14-15), and that Philip is trying to get control of the government, Lysias settles with Judas quickly by granting religious freedom (6:55-59).

A new pretender to the throne, Demetrius son of Seleucus IV, now arrives on the scene and does away with both Antiochus' young son and Lysias (7:1-4). Demetrius sends Alcimus, a legitimate priest, to assume the high priesthood. Many Jews, satisfied that religious freedom is restored and a legitimate priest appointed high priest, consider the war over. But Judas takes to the wilderness again (7:23-24). His struggles now are against not only the Seleucids, but also Jews who have made peace with them. Alcimus makes a trip to the king to ask for help against Judas (7:25). Judas takes the opportunity to recapture Jerusalem, defeating the general Nicanor, who was sent against him (7:39-50). He then sends an emissary to Rome and concludes a treaty with that rising power (8:1-32). Rome gives the Maccabees no direct help, although when the Seleucids make concessions to the Jews, the Romans may enter into their calculations. Judas later meets his end in battle (9:18; 161 BCE).

Another Maccabean brother, Jonathan, inherits the leadership of the band still committed to revolution (9:28-31). He achieves an uneasy coexistence with the Seleucids. When Demetrius later finds himself confronted by another royal pretender, Alexander, he turns to Jonathan for help. Jonathan agrees, but then switches his allegiance to Alexander and is rewarded with the high priesthood (152 BCE), even though he is not of the Zadokite line and so strictly speaking is not qualified for the office (10:15-21). He later loses his life (143 BCE), caught in further Seleucid scheming (12:48).

Confirmation of the Hasmoneans

When Jonathan dies, his brother Simon, the last of the Maccabean brothers (the other two died in battle), comes to power (1 Maccabees 13). Under Simon the Jews finally get control of the Akra (13:49-52; 142 BCE). With the garrison in Jerusalem gone, the Jews are more independent than before. Later there is a solemn declaration by the Jewish leaders and people that Simon is valid high priest and leader of the nation (140 BCE). Through this declaration, the nation officially confirms the honors the Maccabees gained by force and diplomacy from the Seleucids. The following are excerpts from the declaration in 1 Maccabees 14:27-45.

In the great assembly of the priests and the people and the rulers of the nation and the elders of the country, the following was proclaimed to us: "Since wars often occurred in the country, Simon son of Mattathias, a priest of the sons of Joarib, and his brothers, exposed themselves to danger and resisted the enemies of their nation, in order that their sanctuary and the law might be preserved; and they brought great glory to their nation. . . . The people saw Simon's faithfulness and the glory that he had resolved to win for his nation, and they made him their leader and high priest, because he had done all these things and because of the justice and loyalty that he had maintained toward his nation. . . . In view of these things King Demetrius confirmed him in the high priesthood, made him one of his Friends, and paid him high honors. For he had heard that the Jews were addressed by the Romans as friends and allies and brothers, and that the Romans had received the envoys of Simon with honor. The Jews and their priests have resolved that Simon should be their leader and high priest forever, until a trustworthy prophet should arise, and that he should be governor over them and that he should be obeyed by all, and that all contracts in the country should be written in his name, and that he should be clothed in purple and wear gold." (14:27-29, 35, 38-43)

Simon receives far-reaching powers. He is in full control of Temple, city, and countryside. His high office is conferred on him in view of the service he and his family have rendered the nation and the Torah. Though not of the line of Zadok, the Hasmoneans become the established high priestly family. Though not of the line of David, they exercise what amounts to royal power, and several decades later actually assume royal title as well.

Hasmonean Rule

When Simon was assassinated in 134 BCE his son, John Hyrcanus, took the throne (ruled 134–104 BCE). Under John the Jewish state looked more and more like a monarchy, although the title "king" was still not used. John's son Aristobulus I (ruled 104–103 BCE) was the first to use the title "king." John and his successors expanded the empire through conquest. By the time of Alexander Jannaeus (ruled 103–76 BCE), it had attained a size comparable to that of the united kingdom under David and Solomon. Among John's conquests was Samaria. In 128 BCE, he destroyed the temple the Samaritans had built on Mount Gerizim at the beginning of the Hellenistic era. This step contributed greatly to worsening the already hostile relations between Jerusalem and Samaria. Another significant conquest was Idumea, a land to the south of Judea. There John followed the Hasmonean practice of forcibly circumcizing the conquered peoples.

A great irony of the Hasmonean monarchy was that as time went by the Hasmoneans themselves became more and more Hellenized. Having begun by fighting the Hellenizers on the platform of defending the Temple and the Torah against them, they ended by being Hellenizers themselves. Their Greek names—Hyrcanus, Aristobulus, Alexander, Alexandra—bear witness to Greek influence on the Hasmonean court. They hired Greek mercenaries, and their courts acquired the trappings of a typical Hellenistic court. More conservative elements of the population began to resent their rule. A consequence of the resentment aroused by Hasmonean rule was a terrible civil war that broke out in the reign of Alexander Jannaeus. Many of the people opposed Alexander's cruel leadership. They went so far as to call on the Seleucid army for help against Alexander and his mercenary forces in 88 BCE. However, a sizable portion of the anti-Alexander Jews switched their allegiance back to the king when they realized that fighting him might result in the reestablishment of Seleucid rule over Judea. Alexander won the war and punished those who had rebelled against him.

EXCURSUS: THE HASIDIM

A group called the "Hasideans" appears in 1 and 2 Maccabees. Their name derives from the Hebrew word *ḥăsîdîm* meaning "pious." It is the same word that lies behind today's designation of some Jews as "hasidic." Some scholars picture the Hasideans as a coherent group, either scribes or with a strong scribal contingent, who were strong warriors allied with the Maccabees for a time, but who then accepted the Seleucid terms of religious freedom in return for stopping the revolt. The group later reacted negatively to the rule of the Hasmoneans and split into two factions, both opposed to Hasmonean rule—the Pharisees and the Essenes. This hypothesis is attractive, especially because it explains the origin of the Pharisees and Essenes, but there is not enough evidence to prove or disprove it.

In 1 Maccabees 2:42, it is reported that joining the Maccabees in the wilderness was "a company of Hasideans, mighty warriors of Israel, all who offered themselves willingly for the law." The text says that the Hasidim were conservative law-observers who were willing to fight and die for the Torah. It does not tell us to what degree they were organized, whether they existed as a fixed group before the revolt, or whether they had anything in common besides zeal for Torah.

The word "Hasideans" occurs again in 1 Maccabees 7. The Seleucids appear ready to grant religious freedom to the Jews, and send a legitimate priest named Alcimus to offer terms. "Then a group of scribes appeared in a body before Alcimus and Bacchides to ask for just terms. The Hasideans were first among the Israelites to seek peace from them, for they said, 'A priest of the line of Aaron has come with the army, and he will not harm us'" (1 Macc 7:12-14). Many scholars take "scribes" to describe the Hasidim here, but that is not clearly stated. The Hasideans were an identifiable group, but beyond their devotion to Torah they remain a mystery. Their policy here differs from that of the Maccabees, because the latter continued the struggle.

The final reference to the Hasideans occurs in 2 Maccabees 14:6. Judea is ruled by Alcimus, but the Maccabees have continued the fight. Alcimus says to King Demetrius, ''Those of the Jews who are called Hasideans, whose leader is Judas Maccabeus, are keeping up war and stirring up sedition, and will not let the kingdom attain tranquility.'' This statement is incompatible with what is known of the Hasideans from 1 Maccabees. There the Hasideans acted contrary to the wishes of Judas Maccabeus and made peace with Alcimus (1 Macc 7:13). Judas was not their leader.

What is clear is that under the Maccabees, a coalition was formed between various segments of the population to battle what was perceived as an attack on the divinely ordained Jewish way of life. When that immediate threat was overcome, a number of groups emerged in Jewish society, not all of which were satisfied with the new state of affairs in the Hasmonean state.

THE BOOK OF SIRACH

The book of Sirach, a work of Israel's wisdom tradition, was written early in the second century BCE by the scribe Joshua ben Sira (the Greek form of his name is Jesus ben Sirach).[1] He was probably of the upper class, and he lived in Jerusalem. Ben Sira's book is examined here for the light it sheds on scribes and scribal activity in Jerusalem just before the Hellenistic reform. Sirach paints a portrait of the ideal scribe, making little distinction between the scribe and the wise man. Investigation of passages dealing with what a wise man should be yields a portrait of what the ideal upper-class, well-educated scribe should be. Torah is seen as the epitome of wisdom, and divine inspiration as the root of all wisdom. But there is also a basic openness to the larger Hellenistic world in ben Sira. A scribe does not scorn foreign wisdom (39:4), but rather is open to knowledge wherever it may be found. Sirach thus occupies a middle ground between the Jewish Hellenizers like Jason the high priest, and the groups who allied against the Hellenizing reformers. The very fact that ben Sira writes in his own name (50:27) is unusual in a Jewish context, but common in a Hellenistic one.

The book's prologue indicates that it was brought to Egypt by Sirach's grandson and translated into Greek. The grandson begins his prologue:

Many great teachings have been given to us through the Law and the Prophets and the others that followed them, and for these we should praise Israel for instruction and wisdom. Now, those who read the scriptures must not only themselves understand them, but must also as lovers of learning be able through the spoken and written word to help the outsiders. So my grandfather Jesus, who had devoted himself especially to the reading of the Law and the Prophets and the other books of our ancestors, and had acquired considerable proficiency in them, was himself also led to write something pertaining to instruction and wisdom, so that by becoming familiar also with his book those who love learning might make even greater progress in living according to the law.

156

True learning lies in the study of God's Torah, although ben Sira's learning draws on sources outside Scripture, as is common in wisdom works. Ben Sira's vocation is to study and to write and teach about the wisdom that comes from God.

Sirach contains a long meditation on the ideal scribe in 38:24–39:11. It begins with the words, "The wisdom of the scribe depends on the opportunity of leisure; only the one who has little business can become wise" (38:24). Other occupations take up too much time for there to be any opportunity for study. Sirach goes through the occupations of farmer, craftsman, blacksmith, and potter. All are consumed with perfecting the skills required for their jobs, and in being productive. Sirach allows them their integral role in society, but they have no place in the upper echelons of the social structure. Sirach's words illustrate the social stratification typical of his society.

> All these rely on their hands,
>   And all are skillful in their own work.
> Without them no city can be inhabited,
>   and wherever they live, they will not go hungry.
> Yet they are not sought out for the council of the people,
>   nor do they attain eminence in the public assembly.
> They do not sit on the judge's seat,
>   nor do they understand the decisions of the courts;
> they cannot expound discipline or judgment,
>   and they are not found among the rulers.
> But they maintain the fabric of the world,
>   and their concern is for the exercise of their trade. (38:31-34)

Tradespeople are essential for a city, but they are not prominent in the community, nor do they administrate the Law, which organizes society. There follows a passage describing the nature of the wise scribe.

> How different is the one who devotes himself
>   to the study of the law of the Most High!
> He seeks out the wisdom of all the ancients,
>   and is concerned with prophecies;
> he preserves the sayings of the famous
>   and penetrates the subtleties of parables;
> he seeks out the hidden meanings of proverbs
>   and is at home with the obscurities of parables.
> He serves among the great
>   and appears before rulers;
> he travels in foreign lands
>   and learns what is good and evil in the human lot.

He sets his heart to rise early
  to seek the Lord who made him,
  and to petition the Most High;
he opens his mouth in prayer
  and asks pardon for his sins.
If the great Lord is willing,
  he will be filled with the spirit of understanding;
he will pour forth words of wisdom of his own
  and give thanks to the Lord in prayer.
The Lord will direct his counsel and knowledge,
  as he meditates on his mysteries.
He will show the wisdom of what he has learned,
  and will glory in the law of the Lord's covenant.
Many will praise his understanding;
  it will never be blotted out.
His memory will not disappear,
  and his name will live through all generations.
Nations will speak of his wisdom,
  and the congregation will proclaim his praise.

(38:34b–39:10)

This passage on the wise scribe illustrates the centrality of Torah and of explicitly religious motivations in scribal activity. The first duty of the scribe is to study "the law of the Most High." Seeking out the "wisdom of all the ancients" as well as "prophecies" probably also deals with Scripture. Inspiration direct from God is central to scribal activity, according to this passage. The scribe rises early to pray, to open his heart to God, and to await inspiration. For the true scribe, Torah is always central, for he will "glory in the law of the Lord's covenant." The upper-class scribe also preserves and passes on the teachings of notable men, just as it is the job of the Hellenistic schools of philosophy to preserve and transmit the teachings of Plato, Aristotle, and Zeno. Reflection on parables and proverbs is typical of wisdom teachers.

The political function of upper-class scribes also is evident in this passage. In 38:33, it is implied that unlike craftsmen, scribes are eminent in the public assembly, and the people follow their advice. They act as judges because they know the Law. They perform their duties among "the great" and they appear "before rulers" (39:4). Certain scribes are advisors to the ruling class. Some are even members of the ruling class. They are well educated, knowledgeable in international affairs and in understanding of the bureaucracy, learned in the histories of great empires, and so on. Ideally, they have traveled "in foreign lands." Foreign wisdom is examined for the fruit it could bear domestically. The ideal of foreign travel was typical of the Hellenistic age when acquaintance with various cultures was desirable.

In 51:13-30 there is an advertisement for a wisdom school. The passage is found at Qumran in a somewhat different version, so there is some question whether it is from the pen of ben Sira. In any case, it supplies information about second-century schools. It begins, "While I was still young, before I went on my travels, I sought wisdom openly in my prayer. Before the temple I asked for her, and I will search for her until the end" (51:13-14). Wisdom comes from God, who dwells in the Temple. The search for wisdom begins at the Temple. Then the quest involves travel and any other activity that leads to knowledge. The next verses describe the constant search for wisdom in rather abstract terms. A school is mentioned in 51:23: "Draw near to me, you who are uneducated, and lodge in the house of instruction." The Hebrew here is *bêt midrāš*, a term used later by rabbis to designate their schools. Later in the passage money is mentioned: "Hear but a little of my instruction, and through me you will acquire silver and gold" (51:28). This verse may be purely figurative, but it raises the question of how a scribal or wisdom school would be supported. Wealthy citizens who sent their sons to a prominent wise scribe would probably pay him for their education.

Judging from the political functions the scribe performed, it is likely that ben Sira was sympathetic to the government headed by the high priest. He wrote before the Hellenistic reform under Jason. Ben Sira ends his book with a lengthy praise of Israel's illustrious (translated from the Hebrew and Syriac manuscripts as "pious") men. The list culminates in an encomium on Simon son of Onias, the high priest. Ben Sira lists Simon's accomplishments, including repair and fortification of the Temple, digging a cistern for water, and reinforcing Jerusalem's defenses. There follows a long passage in which ben Sira glories in Simon's cultic role and its significance for Israel. Ben Sira expresses his devotion to Israel's priestly religion extravagantly (50:1-21).

> How glorious he was, surrounded by the people,
>   as he came out of the house of the curtain.
> Like the morning star among the clouds,
>   like the full moon at the festal season;
> like the sun shining on the temple of the Most High,
>   like the rainbow gleaming in splendid clouds. . . .
> When he put on his glorious robe
>   and clothed himself in perfect splendor,
> when he went up to the holy altar,
>   he made the court of the sanctuary glorious.

When he received the portions from the hands of the priests,
　　as he stood by the hearth of the altar
with a garland of brothers around him,
　　he was like a young cedar on Lebanon
　　surrounded by the trunks of palm trees.
All the sons of Aaron in their splendor
　　held the Lord's offering in their hands
　　before the whole congregation of Israel.
Finishing the service at the altars,
　　and arranging the offering to the Most High, the Almighty,
he held out his hand for the cup
　　and poured a drink offering of the blood of the grape;
he poured it out at the foot of the altar,
　　a pleasing odor to the Most High, the king of all.
Then the sons of Aaron shouted;
　　they blew their trumpets of hammered metal;
they sounded a mighty fanfare
　　as a reminder before the Most High.
Then all the people together quickly
　　fell to the ground on their faces
to worship their Lord, the Almighty, God Most High.
Then the sinners praised him with their voices
　　in sweet and full-toned melody.
And the people of the Lord Most High offered
　　their prayers before the Merciful One,
until the order of worship of the Lord was ended,
　　and they completed his ritual.
Then Simon came down and raised his hands
　　over the whole congregation of Israelites,
to pronounce the blessing of the Lord with his lips,
　　and to glory in his name;
and they bowed down in worship a second time,
　　to receive the blessing from the Most High. (50:5-7, 11-21)

In this poem one glimpses the Temple service through the eyes of a participant.
The eyewitness is a member of Israel's upper class, a resident of Jerusalem, an
intimate of the government, and a supporter of the political and economic
structures replicated in the Temple service. One can appreciate the impression
made by the worship, especially on pilgrims who had to make lengthy journeys
to get to Jerusalem. The power of the liturgy and the centrality of the high priest
comes across forcefully. The high priest is the conduit for God's blessing, and so
occupies a crucial role in Israel's life. Political power and religious function
coincide in this system.

CONCLUSION

The conquests of Alexander the Great changed the world forever. The Jews under Greek rule were faced with a political and cultural imperialism that challenged not only their political institutions but also their religious faith and customs. Jews reacted in varied ways to the new situation. In the Diaspora, Jews were able to undergo extensive integration into the Hellenistic world without losing their Jewish identity. In Jerusalem, tension mounted between Jews who wanted to turn the city into a Greek *polis,* and those who thought that such a transformation would be a violation of Torah. That tension, combined with the unstable situation of the Seleucid empire, resulted in a revolt. Within the space of several decades, the Jews had won not only religious freedom, but political independence under the leadership of the priestly Hasmoneans. That independence was to last until the coming of the Romans in 63 BCE.

SELECT BIBLIOGRAPHY

This chapter makes extensive use of Tcherikover's work listed below.

Attridge, Harold. "Jewish Historiography," in *EJMI,* 311-43.

Bickerman, Elias. *The God of the Maccabees: Studies on the Meaning and Origin of the Maccabean Revolt.* Leiden: Brill, 1979.

_____. *From Ezra to the Last of the Maccabees: Foundations of Postbiblical Judaism.* New York: Schocken Books, 1962.

Collins, John J. *Between Athens and Jerusalem: Jewish Identity in the Hellenistic Diaspora.* New York: Crossroad, 1983.

Cumont, Franz. *Astrology and Religion Among the Greeks and Romans.* New York: Dover, 1960.

Davies, Philip R. "Hasidim in the Maccabean Period," *JSJ* 28 (1977): 127-40.

Eddy, Samuel K. *The King Is Dead: Studies in the Near Eastern Resistance to Hellenism 334–31 B.C.* Lincoln, Neb.: University of Nebraska Press, 1961.

Goldstein, Jonathan. "Jewish Acceptance and Rejection of Hellenism," in E. P. Sanders ed., with A. I. Baumgarten and Alan Mendelson, *Jewish and Christian Self-Definition: Volume Two: Aspects of Judaism in the Graeco-Roman Period.* Philadelphia: Fortress Press, 1981, 64-87.

Hadas, Moses. *Hellenistic Culture: Fusion and Diffusion.* New York: W. W. Norton & Co., 1972.

Harrington, Daniel J. *The Maccabean Revolt: Anatomy of a Biblical Revolution.* Wilmington, Del.: Michael Glazier, 1988.

_____. "The Wisdom of the Scribe According to Ben Sira," in *IFAJ,* 181-88.

Hengel, Martin. *Judaism and Hellenism: Studies in Their Encounter in Palestine During the Early Hellenistic Period.* 2 vols. Philadelphia: Fortress Press, 1974.

Jones, A. H. M. *The Greek City: From Alexander to Justinian.* Oxford: Clarendon Press, 1940.

Lieberman, Saul. *Greek in Jewish Palestine.* New York: Jewish Theological Seminary, 1942.

———. *Hellenism in Jewish Palestine.* New York: Jewish Theological Seminary, 1950.

Martin, Luther H. *Hellenistic Religions: An Introduction.* Oxford: Oxford University Press, 1987.

Meyers, Eric M., and A. Thomas Kraabel. "Archeology, Iconography, and Non-literary Remains," in *EJMI,* 175-210.

Peters, F. E. *The Harvest of Hellenism: A History of the Near East from Alexander the Great to the Triumph of Christianity.* New York: Simon and Schuster, 1970.

Sanders, E. P. "The Covenant as a Soteriological Category and the Nature of Salvation in Palestinian and Hellenistic Judaism," in *Jews, Greeks, and Christians: Studies in Honor of W. D. Davies.* Ed. R. Hamerton-Kelly and R. Scroggs. Leiden: Brill, 1976, 11-44.

Skehan, P. W., and Alexander DiLella. *The Wisdom of Ben Sira,* AB 39. Garden City, N.Y.: Doubleday, 1987.

Smith, Jonathan Z. "Hellenistic Religions," in *The Encyclopedia Britannica,* 15th ed. Chicago: University of Chicago Press, 1985, "Macropedia," vol. 18, 925-27.

———. "Hellenistic Cults in the Hellenistic Period," *HR* 11 (1971): 236-49.

Stone, Michael. "Hellenism and the Diaspora," in *SSV,* 87-98.

Tarn, W. W., and G. T. Griffith. *Hellenistic Civilization,* 3rd. ed. New York: New American Library, 1961.

Tcherikover, Victor. *Hellenistic Civilization and the Jews.* New York: Atheneum Publishers, 1977.

Apocalypticism

Primary Readings: Daniel, 1 Enoch 1–36, 72–108

TERMINOLOGY

Recent research on apocalypticism has clarified the terminology used to discuss it. (1) The word "apocalypse" denotes a literary genre (type). (2) "Apocalypticism" is a world view common to apocalypses. (3) The adjective "apocalyptic" means something typical of apocalypses or apocalypticism.

There are only two apocalypses in the Bible—Daniel and Revelation (also called the Apocalypse)—but much of post-biblical Jewish literature was in the form of apocalypses or contained apocalyptic elements. Christianity developed in an apocalyptic matrix. An understanding of apocalypticism is essential for appreciating both Second Temple Judaism and Christian origins.

LITERARY GENRE: APOCALYPSE

In 1979 a team of scholars published a definition of "apocalypse":

> A genre of revelatory literature with a narrative framework, in which a revelation is mediated by an otherworldly being to a human recipient, disclosing a transcendent reality which is both temporal, insofar as it envisages eschatological salvation, and spatial insofar as it involves another, supernatural world.[1]

An apocalypse is a story about a human who receives a revelation. The human is often called a "seer", because he or she frequently sees visions. What is seen is usually not self-explanatory, but needs interpretation by a supernatural being, usually an angel. The temporal aspect of the revelation deals with the future, in which evil is punished and good rewarded. Most apocalypses see this judgment as coming fairly soon. The revelation is spatial in that there is a supernatural world in which decisions are made and events happen that determine human history. One can understand what occurs in the human sphere only by knowing what is happening in the supernatural sphere.

The revelation conveyed to the seer contains information not generally available. It cannot be attained through reason, by reading sacred writings, or by any of the normal methods of determining God's will. Yet it is crucial to the fate of humans because it concerns the criteria for final judgments on humans, angels, and demons. Because right action depends on right knowledge, wisdom terminology ("wisdom," "the wise," "knowledge," "understanding") abounds in apocalypses. But apocalyptic wisdom is very different from the wisdom of the wisdom tradition. In the latter, human reason applied to everyday life produces knowledge of how the world works and how humans should behave. Apocalyptic wisdom is available only through direct revelation. Because of its esoteric nature, the revelation is often called a "mystery" or a "secret." The means of revelation point to the mysteriousness of the knowledge. The seer travels to where others have not gone, or sees visions others have not seen. He or she does not understand what is seen. Someone from the supernatual world must explain the vision. God is mysterious and remote.

Most apocalypses fall into one of two principal types: those with an other-worldly journey, and those with a review of history. Broadly speaking, the former type is characterized by speculation about the workings of the universe. This is called "cosmological speculation," from the Greek word *kosmos,* which denotes an ordered universe whose order is knowable. Apocalypses with reviews of history tend to be less interested in the cosmos and more interested in history. Both types of apocalypses assume an intimate connection between the workings of the universe and the events of human history.

An almost universal feature of apocalypses is pseudonymity. "Pseudonymity" means "false name." The person whose name an apocalypse bears is usually not its real author, but a prominent figure of the distant past. Pseudonymity imparts authority to the apocalypse, especially given the Hellenistic world's respect for the past. In apocalypses containing a historical review, most of the review is a prediction *ex eventu,* that is, after the events. When the fictitious author accurately "predicts" events that are really past events for the author, actual predictions of the near future have greater credibility.

THE APOCALYPTIC WORLD VIEW

An important aspect of the apocalyptic world view is its eschatology. The word "eschatology" derives from the Greek word *eschaton* meaning "end." Eschatology is teaching about the end of something, usually the end of the world as presently constituted. Apocalyptic eschatology involves a transcendence of death, thus furnishing an answer to the age-old dilemma of why the good suffer and the wicked prosper. The answer is that there will be rewards and punishments after death.

Apocalypses with historical reviews often contain the following elements, although not all elements are present in each apocalypse.

(1) urgent expectation of the end of earthly conditions in the immediate future; (2) the end as a cosmic catastrophe; (3) periodization and determinism; (4) activity of angels and demons; (5) new salvation, paradisal in character; (6) manifestation of the kingdom of God; (7) a mediator with royal functions; (8) the catchword "glory."[2]

Each element deserves comment.

1) The world as presently known will end soon. Such a view assumes that something is wrong with the world. The eschaton brings the end of what is bad in the world and the reconstitution of things so that everything is as it should be.

2) The entire universe is involved in the eschaton. Stars fall, the sun and moon stop giving light, mountains melt, and so on. The cosmos is intimately tied up with the fate of humanity. Such a view is not peculiar to apocalypticism. In the creation stories in Genesis 1–2, humans are part of God's creation. When Adam and Eve disobey God, it is not just they who are cursed but the earth itself (Gen 3:17).

3) Many apocalypses divide history into periods whose progression is foreordained by God and unchangeable. The real author of a given apocalypse sees himself or herself as living at the end of the succession of periods, "the end of times." "Determinism" means that God's plans are set and cannot be changed. Repentance may put one on the right side of God when the end finally comes, but it will not stop the end from coming.

4) Angels and demons are inferior to God but greater than humans. Belief in the extensive activity of such figures implies that God is distant from humans. Humans spend more time interacting with intermediate figures than with God. Evil is personified in supernatural beings, demons, or evil angels, often with a single demon at their head. The Hebrew word *śāṭān* means "accuser." Early traditions about Satan see him as the prosecuting attorney in the heavenly courtroom (*see* Zechariah 3), his task being to accuse humans. By the late Second Temple period, the figure has become completely evil and opposed to God: He is leader of the demons. Other figures earn this dubious honor in other Jewish traditions—Beelzebul, Mastema, Shemihazah, 'Asael, and others.

5) Salvation may mean a rectification of earthly wrongs, such as the overthrow of Israel's enemies and the setting up of an earthly kingdom in Jerusalem, but it does not necessarily mean that. Apocalyptic salvation always means transcendence of death, punishment of the wicked and reward of the righteous, and the banishment of all that is bad. The new world is "paradisal," meaning that everything is as it should be. Creation will be as it was in the garden of Eden before sin.

6) "Kingdom of God" means "God's rule." Humanity and creation itself have not obeyed God's will. Evil powers have taken over God's creation. But God's rule will be restored in the universe at the appropriate time.

7) The "mediator with royal functions" has been taken by Christians to refer to Jesus, the Davidic descendant who rules the universe as messiah. Element seven is not really common in Jewish apocalypses. There is not always a mediator, and when there is, he is not always "royal."

8) The word "glory" recalls the terminology of the priestly writer, in which "glory" indicates the presence of God. The word is frequent in apocalyptic literature because that literature speaks of the divine becoming present to a world alienated from God. God's world is revealed, which is by definition glorious.

THE ORIGINS OF JEWISH APOCALYPTICISM

Jewish apocalypticism was neither simply imported from outside Israel, nor was it fully home-grown. Cultures in contact with Hellenism tended to contain both native and foreign elements. Jewish roots of apocalypticism have been discerned in both the wisdom and the prophetic traditions. Wisdom and apocalypticism share the idea that right understanding is required for right action. Like wisdom, apocalypticism relates the structure of the universe to human life. But wisdom sees that understanding as accessible to human reason, whereas for apocalypticism special revelation is necessary.

Like prophecy, apocalypticism anticipates God's imminent intervention in history. However, prophecy does not expect the cosmic transformation typical of apocalypticism, nor does it speak of the transcendence of death. For the prophets, whether divine punishment will occur depends upon the people's reaction to God's word. Repentance can avert disaster. But for apocalypticism, the end is inevitable. Like prophecy, apocalypticism sees the information necessary for right action as accessible through direct revelation. Later prophets, such as Ezekiel and Zechariah, were moving toward apocalyptic means of revelation by the interpretation of mysterious visions. Trips taken by some seers to heaven to discover God's plans are not unlike Micaiah ben Imlah's journey to the heavenly council in 1 Kings 22, or Isaiah's vision of God's throne in Isaiah 6. But interest in cosmology, shared by wisdom and apocalypticism, is not found in prophecy.

Much research has focused on foreign influences on apocalypticism. It has been shown that Persian writings of the Hellenistic period share elements with Jewish apocalypses. Studies have demonstrated that periodization of history, sufferings caused by eschatological battles, resurrection, and good and evil supernatural forces are present in both bodies of writing. Both Jewish and Persian apocalyptic writings offer an explanation for and a solution to the foreign domination typical of the Hellenistic period. Furthermore, the activity of apocalyptic seers has been compared to the activities of Babylonian wise men. Such studies recall that the Hellenistic world was one in which cultures interacted extensively with one another. Apocalypticism combined old elements in new ways, and introduced new ideas into the mixture. It was neither simply a product of what went before in the life of Israel, nor was it unconnected with Israel's past.

THE NATURE OF APOCALYPTIC DISCOURSE

Apocalypses are full of strange images—beasts that combine frightening traits of many animals including some with human features, forbidding abysses, marvelous heavenly structures, cosmic struggles, and so on. Apocalyptic language is not simple and straightforward. The strangeness of apocalyptic discourse makes it hard to determine exactly what some apocalypses mean. Apocalypses use complicated codes in which referents are masked rather than specified. That has suggested to some that apocalypses are meant to convey information to those who understand the codes, while hiding the message from others. The message would be clear to those holding the key to its imagery, but gibberish to others. According to this view, the code must be broken so as to translate apocalyptic images into intelligible language. Unquestionably, there are codes in apocalypses. The fact that the apocalypses themselves often supply interpretations for their visions proves that. Understanding each work includes discovering the situation it addresses and decoding the sections of the apocalypse that reflect and speak to that situation, a task performed by finding one-to-one correspondence between elements of the texts and entities in the "real world." But that does not imply that the works were meant to hide information from hostile inquirers.

Apocalypticism uses ancient traditions and mythologies in a symbolically expressive way. The objective is not simply to transmit information. Apocalyptic language is akin to poetry. Just as a poem cannot be reduced to simple propositions without losing its essence, so an apocalypse cannot be reduced to the description of a historical situation. The case is analogous to that of mythology. Ancient myth is not simply fantasy, but is the narrative expression of deeply held convictions and feelings about the universe and human experience. Myth is narrative metaphor used to express realities that can only be spoken of metaphorically. Apocalypses usually do not quote myths or biblical traditions directly, but allude to them. A range of associations, analogies, and resonances is set up that appeals to the most profound depths of thought and feeling in those whose cultures contain those myths and traditions. By putting this into narrative form, apocalypses implicate readers as only narrative can. Readers experience the fear, dread, hope, exultation that the story evokes. Even in the midst of a world dominated by sin, they feel the reality of the victory of good over evil. Apocalypses do not just supply new data; they reveal patterns in events, patterns with deep cultural roots, so as to provide a new way of experiencing the world.

167

There are far too many apocalypses to discuss them all. Two are treated here—*1 Enoch* and the book of Daniel. Only those parts of *1 Enoch* that date from the third and second centuries BCE are examined.

THE ENOCH LITERATURE: A COMPILATION

Since the Ethiopic church preserved *1 Enoch* (also called *Ethiopic Enoch*), the manuscript of the full text is in Ethiopic. There exist fragments of the Greek, from which the Ethiopic was translated, and extensive Aramaic fragments. Enoch is really five different works combined.

Book of the Watchers	Chapters 1–36	third century BCE
Similitudes of Enoch	Chapters 37–71	first century CE
Astronomical Book	Chapters 72–82	third century BCE
Book of Dreams	Chapters 83–90	second century BCE
Epistle of Enoch	Chapters 91–108	second century BCE

The *Book of Enoch* is pseudonymous, claiming to have been written by one who lived in the seventh human generation, according to Genesis 5. There is an obscure statement about Enoch in Genesis 5:24: "Enoch walked with God; then he was no more, because God took him." Enoch traditions took this verse to refer to Enoch's intimacy with the unseen heavenly world, and to his ascension to heaven. Enoch is the only human in Genesis 5 who is not explicitly said to have died, which is further support for such speculation.

THE *BOOK OF THE WATCHERS:* CHAPTERS 1–36

The *Astronomical Book* and the *Book of the Watchers* are the two oldest extant apocalypses. They come from the third century BCE. The *Book of the Watchers* is in three parts: an introduction (1–5), the watchers and Enoch's heavenly ascent (6–16), and Enoch's cosmic journeys (17–36). The book shows signs of having been put together from originally independent sources. A "watcher" is an angel who watches in heaven (*see* Dan 4:13, 17, 23), a sort of heavenly guard.

As *1 Enoch* now stands, chapters 1–5 introduce both the *Book of the Watchers* in particular and the whole of the *Book of Enoch* in general. The section begins, "The words of the blessing of Enoch, with which he blessed the elect and righteous, who will be living in the day of tribulation, when all the wicked and godless are to be removed" (1:1; *see* Deut 33:1). *1 Enoch* 1:1 sets an eschatological tone. The division of humanity (and angels) into opposed camps is typical of apocalyptic dualism. One is either on the right side or the wrong side, good or bad. "Tribulation" is a common way of thinking about the day of judgment, because it will be a day of turbulence and suffering.

> And he took up his parable and said—Enoch, a righteous man, whose eyes were opened by God, saw the vision of the Holy One in the heavens, which the angels showed me, and from them I heard everything, and from them I understood as I saw, but not for this generation, but for a remote one which is for to come. (1:2)

"Parable" is a general term for figurative language. Enoch receives explanations of his visions through angels, and comes to understand "everything." The ancient seer learns that the revelation is for a much later time. The rest of chapter 1 describes a theophany, an appearance of God.

> The Holy Great One will come forth from His dwelling, and the eternal God will tread upon the earth, on Mount Sinai, and appear from his camp, and appear in the strength of his might from the heaven of heavens. (1:3-4)

God appears as a mighty warrior, recalling holy war imagery (*see* Deut 33:2). Holiness and greatness are attributes of God prominent throughout *1 Enoch*. They show how utterly different God is from humans. Apocalypses often show that earthly powers and the evil forces behind them are inferior to God. God appears on Sinai, but heaven is where God truly is. God's "camp" is military imagery.

Mountains and hills tremble and melt. Destruction falls upon the "ungodly," "but with the righteous he will make peace, and will protect the elect, and mercy shall be upon them" (1:8). The good are "righteous" (obedient to the divine will), and "elect" (God has chosen them). Both terms permeate *1 Enoch*. As in Deuteronomy 33, a heavenly army accompanies God: "And behold! he comes with ten thousand of his holy ones [angels] to execute judgment upon all, and to destroy the ungodly" (1:9).

Chapters 2–5 describe the order of heaven and earth, attributing that order to the obedience of the universe to God's will:

> Observe ye everything that takes place in the heaven, how they do not change their orbits, and observe the luminaries which are in the heaven, how they all rise and set in order each in its season, and do not transgress against their appointed order. Behold ye the earth, and give heed to the things that take place on it from first to last, how steadfast they are, how none of the things upon earth change, but all of the works of God appear to you. (2:1-2)

Nature's order underscores God's greatness and might, which is such that the whole universe follows God's will. The passage then contrasts the obedience of the cosmos with the disobedience of sinners (5:3-4).

Judgment is coming. The passage addresses the sinners, "For all of you sinners there shall be no salvation, but on you all shall abide a curse. But for the

elect there shall be light and joy and peace, and they shall inherit the earth''
(5:6-7).[3] The promise implies an earthly restoration.

Chapters 6–11 tell of the watchers' transgressions. The story probably grew
out of a mysterious passage in Genesis:

> When people began to multiply on the face of the ground, and daughters were born
> to them, the sons of God saw that they were fair; and they took wives for
> themselves of all that they chose. . . . The Nephilim were on the earth in those
> days—and also afterward—when the sons of God went in to the daughters of
> humans, who bore children to them. These were the heroes that were of old,
> warriors of renown. (Gen 6:1-2, 4)

"Sons of God" means heavenly beings. They were originally gods and
goddesses in the heavenly courts of ancient Near Eastern religions. In Israel,
which was monotheistic, such beings were considered angels. The story in
Genesis 6:1-4 is a fragment of a myth about heavenly beings who had intercourse
with human women who bore children who were greater than humans and less
than gods. Two distinct strands of tradition merge in *1 Enoch* 6–11. The first is
introduced with the following words.

> And it came to pass when the children of men had multiplied that in those days were
> born to them beautiful and comely daughters. And the angels, the children of the
> heaven, saw and lusted after them, and said to one another: "Come, let us choose
> wives from among the children of men and beget us children." (6:1-2)

The leader of this group of angels is called "Semjâzâ." The angels carry out their
plan, and, as in Genesis, their offspring are giants. The giants wreak havoc on the
earth and attack humans and animals. This tradition may be an allegorized
account of the successors of Alexander the Great, who claimed divinity and who
ravaged the earth through their wars.[4] Another interpretation notes the priestly
language used to describe the relationship of the angels to the women: "They
began to go in unto them and to defile themselves with them" (7:1). Such
language also shows up in 10:11: "Go, bind Semjâzâ and his associates who
have united themselves with women so as to have defiled themselves with them
in their uncleanness." In this interpretation, the angels symbolize the
priesthood, which does not observe proper purity rules.[5]

The second strand of tradition sees a different angel, "Azâzêl" as the chief
sinner, who conveys knowledge to humans that they should not have.

> And Azâzêl taught men to make swords, and knives, and shields, and breastplates,
> and made known to them the metals of the earth and the art of working them, and
> bracelets, and ornaments, and the use of antinomy, and the beautifying of the

eyelids, and all kinds of costly stones, and all coloring tinctures. And there arose much godlessness, and they committed fornication, and they were led astray, and became corrupt in all their ways. (8:1-2)

As in the Semjâzâ tradition, human violence is blamed on angels. Knowledge of metal-working is evil because it results in warfare. Likewise, knowledge of cosmetics is evil because it results in fornication.

The Semjâzâ and Azâzêl traditions are not easily separable. The fact that they were brought together and so comment on each other demonstrates how apocalypses were written. Material from disparate sources could be combined to employ the strength of multiple traditions. The traditions claim that violence and fornication are caused by angels. This solution to the problem of evil is typically apocalyptic in that it explains phenomena in this world by reference to an unseen world of angels and spirits. In the story of Adam and Eve, the presence of evil in the world is the fault of humans. In the story of the watchers it is due to the angels.

The earth cries to the good angels in heaven for help, and the angels petition God to respond. God imprisons the angelic offenders until the last judgment. The giants kill one another off. There follows an idyllic description of the earth restored to its pristine harmony with the will of God and resultant fertility and peace (10:16–11:2).

Chapters 12–16 form a unit in which Enoch first appears. He is called "scribe of righteousness," "scribe" because writing plays an important role in what he does, "of righteousness" because he obeys God. Enoch is told to declare to the sinful watchers their punishment. When Enoch carries out his commission, the watchers beg him to compose a petition for forgiveness and to present it to God. Enoch writes the petition, and then falls asleep while reading it. As he sleeps he has visions of being carried up to heaven. He sees God's heavenly palace, described in wondrous terms, complete with "fiery cherubim" as guards. The palace is unlike anything on earth, as is clear in the statement that it was as hot as fire and as cold as ice.

Enoch now perceives a second house much greater than the first, so that he cannot describe it. He sees God on a throne.

And I looked and saw a lofty throne: its appearance was as crystal, and its wheels were as the shining sun, and there was the vision of cherubim. And from underneath the throne came streams of flaming fire so that I could not look at it. And the Great Glory sat on it, and his raiment shone more brightly than the sun and was whiter than any snow. None of the angels could enter and behold his face by reason of the magnificence and glory, and no flesh could behold him. The flaming fire was round about him, and a great fire stood before him, and none around could draw close to him. Ten thousand times ten thousand stood before him, yet he needed no counsellor. And the most holy ones who were near him did not leave by night nor depart from him. (14:18-23)

The throne is pictured as a throne-chariot of the type used by the Canaanite god Baal, which explains the presence of wheels. Ezekiel 1 has a similar picture of God on a throne-chariot. Like the theophany at Sinai, Enoch's vision stresses God's might and glory. As the Israelites were warned not to touch Mount Sinai while God was present, here angels and humans cannot come too close to God, nor can they look directly at the vision. Enoch's visit to heaven gives him authority, because it shows that Enoch has received his information from the heavenly realm. In *1 Enoch,* the trip to heaven legitimates the entire book. God now tells Enoch that evil spirits will rise out of the fallen bodies of the giants who have killed one another. They will go throughout the earth, causing evil and suffering. By this means the *Book of the Watchers* explains the presence and activity of evil spirits in the world.

Chapters 17–36 narrate Enoch's trips through the universe. He visits inaccessible places accompanied by angels who explain to him everything he sees. There is an abiding eschatological theme in these chapters. Enoch observes the fiery abysses reserved for the watchers' punishment, and chapter 22 describes the chambers in which dead humans are kept until the final judgment. In chapters 24–25, Enoch sees a mountain at the ends of the earth where God will descend at the end of time. There is a fragrant tree there.

> And as for this fragrant tree no mortal is permitted to touch it till the great judgment, when He shall take vengeance on all and bring everything to its consummation for ever. It shall then be given to the righteous and holy. Its fruit shall be for food to the elect: it shall be transplanted to the holy place, to the temple of the Lord the Eternal King. Then they shall rejoice with joy and be glad, and into the holy place they shall enter; and its fragrance shall be in their bones, and they shall live in a long life on earth, such as your fathers lived. And in their day no sorrow or plague or torment or calamity shall touch them. (25:4-6)

The tree is the tree of life. In the Garden of Eden, Adam and Eve ate of the forbidden tree of knowledge. God threw them out of the garden, fearing that they would also eat of the tree of life and become immortal. *1 Enoch* 25:4-6 says that the tree of life will be available to the elect at the end-time. Its fragrance will penetrate their bones and give them "a long life on earth," free of sorrow. The tree of life does not bring immortality, but rather it restores the long life people were meant to have. The process observable in Genesis in which human life gets shorter as sin spreads will be reversed. Chapters 28–36 fill out Enoch's cosmic journeys and demonstrate his complete knowledge of the universe.

The historical problems faced by *1 Enoch* are not solved by analyzing the problems directly.

Instead, the problem—whatever it was—is transposed to a mythological plane. By telling the story of the Watchers rather than of the Diadochoi or the priesthood, *1 Enoch* 1–36 becomes a paradigm which is not restricted to one historical situation but can be applied whenever an analogous situation arises.[6]

This is what Collins calls "apocalyptic multivalence." The story of the watchers creates a model that can be applied to a variety of circumstances. The story attributes earthly evil to superhuman agents. It gives hope by positing the sovereignty of God over those agents and gives assurance of God's eventual judgment on them. Thus an interpretive framework is created which is spatial in that there is a superhuman world that determines what happens in this one, and temporal in that a final judgment is coming.

THE *ASTRONOMICAL BOOK:* CHAPTERS 72–82

The *Astronomical Book* tells of Enoch's journey through the heavens and to the ends of the earth. He is guided by the angel Uriel, who explains what Enoch sees. The book assumes an ascent by Enoch to the heavens, although that is not narrated within chapters 72–82, perhaps because the ascent was deleted when the *Astronomical Book* was incorporated into *1 Enoch*. Apocalypses with heavenly journeys usually show cosmological interest, as holds true for the *Astronomical Book*. Enoch observes the movements of the sun, moon, and stars, and the places of the winds. The description of the universe in the *Astronomical Book* stresses cosmic order. Angels oversee the movements of the heavenly bodies and the winds.

The *Astronomical Book*'s cosmological interest goes beyond simple curiosity about the universe. It is concerned to prove that Israel should be following a 364-day calendar. Priestly religion organized time by dividing the year into set periods, marked by sabbaths and feasts. Jewish communities could agree on how to live the liturgical year properly only by agreeing on those temporal boundaries. Groups using different calendars might share the same set of assumptions about how the world works, but be deeply opposed to one another because of the specifics of God's will. They could not even celebrate the principal feasts together and so would be socially, religiously, and politically incompatible.

Another concern of the *Astronomical Book* is eschatology, most evident in chapter 80 where cosmic order breaks down. The sun and moon do not behave as they ought, rain is withheld, crops fail, and the stars stray from their paths. As is common in apocalypticism, cosmic disorder is connected to human transgression. Humans err in how they understand the cosmos and end up worshiping the stars (stars were thought to be supernatural beings). It is not clear whether human sin causes cosmic disorder, or humans sin because they are misled by the stars (the sequence of 80:6-7 seems to blame the situation on the stars). But cosmic disorder and human sin are linked. Judgment comes in 80:8: "And evil shall be multiplied upon them, and punishment shall come upon them so as to destroy all."

Chapter 81 seems to be an addition to the *Astronomical Book* because it does not mention heavenly bodies or calendrical disputes. Enoch discovers that the "deeds of mankind" are written in a heavenly book, and that the righteous will be rewarded and the evil punished. The idea that human actions are recorded in heavenly books is common in the ancient Near East. At the judgment, the books will be evidence against the wicked and for the righteous.

THE *APOCALYPSE OF WEEKS:* 93:1-10 AND 91:11-17

The *Apocalypse of Weeks* is a complete unit that may have originally existed independent of *1 Enoch.* In its present form the sequence of weeks has been disturbed. The first seven weeks occur in *1 Enoch* 93:1-10 and the last three in 91:11-17, and so the entire *Apocalypse of Weeks* is found within the *Epistle of Enoch.* The *Epistle* was written before 160 BCE, since it is mentioned in another work dated to about that time, the *Book of Jubilees,* so the *Apocalypse of Weeks* must predate 160 BCE as well.

At the beginning of the *Apocalypse of Weeks,* Enoch reveals the source of his information: "According to that which appeared to me in the heavenly vision, and which I have known through the word of the holy angels, and have learned from the heavenly tablets" (93:2). The *Apocalypse of Weeks* divides history into ten periods called weeks. Within the fictional framework of the *Apocalypse* Enoch lives in the first of the periods and foretells the other nine. The real author of the Apocalypse lived in the seventh week. The fact that Enoch could foresee all history because he has seen the heavenly tablets implies that history is determined in heaven and is well ordered, composed of alternating good and bad periods. Such periodization of history lets readers locate themselves historically and so make sense of their own experience.

The seventh is the period of the Second Temple, although the author does not deem the rebuilding of the Temple worth mention. The period is evil: "And after that in the seventh week shall an apostate generation arise, and many shall be its deeds, and all its deeds shall be apostate" (93:9). An apostate is one who renounces one's religion or is disloyal to God. "And at its close shall be elected the elect righteous of the eternal plant of righteousness, to receive sevenfold instruction concerning all his creation" (93:10). A group arises called "elect" and "righteous," characterized by its special knowledge. The special knowledge sets the elect apart from the rest of Israel and from the rest of the world.

The *Apocalypse of Weeks* locates the elect in the sweep of history. Its schematization shows that history is driven by a pattern in which evil flourishes and God separates from the world an elect individual or group. Noah was separated from the first evil period, Abraham from the next, Elijah from the next. Now the ''elect'' of the author's own time are separated from the ''apostate generation.'' To know that they are the elect of God is to anticipate vindication. The rest of the *Apocalypse* confirms the anticipation.

''And after that there shall be another, the eighth week, that of righteousness, and a sword shall be given to it that a righteous judgment may be executed on the oppressors, and sinners shall be delivered into the hands of the righteous'' (91:12). The text expects the righteous to avenge themselves on their oppressors. The next verse describes the result of their victory: ''And at its close they shall acquire houses through their righteousness, and a house shall be built for the Great King in glory for evermore'' (91:13). The righteous prosper because of their righteousness, the Temple is rebuilt, and the entire human race looks to ''the path of righteousness,'' meaning the will of God as it is seen by the elect group. The ninth and tenth weeks see the punishment of wicked humans and angels, and an idyllic future untainted by sin.

THE *BOOK OF DREAMS:* CHAPTERS 83–90

The *Book of Dreams* consists of two visions that Enoch tells to his son, Methuselah. In the first vision Enoch sees cosmic destruction, and is informed that his vision concerns ''the secrets of all the sin of the earth: it must sink into the abyss and be destroyed with a great destruction'' (83:7). In chapter 84, Enoch prays that a remnant be spared.

The rest of the book consists of an extended allegory called the *Animal Apocalypse* in which the history of the world is told in terms of animals. As is frequent in apocalypses, names of historic figures are not supplied, but must be inferred from the narrative. Chapter 86 tells the story of the descent of the angels (represented by stars) to have intercourse with human women (*see* Genesis 6 and the *Book of the Watchers*). In chapters 87–88, angels descend to bind the fallen watchers and cast them into the abyss. Throughout the narrative, angels are distinguished from humans in that the humans are depicted as animals whereas the angels look like humans. In the ensuing history, Noah and Moses are transformed into human figures (angels).

Israel is represented by sheep. When wild animals (the Philistines) ravage them, a ram (David) arises who saves them. When the sheep sin, their ''house'' (Jerusalem) is destroyed. God appoints seventy shepherds whom scholars have identified as the angelic patrons of the nations, to rule over them. The rule of the shepherds is divided into four periods, reminiscent of the four kingdoms of Daniel 2 and 7 (*see* below). The sheep become blind and their shepherds abuse their rule. But then lambs are born to some of the sheep, and the lambs can see

(90:6). The sighted lambs are Jews who opposed the Hellenistic reform in Jerusalem. Then follows a reference to the Maccabean revolt, in which Judas Maccabeus is portrayed as a hero. A sword is given to the sheep (90:19), which indicates that this apocalypse favors the military means used by the Maccabees. When the enemies of the sheep are defeated, an idyllic future is described in which Jerusalem is rebuilt, "greater and loftier than at first" (90:29). The wild animals who had oppressed the sheep now are included in Israel's house, but they are subject to Israel (90:30).

The *Animal Apocalypse* provides a typically apocalyptic solution to the problems of the Hellenistic reform. The reform is located in the sweep of world history, so that readers can see that all history has led up to their own period and can observe the supernatural forces at work in that history. They can take comfort in the fact that their oppressor will soon be overthrown by the Maccabees and the sighted lambs who support the Maccabean revolution. The result will be a transformed Jerusalem in which true worshipers of God have their rightful place.

THE *EPISTLE OF ENOCH:* CHAPTERS 91–108

The most likely date for the *Epistle of Enoch* is the period of Hellenization preceding the Maccabean revolt. The *Epistle* specifies that the main sins to be punished are idolatry and social abuses. The two kinds of sins are connected: "Woe to you, you rich, for you have trusted in your riches, and from your riches you shall depart, because you have not remembered the Most High in the days of your riches" (94:8). The wealth of the rich deludes them into thinking that they are self-sufficient, and they forget God. In later verses riches are associated with oppression of those obedient to God: "Woe to you, you mighty, who with might oppress the righteous; for the day of your destruction is coming" (96:8).

The social concerns of the *Epistle of Enoch* emerge in the following verses. "Woe to those who build their houses with sin; for from all their foundations they shall be overthrown, and by the sword they will fall. And those who acquire gold and silver in judgment suddenly shall perish" (94:7). The verse attacks those who live in grand houses bought with ill-gotten gain, and those who take bribes in legal proceedings.

> Woe to you, you sinners, for your riches make you look like the righteous, but your hearts convict you of being sinners, and this fact shall be a testimony against you for a memorial of your evil deeds. Woe to you who devour the finest of the wheat, and drink wine in large bowls, and tread underfoot the lowly with your might. Woe to you who drink water from every fountain, for suddenly you shall be consumed and wither away, because you have forsaken the fountain of life. (96:4-6)

The sinners appear righteous. They are well-to-do, prominent in the community, and respected for their wealth and power. Their exalted status is taken to be proof of their righteousness, since God has blessed them so bountifully. Nonetheless, their actions are unjust. They live well and exploit those less fortunate. "Drink water from every fountain" may mean that they profit from the labor of those beneath them in society. They do not drink from the fountain that really counts, the fountain that comes from God and can truly give life. The text sees social stratification as the basis for sins of the rich against the poor.

The *Epistle* insists on human responsibility for sin: "Sin has not been sent upon the earth, but humans have of themselves created it, and under a great curse shall they fall who commit it" (98:4). Those who suffer oppression are promised that they will be rewarded and their oppressors punished.

> And the righteous shall arise from sleep and walk in the paths of righteousness, and all their path and conversation shall be in eternal goodness and grace. (92:3)

> I swear to you, that in heaven the angels remember you for good before the glory of the Great One; and your names are written before the glory of the Great One. Be hopeful; for aforetime you were put to shame through ill and affliction; but now you shall shine as the lights of heaven, you shall shine and you shall be seen, and the portals of heaven shall be opened to you. And in your cry, cry for judgment, and it shall appear to you; for all your tribulation shall be visited upon the rulers, and on all who helped those who plundered you. (104:1-3)

Enoch can console the suffering righteous because he knows what is happening in heaven and what is written in the heavenly books. The reward of the righteous includes resurrection (92:3).

THE BOOK OF DANIEL

Daniel was put together during the Maccabean revolt. The stories in Daniel 1–6 predate the revolt. They tell of a Daniel who was influential in the royal courts of the kings of Babylonia, then Media, then Persia. Daniel is a "wise man" in the technical sense of one who can interpret dreams, an important medium of communication between the divine and human worlds.

Daniel's position in the royal courts implies a social situation for which there is other evidence. The Jews deported east by the Babylonians settled into their new surroundings and were successful economically, politically, and socially. Those who returned to Judah did so under the patronage of the Persian empire, and when the Greeks took over, many Jews cooperated with the new rulers. There was no innate antipathy between the Jews and their rulers. The situation changed dramatically during the persecution of Judaism by Antiochus IV in the second century BCE. The experience caused some Jews to see Gentile rule as evil, even demonic. The new situation finds expression in Daniel 7–12. The difference between chapters 1–6 and 7–12 is also marked by a change of form. Daniel 1–6 is

177

in the form of stories about Daniel's interpretation of others' dreams, whereas Daniel 7–12 is a first-person narration by Daniel concerning his own dreams and visions. Chapters 7–12 are an apocalypse. Chapters 1–6 are an extended prologue to the apocalypse.

Chapters 1–6

In chapter 1 Daniel and three other Jewish youths are recruited for royal service. They are to be trained in the wisdom of the Chaldeans (another name for Babylonians). The Chaldeans were known especially for divination, the art of predicting the future or discovering hidden knowledge through decoding natural events such as the movements of stars, or through the interpretation of dreams. This art was passed down through successive generations of "wise" ones. Daniel and his fellow Jewish students are expected to share the life of the court, including eating foods prohibited by Jewish law. Their overseer is reluctant to allow them a different diet, lest they suffer from an ascetic regimen. The Jewish youths convince him to let them live according to their own customs. The result is described in 1:17-20:

> To these four young men God gave knowledge and skill in every aspect of literature and wisdom; Daniel also had insight into all visions and dreams. At the end of the time that the king had set for them to be brought in, the palace master brought them into the presence of Nebuchadnezzar, and the king spoke with them. And among them all, no one was found to compare with Daniel, Hananiah, Mishael, and Azariah; therefore they were stationed in the king's court. In every matter of wisdom and understanding concerning which the king inquired of them, he found them ten times better than all the magicians and enchanters in his whole kingdom.

Adherence to God's laws brings success. Forgoing the forbidden luxuries of the court results in prominence and recognition for the Jewish students. Such a story would be meaningful to those forced by Antiochus IV to either abandon the Torah or die. Daniel and the others do well not because of their intelligence or hard work, but because God gives them wisdom. Such a view of Daniel's wisdom accords well with his portrayal in chapters 7–12 as receiver of esoteric wisdom. Interpretation of visions and dreams is at stake, an activity characteristic of the Chaldeans. The Jews end up being much better at that activity than the Chaldeans themselves.

Daniel 2 narrates another episode in the life of Daniel in which the appropriateness of Daniel as the receiver of apocalyptic visions and explanations is clarified. The Babylonian king Nebuchadnezzar has a troubling dream. When the king summons his wise men to explain the dream, he refuses to divulge its contents to them. He is testing them, to see if they have the ability to know the dream without his disclosing it. The wise are unable to tell the king his dream, so he orders their execution. Daniel requests an appointment with the king, and then prays to God. The prayer brings results: "Then the mystery was revealed to Daniel in a vision of the night" (2:19). Daniel emphasizes the divine origin of his wisdom in 2:27-28: "No wise men, enchanters, magicians, or diviners can show to the king the mystery that the king is asking, but there is a God in heaven who reveals mysteries, and he has disclosed to King Nebuchadnezzar what will happen at the end of days."

In 2:31-35, Daniel tells the king his dream, and in 2:36-45 he gives its interpretation. The dream concerns a succession of four kingdoms, declining in quality with time. The first kingdom is that of Nebuchadnezzar and is represented by gold. The second kingdom (probably that of the Medes) is silver, the third (of the Persians) is bronze, and the last (of the Greeks) is a mixture of iron and clay. The four kingdoms are smashed by a rock that is interpreted in verse 44: "And in the days of those kings the God of heaven will set up a kingdom that shall never be destroyed, nor shall this kingdom be left to another people. It shall crush all these kingdoms and bring them to an end, and it shall stand forever." The four-kingdom schema was adopted from Hellenistic political prophecy. Its point is that history is determined, and that the present kingdom is the last. After the last kingdom, a proper kingdom will be established, a kingdom of which God approves. The prophecy gives hope that foreign domination will not last forever, and that native rulers will soon assume their rightful place. In Daniel, the prophecy is that the Seleucid empire ruled by Antiochus IV will be ended by an act of God, and an everlasting kingdom will replace it.

Chapters 7–12

At the beginning of chapter 7, Daniel has a dream, awakens, and writes it down. He then narrates his vision. "He saw the four winds of heaven stirring up the great sea, and four great beasts came up out of the sea, different from one another" (7:2-3). The beasts are strange and terrifying. They are more frightening than earthly beasts, and represent supernatural forces. The interpretation of the vision explains that the beasts stand for oppressive kings and their kingdoms (7:17, 23). This is another instance of the four-kingdom schema encountered in Daniel 2. A climax is reached with the fourth beast, representing the Seleucid kingdom: "A fourth beast, terrifying and dreadful and exceedingly strong. It had great iron teeth and was devouring, breaking in pieces, and stamping what was left with its feet. It was different from all the beasts that preceded it" (7:7). A king arises in the fourth kingdom who challenges God. As is typical in apocalyptic literature, history is seen as leading up to the time in which the author writes, and that time is the culmination of history. Things are bad because history has reached its culmination.

In the ancient Near East the sea often symbolized the forces of chaos. Myths were told in which a god had to fight the sea, enemy of good order, and defeat it so that creation could exist. In Daniel 7, present events are assimilated to ancient mythic patterns symbolizing the battle between good and evil in the world and in the cosmos. Events in Judea are seen as a result of a much larger conflict that encompasses history and the cosmos. The use of the pattern evokes the conviction that the forces of good will conquer the forces of evil.

The scene now shifts to heaven.

> Thrones were placed and one that was ancient of days took his seat;
> his raiment was white as snow, and the hair of his head like pure wool;
> his throne was fiery flames, its wheels were burning fire.
> A stream of fire issued and came forth from before him;
> a thousand thousands served him, and ten thousand times ten thousand stood before him;
> the court sat in judgment, and the books were opened. (7:9-10 RSV)[7]

Judgment by the heavenly court effects the downfall of the blasphemous king on earth: "The beast was put to death, and its body destroyed and given over to be burned with fire" (7:11). God judges the king, and that issues in the destruction of his kingdom. Decisions made in heaven determine what happens on earth.

After the fourth beast is punished, there is a scene that influenced later Jewish and Christian apocalyptic literature.

> I saw in the night visions,
> and behold, with the clouds of heaven there came one like a son of man,
> and he came to the Ancient of Days and was presented before him.
> And to him was given dominion and glory and kingdom,
> that all peoples, nations, and languages should serve him;
> his dominion is an everlasting dominion, which shall not pass away,
> and his kingdom one that shall not be destroyed. (7:13-14 RSV)

The identification of the one like a son of man has caused disagreement among scholars. Christians can too easily assume that "son of man" is a title and take it as *the* Son of Man, as if it were clear just what or who that Son of Man is. But there is no text predating Daniel that gives clear content to the term, aside from the general meaning "human." In Daniel 7, the appearance of the one who comes on the clouds is *like* that of a human being: "There came one *like* a son of man" (7:13 RSV). Except for the use of the singular, the use here is exactly parallel to that in 10:16 (RSV), where the angel Gabriel is "in the *likeness* of the sons of men." Therefore in Daniel, the phrase "son of man" means "human." In Daniel 7, the one like a son of man is a being *resembling* a human.

180

The solution to the question of the identity of the one like a son of man in Daniel 7 must also take into account its mythological parallels. Ancient Canaanite mythology supplies comparable material. El, the Canaanite father of the gods, is called *abu shanima,* probably meaning "father of years." This parallels the phrase applied to the Jewish God in Daniel (rsv), "Ancient of Days." Baal, head god of the Canaanite pantheon when the Israelites settled in Palestine, was son of El, and is traditionally depicted as riding on the clouds. Baal defeats the god Yamm, whose name means "sea," when Yamm challenges Baal's power. Baal thus secures his kingdom. In Daniel 7, the figure of one like a son of man riding the clouds into the presence of the Ancient of Days to receive the kingdom after the slaying of the beasts parallels the Canaanite story.

There are three notable suggestions concerning how the son of man is used in Daniel 7. One is that he is a messianic figure. But the only mentions of messiahs in Daniel are in 9:25-26, where they refer to the high priest of the restoration, Joshua, and to the assassinated high priest Onias III. The one like a son of man is not called "messiah." This first suggestion, therefore, has little to recommend it. The second is that the son of man is a corporate figure symbolizing Israel as a whole. Such a suggestion is possible, but there is a still more plausible suggestion. The third suggestion is that the son of man is an angel. Throughout Daniel, angels are said to have the appearance of human beings (8:15, 16; 9:21; 10:5, 16, 18; 12:6, 7). One angel is spoken of as "one in the likeness of the sons of men" in 10:16. Furthermore, the son of man receives power once exercised by the beasts. The beasts represent kings and kingdoms, but they also symbolize the forces of chaos as ancient as the sea. They are not only earthly kingdoms but cosmic forces behind those kingdoms. This "more" must also apply to the son of man. If he also is a cosmic force, then he stands for more than the Jewish community under persecution. The most plausible solution is that he is an angelic power. If that is so, then he is probably Michael, Israel's angel (10:21).

The idea that nations are represented by supernatural beings whose fate in heaven determines the fate of the nation on earth comes from Israel's ancient Near Eastern setting. It surfaces in Deuteronomy 32:8-9 (rsv): "When the Most High gave to the nations their inheritance, when he separated the sons of men, he fixed the bounds of the peoples according to the number of the sons of God. For the Lord's portion is his people, Jacob his allotted heritage." In earlier, non-Israelite myth these "sons of gods" were divinities. In Deuteronomy they are heavenly beings less than gods, probably angels (*see* Gen 6:2). Each son of god is assigned a people, so that each nation has an angelic representative. Each nation's history is a reflection of the fate of its angel in the supernatural realm.

Daniel asks an angel to interpret the vision of Daniel 7. The angel says: "As for these four great beasts, four kings shall arise out of the earth. But the holy ones of the Most High shall receive the kingdom, and possess the kingdom forever—forever and ever" (7:17-18). The word translated "holy ones" here is the Aramaic *qaddîšîn*. The holy ones "shall receive the kingdom." In Daniel 7:14, the one like a son of man receives the kingdom, so the interpretation associates the one like a son of man with the holy ones. "Holy ones" usually means "angels" in the Hebrew Bible. The same usage occurs in *1 Enoch* 14:22-23, where it refers to angels in a context similar to that of Daniel 7. "Holy ones" means "angels" in Daniel 4:10, 14, 20, and 8:13. The identification of holy ones with angels sheds light on 7:27: "The kingship and dominion and the greatness of the kingdoms under the whole heaven shall be given to the *people of the holy ones* of the Most High." The "people of the holy ones" are the people of the angels, the Jews.

The vision continues: "As I looked, this horn made war with the holy ones and was prevailing over them, until the Ancient One [Ancient of Days] came; then judgment was given for the holy ones of the Most High, and the time arrived when the holy ones gained possession of the kingdom" (7:21-22). If the interpretation of the holy ones as angels is correct then the claim is made here that the fourth king, Antiochus IV, makes war against the angels. His persecution of Judaism is an attack on heaven itself: "He shall speak words against the Most High, shall wear out the holy ones of the Most High, and shall attempt to change the sacred seasons and the law; and they shall be given into his power for a time, two times, and half a time" (7:25). Changing the sacred seasons refers to outlawing the appointed feasts and the sabbaths of the Jews. Changing the Law is outlawing Torah. Antiochus' persecution will last "a time, two times, and half a time," probably meaning three and a half years.

Chapter 8 is a vision and interpretation concerning the history of the world from the Persian empire to the death of Antiochus IV. Daniel 9:2 says, "In the first year of his reign, I, Daniel, perceived in the books the number of years that, according to the word of the LORD to the prophet Jeremiah, must be fulfilled for the devastation of Jerusalem, namely, seventy years." Later in the chapter an angel tells Daniel that Jeremiah's prediction (Jer 25:11-12; 29:10) really refers to "seventy weeks" (9:24). Scholars interpret "seventy weeks" to mean seventy weeks of years, that is, seventy times seven, or 490 years: "Seventy weeks are decreed for your people and your holy city: to finish the transgression, to put an end to sin, and to atone for iniquity, to bring in everlasting righteousness, to seal both vision and prophet, and to anoint a most holy place" (9:24). The meaning is that the destruction of the Temple in 587 BCE was a punishment for Israel's transgressions, and atonement would not be complete until 490 years passed. The anointing of a "most holy place" refers to a full restoration of the Temple. If that is not to take place until such a long period after the prophecy of Jeremiah (dated between 597 and 587 BCE), it implies that the Second Temple was not a full restoration. Jeremiah's prediction was yet to be fulfilled. Such reinterpretation of prophecy is common in Second Temple Judaism.

The building of the Second Temple is mentioned in 9:25: "Know therefore and understand: from the time that the word went out to restore and rebuild Jerusalem until the time of an anointed prince, there shall be seven weeks; and for sixty-two weeks it shall be built again with streets and moat, but in a troubled time." The anointed one may be Joshua, the high priest of the restoration. The rebuilding of Jerusalem is acknowledged, but the entire period is "a troubled time."[8] The next 62 weeks of years (434 years) are rapidly dismissed: "After the sixty-two weeks, an anointed one shall be cut off and shall have nothing, and the troops of the prince who is to come shall destroy the city and the sanctuary" (9:26). The "anointed one" is probably the high priest Onias III, assassinated in 171 BCE. The "prince who is to come" is Antiochus IV. There follows a short account of his actions against the sanctuary. Again, Daniel's interest is in the crisis under Antiochus IV.

Daniel 10 shows that conflicts experienced by the Jews on earth result from battles fought in the supernatural realm. An angel appears to Daniel and speaks of the supernatural battles.

> The prince of the kingdom of Persia opposed me twenty-one days. So Michael, one of the chief princes, came to help me, and I left him there with the prince of the kingdom of Persia, and have come to help you understand what is to happen to your people at the end of days. For there is a further vision for those days. . . . Do you know why I have come to you? Now I must return to fight against the prince of Persia, and when I am through with him, the prince of Greece will come. But I am to tell you what is inscribed in the book of truth. There is no one with me who contends against these princes except Michael, your prince. (10:13-14, 20-21)

The princes of kingdoms are the angels in charge of specific nations. The angels' fate determines the fate of the nations they represent. In Daniel's fictitious time the Persians rule, and Gabriel and Michael (Israel's angel) are fighting Persia's angel. They know they will win and then have to fight the angel of Greece. History is determined by God and has only to be played out in heaven and on earth.

Chapter 11 again traces the course of history from the Persian empire to the death of Antiochus. Such reduplication is common in apocalypses and helps to reinforce a message or a pattern. The story of Antiochus occupies more than half the chapter. The king gives "heed to those who forsake the holy covenant" (11:30), meaning the Hellenizers who want to make Jerusalem a Greek city. There is a contrast between Jews who go along with this apostasy and those who remain faithful to Torah in 11:32: "He shall seduce with intrigue those who violate the covenant; but the people who are loyal to their God shall stand firm and take action."

The next verses offer a glimpse of the group behind the book of Daniel.

> The wise among the people shall give understanding to many; for some days, however, they shall fall by sword and flame, and suffer captivity and plunder. When they fall victim, they shall receive a little help, and many shall join them insincerely. Some of the wise shall fall, so that they may be refined, purified, and cleansed, until the time of the end, for there is still an interval until the time appointed. (11:33-35)

The word translated "wise" (Hebrew: *maśkîlîm*) could be rendered "those who make wise," those who teach others. "Wisdom" here means understanding of the secret plans of God available through Daniel's visions and their angelic interpretations. The book of Daniel itself is probably one of the ways by which the wise "make many understand." Those faithful to Torah will be vindicated and those who abandon it will see their "seducer," Antiochus, suffer the penalty of death at God's hands. In the meantime, some of the wise will fall in the persecution, but this is only a purification.

The reference to a "little help" given to the wise (11:34) has traditionally been taken to mean the Maccabees. The phrase "little help" devalues the Maccabean revolt. Nowhere in Daniel are Jews urged to fight the Seleucids. Daniel wants them simply to remain faithful to Torah and await the defeat of Antiochus by supernatural forces. Militant resistance to Seleucid rule and to Antiochus' persecution is of minimal use. Matters are ultimately decided on another level.

The climactic passage in Daniel is 12:1-3.

> At that time Michael, the great prince, the protector of your people, shall arise. There shall be a time of anguish, such as has never occurred since nations first came into existence. But at that time your people shall be delivered, everyone who is found written in the book. Many of those who sleep in the dust of the earth shall awake, some to everlasting life, and some to shame and everlasting contempt. Those who are wise shall shine like the brightness of the sky, and those who lead many to righteousness, like the stars forever and ever.

At the end of time, Israel's angel, Michael, dominates the scene. As in other apocalyptic scenes, the final struggle between good and evil brings great suffering. Michael's appearance means that those people whose names are written in the heavenly book are delivered. Presumably they are those who have remained faithful to Torah in the final trials. Verse 2 is the only clear affirmation of resurrection in the Hebrew Bible. It is significant that it occurs in the only apocalypse in the Hebrew Bible. Belief in resurrection probably entered Jewish belief through apocalypticism. But Daniel 12 does not envisage general resurrection. Those who are raised are only the very good and the very bad, that is, those who resisted persecution, perhaps to the point of martyrdom, and those who inflicted or aided persecution. The wise get a special reward. They shine like stars for all eternity. Since the stars represent the angels, the wise will join the company of angels. The elect receive the same promise in *1 Enoch* 104:2.

In Daniel 12:4, the angel says, "But you, Daniel, keep the words secret and the book sealed until the time of the end" (*see* 12:9). The literary fiction is maintained. The sealing of the books explains how the words of the seer from the sixth century BCE were unknown until the second.

CONCLUSION

Apocalypticism was an important addition to the world view of ancient Judaism. Apocalypticism offered a way of reconciling the perception of a world opposed to God's will and God's people, with the belief in an all-powerful God, Creator of the universe. The solution was to see the present world as under dominion of evil forces, which would soon be defeated in a decisive battle with the forces of good. Apocalyptic seers claimed direct, esoteric revelation from the supernatural world. The revelation was made known to the chosen few who would be saved when God's wrath finally descended on the universe. Apocalyptic eschatology features transcendence of death, an idea that provided an answer to the age-old question about why the good suffer and the wicked prosper in this life. Different apocalypses responded in varied ways to their own specific historical circumstances, but all embodied the basic world view described in this chapter. Apocalypticism was to furnish key symbols, concepts, and literary forms to late Second Temple Judaism and early Christianity.

SELECT BIBLIOGRAPHY

This chapter depends heavily on the work of John J. Collins, especially *The Apocalyptic Imagination*.

Barr, James. "Jewish Apocalyptic in Recent Scholarly Study," *BJRL* 58 (1975): 9-35.

Collins, John J., ed. *Apocalypse: The Morphology of a Genre, Semeia* 14. Missoula, Mont.: Scholars Press, 1979.

———. *AI*.

———. *The Apocalyptic Vision of the Book of Daniel*, HSM 16. Missoula, Mont.: Scholars Press, 1977.

———. "Apocalyptic Eschatology as the Transcendence of Death," *CQB* 36 (1974): 21-43.

———. "The Apocalyptic Technique: Setting and Function in the Book of the Watchers," *CBQ* 44 (1982): 91-111.

———. *The Apocalyptic Vision of the Book of Daniel*, HSM 16. Missoula, Mont.: Scholars Press, 1977.

———. "Cosmos and Salvation: Jewish Wisdom and Apocalyptic in the Hellenistic Age," *HR* 17 (1977): 121-42.

————. "Jewish Apocalyptic Against Its Ancient Near Eastern Environment," *BASOR* 220 (1975): 27-36.

Eddy, Samuel K. *The King Is Dead: Studies in the Near Eastern Resistance to Hellenism.* Lincoln, Neb.: University of Nebraska Press, 1961.

Hamerton-Kelly, R. G. "The Temple and the Origins of Jewish Apocalyptic," *VT* 20 (1970): 1-15.

Hanson, Paul D. *The Dawn of Apocalyptic.* Philadelphia: Fortress Press, 1975.

Hellholm, David, ed. *Apocalypticism in the Mediterranean World and the Near East: Proceedings of the International Colloquium on Apocalypticism, Uppsala, August 12-17, 1979.* Tübingen: Mohr (Siebeck), 1983.

Knibb, Michael A. "The Exile in the Literature of the Intertestamental Period," *HeyJ* 17 (1976): 253-72.

Koch, K. *The Rediscovery of Apocalyptic,* SBT 2/22. Naperville, Ill.: Allenson, 1972.

Lacocque, Andre. *The Book of Daniel.* Atlanta, Ga.: John Knox Press, 1979.

Nickelsburg, George W. E. "Apocalyptic and Myth in 1 Enoch 6-11," *JBL* 96 (1977): 383-405.

————. *Resurrection, Immortality, and Eternal Life in Intertestamental Judaism.* Cambridge, Mass.: Harvard University Press, 1972.

————. "Social Aspects of Palestinian Jewish Apocalypticism," in *AMW*, 639-52.

Plöger, O. *Theocracy and Eschatology.* Richmond, Va.: John Knox Press, 1968.

Rad, Gerhard von, "Daniel and Apocalyptic," *OTT,* vol. 2, 301-15.

Rowland, Christopher. *The Open Heaven: A Study of Apocalyptic in Judaism and Christianity.* New York: Crossroad, 1982.

Russell, D. S. *The Method and Message of Jewish Apocalyptic.* Philadelphia: Westminster Press, 1964.

Smith, Jonathan Z. "Wisdom and Apocalyptic," in *Religious Syncretism in Antiquity,* ed. B. Pearson. Missoula, Mont.: Scholars Press, 1975, 131-56.

Stone, Michael. "New Light on the Third Century," and "Enoch and Apocalyptic Origins," in *SSV,* 27-47.

Suter, David W. "Fallen Angel, Fallen Priest: The Problem of Family Purity in 1 Enoch 6-16," *HUCA* 50 (1979): 115-35.

Vanderkam, James. *Enoch and the Growth of an Apocalyptic Tradition,* CBQMS 16. Washington, D.C.: Catholic Biblical Association, 1984.

Qumran: A Priestly, Apocalyptic Community

Primary Readings: From DSSE: Damascus Document, Community Rule, The Messianic Rule, The War Rule, Commentary on Habakkuk, Commentary on Psalm 37, Commentary on Nahum, The Thanksgiving Hymns

THE DISCOVERY OF THE SCROLLS

In 1947 an amazing discovery of ancient manuscripts was made by a young Bedouin shepherd. In some caves in a cliff near the northwestern shore of the Dead Sea, Muhammad Ahmed el-Hamed found large earthen jars containing mysterious bundles of cloth and leather. The bundles found their way into the hands of experts and were identified as manuscripts dating from the last two centuries BCE and the first century CE. The find became known as the "Dead Sea Scrolls." Further searches turned up many more manuscripts in neighboring caves. Archaeologists came to recognize that the manuscripts were the library of an ancient Jewish group resident at some nearby ruins called Qumran. The resultant interest in the scrolls and the ruins has produced enough studies to fill a library.

There is consensus that the scrolls were the possession of a group of Essenes. The Essenes were a Jewish sect known from the writings of Josephus, Philo of Alexandria (a Jewish philosopher at the turn of the era), and Pliny the Elder (a Roman author writing shortly after 70 CE). Although the scrolls themselves never use the word "Essene," there are so many similarities between the descriptions of the sect in the scrolls and the characteristics of the group behind the scrolls that few still contest the identification.

Vermes characterizes the scrolls as follows: "Altogether, the eleven more or less complete Dead Sea Scrolls and the thousands of fragments belonging originally to almost six hundred manuscripts, amount to a substantial body of literature covering the Hebrew Bible, other religious compositions, and works proper to a particular Jewish sect" (*DSSE*, xiii-xiv). The Qumran library covers all books of the Hebrew Bible except Esther. The biblical manuscripts show that the biblical text was somewhat fluid before it was standardized in the wake of the destruction of Jerusalem in 70 CE. Some of the nonbiblical documents were written by the members of the Qumran community or their predecessors, while others originated outside the sect. Prominent among the nonsectarian documents are fragments from every section of *1 Enoch* except the *Similitudes*. The present chapter will limit itself to texts produced by members of the sect. There is one significant document, the *Temple Scroll* (11QTemple), on which there is no general agreement with respect to its origin. It is the longest of the scrolls and consists mostly of detailed regulations for the Temple and its cult. Most of the laws are from the Bible, but some are not. Whether or not the *Temple Scroll* is from the pen of a member of the Qumran community, its presence at Qumran attests to the group's interest in the Temple and cult. The scroll will not be analyzed in detail in this chapter.

HISTORY OF THE SECT

The scrolls are not concerned with history in the modern sense, but with the *meaning* of history. During the past four decades scholars have tried to reconstruct Qumran's history using archaeological evidence, clues in the texts, and what is known of the period from other sources. The result is one main theory concerning Qumran's history, the Maccabean theory (followed here), and other theories that attract fewer advocates but are possible. It is not feasible to argue for each piece of evidence here. This chapter provides a brief summary of the reconstructed history of the community, and then examines the texts. This approach gives a general framework within which to read the texts, while fostering an appreciation of each text in its individuality.

Archaeological investigation of Qumran indicates three main periods of occupation. First, Qumran was settled on a modest scale in the middle of the second century BCE. Second, it grew substantially during the reign of John Hyrcanus (134–104 BCE). Finally, it was resettled, probably during the reign of Archelaus (4 BCE to 6 CE), and was eventually destroyed in the Jewish war against the Romans, around 68 CE.

The main lines of the Maccabean theory of Qumran origins are as follows. The Maccabean rebellion against the Seleucids united diverse Jewish groups, who split again into separate entities when Hasmonean rule was established. The group that eventually settled at Qumran should be seen as part of the anti-Seleucid coalition. The group may have split with its Hasmonean allies when the latter assumed the high priesthood. The Hasmoneans were priests, but not of the line of Zadok, the proper high priestly family. At the end of the second century BCE, the Hasmoneans also claimed the title of king, reserved, according to some, for Davidic descendants.

Early in the history of the Qumran group, a leader arose called the "Teacher of Righteousness." The Hebrew word translated "teacher" (*môreh*) is from the same root as "Torah," whose basic meaning is "instruction." In some of the scrolls the Teacher opposes the "Wicked Priest," who was once looked upon favorably by the Teacher's group, but was considered wicked when he became high priest in Jerusalem. Two candidates for identification as the Wicked Priest were brothers of Judas Maccabeus. The first is Jonathan, appointed high priest by a Seleucid king in 152 BCE, and the other is Simon, who assumed the high priesthood upon Jonathan's death in 142 BCE. It is plausible that the Teacher's community fled Jerusalem when Jonathan became high priest. This would be the beginning of the first period of settlement at Qumran.

THE NATURE OF THE COMMUNITY

Pliny the Elder says that the Essenes were "a solitary people, the most extraordinary in the world since there are no women (they renounce all sexual desire), they have no money, and they enjoy only the society of the palm-trees" (*AI*, 117). He locates them in the vicinity of Qumran. Both Josephus and Philo say that Essenes were celibate and lived in many towns. Josephus adds that there were also married Essenes. The apparent contradictions in these reports may be resolved when the scrolls are taken into account.

Among the Dead Sea Scrolls are two community rules which speak of the nature of the community, its rules, its structure, and so on. One of these documents, called the *Community Rule* (1QS), pictures a self-contained, celibate community.[1] The other, the *Damascus Document* (CD), envisages a series of smaller groups living in towns, marrying, and in contact with society at large.[2] Despite the differences, the communities reflected in the two scrolls are very similar. These communities may have been two branches of the Essene movement, one located at Qumran, isolated, and celibate, the other living in towns, marrying, and having contact with the surrounding society.

The Qumran community was priestly, centered on Torah, a sect, based on special esoteric revelation, apocalyptic, and highly structured. Each of these characteristics is discussed below.

Priestly

The Qumran community was strictly ordered, with priests at the top of the order. Purity was a strong concern. Relations between persons of different categories were strictly regulated. The scrolls speak of atonement in terms of temple functions, but there was no temple at Qumran. There is a continuing debate about whether members of the sect participated in the sacrifices at Jerusalem. It is possible that the town branch did sacrifice at the Temple, but those at Qumran did not. There may also have been times in the sect's history when it frequented the Temple and other times when it did not. The scrolls speak of effecting atonement *apart* from sacrifices at Jerusalem. Prayer and Torah observation were considered equivalent to sacrifices in their effect. Such ideas made it possible for the sect to be cut off from the religious establishment in Jerusalem without being deprived of the benefits of the sacrificial system. The community conceived of itself as a temple. God was present within it. One way of expressing this was that the angels were present in the community. God was attended by angels, who were divine bodyguards, messengers, worshipers, and other things. To be among the assembly of the angels was to have access to God.

Several allusions to ritual washings and the existence of facilities for such washings at the Qumran ruins suggest that they were an important feature of the sect's practice. Washing symbolized the leaving behind of sin and its effects, but only if one's inner disposition was proper.

Centered on Torah

All Jewish groups were in some way centered on Torah. The people of Qumran interpreted Torah in ways that distinguished them from other Jews. Those interpretations, many of which may go back to the Teacher of Righteousness, were multifaceted. Some were halakhic. Halakhah, a word derived from the Hebrew word *hālak*, "walk," refers to rules of behavior, laws. Another more basic dispute over Torah concerned who had the right to interpret it authoritatively. Qumran claimed that only the Teacher of Righteousness and his community held the key to Torah. Since they had been granted the correct interpretation of Torah, only they could authentically fulfill Torah. The Qumran community was the true Israel. Since the community was recently founded, it had a "New Covenant" with God. The new covenant was based on the Mosaic covenant, but it was new because it involved the true interpretation of Torah given only to the Teacher of Righteousness and his community. For a Jew to join the sect, conversion was necessary. One had to recognize the futility of one's former life and to accept Qumran as the one way to relate to God. The term "New Covenant" may come from Jeremiah 31:31, "The days are surely coming, says the LORD, when I will make a new covenant with the house of Israel and the house of Judah." The Qumran community may have seen itself as a fulfillment of this verse, as did the Christian church later.

A fundamental halakhic dispute between the sect and the Jerusalem establishment involved the calendar. At Qumran a solar calendar was followed, but in Jerusalem the moon determined the divisions of the year. This was a serious disagreement, because proper categorization of time was central in priestly religion. It meant that Qumran considered the rest of Judaism in violation of God's will concerning worship, and, conversely, that other Jewish groups could level the same accusation at Qumran.

QUMRAN: A PRIESTLY, APOCALYPTIC COMMUNITY

Sect

"Sect" has a very specific meaning. It denotes a minority group conscious of itself as separate from those around it and not in harmony with the dominant religious establishment. Sects have clearly defined social boundaries, often reinforced by stringent purity rules. Contact with outsiders is rigidly regulated. Marriage is endogamous, meaning that one finds one's spouse inside the sect.

Esoteric Revelation

Only members of the community knew God's will. It was disclosed to the Teacher of Righteousness and his successors, and it was not generally available. The revelation concerned the role of the community as the true Israel, eschatological teaching, interpretation of the Torah, and other matters.

Apocalyptic

Although there are no apocalypses among the documents attributed to the Qumran sectaries (members of the sect), there were several apocalypses in their library. Daniel was especially popular. Qumran shared with apocalypses an interest in both angelology and eschatology. Qumran was also apocalyptic in its dualism, believing that the world was in the grips of a cosmic battle between good and evil. Humanity was likewise divided into good and bad. The sectaries looked forward to an imminent eschatological battle in which the powers of good would overcome the powers of evil. The victory of the good was ensured because God was all-powerful, and God had planned the entire course of history in advance.

The sect's beliefs concerning the afterlife are unclear. There are no unambiguous references to resurrection, although some passages seem to imply resurrection. Since the community already lived in the presence of the angels, in a sense resurrection would be anticlimactic. "Everlasting life" is mentioned in the scrolls, and this phrase may mean some sort of immortality. Josephus says that the Essenes did not believe in the resurrection of the body but in the immortality of the soul. In any case, the sect was more interested in the defeat of Satan, the overthrow of the unrighteous in Jerusalem, and the restoration of the proper role of the sons of Zadok than in the afterlife.

Qumran expected two messiahs, one priestly and the other royal. They were not to be divine beings, but fully human. These messiahs were not said to bring in the endtime. Their significance resided in the idea that when God would visit the earth, Israel would come to be what it was meant to be. Properly constituted, Israel had at its head a king and a high priest. Both were anointed, so both were messiahs, just as David and Aaron were messiahs. The priestly messiah was seen as superior to the royal one.

The community's view of Scripture corresponded to its apocalyptic world view. Qumran took special interest in prophetic writings and saw them as predictive of the sect itself. Their exegesis consisted of showing in detail how prophetic texts referred to Qumran.

Highly Structured

The community was divided into three main parts—priests (also called the "sons of Zadok"), Levites, and laypeople. The priests were the leaders, responsible for right doctrine and practice. Priests had to be present in any significant gathering. The top officer was called the "Guardian," elsewhere called the "Master." He was to teach the sect how to live in conformity with correct understanding of the Torah, to preside over important meetings, and to rank each of the members on the basis of adherence to the rule. The "Council of the Community" seems to have been a formal gathering of the members. In the *Community Rule,* a smaller council of fifteen men is mentioned, but its place in the structure of the community is uncertain. There was a bursar to attend to the community's finances.

THE *DAMASCUS DOCUMENT* (CD)

This document is dated by Vermes to around 100 BCE. It is a good place to begin because it starts with a "history" of the world. This history is in the form of an exhortation to the sectaries to remain faithful to their calling. The theme is that obedience to God brings blessing and disobedience brings punishment. The history is prefaced by a brief description of the emergence of the sect. All history is seen as leading up to the formation of the sect; it is something that God planned from all eternity. The second part of the text consists of rules for the community.

Exhortation Through History

The preacher reminds the hearers that the Temple was destroyed and the people killed because of Israel's sins, but God, "remembering the Covenant of the forefathers," let a remnant survive. Then he says,

> And in the age of wrath, three hundred and ninety years after He had given them into the hand of king Nebuchadnezzar of Babylon, He visited them, and He caused a plant root to spring from Israel and Aaron to inherit His Land and to prosper on the good things of His earth. And they perceived their iniquity and recognized that they were guilty men, yet for twenty years they were like blind men groping for the way.
>
> (CD 1)[3]

"Wrath" means God's anger at sins. Nebuchadnezzar exiled Israel in 587 BCE. Three hundred and ninety years after that would be 197 BCE, just before the Hellenizing reform in Jerusalem. Such a view assumes that the whole period from 587 to the foundation of the sect was a time of exile. It is a view that denigrates the Second Temple and its establishment as not a true restoration at all. The true restoration of the covenant community is the Qumran sect itself, four centuries after Nebuchadnezzar's destruction of the Temple.

The summary in CD 1 implies that the group was not very organized or sure of its goals when it first arose. "For twenty years they were like blind men groping for the way." That could be a period during which they were allied with the Maccabees, first in war and then in the Maccabees' control of Jerusalem. The next stage is crucial for the community: "And God observed their deeds, that they sought Him with a whole heart, and He raised for them a Teacher of Righteousness to guide them in the way of His heart" (CD 1). Through the Teacher, God reveals that Israel continues to suffer because it is a "congregation of traitors," which was departed from God's way. The Teacher is opposed by one who "shed over Israel the waters of lies" and was engaged in "abolishing the ways of righteousness." The opponent is pictured as attacking the Torah itself, and thus bringing on Israel "the curses of His Covenant" and delivering it to "the avenging sword of the Covenant." The one who opposes the Teacher and misleads Israel brings curses upon Israel. The wicked leader is elsewhere called "the Scoffer" because he scoffs at Torah.

The Scoffer pursues the Teacher and his followers. Since Torah is not just religious but affects every aspect of life, including politics, the existence of a group challenging the established order is a religious and a political threat. The acts of the Scoffer and his supporters are summed up by the *Damascus Document* with the sentence, "Their deeds were defilement before Him" (CD 2). Priestly terminology is employed to categorize their behavior as abominable to God. Of course, the scrolls give only one side of the argument. The "Scoffer" probably thought that the Teacher was the one threatening the covenant by rebelling against God's representatives in Jerusalem.

The exhortation again addresses the hearers directly, saying, "Hear now, all you who enter the Covenant, and I will unstop your ears concerning the ways of the wicked" (CD 2). The covenant is now congruent with the community. To be outside the sect is to be outside the covenant, even if one is Jewish or worships in the Temple. Joining the sect is entering the covenant. After this new address the preacher launches into a narrative demonstrating that obedience to God brings divine favor and disobedience brings anger. The preacher states this principle, and then, before showing how it applies to the history of the world, asserts that God foreknew everything. The sinners

shall have no remnant or survivor. For from the beginning God chose them not; He knew their deeds before ever they were created and He hated their generations, and He hid His face from the Land until they were consumed. For He knew the years of their coming and the length and exact duration of their times for all ages to come and throughout eternity. He knew the happenings of their times throughout all the everlasting years. And in all of them He raised for Himself men called by name, that a remnant might be left to the Land, and that the face of the earth might be filled with their seed. And He made known His Holy Spirit to them by the hand of His anointed ones, and He proclaimed the truth (to them). But those whom He hated He led astray. (CD 2)

The sinners have already experienced punishment for their sins in the misfortunes that have overtaken Israel, but since they still sin, they will continue to be punished until not a single survivor is left of their number. God even allowed the land of Israel to be punished. God knew everything that was to happen beforehand, and provided for the preservation of the covenant by leaving a remnant. That remnant is called by God; it is an elect group. To this elect group God makes known the truth through people chosen for the task who are called anointed ones (messiahs).

The review of history shows that those (both humans and angels) who obey God prosper, while those who "follow after thoughts of the guilty inclination and after eyes of lust" are punished (CD 2). The idea that there is a guilty inclination in humanity and even in angels is also found elsewhere in post-biblical Judaism. Through the guilty inclination "their sons perished, and through it their kings were cut off; through it their mighty heroes perished and through it their land was ravaged" (CD 3).

At the end of this dismal history comes the glory of the community of the covenant.

But with the remnant which held fast to the commandments of God He made His Covenant with Israel for ever, revealing to them the hidden things in which all Israel had gone astray. He unfolded before them His holy Sabbaths and His glorious feasts, the testimonies of His righteousness and the ways of His truth, and the desires of His will which a man must do in order to live. (CD 3)

The remnant is coterminous with the Qumran community. God has revealed to them mistakes and sins that Israel is making that no one else knows. To Qumran has been revealed the correct cultic year with its feasts. Only the community of the covenant truly knows God's will, because only to them has it been revealed. Since the prosperity and even the survival of humans depends on God, knowledge of the divine will is something that one must have "in order to live."

Speaking of the first members of the community CD says,

(They were the first men) of holiness whom God forgave, and who justified the righteous and condemned the wicked. And until the age is completed, according to the number of those years, all who enter after them shall do according to that interpretation of the Law in which the first were instructed. According to the

Covenant which God made with the forefathers, forgiving their sins, so shall He forgive their sins also. But when the age is completed, according to the number of those years, there shall be no more joining the house of Judah, but each man shall stand on his watchtower. (CD 4)

The community sees as God sees, and so they know who is truly righteous and who is truly wicked. All who convert to the sect must follow the sect's interpretation of Torah just as the first members did. Conversion is open to anyone during the present age, but when the age draws to a close it will be too late to convert, for the eschatological battle will have begun. The thought that history consists of a succession of preordained ages is typical of apocalypticism.

During the time before the eschaton, "Satan[4] shall be unleashed against Israel, as He spoke by the hand of Isaiah, son of Amoz, saying, *Terror and the pit and the snare are upon you, O inhabitant of the land* (Isa. xxiv, 17)" (CD 4). In typical fashion, an ancient prophecy is taken to refer directly to the community's own time. Satan dominates the present age and makes war against Israel. "Terror," "pit," and "snare" are taken as cryptic allusions to sins committed by the Jerusalem priestly establishment. The sins involve "fornication," "riches," and "profanation of the Temple." Fornication really means failure to conform to the marriage laws advocated by the sect.

The legal disputes between the sect and the establishment are summarized from the sectarian point of view as follows: "They defile their holy spirit and open their mouth with a blaspheming tongue against the laws of the Covenant of God saying, 'They are not sure'" (CD 5). "Not sure" may mean that the opponents do not see Qumran's interpretation as based on Torah.

At the end of CD 6 is a paragraph dealing with the Temple.

None of those brought into the Covenant shall enter the Temple to light His altar in vain. They shall bar the door, forasmuch as God said, *Who among you will bar its door?* And, *You shall not light my altar in vain* (Mal. i, 10). They shall take care to act according to the exact interpretation of the Law during the age of wickedness. They shall separate from the sons of the Pit, and shall keep away from the unclean riches of wickedness acquired by vow or anathema or from the Temple treasure; they shall not rob the poor of His people, to make of widows their prey and of the fatherless their victim (Isa. x, 2). They shall distinguish between clean and unclean, and shall proclaim the difference between holy and profane. They shall keep the Sabbath day according to its exact interpretation, and the feasts and the Day of Fasting according to the finding of the members of the New Covenant in the land of Damascus.[5] They shall set aside the holy things according to the exact teaching concerning them. They shall love each man his brother as himself; they shall succour the poor, the needy, and the stranger. (CD 6)

This text says that because the Temple in Jerusalem was defiled it would be futile to send sacrifices there. Through Isaiah God decreed that the altar not be lit in vain. What the community should do during the "age of wickedness," the age in which Satan's allies rule Jerusalem, is to obey the Torah strictly, and to do so "according to the finding of the members of the New Covenant." True to the community's priestly nature, decisions about clean and unclean are crucial. The point is reemphasized a few lines farther on: "They shall keep apart from every uncleanness according to the statutes relating to each one, and no man shall defile his holy spirit since God has set them apart" (CD 7). Holiness means to belong to God, which implies separation from everything that is profane. Determination of the dates of feasts and of exactly how they are to be observed is also central to living as God wants. But attention to ritual and cultic matters is not incompatible with ethical concerns. Love of one another and social justice issues are highlighted here, as they are in other priestly writings. The text elaborates on how sectaries are to relate to one another. They are to be open, not holding grudges.

Separation from those who do not follow the proper interpretation of Torah is envisaged in this passage. Others are "sons of the Pit." "The Pit" is a biblical term originally denoting Sheol, a shadowy place where humans go when they die. In the context of the scrolls, it probably means the place of punishment of the angels and humans who do not follow the sect's life-style. The separation enjoined on covenant members functions on several levels. It allows the sect to maintain ritual purity and so guard God's presence among them. It helps to maintain strong social boundaries and so avoid any threat to its identity from dissenting ideas and practices. It also allows for social control in that the threat of separation from the holy community can keep members in line. That the concept of separation operates in this last way is confirmed by the fact that the punishment imposed on transgressors is often separation from certain aspects of community life, or from the community in general.

The next section of the *Damascus Document* shows that the sect had a branch that lived in various locations and was noncelibate. It lays down certain rules for members, "If they live in camps according to the rule of the Land . . . , marrying . . . and begetting children" (CD 7).

Mere membership in the community does not ensure God's favor. Adherence to the Torah is necessary. The preacher warns,

At the time of the former Visitation they were saved, whereas the apostates were given up to the sword; and so shall it be for all the members of His Covenant who do not hold steadfastly to these. . . . They shall be visited for destruction by the hand of Satan. That shall be the day when God will visit. (CD 7–8)

The day of judgment is a threat to those insincere in their membership in the sect. God will come to judge, and transgressors will be given over to Satan for destruction. "The former Visitation" must refer to some period of severe punishment of Israel which the sect escaped. It may allude to the persecution of Judaism by Antiochus IV seen as a punishment for the Hellenistic reform. That reading is supported by the next section, which speaks of "the kings of Greece who came to wreak vengeance upon them" (CD 8).

Later in CD 8 the warning to those not serious about following the rules is put in terms that provide a frame for the existence of the sect.

> None of the men who enter the New Covenant in the land of Damascus, and who again betray it and depart from the fountain of living waters, shall be reckoned with the Council of the people or inscribed in its Book from the day of the gathering in of the Teacher of the Community until the coming of the Messiah out of Aaron and Israel.

The "gathering in" of the Teacher is his death. The Teacher's death is apparently in the past for the *Damascus Document*. The document anticipates a messianic age. Throughout the scrolls, a juxtaposition of terms for priests with terms for Israel in general means that the group is being broken up into its priestly and lay components. It is reasonable, therefore, to interpret this verse as referring to *two* messiahs, one a priest (out of Aaron) and one a layperson (out of Israel). In Israel, both kings (laymen) and priests were anointed, so the text probably anticipates priestly and royal messiahs.

The *Damascus Document* is more specific about its timetable in the following passage.

> From the day of the gathering in of the Teacher of the Community until the end of all the men of war who deserted to the Liar there shall pass about forty years (Deut. ii, 14). And during that age the wrath of God shall be kindled against Israel; as He said, *There shall be no king, no prince, no judge, no man to rebuke with justice* (Hos. iii, 4). But those who turn from the sin of Jacob, who keep the Covenant of God, shall then speak each man to his fellow, to justify each man his brother, that their step may take the way of God. . . . And every member of the House of Separation who went out of the Holy City and leaned on God at the time when Israel sinned and defiled the Temple, but returned again to the way of the people in small matters, shall be judged according to his spirit in the Council of holiness. (CD 8)

There are only forty years between the death of the Teacher and the eschatological judgment. The only ones to escape God's wrath are the members of the covenant who have turned their backs on the rest of Israel. Thus, an appropriate name for the sect is the "House of Separation." They have fled the "Holy City," Jerusalem, because the Temple establishment did not follow the teaching of the Teacher of Righteousness and so was defiling the Temple. The "Liar" controls the Temple. This passage is especially negative toward members of the sect who deserted to the Liar. Contrasted with these are "all those who hold fast to these precepts, going and coming in accordance with the Law, who heed the voice of the Teacher" (CD 8).

Rules for the Community

The rest of the *Damascus Document* contains statutes for the community. The statutes begin with safeguarding the sanctity of the name of God (Yahweh).[6] No one may swear by it (CD 15). The document goes farther and prohibits swearing by the Torah as well.[7] Entrance into the sect is returning to the Torah. Speaking of one who has decided to join, the document says, "They shall enroll him with the oath of the Covenant which Moses made with Israel, the Covenant to return to the Law of Moses with a whole heart and soul" (CD 15). Since true knowledge of Torah is something granted to the sect alone, a prospective convert should not be told the statutes until approved by the Guardian.

God is present with the community, which is the true Temple. That means God's angels were present, so purity rules must be stringently observed: "No madman, or lunatic, or simpleton, or fool, no blind man, or maimed, or lame, or deaf man, and no minor, shall enter into the Community, for the Angels of Holiness are with them" (CD 15). The Hebrew Bible contains similar restrictions on who may enter the Temple (Deut 23:1-6, e.g.). Those who are on the fringes of the community cannot be allowed full access to God. Societal structures are replicated in cultic prescriptions.

The concern to celebrate feasts according to the solar calendar is probably behind the following statement: "As for the exact determination of their times to which Israel turns a blind eye, behold it is strictly defined in the *Book of the Divisions of the Time into Their Jubilees and Weeks*" (CD 16). The book alluded to is probably the *Book of Jubilees*. It is in the Qumran library and so was known to the sect. It advocates a solar calendar.

A series of rules safeguards the sanctity of the sabbath (CD 10–11). Sabbath observance became a matter of controversy and was one of the ways Jewish groups distinguished themselves from one another. Characteristic of the statutes in the *Damascus Document* is the stringency of its sabbath rules. Work in any form is prohibited. Nonetheless, a person whose life is in danger may be saved on the sabbath, even if that involves work.[8]

Care for Jerusalem's purity appears in the rule prohibiting the sending of sacrifices to Jerusalem by the hand of one who is unclean (CD 11). The same concern emerges in the forbidding of sexual intercourse in the holy city (CD 12). It is not certain whether these rules assume that members of the sect are actually going to Jerusalem to sacrifice, or are simply "on the books" in anticipation of a time when the sect will control the Temple.

The existence of laws governing relations with Gentiles implies that members were not isolated from society at large. That is confirmed by the heading, "The Rule for the assembly of the towns" (CD 12).

THE *COMMUNITY RULE* (1QS)

The *Community Rule* is considered one of the oldest documents of the sect. Its present form may date to ca. 100 BCE. It is thought to be composed of earlier documents, so its parts are even older. It existed in one form or another during most of the sect's life. Its importance is shown by the fact that twelve copies of it are attested. Vermes sketches its contents as follows.

> It seems to have been intended for the Community's teachers, for its Masters or Guardians, and contains extracts from liturgical ceremonies, an outline of a model sermon on the spirits of truth and falsehood, statutes concerned with initiation into the sect and with its common life, organization and discipline, a penal code, and finally a poetic dissertation on the fundamental religious duties of the Master and his disciples, and on the sacred seasons proper to the Community. (*DSSE,* 61)

Each of these parts—the liturgy, sermon, statutes and penal code, and duties of master and disciples—are examined below.

Liturgy

The first three columns of the *Community Rule* contain what appears to be part of a liturgy for a covenant renewal ceremony. Members pledge themselves to do what is good and right before God, "As He commanded by the hand of Moses and all His servants the Prophets" (1QS 1). The Guardian is to emphasize the importance of the revealed "appointed times," times for feasts and for daily prayers. Qumran's dualism is apparent in this liturgy, as it is in the sermon on the two spirits that follows it. Humanity is divided into two opposing groups, one belonging to light and the other to darkness, and this is all part of God's design. God has placed each person in one camp or the other. Members must pledge to "love all the sons of light, each according to his lot in God's design, and hate all the sons of darkness, each according to his guilt in God's vengeance" (1QS 1).

"All those who embrace the Community Rule shall enter into the Covenant before God to obey all His commandments so that they may not abandon Him during the dominion of Satan because of fear or terror or affliction" (1QS 1). These words assume that the elect are in danger of suffering because of Satan's dominion. Eventual victory is assured the forces of good, though Satan has the upper hand at present.

The scroll speaks of one who enters the covenant with doubt.

He shall not be justified by that which his stubborn heart declares lawful, for seeking the ways of light he looks towards darkness. He shall not be reckoned among the perfect; he shall neither be purified by atonement, nor cleansed by purifying waters, nor sanctified by seas and rivers, nor washed clean with any ablution. Unclean, unclean shall he be. For as long as he despises the precepts of God he shall receive no instruction in the Community of His counsel. (1QS 3)

The scroll admits that the people it condemns seek light and do what their heart declares lawful. That does not excuse the fact that they are in error. Only absolute adherence to the sect's ways brings God's favor. Using the language of priestly religion, the scroll claims that no one who does not give full inner assent to the truth can be purified. Ritual washings are not magic. They are outer signs of an inner conversion. Without the inner conversion, one remains unclean.

The liturgical section ends with a statement of how ritual washing combined with an inner determination to obey Torah effects atonement.

For it is through the spirit of true counsel concerning the ways of man that all his sins shall be expiated that he may contemplate the light of life. He shall be cleansed from all his sins by the spirit of holiness uniting him to His truth, and his iniquity shall be expiated by the spirit of uprightness and humility. And when his flesh is sprinkled with purifying water and sanctified by cleansing water, it shall be made clean by the humble submission of his soul to all the precepts of God. Let him then order his steps to walk perfectly in all the ways commanded by God concerning the times appointed for him, straying neither to right nor to left and transgressing none of His words, and he shall be accepted by virtue of pleasing atonement before God and it shall be to him a Covenant of the everlasting Community. (1QS 3)

The first step to following the right path is to understand humanity correctly. If one receives "true counsel concerning the ways of man," one can comprehend the meaning of human life and the content of God's will. As was indicated at the beginning of the *Community Rule,* true understanding of humanity rests upon the recognition that it is divided into two parts, the good and the bad.

Sermon

The *Community Rule* now begins a dissertation on the "nature of all the children of men" (1QS 3). The scroll itself supplies a table of contents for the presentation: "the kind of spirit which they possess, the signs identifying their works during their lifetime, their visitation for chastisement, and the time of their reward" (1QS 3). The section goes on to a general statement that even before creation came into being, God had planned the entire course of it. "From the God of Knowledge comes all that is and shall be. Before ever they existed He established their whole design, and when, as ordained for them, they come into being, it is in accord with His glorious design that they accomplish their task without change'' (1QS 3).

Then comes a section that states in the clearest possible terms the division of humanity into two parts.

> He has created man to govern the world, and has appointed for him two spirits in which to walk until the time of His visitation: the spirits of truth and falsehood. Those born of truth spring from a fountain of light, but those born of falsehood spring from a source of darkness. All the children of righteousness are ruled by the Prince of Light and walk in the ways of light, but all the children of falsehood are ruled by the Angel of Darkness and walk in the ways of darkness. (1QS 3)

The text asserts the unqualified sovereignty of God over all creation, including the Prince of Light (Michael) and the Angel of Darkness (Satan). God created the good and evil spirits, and assigned individuals to one or the other. This appears to be a statement of individual predestination. What follows qualifies this extreme position, as does the content of the rest of the scrolls, in which it is assumed that individuals choose which path they will take. The tension between determinism and free will, implied in the extreme position and its qualification, is a tension present in other writings of the period, Jewish and non-Jewish.

The Angel of Darkness influences not only the children of darkness, but also tempts the children of righteousness: ''The Angel of Darkness leads all the children of righteousness astray, and until his end, all their sin, iniquities, wickedness, and all their unlawful deeds are caused by his dominion in accordance with the mysteries of God'' (1QS 3). This sentence explains how it can be that even the righteous can stumble at times. It is because the Angel of Darkness tempts them, too. But the Angel of Darkness has power only because God has allowed it. ''But the God of Israel and His Angel of Truth will succour all the sons of light. For it is He who created the spirits of Light and Darkness and founded every action upon them and established every deed [upon] their [ways]'' (1QS 3).

The next column takes a remarkable turn. It claims not only that humans are in the camp of either the good or the bad angel, but also that those spirits struggle in the heart of each individual. Each person has a certain measure of each spirit, and the size of the portion determines the ultimate orientation of the individual. ''And the whole reward for their deeds shall be, for everlasting ages, according to whether each man's portion in their two divisions is great or small'' (1QS 4).

There follow catalogs of the deeds of the righteous and of the unrighteous. Notable among the deeds of the righteous is the emphasis on ''zeal for just laws'' and ''faithful concealment of the mysteries of truth'' (1QS 4). This last element points to the esoteric revelation granted to the sect. The ''visitation'' of the righteous, their reward at the Lord's visit, is ''healing, great peace in a long life, and fruitfulness, together with every everlasting blessing and eternal joy in life without end, a crown of glory and a garment of majesty in unending light'' (1QS 4). The visitation of the wicked is

> a multitude of plagues by the hand of all the destroying angels, everlasting damnation by the avenging wrath of the fury of God, eternal torment and endless disgrace together with shameful extinction in the fire of the dark regions. The times of all their generations shall be spent in sorrowful mourning and in bitter misery and in calamities of darkness until they are destroyed without remnant or survivor.
>
> (1QS 4)

When the end comes, the evil parts of the righteous will be wiped away and evil will be destroyed completely. This description is put in priestly and apocalyptic terminology. A time is appointed for judgment in which

> God will then purify every deed of man with his truth; He will refine for Himself the human frame by rooting out all spirit of falsehood from the bounds of his flesh. He will cleanse him of all wicked deeds with the spirit of holiness; like purifying waters He will shed upon him the spirit of truth (to cleanse him) of all abomination and falsehood. And he shall be plunged into the spirit of purification that he may instruct the upright in the knowledge of the Most High and teach the wisdom of the sons of heaven to the perfect of way. (1QS 4)

Statutes and Penal Code

The rules section begins with the statement that converts must separate

> from the congregation of the men of falsehood and shall unite, with respect to the Law and possessions, under the authority of the sons of Zadok, the Priests who keep the Covenant, and of the multitude of the men of the Community who hold fast to the Covenant. Every decision concerning doctrine, property, and justice shall be determined by them. (1QS 5)

This passage reaffirms the absolute authority of the Zadokite priests. It puts full jurisdiction even for possessions under their control. The text goes on to say that the one entering must take an oath to ''return with all his heart and soul to every commandment of the Law of Moses in accordance with all that has been revealed of it to the sons of Zadok, the Keepers of the Covenant and Seekers of His will'' (1QS 5).

Members are strictly enjoined not to associate with any member who does not conform completely to Qumran's rule. Eschatological punishment is threatened against such people, and they are excluded from the sect. This is symbolized especially by their exclusion from the common meal that must be eaten in a state of purity effected by ablution. Further rules specify the complete isolation of the wicked individual.

There follow regulations stressing the hierarchy of the community. Assemblies are run with strict decorum. Every year each member is ranked according to knowledge and practice of Torah. Study of the Law is a priority: "There shall never lack a man among them who shall study the Law continually, day and night, concerning the right conduct of a man with his companion. And the Congregation shall watch in community for a third of every night of the year, to read the Book and to study Law and to pray together" (1QS 6).

Full membership in the community is attained only after a period of probation.[9] A candidate must be examined by the Guardian "concerning his understanding and his deeds." If found acceptable, he enters a period of instruction in the sect's rules. Then he is examined by the entire congregation. If he passes this test, he lives as a member for a year, but he is still excluded from the pure common meal and retains his personal property. If the assembly finds that he has lived the life satisfactorily, then he is admitted to the meal but not to the "Drink of the Congregation." Precisely what this means is unclear, but it is a use of food to mark the degree of integration of the candidate into the sect. During the second year his property is given over to the bursar, who keeps it separate from the common property. This is an arrangement allowing the person to sample the community and the sect to observe the person without either making a definitive commitment to the other. Then the candidate is again examined. If found worthy, "He shall be inscribed among his brethren in the order of his rank for the Law, and for justice, and for the pure Meal; his property shall be merged and he shall offer his counsel and judgement to the Community" (1QS 6).

Next are a number of rules to ensure that the community runs smoothly and that members are at peace with one another and subject to the proper Zadokite authorities. Column 8 begins,

In the Council of the Community there shall be twelve men and three Priests, perfectly versed in all that is revealed of the Law, whose works shall be truth, righteousness, justice, loving kindness and humility. They shall preserve the faith in the Land with steadfastness and meekness and shall atone for sin by the practice of justice and by suffering the sorrows of affliction. They shall walk with all men according to the standard of truth and the rule of the time.

When these are in Israel, the Council of the Community shall be established in truth. It shall be an Everlasting Plantation, a House of Holiness for Israel, an Assembly of Supreme Holiness for Aaron. They shall be witnesses to the truth at the Judgement, and shall be the elect of Goodwill who shall atone for the Land and pay to the wicked their reward.

The Council of the Community

shall be a Most Holy Dwelling for Aaron, with everlasting knowledge of the Covenant of justice, and shall offer up sweet fragrance. It shall be a House of Perfection and Truth in Israel that they may establish a Covenant according to the everlasting precepts. And they shall be an agreeable offering, atoning for the Land and determining the judgement of wickedness, and there shall be no more iniquity. When they have been confirmed for two years in perfection of way by the authority of the Community, they shall be set apart as holy within the Council of the men of the Community. And the Interpreter shall not conceal from them, out of fear of the spirit of apostasy, any of those things hidden from Israel which have been discovered by him. (1QS 8)

Qumran is a priestly group, and it is important that it have a means of effecting atonement. The community itself functions as a temple. When its members study and observe the Law, and when they suffer for their obedience to the will of God, this brings about atonement for the land and ensures that God will remain there. Without the existence of Qumran, God would leave the land of Israel because it would be completely unclean. The frequent use of the word "house" in this passage is due to the fact that the Temple is called a "house." The community now becomes the house (Temple) where Aaron, the true priests, can dwell. It is a house of holiness because it belongs to God. It "shall offer up sweet fragrance" because it does what the Temple was intended to do through its sacrificial system—send the pleasing odor of sacrifices up to God in heaven.

A later passage shows that all sectaries effect atonement.

When these become members of the Community in Israel according to all these rules, they shall establish the spirit of holiness according to everlasting truth. They shall atone for guilty rebellion and for sins of unfaithfulness that they may obtain lovingkindness for the Land without the flesh of holocausts and the fat of sacrifice. And prayer rightly offered shall be as an acceptable fragrance of righteousness, and perfection of way as a delectable free-will offering. At that time, the men of the Community shall set apart a House of Holiness in order that it may be united to the most holy things and a House of Community for Israel, for those who walk in perfection. The sons of Aaron alone shall command in matters of justice and property, and every rule concerning the men of the Community shall be determined according to their word. (1QS 9)

The passage ends with the declaration that members "shall be ruled by the primitive precepts in which the men of the Community were first instructed until there shall come the Prophet and the Messiahs of Aaron and Israel" (1QS 9). When Israel is properly constituted at the end of time, it will have a king and a high priest, both anointed. In Deuteronomy 18:15-19, Moses promises that the

Lord will send another prophet like him. The prophet awaited by Qumran is probably the prophet promised by Moses. That is supported by *A Messianic Anthology* (4QTest), which collects biblical passages concerning three figures, a prophet (Deut. 5:28-29; 18:18-19), a king (Num 24:15-17), and a priest (Deut 33:8-11).

Duties of Master and Disciples

The prose section of the Community Rule ends with rules for the Master. The scroll ends with a poetic section similar to a psalm. It assumes the singer is a teacher. It begins with a declaration that the psalmist will keep all of God's appointed holy days and times for prayer. The keeping of God's prescribed order for worship reflects God's order in creation and so demonstrates a concern for order typical of priestly religion:

> I will sing with knowledge and all my music shall be for the glory of God.
> (My) lyre (and) my harp shall sound for His holy order
> and I will tune the pipe of my lips to His right measure. (1QS 10)

The psalmist then praises God's judgment of his sins and calls God "My Righteousness." There is a profound sense in many places in the scrolls, but especially in the psalms, of the unworthiness of all humanity. Unworthiness characterizes the sectaries, too, but God has chosen them and made them worthy to stand in the divine presence.

> As for me, my justification is with God.
> In His hand are the perfection of my way and the uprightness of my heart.
> He will wipe out my transgression through His righteousness. (1QS 11)

Consciousness of having been elected by God despite lack of merit is a hallmark of the thought of the apostle Paul, which is often contrasted with a monolithic "Judaism," thought to believe it earns its own salvation. Qumran is but one piece of evidence that this Christian-Jewish contrast is unfair and anti-Jewish.

The psalm goes on to praise God for the essential element of the sect, the revelation of God's way hidden from all others.

> From the source of His righteousness is my justification,
> and from His marvellous mysteries is the light in my heart.
> My eyes have gazed on that which is eternal,
> on wisdom concealed from men, on knowledge and wise design (hidden) from the
> sons of men;
> on a fountain of righteousness and on a storehouse of power,
> on a spring of glory (hidden) from the assembly of flesh.
> God has given them to His chosen ones as an everlasting possession,

and has caused them to inherit the lot of the Holy Ones.
He has joined their assembly to the Sons of Heaven
to be a Council of the Community,
a foundation of the Building of Holiness,
and eternal Plantation throughout all ages to come. (1QS 11)

The revelation to the sectaries is a gracious act of God. Self-righteousness is inappropriate because one's graced status is not something earned. God's grace allows the psalmist to stand in the midst of the "Holy Ones," the "Sons of Heaven," both terms for angels. The psalmist is rescued from the power of Satan and placed in a new, proper relationship with God.

THE *MESSIANIC RULE* (1QSa)

Vermes dates this document to around the turn of the first century CE. It is a brief text containing rules for the community in the last days when the messiahs are present. It illustrates the fact that the present structure and operation of the community accords with an ideal to be fully implemented at the end of time. Although the rule is for the messianic age, the community appears essentially as it does in the *Community Rule* and the *Damascus Document*. It specifies the status of an individual in the community at each stage of life. It reaffirms the absolute authority of the sons of Zadok, also called the sons of Aaron. It recalls the angels' presence in the community and the need for strict limits on who may enter it and on how one is to act while belonging to it. Finally, it briefly describes a common meal at which the messiahs of Aaron and of Israel preside. The priestly messiah takes precedence over the royal one. It is significant that the meal resembles the regular common meal of the community. The community even now lives the ideal life desired by God, which will be fully implemented at the end of times.

THE *WAR RULE* (1QM, 4QM)

The *War Rule* is a composite work. It was probably written when Israel was dealing with the Seleucids and was later adapted to the Roman period. The scroll describes the final war between the forces of good and evil, cosmic and earthly. The main earthly opponents of the righteous are the "Kittim." The word originally denoted the inhabitants of Citium in Cyprus, was later applied to the Greek overlords of Palestine, and finally meant the Romans. As they do in apocalypticism in general, earthly and heavenly events correspond. In the book of Daniel, the fate of Israel depends on the fate of its heavenly prince, Michael. When Michael conquers the angel of another nation, Israel prevails over that nation on earth. In the *War Rule* the heavenly and earthly levels are more mixed. Spiritual and human forces fight side-by-side.

The first lines of the document state that it is for "the unleashing of the attack of the sons of light against the company of the sons of darkness, the army of Satan." Then the human enemies are listed, including traditional biblical enemies of Israel such as Edom, Moab, and the Philistines. Also present are the Kittim and the "ungodly of the Covenant." In other words, on one side of the battle is the sect, and on the other everyone else, including Jews who do not belong to the sect and are therefore the "ungodly of the Covenant."

The battle starts when the "exiled sons of light return from the Desert of the Peoples to camp in the Desert of Jerusalem; and after the battle they shall go up from there (to Jerusalem?)" (1QM 1).[10] Victory is ensured because God sides with the righteous. "This shall be a time of salvation for the people of God, an age of dominion for all the members of His company, and of everlasting destruction for all the company of Satan." The battle is waged by human and superhuman forces:

> On the day when the Kittim fall, there shall be battle and terrible carnage before the God of Israel, for that shall be the day appointed from ancient times for the battle of destruction of the sons of darkness. At that time, the assembly of gods and the hosts of men shall battle, causing great carnage; on the day of calamity, the sons of light shall battle with the company of darkness amid the shouts of a mighty multitude and the clamour of gods and men to (make manifest) the might of God. (1QM 1)

The war unfolds as predetermined by God. This first column says that the war will take place in seven phases. In three the righteous will prevail, in three the wicked will win, but in the seventh God will destroy the power of the wicked forever. This implies a dualism in which good and evil are equally balanced until God's intervention.

The eschatological war is a holy war in which people and angels fight alongside one another. As a holy war its description mixes realistic with unrealistic elements. Prayers, sacrifices, and liturgy are as important as the fighting itself. Military arrangements are determined by purity rules.

> No boy or woman shall enter their camps, from the time they leave Jerusalem and march out to war until they return. No man who is lame, or blind, or crippled, or afflicted with a lasting bodily blemish, or smitten with a bodily impurity, none of these shall march out to war with them. They shall all be freely enlisted for war, perfect in spirit and body and prepared for the Day of Vengeance. And no man shall go down with them on the day of battle who is impure because of his "fount", for the holy angels shall be with their hosts. And there shall be a space of about two thousand cubits between all their camps for the place serving as a latrine, so that no indecent nakedness may be seen in the surroundings of their camps. (1QM 7)

Ritual purity must be constantly maintained in the camps because of the presence of the angels. Purity rules about who can be in the war camp resemble such rules for the Temple as are found in Deuteronomy 23 and elsewhere.

In 1QM 10–12, the officers deliver a long speech recalling the mighty battles of Israel in the past and God's saving of the people. It has been revealed to the "messiah" (probably the Teacher of Righteousness) that in the final battle the hordes of Satan will be defeated because God is on the side of the righteous: "For thou wilt fight with them from heaven" (1QS 11).

> For Thou art [terrible], O God, in the glory of Thy kingdom, and the congregation of Thy Holy Ones is among us for everlasting succour. We will despise kings, we will mock and scorn the mighty; for our Lord is holy, and the King of Glory is with us together with the Holy Ones. Valiant [warriors] of the angelic host are among our numbered men, and the Hero of war is with our congregation; the host of His spirits is with our foot-soldiers and horsemen. (1QM 12)

The priests are noncombatants in the final struggle. They sacrifice, pray, and deliver sermons. They are the cultic leaders of the war. The role of the archangel Michael, Israel's prince, is detailed in column 17.

> This is the day appointed by Him for the defeat and overthrow of the Prince of the kingdom of wickedness, and He will send eternal succour to the company of His redeemed by the might of the princely Angel of the kingdom of Michael. . . . He will raise up the kingdom of Michael in the midst of the gods, and the realm of Israel in the midst of all flesh. Righteousness shall rejoice on high, and all the children of his truth shall jubilate in eternal knowledge.

Michael victorious among the gods (angels) corresponds to Israel exalted among the nations.

BIBLICAL INTERPRETATION

Biblical interpretation at Qumran is guided by the principle that the Hebrew Bible was written in reference to the sect. Prophetic literature was especially rich in allusions to the sect. This is precisely the position of Christians with respect to their own religion. They interpret the Hebrew Bible as if its purpose is to point to Christ and the Christian religion. A good example of Qumran's use of biblical prophecy is found in 1QS 8. It quotes Isaiah 40:3, a verse written during the Exile that prophesied that God would soon be traveling from Babylon back to Jerusalem, signifying the restoration of Zion. Qumran interprets it in terms of itself.

> And when these become members of the Community in Israel according to all these rules, they shall separate from the habitation of ungodly men and shall go into the

wilderness to prepare the way of Him; as it is written, *Prepare in the wilderness the way of . . . , make straight in the desert a path for our God* (Isa. xl, 3). This (path) is the study of the Law which He commanded by the hand of Moses, that they may do according to all that has been revealed from age to age, and as the Prophets have revealed by His Holy Spirit. (1QS 8)

Christians later took the same passage to refer to John the Baptist (Mark 1:2-4; Matt. 3:3; Luke 3:3-6; John 1:22-23). For them John was the forerunner of Jesus, preparing his way by his baptizing in the desert. Qumran took it to refer to their own community, living in the desert and preparing the way of the Lord by study and observance of Torah.

The Qumran library contains several texts whose literary genre is a commentary on Scripture. They cite and comment on a biblical book verse by verse. Each verse is usually followed by the formula "It's interpretation," followed by a decoding of the verse to show its application to the sect. This sort of interpretation is called "pēšer," a Hebrew word meaning "interpretation." The sect does not assume that the author of the biblical text understood its full implications. It was the Teacher of Righteousness who was given knowledge of what the deeper meanings of the prophecies were, as is claimed in the commentary on the prophet Habakkuk:

God told Habakkuk to write down that which would happen to the final generation, but He did not make known to him when time would come to an end. And as for that which He said, *That he who reads may read it speedily:* interpreted this concerns the Teacher of Righteous, to whom God made known all the mysteries of the words of His servants the Prophets. (1QpHab 7)[11]

COMMENTARY ON HABAKKUK (1QpHab)

This document quotes Habakkuk verse by verse and explains it in terms of the sect. Although the prophet Habakkuk lived under Babylonian rule, probably 608–598 BCE, and addressed his own times, Qumran is not interested in the original setting of the prophecies. The true meaning of the prophecies is not what they meant to Habakkuk, but what they mean to the sect. The verse-by-verse decoding of Habakkuk is a method followed by all of the pesharim (plural of "pesher"). It is not simply that the sectaries conceive of themselves as adapting prophecy to the sect's needs. They believe that God was foretelling specific events in the life of the community, so the pesharim are an important place to look for reconstructing the history of the Qumran community. The analysis will be confined to several important points in the pesher.

O traitors, why do you stare and stay silent when the wicked swallows up one more righteous than he? (i, 13b)

> Interpreted, this concerns the House of Absalom and the members of its council who were silent at the time of the chastisement of the Teacher of Righteousness and gave him no help against the Liar who flouted the Law in the midst of their whole [congregation]. (1QpHab 5)

The identity of the House of Absalom is not known. "Absalom" may refer to the son of David who revolted against his father (2 Samuel 15–19), or it may refer to a contemporary of the Teacher of Righteousness. In any case, Habakkuk 1:13*b* is taken to refer to an incident when the Teacher was abandoned by a group from whom he expected support. The Liar seems to be a prominent public figure who disagreed with the Teacher on Torah. He may be the same person as the Wicked Priest and the Scoffer. This event may be one of the occurrences leading to the Teacher's withdrawal from Jerusalem to the desert.

In column 6, Habakkuk 1:14-16 is taken to refer to the Kittim, who "sacrifice to their standards." This describes the Romans well. Josephus says that when the Romans captured the Temple in the war of 66–70 CE they set up their standards in the Temple court and sacrificed to them (*War* 6.6.1 § 316).

> *If it tarries, wait for it, for it shall surely come and shall not be late* (ii, 3b).
> Interpreted, this concerns the men of truth who keep the Law, whose hands shall not slacken in the service of truth when the final age is prolonged. For all the ages of God reach their appointed end as He determines for them in the mysteries of His wisdom. (1QpHab 7)

This commentary may have been written when the eschatological battle did not happen when the sect expected. It uses the prophetic word to show the delay was anticipated in Scripture, and reaffirms the belief that God's mysterious plans will be put into effect without fail.

> [*But the righteous shall live by his faith*] (ii, 4b).
> Interpreted, this concerns all those who observe the Law in the House of Judah, whom God will deliver from the House of Judgement because of their suffering and because of their faith in the Teacher of Righteousness. (1 QpHab 7–8)

This is only one of many references in the scrolls to the suffering undergone by the sectaries. Faith in the Teacher of Righteousness is necessary for deliverance (salvation) here. It is striking that Paul uses the same verse to show that salvation comes through faith in Jesus Christ (Gal 3:11).

In column 8, Habakkuk 2:5-6 is interpreted as follows.

> Interpreted, this concerns the Wicked Priest who was called by the name of truth when he first arose. But when he ruled over Israel his heart became proud, and he forsook God and betrayed the precepts for the sake of riches. He robbed and

amassed the riches of the men of violence who rebelled against God, and he took the wealth of the peoples, heaping sinful iniquity upon himself. And he lived in the ways of abominations amidst every unclean defilement.

This passage applies to a priest originally approved by the Teacher's group, who then assumed power and went astray. The Hasmoneans are likely candidates for this description. Vermes thinks that the Wicked Priest is the first Hasmonean to assume the title of High Priest, Jonathan, who ruled from 152 to 142 as high priest. The pesher considers the Wicked Priest guilty of the kinds of crimes typical of rulers—violence and amassing of riches. He and his allies are spoken of as rebels against God. The last line puts all of this into the language of priestly religion—abomination, uncleanness, defilement.

The condemnation is repeated in the following passage, an interpretation of Habakkuk 2:7-8*a*.

> Interpreted, this concerns the last Priests of Jerusalem, who shall amass money and wealth by plundering the peoples. But in the last days, their riches and booty shall be delivered into the hands of the army of the Kittim. (1QpHab 9)

John Hyrcanus and Alexander Jannaeus both conquered substantial portions of territory in Palestine and surrounding areas. "Plundering the peoples" would fit their reigns. The army of the Kittim is probably the Roman army that took over Palestine in 63 BCE.

The next section of the commentary speaks of the death of the Wicked Priest as a fulfillment of Habakkuk 2:8*b*.

> Interpreted, this concerns the Wicked Priest whom God delivered into the hands of his enemies because of the iniquity committed against the Teacher of Righteousness and the men of his Council, that he might be humbled by means of a destroying scourge, in bitterness of soul, because he had done wickedly to His elect. (1QpHab 9)

If the Wicked Priest is Jonathan, then the enemies are the Seleucids who killed him by treachery in 142 BCE. The Habakkuk Commentary considers his death a punishment for the way he treated the Teacher and his followers, who were God's elect.

In column 11 a confrontation between the Teacher and the Wicked Priest is seen as a fulfillment of Habakkuk 2:15.

> Interpreted, this concerns the Wicked Priest who pursued the Teacher of Righteousness to the house of his exile that he might confuse him with his venomous fury. And at the time appointed for rest, for the Day of Atonement, he appeared before them to confuse them, and to cause them to stumble on the Day of Fasting, their Sabbath of repose.

Because Qumran followed a solar calendar and Jerusalem a lunar one, the day on which the Day of Atonement was observed at Qumran did not correspond to that of the observance of the Jerusalem establishment. The Wicked Priest may have used this discrepancy to confront the Qumran community when it was most vulnerable. The horror with which the Qumran viewed this desecration is expressed in the many titles given to the feast—time appointed for rest, Day of Atonement, Day of Fasting, Sabbath of repose. Precisely what happened is unknown, but it certainly made an impression on the sect and illustrates how seriously the priestly establishment took the existence of the Qumran settlement.

A final passage indicating the wickedness of the Jerusalem establishment interprets Habakkuk 2:17. Because the priest tried to harm the "Poor" (here it seems to be a designation of the sectaries), then he will be treated as he wished to treat them. The passage continues,

> And as for that which He said, *Because of the blood of the city and the violence done to the land:* interpreted, *the city is* Jerusalem where the Wicked Priest committed abominable deeds and defiled the Temple of God. *The violence done to the land:* these are the cities of Judah where he robbed the Poor of their possessions.
>
> (1QpHab 12)

The Wicked Priest is in Jerusalem and in charge of the Temple. His rule defiles the Temple. He uses his power to wreak violence against the Poor, the sectaries.

COMMENTARY ON PSALM 37 (4QpPs37, 4Q171)

Two points in this short document are of interest here. Psalm 37 is a generalized reflection on the injustices of the world and the justice of God. Interpreting Psalm 37:21-22, the commentary says, "Interpreted, this concerns the congregation of the Poor, who [shall possess] the whole world as an inheritance. They shall possess the High Mountain of Israel [for ever], and shall enjoy [everlasting] delights in His Sanctuary" (4Q171 3). This implies that the sect will control Jerusalem in the end. The second point concerns the Wicked Priest, who is said to have tried to put the Teacher of Righteousness to death, a point that if accurate would add to knowledge about the relations between the Priest and the Teacher.

COMMENTARY ON NAHUM (4QpNah, 4Q169)

This commentary is of special interest because it mentions names of historical figures in the context of the interpretation of Nahum 2:11b. Nahum was originally written in reaction to the fall of the Assyrian empire, which destroyed the northern Israelite kingdom. The pesher takes the prophetic text to refer to Hasmonean times.

[Interpreted, this concerns Deme]trius king of Greece who sought, on the counsel of those who seek smooth things, to enter Jerusalem. [But God did not permit the city to be delivered] into the hands of the kings of Greece, from the time of Antiochus until the coming of the rulers of the Kittim. But then she shall be trampled under their feet. (4Q169 1)

Antiochus is undoubtedly Antiochus IV, and the rulers of the Kittim are the Romans. Demetrius is a Seleucid who ruled between Antiochus and the coming of the Romans in 63 BCE. Jerusalem was plundered by Antiochus, but then evaded further capture until the coming of Pompey in 63 BCE. The commentary must date from some time after 63 BCE.

The "seekers of smooth things" are probably the Pharisees, as is supported by the next passage: "Interpreted, this concerns the furious young lion [who executes revenge] on those who seek smooth things and hangs men alive, . . . formerly in Israel" (4Q169 1). Many scholars find in the lion a reference to the Hasmonean king Alexander Jannaeus (ruled 103–76 BCE). The reference accords well with Josephus' story about eight hundred Pharisees who were crucified by Jannaeus for conspiring with Demetrius III to overthrow him (*Ant.* 13.14.2 §§ 380–83; *War* 1.4.6 §§ 96–98).

THE *THANKSGIVING HYMNS* (1QH)

This is a collection of about 25 psalms (according to Vermes' counting) similar to those in the Hebrew Bible, echoing the biblical psalms in language and ideas. The hymns of Qumran may have been used in the sect's worship. The hymns are in the form of individual thanksgivings. Several of them describe the experience of a teacher who is betrayed by his own group and persecuted by opponents.[12] It is possible that those hymns were written by the Teacher of Righteousness, but that cannot be known for sure. The focus here is on what the hymns show about the assumptions behind the way the sect prayed. The hymns claim that God controls everything.

By Thy wisdom [all things exist from] eternity,
　　and before creating them Thou knewest their works for ever and ever.
[Nothing] is done [without Thee]
　　and nothing is known unless Thou desire it.
Thou hast created all the spirits
　　[and hast established a statute] and law
　　for all their works. (1QH 1)

The hymns often contrast humanity and God. The following passage is prefaced by the psalmist saying that he understands how things really are, not through his own reason, but through God's gracious revelation.

These things I know by the wisdom which comes from Thee,
for Thou hast unstopped my ears to marvellous mysteries.
And yet I, a shape of clay kneaded in water,
a ground of shame and a source of pollution,
a melting-pot of wickedness and an edifice of sin,
a straying and perverted spirit of no understanding, fearful of righteous
    judgements,
what can I say that is not foreknown, and what can I utter that is not foretold?
All things are graven before Thee on a written Reminder for everlasting ages,
and for the numbered cycles of the eternal years in all their seasons;
they are not hidden or absent from Thee. (1QH 1)

The psalmist goes on to say that God has purified him of his sins and placed him
in the company of angels. Because of secret knowledge given him by God, he
represents the truth and so is ill-treated by sinners. "But to the elect of
righteousness Thou hast made me a banner, and a discerning interpreter of
wonderful mysteries" (1QH 2). Differing interpretations of Torah are at stake,
as is clear from the following: "To the interpreters of error I have been an
opponent, [but a man of peace] to all those who see truth" (1QH 2). Opponents
of the psalmist and his revealed message are considered to be anti-God and
partisans of Satan.

    Through knowledge of God's will and submission to it, the psalmist has been
saved from the lot of Satan and brought into the company of angels.

I thank Thee, O Lord,
    for Thou hast redeemed my soul from the Pit,
and from the hell of Abaddon
    Thou hast raised me up to everlasting height.
I walk on limitless level ground,
and I know there is hope for him
    whom Thou hast shaped from dust
    for the everlasting Council.
Thou hast cleansed a perverse spirit of great sin
    that it may stand with the host of the Holy Ones,
and that it may enter into community
    with the congregation of the Sons of Heaven. (1QH 3)

This passage is immediately followed with one that begins, "And yet I, a
creature of clay, what am I?" (1QH 3).

    The "seekers of smooth things" receive much criticism from the psalmist, for
they lead Israel astray regarding Torah.

And they, teachers of lies and seers of falsehood,
    have schemed against me a devilish scheme,

214

> to exchange the Law engraved on my heart by Thee
>> for the smooth things (which they speak) to Thy people.
> And they withhold from the thirsty the drink of Knowledge,
>> and assuage their thirst with vinegar,
> that they may gaze on their straying,
>> on their folly concerning their feast-days,
>> on their fall into their snares.
> But Thou, O God,
>> dost despise all Satan's designs;
> it is Thy purpose that shall be done
>> and the design of Thy heart
>> that shall be established for ever. (1QH 4)

The seekers of smooth things are teachers (probably Pharisees), and their teaching concerns the Torah, particularly the feast-days. The psalmist admits that they seek God, but he claims that "they seek Thee with a double heart and are not confirmed in Thy truth" (1QH 4).

The road of the psalmist, who is perhaps identical in this case with the Teacher of Righteousness, has not been easy. Not only has he faced fierce opposition from others in Israel; members of his own group have not always been faithful to him.

> But I have been [iniquity to] those who contend with me,
> dispute and quarreling to my friends,
> wrath to the members of my Covenant
> and murmuring and protest to all my companions.
> [All who have ea]ten my bread
>> have lifted their heel against me,[13]
> and all those joined to my Council
>> have mocked me with wicked lips.
> The members of my [Covenant] have rebelled
>> and have murmured round about me;
> they have gone as talebearers
>> before the children of mischief
>> concerning the mystery which Thou hast hidden in me.
>> (1QH 5)

God will not allow Satan to hold sway forever. There will be a great battle, and the unrighteous will fall.

> And then at the time of Judgement
> the Sword of God shall hasten,

and all the sons of His truth shall awake
  to [overthrow] wickedness;
all the sons of iniquity shall be no more.
The Hero shall bend his bow;
  the fortress shall open on to endless space
and the everlasting gates shall send out weapons of war. (1QH 6)

The teacher claims that he is the touchstone by which each one will be judged righteous or unrighteous. "For Thou wilt condemn in Judgement all those who assail me, distinguishing through me between the just and the wicked" (1QH 7). This recalls the idea that one will be saved through faith in the Teacher of Righteousness.

Something of the structure of the community is visible in column 14. Rank within one's category (priest, Levite, layperson) is determined by understanding of the Torah and by observance of it.

And thus do I bring into community
  all the men of my Council.
I will cause each man to draw near
  in accordance with his understanding,
and according to the greatness of his portion
  so will I love him. (1QH 14)

The prayer in column 16 shows how far the psalmist is from self-righteousness. Although he considers himself to have attained a high station in God's eyes, he deserves none of the credit.

And I know that man is not righteous
  except through Thee,
and therefore I implore Thee
  by the spirit which Thou hast given [me]
  to perfect Thy [favours] to Thy servant [for ever],
purifying me by Thy Holy Spirit,
  and drawing me near to Thee by Thy grace
  according to the abundance of Thy mercies.

CONCLUSION

The Qumran community was a sect—a religious group that opposed the religious establishment and the dominant religious culture. The people of Qumran withdrew to the shores of the Dead Sea and waited for the coming of the Lord. They made atonement for the land and prepared the Lord's way through perfect obedience to Torah as interpreted by their founder, the Teacher of

Righteousness, and the Zadokite priests who ran the community. Qumran's priestly orientation was expressed in its social structure, which was dominated by Zadokite priests, and in its theology and ritual, which stressed atonement and cleanness. Its world view was heavily influenced by apocalypticism, expressed in its expectation of an imminent final battle, its belief in esoteric revelation granted to its founder, and in the detailed belief in a supernatural world whose struggles between good and evil were reflected in the earthly realm. The Qumran library is extremely important for the information it contains about a concrete apocalyptic community of the late Second Temple period. Although the community's particular way of living out Judaism is quite different from that of the groups to be studied in the next chapters, it has many things in common with them, including a devotion to Torah, and a common cultural milieu in which it devised its ideas and social structures.

SELECT BIBLIOGRAPHY

Brown, Raymond. "The Messianism of Qumran," *CBQ* 19 (1957): 53-82.

Callaway, Phillip R. *The History of the Qumran Community: An Investigation.* Sheffield: Sheffield Academic Press, JSOT Press, 1988.

Charlesworth, James H. "The Original and Subsequent History of the Authors of the Dead Sea Scrolls: Four Transitional Phases Among the Qumran Essenes," *RevQ* 10 (1979–81): 213-33.

Collins, John J. "Patterns of Eschatology at Qumran," in *Traditions in Transformation,* B. Halpern and J. D. Levenson, eds. Winona Lake, Ind.: Eisenbrauns, 1981.

————. "Qumran," chap. 5 in *AI.*

Cross, Frank M. *The Ancient Library of Qumran,* rev. ed. Garden City, N.Y.: Doubleday, 1961.

Davies, Philip R. *Qumran,* Cities of the Biblical World Series. Guildford, Surrey: Lutterworth, 1982.

Fitzmyer, Joseph A. *The Dead Sea Scrolls: Major Publications and Tools for Study,* 2nd ed. Missoula, Mont.: Scholars Press, 1977.

Gärtner, Bertil. *The Temple and the Community in Qumran and the New Testament.* Cambridge: Cambridge University Press, 1965.

Knibb, Michael A. "The Exile in the Literature of the Intertestamental Period," *HeyJ* 17 (1976): 253-72.

Murphy-O'Connor, Jerome. "The Essenes and Their History," *RB* 81 (1974): 215-44.

Smith, Morton. "The Dead Sea Sect in Relation to Ancient Judaism," *NTS* 7 (1960–61): 347-60.

DeVaux, Roland. *Archeology and the Dead Sea Scrolls.* London: Oxford University Press, 1973.

Vermes, Geza. *The Dead Sea Scrolls in English,* 3rd ed. London: Penguin Books, 1987.

_____. *The Dead Sea Scrolls: Qumran in Perspective.* Philadelphia: Fortress Press, 1981.

Wilson, Bryan. *Magic and the Millennium: A Sociological Study of Religious Movements of Protest Among Tribal and Third-World Peoples.* London: Heinemann, 1973.

_____. *Patterns of Sectarianism: Organization and Ideology in Social and Religious Movements.* London: Heinemann, 1967.

Scribes, Pharisees, and Sadducees

Primary Readings: Matthew, Mark, Luke, John

This chapter investigates three groups familiar to readers of the New Testament—scribes, Pharisees, and Sadducees. That very familiarity can be problematic, since the New Testament does not give a balanced picture of the groups. Since some members of each group belonged to the Jewish council in Jerusalem, the Sanhedrin, that institution is treated at the end of the chapter.

SCRIBES

The Scribal Profession

"Scribe" is a diffuse term denoting an occupation based upon the knowledge of reading and writing.[1] Since the literacy rate was low in ancient times, the scribal function was crucial. Scribes did not constitute a coherent, organized group with a consistent point of view, and so were not a group like the Essenes, Pharisees, or Sadducees.

Scribes populated the bureaucracy at every level, from the royal court to the peasant village. Village scribes probably had little education, and performed functions such as writing out contracts. At a higher level, scribes were advisors to the ruler, took care of correspondence, and kept official records of all sorts—financial, military, and so forth. Scribes at the highest level may have been members of the ruling class. Most scribes were in the middle level of the bureaucracy. The English word that best conveys what "scribe" meant in ancient societies is probably "secretary." Secretaries exist at every level of every bureaucracy. Relatively few of them are at the highest level of government (there is but one Secretary of State, for example). Secretaries attain and keep their position because of their skills, but they are always subordinate to someone else. They are retainers, members of a class that exists to serve the governing class. There must have been mechanisms to train scribes. The highest scribes required extensive education, extending well beyond the ability to read and write. There were probably scribal schools.

There were also scribes within most Jewish groups. Pharisees who interpreted

Torah must have been scribes. Essene society, which was centered around Torah and its interpretation, needed scribes. The priestly establishment required many scribes. Hasmonean and Herodian rulers needed scribes. Scribes also wrote and copied apocalypses, including those critical of the Jerusalem establishment. Consequently, scribes had no single social or political viewpoint.

Jewish Writings

In Jewish writings, scribes are often associated with Torah, since Torah and attendant writings are the repository of Israel's legal and narrative traditions. Scribes were responsible for the writing, editing, preserving, and transmitting of sacred traditions, and so were involved in the production of the Bible itself. Likewise, the teaching of the Law must also have been a scribal activity. One of Israel's most famous scribes was Ezra, who brought the Torah from Persia to Judah around the turn of the fourth century BCE. "He was a scribe skilled in the law of Moses that the LORD the God of Israel had given" (Ezra 7:6). In rabbinic literature (literature created by rabbis beginning around 200 CE), the scribes are also not a coherent group. They often appear simply as copyists; however, they are also cited as legal experts. In those cases they are treated as ancient teachers whose rulings on legal matters are authoritative, but do not have the weight of Scripture.

Josephus, the first-century CE Jewish historian, confirms the notion that scribes occupied every level of the bureaucracy, and they do not appear as a single, organized group in his writings. He speaks of the "scribes of the Temple" as a recognizable group (*Ant.* 11.5.1 § 128; 12.3.3 § 142). In the war against the Romans (66–70 CE), many prominent citizens were executed by the rebels. Among these is a scribe: "After these a priest named Ananias, son of Masbalus, a person of distinction, and Aristeus, the secretary [scribe] of the council, a native of Emmaus, and along with them fifteen eminent men from among the people were executed" (*War* 5.13.1 § 532). Aristeus the scribe is included here among the most eminent men of the city, and so belongs to the upper classes.

The New Testament

Ancient Jewish scribes are perhaps most famous for their role in the New Testament. There they are portrayed as a unified group, almost unanimously opposed to Jesus (Mark 12:28-34 is an exception). The New Testament is not an unbiased source, however. Its main interest is in Jesus and how people reacted to him. It does not give a balanced, comprehensive account of Jewish society. Jewish leadership groups are lumped together with little regard for their interrelations and social functions. The New Testament does supply some good historical information about the scribes, but it must be used critically.

The gospels do concur with the other sources in associating scribes with Torah and with government. Saldarini summarizes the roles played by scribes in the gospels.

> The gospels testify most reliably to scribes connected to the government in Jerusalem where their role seems to be as associates of the priests both in judicial proceedings, enforcement of Jewish custom and law and ongoing business in the Sanhedrin. The gospel traditions about scribes may reflect the opposition of many scattered local officials to early Christian communities before and after the war, and perhaps opposition to Jesus also. (268)

PHARISEES

There are several common misconceptions about the Pharisees which derive from an uncritical reading of the New Testament. The first is that the Pharisees were all hypocrites. Historical research will never be able to prove or disprove this because such a judgment depends upon getting inside the minds and hearts of persons who lived two millennia ago. Nonetheless, it stretches the imagination to think that the thousands of members of a group whose difficult goal was to implement the Torah in their daily lives were each and every one of them hypocrites. That would be remarkable indeed. Second, many are under the impression that the Pharisees were the foremost political power in Palestine during the time of Jesus. That is not true. During the time of Jesus their influence was limited. Finally, it is very unlikely that the Pharisees brought about the death of Jesus.

There are three sources of information on the Pharisees: Josephus, the New Testament, and rabbinic documents. None of the three is an objective source of information. Josephus claims to be a Pharisee. The New Testament sees the Pharisees as opponents of Jesus. The rabbis see the Pharisees as their predecessors. None of the sources can claim to be disinterested, so each must be critically assessed.

Josephus

Although Josephus treats the Pharisees, Sadducees, and Essenes together in several places, the Essenes differed from the other two groups in that they had much less to do with Jerusalem politics and religious life. The Qumran branch of the movement separated itself entirely from the rest of Israel. The Qumran community also differed from the Pharisees and the Sadducees in that Qumran left an extensive library, including works by members of the group, whereas there is no extant work that can be traced with confidence to the Sadducees or

Pharisees. Information about Essenes and Sadducees is introduced in this section only if it contributes directly to the discussion of the Pharisees.

In both *War* and *Antiquities,* Josephus tries to use terms Hellenistic audiences understand. He presents Palestinian Jewish society as divided into three "sects"—Sadducees, Pharisees, and Essenes. The word "sect" is a misleading translation of the Greek word *hairesis* here. "Sect" denotes a religious minority that is in conscious opposition to the dominant religious establishment. *Hairesis* denotes a particular option or choice from among prevailing Hellenistic philosophies. The word "school" would be a better translation of *hairesis.* In the following passages the groups are defined in terms of their positions on philosophical problems understandable to Josephus' Hellenistic audience.

> The Pharisees, who are considered the most accurate interpreters of the laws, and hold the position of the leading sect, attribute everything to Fate and to God; they hold that to act rightly or otherwise rests, indeed, for the most part with men, but that in each action Fate co-operates. Every soul, they maintain, is imperishable, but the soul of the good alone passes into another body, while the souls of the wicked suffer eternal punishment. (*War* 2.8.14 §§ 162–63)

> As for the Pharisees, they say that certain events are the work of Fate, but not all; as to other events, it depends upon ourselves whether they shall take place or not. The sect of Essenes, however, declares that Fate is mistress of all things, and that nothing befalls men unless it be in accordance with her decree. But the Sadducees do away with Fate, holding that there is no such thing and that human actions are not achieved in accordance with her decree, but that all things lie within our own power, so that we ourselves are responsible for our well-being, while we suffer misfortune through our own thoughtlessness. (*Ant.* 13.5.9 §§ 172–73)

> They [Pharisees] follow the guidance of that which their doctrine has selected and transmitted as good, attaching the chief importance to the observance of those commandments which it has seen fit to dictate to them. They show respect and deference to their elders, nor do they rashly presume to contradict their proposals. Though they postulate that everything is brought about by fate, still they do not deprive the human will of the pursuit of what is in man's power, since it was in God's good pleasure that there should be a fusion and that the will of man with his virtue and vice should be admitted to the council-chamber of fate. They believe that souls have power to survive death and that there are rewards and punishments under the earth for those who have led lives of virtue or vice: eternal imprisonment is the lot of evil souls, while the good souls receive an easy passage to a new life. Because of these views they are, as a matter of fact, extremely influential among the townsfolk; and all prayers and sacred rites of divine worship are performed according to their exposition. This is the great tribute that the inhabitants of the cities, by practicing the highest ideals both in their way of living and in their discourse, have paid to the excellence of the Pharisees. . . .

Whenever [the Sadducees] assume some office, though they submit unwillingly and perforce, yet submit they do to the formulas of the Pharisees, since otherwise the masses would not tolerate them. (*Ant.* 18.1.3 §§ 12–15, 17)

The theme common to all three passages is that of fate. Hellenistic philosophers debated whether the gods were concerned with human history. Stoics defended the idea of God's providence (oversight of human affairs), and Epicureans denied it. Josephus claims belief in fate for the Pharisees, and he says in his *Life* 2 § 12 that they are like the Stoics.

Antiquities 13 divides the groups neatly between three alternatives: Essenes say that fate rules all, Sadducees deny fate, and Pharisees believe in a compromise between fate and free will. These positions could be translated into issues more familiar to Palestinian Judaism. When Josephus says that the Essenes see fate as "mistress of all things," he may have in mind the apocalyptic determinism of Qumran. The Sadducees, who Josephus says deny fate and believe in free will, are usually seen as resisting messianic hopes and apocalyptic expectations. Rewards and punishments are a matter for this life and are due to one's own actions. The Pharisees, who according to Josephus fall between the other two groups on this issue, might hold apocalyptic views and so be seen to believe in fate, but they defend each individual's freedom to range himself or herself on the side of God or of Satan. Josephus probably has resurrection in mind in *War 2* and *Antiquities* 18 when he says that the Pharisees believe in an afterlife. Belief in resurrection probably entered Judaism through the medium of apocalypticism.

In *War 2* Josephus credits the Pharisees with being "the most accurate interpreters of the laws." In *Antiquities* 18 this is rephrased: "They follow the guidance of that which their doctrine has selected and transmitted as good, attaching the chief importance to the observance of those commandments which it has seen fit to dictate to them." In an earlier chapter Josephus says, "The Pharisees had passed on to the people certain regulations handed down by former generations and not recorded in the Laws of Moses" (*Ant.* 13.10.6 § 297). At issue is Torah interpretation. The Pharisees built up a substantial body of tradition that was as binding for them as written Torah. This tradition probably corresponds to the later rabbinic idea of Oral Torah. For the rabbis, Oral Torah was an integral part of the Torah given to Moses on Sinai, but it was passed down orally through the generations.

Josephus' bias regarding the Pharisees apparently changed over time. He writes of them in both *The Jewish War* (ca. 75 CE) and *Jewish Antiquities* (ca. 94 CE). In the *Antiquities* the Pharisees are credited with more political clout than in the *War*. A possible reason for the change in Josephus' presentation is that in the nineties the Pharisees, who were an important contingent among those who became the rabbis, were in a position to rule Palestine for the Romans and were making a bid to do so. Josephus may have supported them in this bid and rewritten his descriptions of them to make the Romans see them as a potent political force and so qualified to rule. If this is correct, then where the two sources diverge, *War* has a greater claim to historicity, at least where the divergence involves increasing the power of the Pharisees in the later source.

In *Antiquities* 18.1.2-3 §§ 11–17 (*see* above), Josephus presents the Pharisees as all-influential. Their interpretation of the law prevails. But it is questionable whether the Pharisees really did control the masses, since in the years leading up to the Jewish revolt against Rome they play no role Josephus finds worth mentioning, nor do they appear as a group in the account of the revolt in *War*.

Suspicions of Josephus' bias are confirmed when the two accounts of their role in the reign of Alexandra Salome (76–67 BCE) are examined. In *War* 1.5.1-3 §§ 107–14, the earlier source, the account is as follows. When King Alexander Jannaeus died he left the kingdom to his wife, Alexandra Salome. Josephus says that she was "the very strictest observer of the national traditions and would deprive of office any offenders against the sacred laws." He goes on:

> Beside Alexandra, and growing as she grew, arose the Pharisees, a body of Jews with the reputation of excelling the rest of their nation in the observances of religion, and as exact exponents of the laws. To them, being herself intensely religious, she listened with too great deference; while they, gradually taking advantage of an ingenuous woman, became at length the real administrators of the state, at liberty to banish and to recall, to loose and to bind, whom they would. In short, the enjoyments of royal authority were theirs; its expenses and burthens fell to Alexandra. She proved, however, to be a wonderful administrator in larger affairs, and, by continual recruiting doubled her army, besides collecting a considerable body of foreign troops; so that she not only strengthened her own nation, but became a formidable foe to foreign potentates. But if she ruled the nation, the Pharisees ruled her.
>
> Thus they put to death Diogenes, a distinguished man who had been a friend of Alexander, accusing him of having advised the king to crucify his eight hundred victims. They further urged Alexandra to make away with the others who had instigated Alexander to punish those men; and as she from superstitious motives always gave way, they proceeded to kill whomsoever they would.
>
> (*War* 1.5.2-3 §§ 110–13)

During Alexandra's reign the Pharisees were influential, but they do not seem to have been in office. Josephus implies that Alexandra carried out their desires through administrators, even if the Pharisees were the "real" administrators. Josephus' distinction is between "real" and apparent administrators. The Pharisees were expert in the laws and fulfilled the laws zealously. But in other respects this is not a flattering portrait. They took advantage of a "superstitious" woman, who listened to them with "too great deference," and used their power to wreck vengeance on their enemies. Their vengeance sounds almost indiscriminate. But Josephus does not explain how a woman who was "a wonderful administrator in larger affairs," doubled her army, and earned the respect of neighboring rulers, could be deceived by the Pharisees. Here Josephus' bias interferes with his reporting, but his bias seems to be against the Pharisees.

Earlier in the passage Josephus gives the real reason for Alexandra's support among the people: "Alexander bequeathed the kingdom to his wife Alexandra, being convinced that the Jews would bow to her authority as they would to no other, because by her utter lack of his brutality and by her opposition to his crimes she had won the affections of the populace" (*War* 1.5.1 § 107).

Alexandra's support had nothing to do with the Pharisees. She did consult them because she followed the laws and knew the Pharisees to be expert in their interpretation. This is Pharisaic influence, not direct power.

The story is retold in *Antiquities* 13.15.5–16.3 §§ 399–418. The essential facts remain the same, but in *Antiquities* it is Alexander's death-bed idea to place the Pharisees in power. Alexander says that Alexandra

> should yield a certain amount of power to the Pharisees, for if they praised her in return for this sign of regard, they would dispose the nation favourably toward her. These men, he assured her, had so much influence with their fellow-Jews that they could injure those whom they hated and help those to whom they were friendly; for they had the complete confidence of the masses when they spoke harshly of any person, even when they did so out of envy; and he himself, he added, had come into conflict with the nation because these men had been badly treated by him.
>
> (*Ant.* 13.5.5 §§ 401–2)

Josephus now stresses the Pharisees' influence with the people, whereas in *War* he stresses their knowledge of the Torah. Alexandra brought in the Pharisees because her husband told her that they controlled the people and she could not rule without their support. Even here, however, what was probably the real reason for her support among the masses surfaces: "As for the queen herself, she was loved by the masses because she was thought to disapprove of the crimes committed by her husband" (*Ant.* 13.16.1 § 407).

The following incident occurred in the time of Herod the Great (37–4 BCE).

> There was also a group of Jews priding itself on its adherence to ancestral custom and claiming to observe the laws of which the Deity approves, and by these men, called Pharisees, the women (of the court) were ruled. These men were able to help the king greatly because of their foresight, and yet they were obviously intent upon combating and injuring him. At last when the whole Jewish people affirmed by an oath that it would be loyal to Caesar and to the king's government, these men, over six thousand in number, refused to take this oath, and when the king punished them with a fine, Pheroras' wife paid the fine for them. (*Ant.* 17.2.4 §§ 41–42)

The passage assumes that the Pharisees were not in power. Herod ruled. He merely wanted their support.

In *War* the first mention of the Pharisees is in the passage about Alexandra Salome. In *Antiquities* 13.10.5-6 §§ 288–98, they enter the narrative at an earlier point, during the reign of John Hyrcanus (ruled 134–104 BCE).

> As for Hyrcanus, the envy of the Jews was aroused against him by his own successes, and those of his sons; particularly hostile to him were the Pharisees, who are one of the Jewish schools, as we have related above. And so great is their influence with the masses that even when they speak against a king or high priest, they immediately gain credence. Hyrcanus too was a disciple of theirs, and was greatly loved by them.

In the space of a few words, Josephus says that the Pharisees were hostile to Hyrcanus, and that they loved him. As might be expected of this later work he stresses their influence with the people.

The story goes on to a banquet given by Hyrcanus at which a certain Eleazer tells Hyrcanus he should give up the high priesthood and be content with the kingship. A Sadducee named Jonathan, a close friend of the king, tells him that the Pharisees support Eleazar, and that the king will discover the truth of this claim if he asks them what penalty Eleazar deserves. The Pharisees recommend a relatively light punishment, as is their custom. Jonathan persuades Hyrcanus to regard this as approval of Eleazar's action. Jonathan "so worked upon him that he brought him to join the Sadducean party and desert the Pharisees, and to abrogate the regulations which they had established for the people, and punish those who observed them. Out of this, of course, grew the hatred of the masses for him and his sons." The passage concludes, "And so Hyrcanus quieted the outbreak, and lived happily thereafter; and when he died after administering the government excellently for thirty-one years, he left five sons." This last bit of information does not fit well with the idea that the people hated him because he no longer followed the Pharisees, and that it was impossible to rule without their support. Again, Josephus exaggerates the influence of the Pharisees, as is indicated by the contradictions in his reports. Whenever Josephus stresses the Pharisees' great power or influence, it contradicts other aspects of his stories.

Josephus' *Life* was written after *Antiquities*, probably around 100 CE. One would surmise, then, that it reflects Josephus' bias in favor of the Pharisees found in the latter work. Such bias is indeed present in his claims about his own youth in *Life* 2 §§ 10–12. He claims to have gained "personal experience" of all three schools: "So I submitted myself to hard training and laborious exercises and passed through the three courses." Then he went to the wilderness and apprenticed himself for three years to a figure named Bannus, who resembled John the Baptist. All this supposedly happened between the time he was sixteen and his nineteenth year. Such a scenario is impossible. Had he spent three years with Bannus he could not have trained "laboriously" in the three schools. The Essenes alone required a lengthy novitiate. Josephus aims to convince his audience of his firsthand knowledge of all other Jewish groups, and therefore of the reliability of his reports. His claim to intimate personal knowledge of the schools would make his choice of a school important to his readers. He says, "Being now in my nineteenth year I began to govern my life by the rules of the Pharisees, a sect having points of resemblance to that which the Greeks call the Stoic school." Now Josephus asserts that he himself was a Pharisee, a "fact" kept hidden in his earlier works. He probably styles himself a Pharisee as part of his effort to support their case to the Romans.

There are passages from *Life* describing a political role for some Pharisees in the war against the Romans (66–70 CE). Josephus was appointed general of the revolutionary forces in Galilee. His rival, John of Gischala, sent word to a certain Simon in Jerusalem to try to have Josephus removed.

> This Simon was a native of Jerusalem, of a very illustrious family, and of the sect of the Pharisees, who have the reputation of being unrivalled experts in their country's laws. A man highly gifted with intelligence and judgement, he could by sheer genius retrieve an unfortunate situation in the affairs of state. He was John's old and intimate friend, and, at the time, was at variance with me. On receiving this application he exerted himself to persuade the high-priests Ananus and Jesus, son of Gamalas, and some others of their party to clip my sprouting wings and not suffer me to mount to the pinnacle of fame. (*Life* 38 §§ 191–93)

Simon the Pharisee is not portrayed as a person in power in his own right. His importance rested upon his ability to persuade. His being a Pharisee meant only that he was expert in the Torah. He had to persuade those who really held power, the high priests and "their party."

> Then calling up John's brother he instructed him to send presents to Ananus and his friends, as a likely method of inducing them to change their minds. Indeed Simon eventually achieved his purpose; for, as the result of bribery, Anaus and his party agreed to expel me from Galilee. (*Life* 39 §§ 195–96)

Simon had no power either through some office he held or through his membership with the Pharisees. His task was to convince the high priests and their party. He failed even in this, so he resorted to bribery. The conclusion must be that the Pharisees did not have power as a group during the war, but individual Pharisees did have influence because of their intelligence, knowledge of the Law, wealthy family connections, or friends.

Such a conclusion is supported in Josephus' words about a delegation sent to Galilee to remove him from his command.

227

The scheme agreed upon was to send a deputation comprising persons of different classes of society but of equal standing in education. Two of them, Jonathan and Ananias, were from the lower ranks and adherents of the Pharisees; the third, Jozar, also a Pharisee, came of a priestly family; the youngest, Simon, was descended from the high priests. Their instructions were to approach the Galileans and ascertain the reason for their devotion to me. If they attributed it to my being a native of Jerusalem, they were to reply that so were all four of them; if to my expert knowledge of their laws, they should retort that neither were they ignorant of the customs of their fathers; if, again, they asserted that their affection was due to my priestly office, they should answer that two of them were likewise priests.

(*Life* 39 §§ 196–98)

The Pharisees dominated the delegation in terms of numbers, but it is not said that their being Pharisees would carry weight with the Galileans. The three reasons for the delegates' influence were their being from Jerusalem, knowing the laws, and being priests. One of the priests in the embassy was a Pharisee, but his influence was due to his knowledge of the Torah or priestly status. Josephus says that the delegation was composed of members from different social classes, and that two of the Pharisees were of the "lower ranks." Presumably this means of the lower ranks of the upper classes. They were perhaps retainers, those who served the ruling class proper. One of the priests is said to be a Pharisee, but the impression is given that he ranked lower than the priest who was of high priestly descent.

Josephus locates the main Pharisaic presence in Jerusalem. They are present in the courts of John Hyrcanus, Alexandra Salome, and Herod the Great. The Pharisee Simon, who was a friend of Josephus' rival John of Gischala, is a citizen of Jerusalem and is influential there. They are depicted as rivals of the Sadducees, a party located in Jerusalem. The Pharisees in the delegation to Galilee discussed above are explicitly said to be inhabitants of Jerusalem, and there is no indication that there is any Pharisaic influence in Galilee of which they can make use in their mission. Josephus leaves the impression that the Pharisees had little if any significant presence in Galilee.

In summary, Josephus represents the Pharisees as politically influential before the time of Herod, but after that time they had much less influence. After Herod's time there were Pharisees who were influential because of knowledge of the laws, wealth, family, social connections, or priesthood. But being a Pharisee was not equivalent to being in public office. Nonetheless, the Pharisees were always involved in politics in a wider sense.

Josephus consistently characterizes the Pharisees as knowing the Torah well and having a body of interpretation that was authoritative for them. Contrary to Josephus' claims in his later works that they held unique sway over the masses and that the Sadducees, kings, and high priests had to obey them, they held power only briefly and indirectly. They may have been a favored party in the early Hasmonean period, but in Hyrcanus' reign they were displaced by the Sadducees. They were influential under Alexandra Salome, but only for a short time, and their power was limited. Josephus gives no evidence that the Pharisees influenced events in the first century CE prior to the war. In his accounts of the war he gives them no role as a group, though prominent Pharisees are among the members of the provisional government in Jerusalem.

Josephus says that the Pharisees served both John Hyrcanus and Alexandra Salome as experts in Torah. The Pharisees who did so must have been scribes, and so belonged to the retainer class. But the Pharisees also were united by a specific way of interpreting Torah. They had an interest in and a program for society at large. They were a political interest group, ''a collectivity which seeks to convert its interests into public law or gain control over social behavior.''[2] Thus they were competitors with the Sadducees and other such political interest groups.

The New Testament

Many Christians take for granted the New Testament picture of the Pharisees as narrow-minded legalists, hypocrites, proud, lovers of money and of prestige, who opposed Jesus even to the extent of bringing about his death, simply because he preached a loving religion. Such a distorted view is reflected even in dictionaries. The following illustration, taken from the *Shorter Oxford English Dictionary,* is typical:

Pharisaic: Resembling the Pharisees in being strict in doctrine and ritual, without the spirit of piety; laying stress upon the outward show of religion and morality, and assuming superiority on that account; hypocritical; formal; self-righteous.

Pharisaism: The character and spirit of the Pharisees; hypocrisy; formalism; self-righteousness.

Pharisee. One of an ancient Jewish sect distinguished by their strict observance of the traditional and written law, and by their pretensions to superior sanctity. A person of this disposition; a self-righteous person; a formalist; a hypocrite.[3]

Such a vilifying view of an important Jewish group results from taking New Testament descriptions of Jews and Jewish society as historical fact, pure and simple, as if those descriptions were wholly unbiased. Using the New Testament in this way is not only naive, it is destructive to Judaism, as has been amply demonstrated over the past two thousand years.

Jesus left no written records. Others report what he said and did. One of the fruits of modern biblical scholarship is the realization that the writers of the

Gospels had their own viewpoints affecting the way they told the story of Jesus. A large majority of scholars think that Mark is the earliest, and that Matthew and Luke used it as a source. Matthew and Luke also used a source called "Q" consisting mostly of sayings of Jesus. Because of their closeness, these three gospels are called "the synoptics" from the Greek meaning "to see together." The material in the Gospel of John is for the most part independent of that in the first three.

Matthew harbors special animosity toward the Pharisees. This is clear through his frequent insertion of the word "Pharisee" in the gospel when it is absent from the source. An example is Matthew 12:22-36, which uses Mark 3:19-30 as a source. In the version in Mark, some scribes come down from Jerusalem when they hear that Jesus is performing exorcisms. Their judgment on his activities is: "He has Beelzebul, and by the ruler of the demons he casts out demons" (Mark 3:22). Matthew changes "scribes" to "Pharisees." Matthew is not content with this change in a story borrowed from Mark, but repeats the charge in 9:34: "But the Pharisees said, 'By the ruler of the demons he casts out the demons.'"

Another example of Matthew's antipathy toward the Pharisees appears in chapter 15. Its source is Mark 7. Mark's Jesus attacks the Pharisees for their purity rules. Matthew adds verses 12-14 to the passage:

> Then the disciples approached and said to him, "Do you know that the Pharisees took offense when they heard what you said?" He answered, "Every plant that my heavenly Father has not planted will be uprooted. Let them alone; they are blind guides of the blind. And if one blind person guides another, both will fall into a pit."

In this passage Matthew's Jesus denies the Pharisees any divine legitimation, for they are a plant not planted by the Father. The passage contradicts Matthew 23:2-3, where Jesus says that the Pharisees reliably interpret the divine will.

Matthew introduces his readers to his view of the Pharisees early in the gospel. He prefaces Jesus' ministry with an account of John the Baptist, as do the other evangelists. Mark says only that John preached repentance and claimed to be the precursor of another. In Matthew and Luke there is more of John's teaching. The latter two gospels share verses in which the Baptist accuses those who come to him of being a "brood of vipers." But in Luke 3:7 the accusation is aimed at "the crowds," whereas in Matthew 3:7 it is the "Pharisees and Sadducees" who are so accused.

One of Matthew's compositional techniques is to collect traditional sayings of Jesus and put them together into connected "sermons." For example, the Sermon on the Mount occurs only in Matthew 5-7, and it consists partly of material found scattered throughout the other gospels and partly of material unique to Matthew. The sermon in Matthew 23 is crafted as an attack on the "scribes and Pharisees," whom Matthew lumps together as a single group. However, scribes were a professional group, whereas Pharisees were not. The majority of scribes were not Pharisees, and it is unlikely that all Pharisees were scribes. Furthermore, Jesus' sayings against the scribes and Pharisees in Matthew 23 are directed against different groups in Mark and Luke. Luke does accuse the Pharisees of hypocrisy (11:39-41), excessive attention to legal details to the detriment of justice and love (11:42), and craving public recognition (11:43). However, Luke directs some of the other accusations not at the Pharisees but at lawyers. Again, lawyers and Pharisees were not identical. Lawyers were a professional class; Pharisees were not. For Luke, it is the lawyers who lay on others burdens that they themselves do not lift, who do not enter the kingdom or let others do so, and who murder those whom God sends to them (11:45-52). In Matthew 23, these accusations are made against the scribes and Pharisees, who are lumped together as the villains.

Perhaps the strongest statement of Matthew 23 is found in priestly terms in verses 27-28. "Woe to you, scribes and Pharisees, hypocrites! For you are like whitewashed tombs, which on the outside look beautiful, but inside they are full of the bones of the dead and of all kinds of filth. So you also on the outside look righteous to others, but inside you are full of hypocrisy and lawlessness." In the course of Matthew 23, Jesus accuses the scribes and Pharisees of doing religious deeds just to be seen by others, of not practicing what they preach, of laying on others burdens they themselves are unwilling to bear, of refusing to enter the kingdom of God and keeping others out as well by their teaching, of engaging in casuistry that mocks the Law of God, of attending to legal details and ignoring the larger demands of faith, justice, and mercy, and of being full of exhortation and rapacity. The chapter reaches a climax in the assertion that the Pharisees murder those whom God sends to them:

> Therefore I send you prophets, sages, and scribes, some of whom you will kill and crucify, and some you will flog in your synagogues and pursue from town to town, so that upon you may come all the righteous blood shed on earth, from the blood of righteous Abel to the blood of Zechariah son of Barachiah, whom you murdered between the sanctuary and the altar. (23:34-35)

The experience of Matthew's community is probably what is being depicted here, not Jesus' attitude toward the Pharisees. Matthew has Jesus speak of *future* acts of killing, blaming the scribes and Pharisees *in advance* for the death of Jesus and all Christian martyrs. Crucifixion here is inflicted on more than one, which makes it likely that the reference is both to Jesus' death and to that of later Christians. Scourging and persecution corresponds to what Jesus predicts for his followers in Matthew 10:17-20. The passage says that God sends prophets and scribes to the Jewish leaders, and in Matthew "prophet" (10:41) and "scribe"

231

(13:52) are titles for Christians. Here Matthew has Jesus say that the blood of all righteous men will fall upon the scribes and Pharisees, and "righteous" is a favorite term of Matthew for Christians (10:41; 5:20). The conclusion must be that Matthew 23 cannot be used uncritically for reconstructing what Jesus thought of the Pharisees, because the material has been reworked by Matthew and perhaps his predecessors in the transmission of the traditions, to address issues of a later time.

In the rewriting of traditions to address a later time, Matthew frequently makes the Pharisees look worse. The tendency to worsen the picture of the Pharisees is not peculiar to Matthew; Luke also adds several hostile references to them (5:17, 21; 7:39; 11:53; 14:3; 16:14; 18:10-14). The same holds for the Gospel of John, which outdoes even Matthew, Mark, and Luke in portraying the Pharisees as the chief enemies of Jesus. As years passed, Christian hostility to the Pharisees increased. Matthew and Luke (written ca. 85 CE) make them look worse than does Mark (ca. 70 CE), and John (probably written after the other three gospels) makes them look worst of all. When one asks why there is such increasing hostility to the Pharisees, a historical answer lies close at hand.

After the destruction of Jerusalem by the Romans in 70 CE, a group of Pharisees, scribes, and others gathered at Jamnia to restructure Jewish society in the absence of the Temple and its establishment. They confirmed the Torah as the center of the life of the Jewish people, and made Pharisaic interpretation normative for all. Torah teachers were now called rabbis. The budding Christian movement now faced not a multiplicity of groups, but a rabbinic Judaism that claimed that it alone was normative. This caused the Christians to define themselves over against rabbinic Judaism.

Many have seen the activity at Jamnia as the background against which to read the Gospel of Matthew. Matthew portrays Jesus as *the* authoritative Torah teacher (*see* chap. 12). Speaking of the scribes and Pharisees, Jewish interpreters of Torah, Jesus says in Matthew 23:6-10:

> They love to have the place of honor at banquets and the best seats in the synagogues, and to be greeted with respect in the marketplaces, and to have people call them rabbi. But you are not to be called rabbi, for you have one teacher, and you are all students. And call no one your father on earth, for you have one Father—the one in heaven. Nor are you to be called instructors, for you have one instructor, the Messiah.

The term "rabbi" probably did not come into general usage until after the destruction of Jerusalem in 70 CE. These verses are probably a Christian attack on rabbinic authority originating after 70 CE, an attack which pits the authority of Jesus Christ, the Torah teacher, against that of the rabbis.

Both the Jewish community at Jamnia and Matthew's community were defining their own identities. Each claimed to embody the true interpretation of Torah. The stage was set for conflict, and it is probably largely this conflict that is reflected in the pages of Matthew more than the conflict between Jesus and the Pharisees. The same can be said of Luke and John. It is especially apparent in John, where the Pharisees assume a degree of power and authority they did not have before 70 CE.

It has been shown that Christian antipathy toward Pharisees (now rabbis) got worse as the first century progressed. Yet even Mark, written earlier than the other three gospels, does not supply an accurate picture of the Pharisees. It has a tendency to cast the Pharisees in the role of the chief opponents of Jesus. For example, in Mark 2 Jesus and his disciples are still in Galilee. One of the stories of the chapter begins in the following way: "One sabbath he was going through the grainfields; and as they made their way his disciples began to pluck heads of grain. The Pharisees said to him, 'Look, why are they doing what is not lawful on the sabbath?'" (Mark 2:23-24). Although it is not unlikely that Jesus and Pharisees clashed over sabbath observance, it is hardly likely that the Pharisees accompanied him on sabbath walks through Galilean grainfields. The narrative was composed to furnish a setting for the sayings of Jesus that follow. Once it was assumed by the early Christians that Pharisees were Jesus' primary opponents, it became natural to transform them to act in a conventional narrative role. Such a process is also at work in Mark 8:15, 12:13-17, 10:2-9, and elsewhere.

If there was an increasingly anti-Pharisaic tendency that informed Christian traditions as early as Mark, then such a tendency existed even before the rabbis at Jamnia began to be influential. The Pharisees' rise to power at Jamnia cannot be blamed for the tendency, only for its aggravation. There is no reason to deny the earliest anti-Pharisaic stories some foundation in the life of Jesus. That Jesus spent a great deal of his time opposing the Pharisees is probably a misconception. That he never encountered them is unlikely. The truth lies somewhere between the two alternatives (*see* chap. 11).

None of the synoptic gospels claims that the Pharisees played an active role in the death of Jesus. The elders, priests, and scribes of Jerusalem are the ones who turn Jesus over to the Romans, and the Romans kill him. John brings the Pharisees closer to the passion by stating that Judas obtained officers to arrest Jesus from the "chief priests and the Pharisees" (John 18:3), but even John lays ultimate blame for the death of Jesus on the chief priest. In view of the antipathy of the Christian tradition toward the Pharisees, it is striking that they do not figure in the passion and death. If they had played a role, later Christians would not have ignored it. Others were responsible for Jesus' death, not the Pharisees. As will be seen in chapter 11, Jesus would hardly have been executed for the kinds of issues about which he clashed with Pharisees.

Another reason to question the dominance of the Pharisees in the career of

Jesus concerns their sphere of influence. Josephus locates the Pharisees in Jerusalem. They go to Galilee as outsiders. That picture conforms with the idea that the Pharisees were retainers of the Jerusalem establishment, an idea that arises from Josephus' narrative. Galilee was under the rule of Herod Antipas, and the Herodians were traditionally not supported by the Pharisees, nor did the Pharisees seem to work for them. As will become clear, Josephus' depiction also accords with the rabbinic idea that the Pharisees were not influential in Galilee. Yet the gospels locate the Pharisees primarily in Galilee. It is there that Jesus has most of his confrontations with them. It may be going too far to deny the stories of Jesus' Galilean clashes with the Pharisees any basis in fact, since there may have been some Pharisees in Galilee. Nonetheless, that was not their sphere of influence, and the gospel stories that contain those clashes are stylized and questionable from a historical point of view.

The Pharisees in the New Testament are pictured as being very concerned about Torah, its interpretation and application. Their concern for the Torah centers on sabbath observance, and on rules relating to table fellowship—tithing, ritual purity, and rules about with whom one may eat. The Pharisees of the gospels attack Jesus and his followers for working on the sabbath. When the disciples pluck grain on the sabbath, the Pharisees criticize them for working on the holy day (Mark 2:23-28; Matt 12:1-8; Luke 6:1-5). There are two instances in the synoptic gospels (Mark 3:1-6 and parallels; Luke 13:10-17) and two in John (5:2-18; 9:1-14; cf. 7:21-24) where Jesus clashes with the Pharisees over whether it is lawful to heal on the sabbath. According to the gospels, the position of the Pharisees is that such healing is not permitted. (Rabbinic literature shows that most Pharisees did permit healing on the sabbath, at least when the person's life was in danger.)

The other disputes between Jesus and the Pharisees concern table fellowship. In Mark 7:1-23 (paralleled in Matt 15:1-20; *see also* Matt 23:25-26), the Pharisees "and all the Jews" (this last is doubtful) have purification procedures for their hands, cups, pots, and bronze vessels before eating. If such rules were followed strictly, then it would have been impossible for Pharisees to eat with those who did not follow such rules. Other eating rules in dispute between Jesus and the Pharisees concern tithing (but Jesus does not take issue with their strict practice: Matt 23:23-24), and fasting (Mark 2:18-22; paralleled in Matt 9:14-17 and Luke 5:33-39). A final issue raised only in Matthew 23:16-22 concerns rules about swearing on sacred things.

What emerges from this brief survey is that the Pharisees as viewed by the New Testament had a narrow range of interests. Sabbath observance and eating in the proper state of purity are most important. However, this characterization should not lead to denying the Pharisees' political interests. Purity rules structure society, and so are political. Further, the Pharisaic claim to interpret the Torah accurately was both a political as well as a religious claim.

Josephus testifies to Pharisaic belief in an afterlife. That testimony is confirmed by the New Testament. In the context of Paul's trial before the Jewish Sanhedrin, it is said: "The Sadducees say that there is no resurrection, or angel, or spirit; but the Pharisees acknowledge all three" (Acts 23:6-8).

There are a few references to the Pharisees in the New Testament that are not negative. In Matthew, 23:2-3, seen above, Jesus portrays them as reliable interpreters of Torah. In Luke 13:31, they are allied with Jesus against Herod. They side with Paul against the Sadducees in Acts 23 on the issue of resurrection. In Acts 15:5 there are Pharisaic Christians. The historical value of these references can be debated, but there was certainly one Pharisee who did become a Christian—the apostle Paul (Phil 3:5). In Acts 5:33-42 Gamaliel, a Pharisaic member of the Sanhedrin, counsels that body to leave the Christian movement alone, lest they interfere with what might be the work of God. Gamaliel is characterized as a "teacher of the law." The passage is evidence for the presence of some Pharisees among the ruling class.

As in Josephus, the Pharisees in the New Testament are Torah experts, which makes it likely that many of them were scribes, but their interpretation of Torah sets them apart from others. They are anxious to have all of Israel obey their interpretation of Torah. Although they are interested in political power, there is no reliable evidence in the New Testament for assigning them official power. They seem to influence those who do hold power, and some Pharisees are found in the upper echelons of Jewish society. Such a picture makes it likely that the majority of Pharisees belonged to the retainer class. Pharisaic interests center on tithing, sabbath observance, table-fellowship, and purity. It is likely that they would clash with Jesus on those issues, but such clashes are exaggerated in the New Testament because of later tensions between the emerging Christian and rabbinic movements.

Rabbinic Traditions

The Pharisees were the predecessors of the rabbis, so information about the Pharisees is preserved in the rabbinic corpus. Rabbinic material relevant to this topic consists of the Mishnah, whose written form dates to about 200 CE but contains older materials; the Tosephta, a collection of traditions supplementary to the Mishnah and put into writing about 250 CE, and the two Talmuds, the Palestinian (400–450 CE) and the Babylonian (500–600 CE), which are commentaries on the Mishnah. These dates suggest a problem in using the sources for historiography. The earliest of the sources appeared at least a century after the destruction of Jerusalem by the Romans. Most material in the sources was handed down orally before being written down, and the stories and legal traditions were altered in the course of their transmission. Furthermore, the material was generated, preserved, and transmitted to fashion and convey a world view, not for the purpose of recording history. Thus the rabbinic sources must be used with caution.

The word *pĕrûŝîm* or *pĕrîŝîn* is the word in rabbinic literature that lies behind the word "Pharisee." Not all occurrences of the word can mean "Pharisee," however. The rabbinic word simply means "separated ones" or "separatists" and is used for various individuals and groups, some clearly not the Pharisees. Neusner limits his investigation to traditions about people who definitely were pre–70 CE Pharisees.[4] He finds 371 separate Pharisaic traditions contained in 655 passages (some traditions occur in more than one passage). Of these, 280 traditions in 462 passages concern a Pharisee named Hillel, and people associated with Hillel, especially Shammai and the houses of Hillel and Shammai. This accounts for 75 percent of the total number of traditions about pre–70 CE Pharisees. Hillel is obviously a dominant figure for the rabbis, and it is likely that he played a crucial role in the Pharisaic movement. He came to Judea from Babylonia, and his school of Torah interpretation, which is depicted as a rival of another important Pharisaic school, the school of Shammai, became the dominant one.

"Most of the nearly 700 pericopae pertaining to pre–70 Pharisees concern legal matters, and the largest number of these pertain to, first, agricultural tithes, offerings, and other taboos, and, second, rules of ritual purity—that is, sectarian interests."[5] A "pericope" is a short unit of tradition. By "sectarian" is meant that which set the Pharisees apart from other Jews. What set the Pharisees apart from other Jews was primarily the principle that purity rules previously applicable only to Temple priests now applied to all Israel, specifically in the area of meals. The implication was that the table was analogous to the altar, and that all Jews were priests. The entire people, or at least that portion of the people that followed Pharisaic purity rules, were the dwelling place of God. This laid the theoretical groundwork for a Judaism without a Temple, although there is no reason to believe that the Pharisees were against the Temple as such. The Pharisaic emphasis on tithing should probably be seen as related to table purity. Tithes applied primarily to agricultural products that composed the bulk of what was eaten in Palestine. Tithing rules thus affected table-fellowship. To eat untithed food would be to violate Torah at one's table.

Pharisees do not seem to have had ritual meals at which they celebrated their community and difference from other groups. They had no analogue to the Christian eucharist or to the Qumran messianic meal. Sanctification, making holy, was now a category that applied not just to cultic acts but to every meal in the home. Every meal became a living reminder of God's presence in the midst of the people.

The name perushim ("separatists") may originally have been a negative appellation conferred by outsiders on the Pharisees, but was later adopted by them as an appropriate title. "Holiness" meant being acceptable to God because of separation from anything unpleasing to God, and therefore being able to participate in the cult. In the course of separating themselves from anything ritually impure, the Pharisees separated themselves from portions of their own society. Pharisaic interpretation of Torah set them apart from other Jews, but they are pictured as wanting at least some of their interpretations to apply to society at large, which means that they were interested in politics. In rabbinic literature, the Pharisees and Sadducees are seen as rivals, as they were in Josephus' story of John Hyrcanus' banquet. That rivalry concerns ritual purity in rabbinic traditions, but as has been stated before, purity laws had political consequences. The rivalry with the Sadducees makes it likely that the Pharisees were present in Jerusalem. Rabbinic tradition implies that Pharisaic interpretation of Torah was not influential in Galilee, an implication that accords with Josephus' presentation.

In summary, rabbinic documents depict the Pharisees as a table-fellowship group. Rules surrounding their meals were what set them apart from others. This setting apart was for the purpose of being holy, so that they could be open to the presence of God among them. Such behavior had social, political, and economic consequences, and was not merely "religious" in the modern sense. In particular, opposition depicted in rabbinic literature between Pharisees and Sadducees over ritual matters had political overtones. Pharisaic influence seems to have been strongest in Jerusalem. Rabbinic literature offers little support for the idea that Pharisees were very influential in Galilee.

Results

Because Josephus, the New Testament, and the rabbinic traditions have varied interests, they present different aspects of the Pharisees. Josephus stresses their relation to the politics of Palestine, the New Testament focuses on their opposition to Jesus, and rabbinic literature preserves material relevant to its own world view. The Pharisees are first mentioned in connection with the rule of the Hasmonean John Hyrcanus. Given the consistent emphasis on devotion to Torah stressed by all the sources, it is plausible that their original program involved a revival of Torah observance to counter the problems raised by the Hellenistic reform, and later the Hasmonean rule. The Pharisees wanted to structure Judaism according to a strict interpretation of Torah. This made the Pharisees a political interest group.

The Pharisees had less influence under Herod the Great, but Herod was unwilling or unable to stamp them out. The Pharisees do not seem to have been politically powerful in the first century CE, although they were somewhat influential. A few may have been members of the ruling class. When other groups lost their power bases or saw them eroded because of the Roman war, the Pharisees, who were experts in Torah and had been devising a consistent interpretation of it, were ready to rebuild Judaism according to their own definition. Their views always had political implications, but now they were able to make those implications a reality. When they were out of power, their interpretations and practices allowed them to maintain their identity and resist assimilation to society at large. Once they gained power, they had a program ready.

Certain features of postexilic Israel explain why the Pharisees concentrated on sabbath observance and table-fellowship. The sabbath set the Jews apart from others. Although it may well have been important before the Exile, it became even more so during the Exile and the Second Temple period. During the Exile the Jews no longer had a Temple and a land of their own. In the absence of a symbolic center that was geographical and architectural, they emphasized one that was "portable" and temporal. The sacred time, the sabbath, assumed more importance because the sacred place, the Temple, no longer existed. Similarly, the Torah assumed a new importance in postexilic Judaism, and took on the form of a book. The Torah was central to Pharisaic thought and practice, as it was for other Jewish groups. The existence of the written Torah made it possible for the Pharisees to evolve their own interpretations of Torah, potentially independent of those of the priests.

The Pharisees were concerned about ritual purity. In priestly religion, priests declared what was clean and unclean, that is, what was acceptable to God and what was not. By the use of purity rules, boundaries were drawn not only between Jews and Gentiles, but also between Jews and Jews. Degrees of purity determined degrees of access to God. Those with most access were the important members of society, and that corresponded with power, influence, and wealth. Contact between classes was limited, which meant that the social structure was less apt to break down. Thus, by declaring what was clean and unclean the priests were potentially in control of society. Although primarily lay-people, Pharisees made oral rulings that applied and reinterpreted Torah. They thus arrogated to themselves influence (and potentially power) that within a priestly world view belonged properly to the priests and their scribes. Their authority came not from heredity, or from being in charge of the Temple, but from an accurate knowledge of and adherence to Torah. The power of the priests was challenged not only by the Pharisees' claim to interpret Torah authoritatively, but also because according to the redefined purity rules the holiest ones of the community were no longer necessarily the priests. Rather, holiness was determined by Pharisaic purity rules. The groundwork was laid for the post–70 CE period when Torah scholars became dominant in Judaism.

The social location of the Pharisees is unclear. Being a Pharisee was not a profession, it was a particular way of living out being Jewish. The question arises about how the Pharisees made their living. There were some Pharisaic priests, and there were Pharisaic members of the ruling class. They seem to have been the exceptions. Most Pharisees occupied a position in society subordinate to the ruling class, but superior to the lower classes (peasants, artisans, et al.). If Pharisees were expert in the Law, many of them must have been scribes (*see* Mark 2:16 and parallels). If this is so, then they would have been in the employ of the priestly establishment. Saldarini suggests the following:

> Though some Pharisees were part of the governing class, most Pharisees were subordinate officials, bureaucrats, judges and educators. They are best understood as retainers who were literate servants of the governing class and had a program for Jewish society and influence with the people and their patrons. When the opportunity arose, they sought power over society. (284)

The recognition that Pharisees were scribes, judges, teachers, and priests leads to three general observations about groups. (1) Groups are not mutually exclusive. Individuals may belong to more than one group simultaneously. The Pharisees cut across more than one social class, and more than one profession. (2) Groups change over time. The Pharisees under the Hasmoneans may not look exactly like the Pharisees in the first century CE. (3) Groups can have several functions. The Pharisees could be both a religious fellowship and a political interest group.[6]

SADDUCEES

Josephus, the New Testament, and rabbinic literature all speak of the Sadducees, but very little is really known about them. All three sources contrast the Sadducees and the Pharisees. In rabbinic literature, ritual purity and sabbath observance are debated by the two groups. The rabbis supply little information for reconstructing Sadducean organization or beliefs. The only two solidly established traits of the Sadducees are that they were members of the ruling class, and that they did not believe in resurrection. Josephus and the New Testament agree on those facts. Further, if the Sadducees were members of the ruling class, they could not have been a sect, a minority group that stands in conscious opposition to the establishment.

Josephus

The Sadducees are first mentioned in the passage about John Hyrcanus discussed in the section above (*Ant.* 13.10.5-6 §§ 288–98). The passage is also the first to mention the Pharisees. Josephus says that John Hyrcanus was a disciple of the Pharisees and followed their interpretation of Torah. The Sadducees persuaded Hyrcanus to turn against the Pharisees and adopt them as advisors. The passage portrays both associations as political interest groups seeking influence with the king. Both groups retained their interest in politics until the fall of the Second Temple.

Josephus gives four descriptions of the Sadducees. The following passage contrasts them with the Pharisees.

> The Pharisees had passed on to the people certain regulations handed down by former generations and not recorded in the Laws of Moses, for which reason they are rejected by the Sadducean group, who hold that only those regulations should be considered valid which were written down (in Scripture), and that those which had been handed down by former generations need not be observed. And concerning these matters the two parties came to have controversies and serious differences, the Sadducees having the confidence of the wealthy alone but no following among the populace, while the Pharisees have the support of the masses.
>
> (*Ant.* 13.10.6 §§ 297–98)

The Sadducees did not accept traditional Pharisaic legal rulings. They accepted as authoritative only written traditions, presumably written down in Torah. Of course, the Sadducees would have had to interpret and apply Torah, but their interpretations were probably less far-reaching and innovative than those of the Pharisees. That conservative tendency would not be surprising if they were associated with the ruling class. Pharisaic rulings applied Torah to everyday life, including parts of Torah previously applied only to priests. Their "democratizing" of the cult might explain Josephus' claim that they were supported by the masses. Most accept Josephus' claim that the Sadducees were supported by the wealthy, which makes it more than likely that they were associated with the ruling class, but not coterminous with it.

Josephus' other three passages discuss the Pharisees, Sadducees, and Essenes in ways comprehensible to a Hellenistic audience. The model is that of philosophical schools with set doctrines.

> The Sadducees hold that the soul perishes along with the body. They own no observance of any sort apart from the laws; in fact, they reckon it a virtue to dispute with the teachers of the path of wisdom that they pursue. There are but few men to whom this doctrine has been made known, but these are men of the highest standing. (*Ant.* 18.1.4 §§ 16–17)

The Sadducees did not have a body of authoritative interpretation to which they were bound in the same way as did the Pharisees, which might explain their readiness to argue. Their arguments were between members of the ruling elite ("men of highest standing"). Josephus' mention of the immortality of the soul might be conceived of in a Palestinian setting as a disagreement over resurrection of the dead. His connection of lack of belief in an afterlife and insistence on written Torah might mean that the Sadducees rejected the idea of resurrection because it was not in written Torah.

> The Sadducees, the second of the orders, do away with Fate altogether, and remove God beyond, not merely the commission, but the very sight, of evil. They maintain that man has the free choice of good or evil, and that it rests with each man's will whether he follows the one or the other. As for the persistence of the soul after death, penalties in the underworld, and rewards, they will have none of them. The Pharisees are affectionate to one another and cultivate harmonious relations with the community. The Sadducees, on the contrary, are, even among themselves, rather boorish in their behaviour, and in their intercourse with their peers are as rude as to aliens. (*War* 2.8.14 §§ 164–66)

> But the Sadducees do away with Fate, holding that there is no such thing and that human actions are not achieved in accordance with her decree, but that all things lie within our own power, so that we ourselves are responsible for our well-being, while we suffer misfortune through our own thoughtlessness. (*Ant.* 13.5.9 § 173)

The Sadducees did not believe in the afterlife. The discussion of Fate should probably be read as a dispute about apocalyptic determinism. That the Sadducees did not accept apocalypticism would not be surprising if they were members of the ruling class. They had a stake in maintaining the status quo, and they would not subscribe to a world view that saw the present state of things as being determined by Satan. If the Sadducees were closely associated with the priestly aristocracy, then Josephus' claim that they remove God beyond the very sight of evil would correspond to priestly concerns with ritual purity. Support of the priestly system does not imply that the Sadducees were actually priests, however.

The New Testament

The New Testament picture of the Sadducees agrees with that of Josephus. The following passage contrasts them with the Pharisees. Paul is on trial before the Sanhedrin.

> When Paul noticed that some were Sadducees and others were Pharisees, he called out in the council, "Brothers, I am a Pharisee, a son of Pharisees. I am on trial concerning the hope of the resurrection of the dead." When he said this, a dissension began between the Pharisees and the Sadducees, and the assembly was divided. (The Sadducees say that there is no resurrection, or angel, or spirit; but the Pharisees acknowledge all three.) (Acts 23:6-8)

The Torah says little about angels and spirits, but apocalyptic literature is full of them. Josephus hints that the Sadducees did not believe in resurrection because it was not in Torah. Their reluctance to believe in a universe populated with spirits might have the same basis. Incidentally, this passage shows that its author thought of the Pharisees and Sadducees as being important in the Sanhedrin, the Jewish council at Jerusalem, to be discussed below.

In Acts 4:1 and 5:17, the Sadducees are associated with, but not identical to, the chief priests and the captain of the Temple. That agrees with Josephus's claim that they were supported by the ruling class. The only time the Sadducees appear in the gospels of Mark and Luke, it is in a controversy over resurrection (Mark 12:18; Luke 20:27). The Sadducees try to persuade Jesus that belief in resurrection is unreasonable, but Jesus refutes them. The Gospel of Matthew pictures the Sadducees in league with the Pharisees against Jesus. The alliance is suspect because only Matthew mentions it. In Acts, Josephus, and rabbinic literature the Sadducees and Pharisees are rivals.

Rabbinic Traditions

Rabbinic literature gives little information about the Sadducees, save that they are rivals of the Pharisees. The two groups argue about purity regulations. Rabbinic traditions are negative toward the Sadducees, which makes sense if the rabbinic movement was dominated by Pharisees.

Results

The Sadducees were a small segment of the ruling class. Not all members of the ruling class were Sadducees. The Sadducees existed at least from the second half of the second century BCE to the destruction of Jerusalem in 70 CE. They are associated with the chief priests in several contexts, and Josephus says that Ananus the high priest was a Sadducee. They were a political interest group who were often rivals to the Pharisees, but the two groups worked together in the Sanhedrin. During Roman rule they probably shared the view of a large portion of the ruling class that Jews should accept the degree of autonomy granted by Rome, and not strive for national independence. The Sadducees were not a sect, because they were part of the establishment.

SANHEDRIN

"Sanhedrin" denotes the aristocratic council of Jerusalem. It derives from the Greek word *synedrion,* meaning "council." Evidence of an aristocratic council, probably the prototype of the Sanhedrin, first emerges in the Greek period. It is mentioned in a letter of Antiochus III (223–187 BCE) under the title *gerousia,* which means a "council of elders" (*see Ant.* 12.3.3 § 138). The *gerousia* is mentioned several times in the books of the Maccabees. There is evidence that the council continued throughout Hasmonean times, although its precise function and status must have depended on the Hasmoneans to some degree. Herod the Great repressed the Jewish aristocracy, so it is unlikely that the council had independent authority during his rule (37–4 BCE). In the first century, the Romans used the Sanhedrin to help administer Judea.

Josephus

Josephus uses the term *synedrion* freely. He applies it to both Jewish and Roman councils, often in the sense of the court of a ruler. He follows Hellenistic use of the term as a variety of councils—political, military, economic, and private.

The New Testament

The Sanhedrin appears in the gospels in connection with the trial of Jesus. The gospels are not concerned to define the Sanhedrin. Their purpose is to demonstrate that the Jewish establishment as a whole opposed Jesus. Mark 14 narrates the capture of Jesus in the Garden of Gethsemane. After capture, "They took Jesus to the high priest; and all the chief priests, the elders, and the scribes were assembled. . . . Now the chief priests and the whole council [Sanhedrin] were looking for testimony against Jesus to put him to death; but they found none" (Mark 14:53, 55). This passage assumes that the Sanhedrin is the principal judicial body in Jerusalem. The high priest is foremost in authority, and throughout the scene he is in charge. The "chief priests" are the leading priests in Jerusalem, perhaps belonging to the families from which the high priest was usually chosen, along with some other prominent families. The "elders" are the prominent citizens, probably where the oldest male was the head of the family. In view of the discussion of scribes above, it is no surprise that they are in the Sanhedrin. The Gospel of John includes Pharisees in the Sanhedrin as it deliberated about Jesus, but one must remember that John intends to increase the presence and power of the Pharisees where possible (John 11:45-53).

In Acts 4 the captain of the Temple and the Sadducees happen upon Peter and John preaching about Jesus in the Temple. Peter and John are brought before the Sanhedrin to be judged: "The next day their rulers, elders, and scribes assembled in Jerusalem, with Annas the high priest, Caiaphas, John, and Alexander, and all who were of the high-priestly family" (4:5-6; *see* 4:15). Here the Sanhedrin consists of rulers, elders, scribes, the high priest, and the high priestly family. They have the authority to judge Peter and John on a matter that is both religious and political, their preaching of Jesus. In Acts 5:34, Gamaliel, a Pharisee and a teacher of Torah, is a member of the Sanhedrin. In Acts 23, both Pharisees and Sadducees are in the Sanhedrin, and Paul pits one against the other on the issue of resurrection from the dead.

Rabbinic Traditions

The rabbis normally use the Hebrew term *bêt dîn*, "house of judgment," for the Sanhedrin. According to them, there was a great Sanhedrin with seventy-one members that met in the Temple, three courts with twenty-three members, and other courts with three members. Their function was to judge and to make legal rulings. Rabbinic sources speak of the Sanhedrin as composed of religious scholars. Because Josephus and the New Testament use the term more widely, assigning judicial and political functions to the council, some scholars have posited two Sanhedrins, one political and one religious. Such a division between politics and religion is highly doubtful. The different functions emphasized by different sources probably reflect the divergent interests of the sources. The ancient Jews did not make such neat distinctions between politics and religion.

Results

The evidence for reconstructing the nature of the Sanhedrin is scarce. Josephus uses the term flexibly, the New Testament evidence is affected by its own agenda, and the rabbinic evidence is questionable because of its date and nature. However, all three sources attest to the existence of a ruling council in Jerusalem. The existence of such a body is likely because the Romans often ruled local areas through aristocratic councils.

CONCLUSION

This chapter has investigated three groups who were important in Jewish Palestine of the late Second Temple period. The scribes were a professional group, and were found within most Jewish groups, and in most strata of society. The Pharisees and Sadducees were political interest groups with specific stands toward Torah and programs for Jewish society, and are often presented as rivals. The Pharisees were probably of the retainer class. Many of them may have been scribes. Their origins may lie in the desire to structure Jewish society according to strict interpretations of Torah, under circumstances of the Hellenization of Palestine. They probably did not hold direct political power before the destruction of Jerusalem in 70 CE, but they were influential because of their knowledge of and adherence to Torah, and because some of the ruling class were of their number. The Sadducees were a faction of the ruling class of Jerusalem. It is likely that some of them were upper-class priests. As a party they were associated with the religio-political establishment centered on the Temple and the Sanhedrin. The Sanhedrin was the aristocratic council of Jerusalem, and included Pharisees, Sadducees, upper-class scribes, and elders (probably rich landowners). Its power varied with political circumstances; it was weak under Herod, yet under direct Roman rule in the first century CE, its power increased because of the Roman policy of depending on local aristocrats to rule subject areas.

SELECT BIBLIOGRAPHY

This chapter depends primarily on Neusner and Saldarini.

Black, Matthew. "Pharisees," in *IDB* 3, 774-81.

Bowker, John. *Jesus and the Pharisees*. Cambridge: Cambridge University Press, 1973.

Cook, Michael J. *Mark's Treatment of the Jewish Leaders*. Leiden: Brill, 1978.

Finkelstein, Louis. *The Pharisees: The Sociological Background of Their Faith*, 3rd. ed. Philadelphia: Jewish Publication Society, 1966.

Gowan, Donald. "The Sadducees" and "The Pharisees," in *BBT*, 139-55.

Lightstone, Jack. "Sadducees *Versus* Pharisees: The Tannaitic Sources," in vol. 3, ed. Jacob Neusner, *Christianity, Judaism, and Other Greco-Roman Cults: Studies for Morton Smith at 60*. Leiden: Brill, 1973, 206-17.

Neusner, Jacob. *From Politics to Piety: The Emergence of Rabbinic Judaism*, 2nd. ed. New York: Ktav, 1979.

––––––. *The Rabbinic Traditions About the Pharisees Before 70*, 3 vols. Leiden: Brill, 1971.

Parsons, Talcott. *Politics and Social Structure*. New York: Free Press, 1969.

Porton, Gary G. "Diversity in Postbiblical Judaism," in *EJMI*, 57-80.

Rivkin, Ellis. *The Hidden Revolution*. Nashville: Abingdon, 1978.

Saldarini, Anthony J. *Pharisees, Scribes, and Sadducees in Palestinian Society: A Sociological Approach*. Wilmington, Del.: Michael Glazier, 1988.

Schürer, Emil. "Torah Scholarship" and "Pharisees and Sadducees," in *HJPAJC* 2, 314-414.

Smith, Morton. "Palestinian Judaism in the First Century," in *Israel: Its Role in Civilization*. ed. Moshe Davis. New York: Jewish Theological Seminary of America, 1956.

CHAPTER NINE

Transition to Roman Rule

Primary Readings: Testament of Moses (also called Assumption of Moses), Psalms of Solomon, 1 Enoch 37–71 (also called Similitudes of Enoch)

This chapter traces Judea's transition from independence to Roman rule. Then three documents are examined, the *Psalms of Solomon,* the *Testament of Moses,* and the *Similitudes of Enoch.* Finally, there is an excursus on the synagogue.

THE HISTORY

From Alexander Jannaeus to Herod the Great

The ruler discussed last in chapter 5 was the Hasmonean Alexander Jannaeus (ruled 103–76 BCE). He was a cruel king whose main interest was in increasing his own power. Much of his reign was marked by warfare, often against fellow Jews. His successor was his wife, Alexandra Salome (ruled 76–67 BCE), who, because she was a woman, could not be high priest. She had two sons, Hyrcanus II and Aristobulus II. The former was rather passive, but the latter was ambitious and aggressive. Alexandra appointed Hyrcanus high priest, possibly because he was more easily controlled than Aristobulus. Aristobulus did not take the appointment of Hyrcanus well, and after Alexandra's death in 67 BCE Aristobulus ousted Hyrcanus and ruled until 63 BCE. At this point the Romans entered Israel's story in a substantial way. The Roman general Pompey was in the eastern Mediterranean extending Roman control over the area. Both Hasmonean brothers appealed to Pompey for help in their dispute, and Pompey decided in favor of Hyrcanus. Pompey put Hyrcanus in charge of Judea and environs, and subordinated the area to the new Roman province of Syria. Appointing Hyrcanus was consonant with Roman policy of ruling through local elites. In 57 BCE Gabinius, governor of Syria, restricted Hyrcanus' authority to the Temple and set up five administrative districts under the control of aristocratic councils.

During the two decades between 49 and 30 BCE, Rome was embroiled in internal power struggles. Hyrcanus and his general Antipater supported Julius Caesar in his war against Pompey, and then against Ptolemy XIII of Egypt. In return Caesar appointed Hyrcanus ethnarch ("leader of the people") in

Jerusalem, and made Antipater procurator of Judea (47 BCE). "Procurator" means a caretaker, that is, one who takes care of a place for someone else. Antipater thus became Caesar's agent in Judea, even though his status as a Jew was questionable. Antipater was an Idumean. Idumea was the area south of Judea that John Hyrcanus conquered and whose inhabitants were forcibly circumcised. Their Judaism was rather recent and was suspect in Judean eyes (*see* Josephus, *Ant.* 14.15.2 § 403). Julius Caesar gave Antipater Roman citizenship and exempted him from tribute. The Jews were granted freedom of religion, allowed to rebuild the walls of Jerusalem, and regained some of the lands they had lost in previous years. Antipater's sons administered various parts of the land under Antipater's jurisdiction. The most famous of his sons was Herod, who administered Galilee. He made a name for himself by his efficiency in controlling resistance forces there.

Julius Caesar was killed in 44 BCE. Pompey had been killed earlier in Egypt. In the new power alignment, Antipater and his sons supported Marc Antony. Marc Antony made Herod and his brother Phasael ethnarchs. In 43 BCE Antipater was killed. It was not long before the upheavals in the Roman Empire tempted the Parthians (rulers of an empire east of the Roman Empire) to invade the eastern reaches of the Empire. In 40 BCE, the Parthians captured Jerusalem and installed the Hasmonean Antigonus Mattathias, son of Aristobulus II, as king and high priest. In that same year, Herod managed to get himself declared king by the Roman Senate. He proceeded to Palestine and finally recaptured Jerusalem in 37 BCE. He was to reign until 4 BCE, and because of his accomplishments he earned the title "Herod the Great." The title does not imply that Herod was morally great or that his rule benefited his subjects but simply recognizes his historical significance.

The Reign of Herod the Great (37–4 BCE)

Herod's first priority was to consolidate his power. Herod had no natural constituency in Jewish Palestine since his father was Idumean and his mother Arab. Many did not consider him a Jew. Furthermore, he lacked the credentials to be ruler of the Jews. He was not a priest, and so could not be high priest. He was not of the Davidic line, and so did not have that claim to kingship. Herod owed his power to his own cunning and that of his father Antipater in supporting the winning sides in Roman power struggles. When Antony was defeated by Octavian (later to be called "Augustus") at Actium in 31 BCE, and then committed suicide with Cleopatra in 30 BCE, Herod adroitly switched his allegiance to Octavian and was reconfirmed in his royal office.

The story of Herod's relations with the Hasmonean family shows his difficulties with legitimacy. In 37 BCE, he executed the Hasmonean Antigonus Mattathias, who had ruled Jerusalem under Parthian patronage from 40 to 37 BCE.

That may have made him unpopular with some Hasmonean supporters. But then Herod married the Hasmonean princess Mariamne, daughter of Alexander Jannaeus and Alexandra Salome. Although he is said to have loved her, this was also a political move to tap into the Hasmonean family. Marriages within the ruling class often had political overtones. In 35 BCE, Herod wanted to import a high priest from among the priestly families in the Jewish community in Babylonia. This was probably because he did not think he could trust the Jerusalem establishment. Instead he was persuaded to appoint Aristobulus III, the young brother of his wife. Later that same year Herod had Aristobulus drowned at Jericho, probably because he saw him as a threat. It seems that Herod vacillated between using the influence of the Hasmoneans and trying to destroy it.

Herod's reign was full of executions of people whom he suspected, sometimes rightly, of conspiring against him. He seems seldom to have felt secure in his position, and became known as a cruel and ruthless ruler, ready to do away with anyone he saw as a menace. Herod put Mariamne to death in 29 BCE. Her two sons by Herod, Alexander and Aristobulus, met the same fate in 7 BCE. Josephus provides a glimpse of life under Herod.

> They [the people] resented his [Herod's] carrying out of such arrangements as seemed to them to mean the dissolution of their religion and the disappearance of their customs. And these matters were discussed by all of them, for they were always being provoked and disturbed. Herod, however, gave the most careful attention to this situation, taking away any opportunities they might have (for agitation) and instructing them to apply themselves at all times to their work. No meeting of citizens was permitted, nor were walking together or being together permitted, and all their movements were observed. Those who were caught were punished severely, and many were taken, either openly or secretly, to the fortress of Hyrcania and there put to death. Both in the city and on the open roads there were men who spied on those who met together. (*Ant.* 15.10.4 §§ 365–66)

Herod was known as a builder. In the Hellenistic world, building was a medium of propaganda, and an ambitious building program signified wealth, power, and stability. Wealth usually came from peasants' toil, the main source of wealth in the ancient world in general and Palestine in particular. To some subjects magnificent buildings were a source of pride. To others they symbolized the power of a well-entrenched ruler. To still others they represented economic oppression. Herod's most famous project was rebuilding Jerusalem's Temple on a scale never before seen in Jerusalem, complete with a massive platform surrounded by Hellenistic porticoes. He began in 20 BCE, and Josephus says that the work did not cease until 64 CE, eighty-four years later. The building was probably substantially finished by the time of Jesus, who is said to have taught under the porticoes. For Herod, the Temple served the dual purpose of advertising the magnificence of his rule, and of placating his Jewish subjects.

Herod may have tried to please Jews by his work in Jerusalem, but he used building for other purposes as well. A strong motivation for building was to flatter Rome. He rebuilt the town of Strato's Tower on the Mediterranean coast and renamed it Caesarea in honor of Caesar.[1] He also rebuilt Samaria and renamed it Sebaste, the Greek form of the name Augustus. Herod had no qualms about erecting a temple to Augustus in the city, showing that Torah had little claim on him. Herod also built for his own defense. He built or rebuilt numerous fortresses to guard his power. Among those fortresses was Masada, northwest of the Dead Sea. Atop a high hill surrounded by precipitous cliffs, it was almost impregnable. In the Jewish-Roman war, a Jewish group held off the Romans there until 74 CE, four years after Jerusalem had been destroyed and the war effectively won by the Romans.

The Herodian Family

At Herod's death, Rome divided his kingdom among three of his sons, Archelaus, Herod Antipas, and Philip.[2] Archelaus ruled Jerusalem, Judea, and some surrounding territories from 4 BCE to 6 CE. At first some Judeans hoped that his rule would be less harsh than his father's, but it was more so (see Matt 2:22). Eventually the Romans admitted that his role was a failure and banished him to the western Mediterranean. They then instituted direct Roman rule over Judea under a procurator accountable to the governor of Syria.

Herod Antipas received Galilee and Perea (a territory east of the Jordan). He ruled from 4 BCE to 39 CE. This was the Herod before whom Jesus appeared just before his crucifixion, according to Luke 23:6-12. Herod Antipas contracted a political marriage with the daughter of King Aretas IV of Nabatea, and then divorced her to marry his own sister-in-law. The gospels say that John the Baptist was beheaded by Herod Antipas because John protested this second marriage. Herod rebuilt the city of Sepphoris in Galilee, which had been destroyed in 4 BCE by the Roman Varus (see chap. 10). He also built the town of Tiberias, named for the reigning emperor Tiberius, on the shores of the Sea of Galilee. Sepphoris and Tiberias were the two principal cities in Galilee in the first century. The Romans banished Antipas to Gaul in 39 CE because Agrippa I (see below) accused him of sedition.

Philip took charge of land north and east of the Sea of Galilee. His rule was apparently uneventful. He built a town named Caesarea, often called Caesarea Philippi (see Mark 8:27). Philip ruled from 4 BCE until 34 CE, at which time his territory was attached to Syria.

Agrippa I was grandson of Herod the Great, and son of Aristobulus, one of the two sons of Herod by Mariamne the Hasmonean. He spent time in Rome and was friendly with several influential Romans. Among his friends was Gaius, nicknamed Caligula,[3] emperor from 37 to 41 CE. In 37 CE, Caligula awarded the former territory of Philip to Agrippa. In 39 CE, Agrippa became king of Judea and Samaria. At the beginning of the reign of the emperor Claudius (ruled 41–54 CE), he became king of the whole country, including those areas previously governed by Herod Antipas. He remained king until his sudden death in 44 CE.[4] During his short reign he did several things that made his loyalty to Rome suspect, such as convening a meeting of local rulers without Rome's permission. When Agrippa died, Claudius decided not to appoint another Jewish king over Judea. Instead, he reinstituted direct Roman rule through procurators. Agrippa I was the last Jewish king to rule over Judea.

Agrippa's son, Agrippa II, became king over some small territories north of Galilee in 48 CE and enjoyed a long rule in spite of the upheavals in Judea and Galilee during that time. He was the last of Herod's descendants to rule.

THE *PSALMS OF SOLOMON*

This text is a collection of eighteen psalms, none of which are from the biblical collection. They date from about the middle of the first century BCE and were originally written in Hebrew, which has been lost, but they are extant in Greek. They represent a firsthand Jewish reaction to the reign of the Hasmoneans in the first century BCE and to the coming of Rome into Palestine in the person of Pompey. The composers of the Psalms cannot be identified as members of any one party in Judaism. They express a negative evaluation of the Hasmoneans because of Hasmonean social sins, and of Pompey for his defilement of the Temple. They look forward to a Davidic Messiah who will reform Israel and bring it into conformity with Torah. This section examines only those psalms that pertain to the events discussed earlier in this chapter.

Psalm 2 describes Pompey's attack on Jerusalem and blames it on Jerusalem's sinful inhabitants.

> When the sinner waxed proud, with a battering-ram he cast down
>   fortified walls,
> And Thou didst not restrain him.
> Alien nations ascended Thine altar,
>   They trampled it proudly with their sandals;
> Because the sons of Jerusalem had defiled the holy things of the
>   Lord,
> Had profaned with iniquities the offerings of God. (2:1-3)

The psalm assumes that if Jerusalem has fallen to foreigners, God must have allowed it. The only reason God would have allowed such an event is that Jerusalem's residents displeased God. This is put in terms of defilement of the sanctuary, "the holy things of the Lord." The "offerings" are the sacrifices

251

offered by the priests in the Temple. The psalm praises God for righteous judgment on the people: "God is a righteous judge, and He is no respecter of persons" (2:19). God does not respect persons in the sense that divine punishment falls on God's own people as well as on Gentile sinners.

The psalmist then complains that Jerusalem's punishment, though just, has lasted long enough, and those who have carried out the punishment (Pompey and the Romans) are insolent toward God and must be prevented from utterly destroying Israel. God soon responds.

> And I had not long to wait before God showed me the insolent one
>> Slain on the mountains of Egypt,
> Esteemed of less account than the least, on land and sea;
> His body . . . borne hither and thither on the billows with much
>> insolence,
>> With none to bury him, because He had rejected him with dis-
>> honor. (2:30-31)

Pompey died in Egypt in war against Julius Caesar in 48 BCE. His body did indeed go unburied for some time, a mark of great dishonor. The insolent and shameful way Pompey was treated is considered a direct punishment for the insolence he showed in dishonoring Jerusalem.

> He reflected not that he was a man,
>> And reflected not on the latter end;
> He said: I will be lord of land and sea;
>> And he recognized not that it is God who is great,
>> Mighty in His great strength.
> He is king over the heavens,
>> And judgeth kings and kingdoms. (2:31-34)

Pompey was called "the Great." The psalm accuses him of forgetting his place as a human and not being humble before the one who is truly great, God.

At the end of Psalm 3, resurrection is mentioned: "But they that fear the Lord shall rise to life eternal, and their life shall be in the light of the Lord, and shall come to an end no more" (3:16). It is not uncommon to find the strongest expressions of belief in resurrection in documents written by the oppressed, or by those who feel that the world is not as it should be (*see* Daniel 12 and 2 Maccabees 7).

Psalm 4 contains a section castigating some of the psalmist's fellow Jews for only pretending to follow Torah.

> Wherefore sittest thou, O profane man, in the council of the pious,
>> Seeing that thy heart is far removed from the Lord,

> Provoking with transgressions the God of Israel?
> Extravagant in speech, extravagant in outward seeming beyond all men,
>   Is he that is severe of speech in condemning sinners in judgement.
> And his hand is first upon him as though he acted in zeal,
>   And yet he is himself guilty in respect of manifold sins and
>   of wantonness. (4:1-3)

The very ones who act as judges and claim to uphold Torah are themselves sinners. This psalm and the *Psalms of Solomon* in general go into some detail about the sins such people commit. They are sexually wanton, they render false judgments in court, and they steal others' property by seemingly legal means. The sinners "utter law guilefully" (4:10). The sins are those of the upper class. The psalm begs for God's punishment on the hypocrites.

The *Psalms of Solomon* claim that Jewish suffering at Roman hands is due to the sins of some members of the Jewish upper class. The psalms plead for the destruction of those sinners, but remind God to remain with the righteous, lest they too perish.

> Make not Thy dwelling afar from us, O God;
>   Lest they assail us that hate us without cause.
> For Thou hast rejected them, O God;
>   Let not their foot trample upon Thy holy inheritance.
> Chasten us Thyself in Thy good pleasure;
>   But give us not up to the nations;
> For, if Thou sendest pestilence,
>   Thou Thyself givest it charge concerning us;
> For Thou art merciful,
>   And wilt not be angry to the point of consuming us.
> While Thy name dwelleth in our midst, we shall find mercy;
>   And the nations shall not prevail against us.
> For Thou art our shield,
>   And when we call upon Thee, Thou hearkenest to us. (7:1-7)

"The nations" are the Gentiles. These are the words of someone who has recently seen Jerusalem captured and defiled by the Romans. The prayer is that God remain with Israel lest it be completely destroyed by the Gentiles.

Psalm 8 bemoans Pompey's defilement of the Temple, caused by the Temple's pollution by those in charge of it. The psalm considers the judgment of God just because it is owing to the behavior of Jerusalem's inhabitants.

> God laid bare their sins in the full light of day;
>   All the earth came to know the righteous judgements of God.
> In secret places underground their iniquities were committed to
>   provoke Him to anger;

They wrought confusion, son with mother and father with daughter;
　They committed adultery, every man with his neighbour's wife.
They concluded covenants with one another with an oath touching
　　these things;
　They plunder the sanctuary of God, as though there was no
　　avenger.
They trode the altar of the Lord, coming straight from all manner
　　of uncleanness;
　And with menstrual blood they defiled the sacrifices, as
　　though these were common flesh.
They left no sin undone, wherein they surpassed not the heathen. (8:8-14)

The psalm condemns what it considers sexual sins of those who attend the altar, who must be priests. The mention of menstrual blood suggests that the priests are not following the Torah as interpreted by the psalmist concerning abstention from intercourse during a woman's menstrual period. The illegitimate crossing of kinship lines in marriage is also listed as a sin of the priests. The charges may be exaggerated, but the psalmist's marriage rules were not being followed by the ruling class. The sinners are also said to have plundered the sanctuary, so there are violations in the economic sphere as well.

The Psalm goes on to the punishment of the Jewish sinners.

He [God] brought him that is from the end of the earth, that
　　smiteth mightily;
　He decreed . . . war against Jerusalem, and against her land.
The princes of the land went to meet him with joy: they said
　　unto him:
　Blessed be thy way! Come ye, enter ye in with peace.
They made the rough ways even, before his entering in;
　They opened the gates to Jerusalem, they crowned its walls.
As a father entereth the house of his sons, so he entered
　　Jerusalem in peace;
　He established his feet there in great safety.
He captured her fortresses and the wall of Jerusalem;
　For God Himself led him in safety, while they wandered.
He destroyed their princes and every one wise in counsel;
　He poured out the blood of the inhabitants of Jerusalem, like
　　the water of uncleanness.
He led away their sons and daughters, whom they had begotten in
　　defilement.
They did according to their uncleanness, even as their fathers
　　had done:
　They defiled Jerusalem and the things that had been hallowed to
　　the name of God. (8:16-26)

The one "from the end of the earth" is Pompey. Rome seemed like the end of the earth to the Palestinian Jews, and Pompey's prowess in war was legendary. Josephus confirms that the princes of Israel invited Pompey in and made his way safe all the way to Jerusalem (*Ant.* 14.4.2 §§ 58–59). Hoping for a favorable decision from Pompey, Aristobulus at first offered him gifts and turned over fortresses. The gates of Jerusalem were opened by Jews who hoped that Pompey would arrange the political situation in their favor. But the Romans' arrival resulted in bloodshed and defilement of the holy city.

Psalms 17 and 18 see the hope of Israel in the expectation of a new Davidic messiah. Psalm 17 opens with the cry that Israel hopes in its God who is its savior (17:3). Salvation is liberation from bondage to foreign and domestic oppressors whose governance of society violates God's Law. The group behind the *Psalms* had somehow to make sense of the fact that, despite their loyalty to the all-powerful God of the universe, they were oppressed and powerless, while the wicked ruled the earth. The solution was to insist still more strongly that God controls all. "The kingdom of our God is for ever over the nations in judgement" (17:4). The Gentiles might *seem* all-powerful, but in reality the kingdom of God is supreme.

The next verses of Psalm 17 probably refer to the Hasmoneans.

> Thou, O Lord, didst choose David to be king over Israel,
> And swore to him touching his seed that never should his
> kingdom fail before Thee.
> But, for our sins, sinners rose up against us;
> They assailed us and thrust us out;
> What Thou hadst not promised to them, they took away from us
> with violence.
> They in no way glorified Thy honourable name;
> They set a worldly monarchy in place of that which was
> their excellency;
> They laid waste the throne of David in tumultuous arrogance.
>
> (17:5-8)

Although the Hasmoneans called themselves kings, they were not of Davidic lineage. Their monarchy was "worldly," and they ruined David's throne through their arrogance. In reaction to Hasmonean abuses the psalm recalls the promises to David. In 2 Samuel 7, God promises David that his posterity will always sit upon the throne of Israel. The psalm reminds God of that fact, but admits that the sinfulness of Israel has led to the absence of a Davidic king.

The next passage recalls the coming of Pompey, "a man that was alien to our race" (17:9). Pompey laid waste the land, exiled the people, and acted proudly in Jerusalem. This was due to the sins of Jerusalem's residents:

> And the children of the covenant in the midst of the mingled
> peoples . . .
> There was not among them one that wrought in the midst
> of Jerusalem mercy and truth.
> They that loved the synagogues of the pious fled from them. (17:17-18*a*)

The reference to "mingled peoples" hints that the mixing of Jews with non-Jews endangers the covenant.

The psalm asks for a Davidic king. The king will "shatter unrighteous rulers" and "purge Jerusalem from nations that trample (her) down to destruction" (17:24-25). Further, he will "thrust out sinners from the inheritance" (17:26). The next verses state the Davidic Messiah's tasks. They allude to biblical traditions about the messiah and the ideal Israel.

> And he shall gather together a holy people, whom he shall lead in
> righteousness,
> And he shall judge the tribes of the people that has been
> sanctified by the Lord his God.
> And he shall not suffer unrighteousness to lodge any more in their
> midst,
> Nor shall there dwell with them any man that knoweth
> wickedness,
> For he shall know them, that they are all sons of their God. (17:28-30)

The king's primary task is to obey Torah and to ensure that Israel does the same. "Sons of their God" means a community that *acts* like children of God, completely obedient. In the Hebrew Bible, Israel is spoken of as God's son or sons, and individual Israelites also are spoken of this way (*see* Isa 1:2; Hos 11:1; Wis 2:13; Ps 2:7; 2 Sam 7:14).

> And he shall divide them according to their tribes upon the land,
> And neither sojourner nor alien shall sojourn with them any
> more.
> He shall judge peoples and nations in the wisdom of his righteous-
> ness. (17:30-31)

The Davidic era is seen as a golden age. It will be restored. The twelve tribes, an anachronistic term in the first century BCE, will once again be living in their allotted areas in Palestine. The theme that the ideal Israel will contain no foreigners emerges, as it did in the critical periods of Josiah's reform (Deuteronomy), and the Restoration (Ezra and Nehemiah). Although Israel will remain pure of foreign influences, the Davidic king will rule over the whole earth "in the wisdom of his righteousness."

The next verses paint a glorious picture of a restored Jerusalem, seat of God's messiah, home to a purified community.

> And he shall have the heathen nations to serve him under his yoke;
>> And he shall glorify the Lord in a place to be seen of . . . all the earth;
>> And he shall purge Jerusalem, making it holy as of old:
> So that nations shall come from the ends of the earth to see
>> his glory,
>> Bringing as gifts her sons who had fainted,
>> And to see the glory of the Lord, wherewith God hath glorified her.
> And he shall be a righteous king, taught of God, over them,
> And there shall be no unrighteousness in his days in their midst,
> For all shall be holy and their king the anointed of the Lord.
> For he shall not put his trust in horse and rider and bow,
>> Nor shall he multiply for himself gold and silver for war,
>> Nor shall he gather confidence from . . . a multitude . . . for the day of battle.
> The Lord Himself is his king, the hope of him that is mighty
>> through his hope in God. (17:32-38)

The messiah's power comes not from military means, but from obedience to God. In terms derived from holy war, battles are won not with cavalry and bows, but through devotion to God. Jerusalem's invincibility will be ensured by its holiness, and the righteousness of its king that ensures the righteousness of the people. Other elements of Zion ideology are present here. When God intervenes in history, the exiles will return, and all nations will recognize the true God and the divine election of Israel and of Jerusalem. Jerusalem will have been delivered from the "uncleanness of unholy enemies" (17:51).

The Davidic Messiah is expected to be "pure from sin" (17:41) and full of God's Holy Spirit. In the Hebrew Bible, "God's Spirit" is a way of speaking of the presence and activity of God. The psalm sees the messiah as possessing the Holy Spirit and therefore having understanding, strength, and righteousness. He will be "shepherd" of God's flock. His words will guide Israel: "His words (shall be) like the words of the holy ones in the midst of sanctified peoples" (17:49). The "holy ones" are the angels.

Psalm 18 speaks of the people's preparation for the messiah.

> Thy chastisement is upon us as upon a first-born, only-begotten son,
>> To turn back the obedient soul from folly that is wrought in ignorance.
> May God cleanse Israel against the day of mercy and blessing,
>> Against the day of choice when He bringeth back His anointed. (18:4-6)

The suffering of the righteous proves that they are the only sons of God, the firstborn. Because God cares for them, they have undergone a purging meant to teach them how to be true sons. When the messiah comes he will continue the chastening so that the community will remain pure. Israel will live "under the rod of chastening of the Lord's anointed in the fear of his God" (18:8).

The *Psalms of Solomon* allow a glimpse of how some Jews of the first century BCE viewed the reign of the Hasmoneans and the coming of the Romans. They knew themselves to be God's worshipers, but they saw the Torah betrayed by their priests and princes. They felt justified when the wicked suffered at the hands of the Romans, but they lamented the injury done their holy city and Temple by Pompey. They looked to their traditions and found hope in God's promises to David, and in the Zion traditions that portrayed a world centered around Jerusalem and its God. They believed that the coming of the Davidic Messiah would mean the fulfillment of the divine promises to Israel and the destruction of their oppressors, Jewish and Gentile. They awaited an Israel restored to its glorious state under David.

THE *TESTAMENT OF MOSES*

The *Testament of Moses* is sometimes called the *Assumption of Moses* because when it was first discovered in the nineteenth century it was thought to be a book referred to by some ancient authors by the latter title. But in the extant document there is no reference to Moses' assumption into heaven. The work lacks its ending, so it is not known whether there was ever such a reference. Since the work's literary genre is that of a testament, a better title for it is the *Testament of Moses*. A testament is the final message of an important figure, framed by narrative that discloses the circumstances of the final words—the figure is about to die, and he gathers his sons or successor to him. The *Testament of Moses* was probably originally written during the persecution of Judaism by Antiochus IV in the second century BCE. But chapters 5–6 refer to the time of Herod the Great and to the War of Varus fought in 4 BCE. The probable solution to this inconsistency is that chapters 5–6 were inserted into a preexisting document to make the entire document address a new situation.

The setting of the *Testament of Moses* is taken from the description of Moses' death in Deuteronomy 34. The use of a death scene of an ancient hero of Israel as a framework for a new composition is common in the Second Temple period. In the *Testament,* Moses is about to die, and he appoints Joshua to succeed him. Moses informs Joshua that the world was created for Israel, but that this fact had been hidden from the Gentiles. Moses instructs Joshua to preserve some books, probably the Pentateuch. The books are to be preserved "until the day of repentance in the visitation wherewith the Lord will visit them in the consummation of the end of the days" (1:18). He then "predicts" the course of history. This is the sort of *ex eventu* prophecy typical of apocalypses. Although the *Testament* is not an apocalypse, it contains apocalyptic elements such as this type of prophecy and its eschatology. The viewpoint of the text is that of Deuteronomistic theology: Suffering is punishment for sin, and obedience to Torah brings success. Historical referents of the text are not always certain because the *Testament* follows the common apocalyptic practice of not naming the figures explicitly.

Chapter 2 predicts the entry into the land, the building of the Temple, and the breaking away of the ten northern tribes. The north is condemned for breaking away from Jerusalem, and for idolatry. The two southern tribes (Judah and Benjamin) are called the "holy tribes." In chapter 3 the destruction of Jerusalem and the Babylonian Exile are described. Remarkably, the exile of the southern tribes is blamed on the sins of the northern tribes (3:5).

In chapter 4 an unnamed person, probably Daniel, prays to God for the people and is heard (*see* Daniel 9). Cyrus arises and allows the people to return to Judah and rebuild Jerusalem. The text says, "The two tribes shall continue in their prescribed faith, sad and lamenting because they will not be able to offer sacrifices to the Lord of their fathers" (4:8). This seems to be a denigration of the Second Temple.[5]

Chapter 5 may describe the time of the Hellenistic reform when it says of the Jews, "They themselves . . . shall be divided as to the truth" (5:2). Because of their sins they will be punished "through the kings who share in their guilt and punish them" (5:1). This probably refers to the Seleucids, who in the person of Antiochus IV were party to the reform, but who were God's instrument of punishment during the persecution and subsequent wars. The desecration of Jerusalem and its altar is described in priestly terms.

> It hath been said: "They shall turn aside from righteousness and approach iniquity, and they shall defile with pollutions the house of their worship," and because "they shall go a-whoring after strange gods." For they shall not follow the truth of God, but some shall pollute the altar with the very gifts which they offer to the Lord, who are not priests but slaves, sons of slaves. (5:3-4)

Chapter 6 deals with the Hasmoneans and Herod.

> Then there shall be raised up unto them kings bearing rule, and they shall call themselves priests of the Most High God: they shall assuredly work iniquity in the holy of holies. And an insolent king shall succeed them, who will not be of the race of the priests, a man bold and shameless, and he shall judge them as they shall deserve. And he shall cut off their chief men with the sword, and shall destroy them in secret places, so that no one may know where their bodies are. He shall slay the old and the young, and he shall not spare. Then the fear of him shall be bitter unto them in their land. And he shall execute judgements on them as the Egyptians

executed upon them, during thirty and four years, and he shall punish them. And he shall beget children, who succeeding him shall rule for shorter periods. Into their parts cohorts and a powerful king of the west shall come, who shall conquer them: and he shall take them captive, and burn a part of their temple with fire, and shall crucify some around their colony.

The Hasmoneans were both kings and priests. Their activity insults the Temple. Herod is not a Hasmonean or even a priest. His harsh treatment of the Hasmoneans and other aristocrats who oppose him is seen as punishment for their sins. The description of Herod's 34-year reign (37–4 BCE) fits what is known of it from other sources. The Roman Varus brutally crushed the upheavals that followed Herod's death, and this reference ends the chapter.

Chapters 7–8 speak of the persecutions under Antiochus IV. Chapter 9 introduces a Levite named Taxo who has seven sons. Taxo remarks upon the severity of the punishment visited on the people. He suggests that the people withdraw to a cave in the wilderness and die there rather than transgress Torah. "For if we do this and die, our blood shall be avenged before the Lord" (9:7). (See 1 Macc 2:29-38 where faithful Jews are slaughtered in the wilderness rather than violate Torah.) Chapter 10 continues his speech with a description of God's expected intervention, provoked by the death of the martyrs. God's action is described in apocalyptic terms as the reassertion of divine sovereignty over all of creation, which had been controlled by Satan. Themes of holy war are recalled as God goes out to battle:

> And then His kingdom shall appear throughout all His creation,
> And then Satan shall be no more,
> And sorrow shall depart with him.
> Then the hands of the angel shall be filled
> Who has been appointed chief,
> And he shall forthwith avenge them of their enemies.
> For the Heavenly One will arise from His royal throne,
> And He will go forth from His holy habitation
> With indignation and wrath on account of His sons.
> And the earth shall tremble: to its confines shall it be shaken:
> And the high mountains shall be made low
> And the hills shall be shaken and fall.
> And the horns of the sun shall be broken and he shall be turned
>   into darkness;
> And the moon shall not give her light, and be turned wholly into
>   blood.
> And the circle of the stars shall be disturbed.
> And the sea shall retire into the abyss,
> And the fountains of waters shall fail,
> And the rivers shall dry up.

> For the Most High will arise, the Eternal God alone,
> And He will appear to punish the Gentiles,
> And He will destroy all their idols.
> Then thou, O Israel, shalt be happy,
> And thou shalt mount upon the necks and wings of the eagle,
> And they shall be ended.
> And God will exalt thee,
> And He will cause thee to approach to the heaven of the stars,
> In the place of their habitation.
> And thou shalt look from on high and shalt see thy enemies in
>   Gehenna,
> And thou shalt recognize them and rejoice,
> And thou shalt give thanks and confess thy Creator. (10:1-10)

God is angry at the treatment of God's "sons," Israel. God's going out to battle has cosmic repercussions. Earth, sun, moon, and stars are all affected. The cosmic scope of the turmoil is a trait of apocalypticism. The withdrawal of the sea into the abyss draws on the symbolism of the sea as that which opposes God, as in Daniel 7. All forces opposing God are destroyed. This chapter was probably originally written during the persecution of Judaism by the Gentile king Antiochus IV, so the basic division of humanity here is Jew and Gentile. The Jews are God's sons, being attacked by the wicked Gentiles. God's intervention means the defeat of the Gentiles and their descent to hell, whereas Israel ascends to heaven and lives with the stars, considered in the ancient world as heavenly beings (in Israel, angels). Israel looks down from its heavenly abode and recognizes its enemies being punished.

In its present form the *Testament* ends with Joshua's distress that Moses is about to leave. Moses strengthens him with words about God's control of history. In chapter 12, Moses asserts that God has foreseen all of history, as is proved by the "predictions" Moses has just uttered.

There are several contacts between chapter 9 and 2 Maccabees 6–7. In 2 Maccabees 6, there was an old man named Eleazar who resisted the persecution of Antiochus IV and was martyred. In 2 Maccabees 7 there is a story about a woman and her seven sons who die for the Torah, and who make speeches expressing the hope that their death will atone for Israel's sins and that they will be vindicated by their resurrection. In *Testament of Moses* 9–10, the old man Taxo has seven sons. He makes a speech urging martyrdom for the sake of the Torah, expressing the hope that their martyrdom will bring about atonement for sins, the defeat of Satan, and vindication for the righteous. The *Testament of Moses* and 2 Maccabees preserve two versions of the same story. If there was an earlier edition of the *Testament* written as a response to Antiochus IV's persecution, then both versions of the story arose from the same historical situation. Both respond to the situation by acknowledging Israel's sin, seeing suffering as an atoning act, and anticipating the defeat of evil and the vindication of the righteous after death. That a later editor could use the same story to reflect on a later situation, that of Herod's reign, is testimony to the process of adapting tradition to explain the present.

THE *SIMILITUDES OF ENOCH* (*1 ENOCH* 37–71)

The *Similitudes of Enoch* do not contain many of the sorts of historical references that contribute directly to Jewish history of the Roman period. Nonetheless it is important to consider the work at this point because it comes from the period and locale under discussion, provides another example of apocalyptic literature, embodies one reaction to events in Jewish Palestine under the Romans, and displays an interest in a savior figure that is important for Christianity and later Judaism.[6]

Most scholars date the *Similitudes of Enoch* to the first century CE. The work survives as part of *1 Enoch*. Like the other parts of that collection it once had an existence independent of *1 Enoch*. Its original language was probably Aramaic, but it is preserved in Ethiopic. The work's title comes from the fact that it consists of three "similitudes" introduced in chapters 38, 45, and 58, framed by an introduction in chapter 37 and two endings, one in chapter 70 and the other in chapter 71. "Similitude," also translated "parable," has a wide range of meaning in ancient Israel. Its basic meaning is any sort of figurative language. Such language operates on the principle of finding similarities between various things. In the context of *1 Enoch,* it denotes revelatory discourse, a meaning derived from a prophetic milieu.[7]

The central concern in the *Similitudes* is the fate of the good and the bad. The good are called "righteous," "elect" ("chosen"), and "holy." They possess the secret wisdom imparted to Enoch. Enoch has traveled to heaven and seen God and God's agent, the "Son of Man," also called the "Righteous One," the "Elect One," and the "Messiah." It is the Son of Man who will judge the good and the bad at the end of time. Enoch's trips to heaven and to various parts of the universe provide him with firsthand views of the punishment of the bad and the reward of the good. Enoch brings this knowledge, available only through direct revelation, to the chosen people. Acceptance of this secret knowledge and hope in the Son of Man will result in salvation.

There is a close relation between the earthly righteous and the heavenly Son of Man. They share the titles "righteous" and "elect." The relationship of the Son of Man to the righteous is like the relationship of the Son of Man to Israel in Daniel 7 and the relationship of the archangel Michael to Israel in Daniel 10. He is the people's heavenly patron. The career of the Son of Man in heaven corresponds to the experience of the righteous on earth. As the Son of Man remains hidden until his glory is fully revealed at the judgment, the righteous are not recognized and suffer oppression on earth, but will share in the Son of Man's glory at the end of time.

Chapter 37 introduces the *Similitudes*. Enoch claims that three parables were given to him in which wisdom was contained. He says, "Till the present day such wisdom has never been given by the Lord of Spirits as I have received" (37:4). The "Lord of Spirits" is a frequent title for God in the *Similitudes*, because the *Similitudes* assume that there is a multitude of spirits, good and bad, operating in the universe. God is sovereign over them all.

The first parable begins in chapter 38. It announces the reward of the good and the punishment of the evil "when the congregation of the righteous shall appear" (38:1). This implies that the righteous are not yet recognized as such. At the end of time, "Those that possess the earth shall no longer be powerful and exalted" (38:4). At that time "shall the kings and the mighty perish" (38:5). The group called the righteous sees as its enemies the kings and the mighty of the earth. The judgment will bring the downfall of rulers. This theme is common in apocalyptic literature.

In chapter 39, Enoch receives "books of zeal and wrath, and books of disquiet and expulsion" (39:2). The content of those books coincides with the revelation imparted in the *Similitudes*. Enoch continues,

> And in those days a whirlwind carried me off from the earth,
> And set me down at the end of the heavens.
> And there I saw another vision, the dwelling-places of the holy,
> And the resting-places of the righteous.
> Here mine eyes saw their dwellings with His righteous angels,
> And their resting-places with the holy.
> And they petitioned and interceded and prayed for the children of
>   men,
> And righteousness flowed before them as water,
> And mercy like dew upon the earth:
> Thus it is amongst them for ever and ever.
> And in that place mine eyes saw the Elect One of righteousness and of
>   faith,
> And I saw his dwelling-place under the wings of the Lord of
>   Spirits.
> And righteousness shall prevail in his days,
> And the righteous and elect shall be without number before Him for
>   ever and ever. (39:3-7)

Enoch speaks of what he witnesses, so his words are authoritative. He has been present in heaven itself where he sees the angels, the righteous who have died, God, and the Elect One resting close to God. Such a vision is comforting to the righteous still oppressed on earth because they can see that those that have gone before them, perhaps in martyrdom, are present with the angels and intercede for them. When the days of the Elect One come, righteousness will prevail, and the righteous will live in glory.

God is the one who "knows before the world was created what is for ever and what will be from generation unto generation" (39:11). Enoch hears "those who sleep not" (probably angels) saying, "Holy, holy, holy, is the Lord of Spirits: He filleth the earth with spirits" (39:12). This is an allusion to the prophet Isaiah's vision in the Temple, when he sees God sitting on a throne and the angels singing: "Holy, holy, holy is the LORD of hosts; the whole earth is full of his glory." The world view of the *Similitudes* is reflected in the change of "hosts" to "spirits" and by the fact that God fills the earth with spirits instead of divine glory. As is typical of apocalypticism, the universe is full of spirits and God rules all of them.

In chapter 40 Enoch says that the angel who accompanies him on his tour of heaven shows him "all the hidden things" (40:2). Enoch sees four angels in the presence of God, a feature recalling Ezekiel 1:4-14. The first angel praises God. The second blesses "the Elect One and the elect ones." The third prays and intercedes for those dwelling on earth. The last angel is seen "fending off the Satans and forbidding them to come before the Lord of Spirits to accuse them who dwell on the earth." The scene recalls Zechariah 3, where Satan (Hebrew for "accuser"), the heavenly "prosecuting attorney," stands before God and accuses the high priest of sin. In *1 Enoch* 40, God's angelic protector fends off the advances of would-be accusers (satans) of the earthly righteous. In *1 Enoch*, the satans are unwelcome in heaven and God must be protected from them. In the development of the tradition, the accuser, the satan, once a member of the heavenly host, has become demonic.

Chapter 41 portrays nature as obedient to God, having taken an oath to remain faithful to its tasks. There is an implicit contrast of nature with the sinners who do not follow God's ways. The next chapter illustrates that apocalyptic wisdom is accessible only by the elect. The form of the chapter is that of a hymn about wisdom, personified as a woman.

> Wisdom found no place where she might dwell;
> Then a dwelling-place was assigned her in the heavens.
> Wisdom went forth to make her dwelling among the children of men,
> And found no dwelling-place:
> Wisdom returned to her place,
> And took her seat among the angels.
> And unrighteousness went forth from her chambers:
> Whom she sought not she found,
> And dwelt with them,
> As rain in a desert
> And dew on a thirsty land. (42:1-3)

When Wisdom toured the nations she found no place to dwell, so she returned to heaven to live with the angels. That is where she is now. One must go to heaven to find Wisdom. There is no other way. Enoch's trip to heaven, which is the origin of the *Similitudes,* establishes him as the sole source of wisdom for those on earth. To accept his testimony contained in the *Similitudes* is to have wisdom, to reject it is to live in darkness.[8] Not only can wisdom not be found on earth, but humanity welcomes her opposite, unrighteousness. The personification of wisdom and her opposite as women wooing men is known from the wisdom tradition (Proverbs 8–9). Humanity's acceptance of unrighteousness and rejection of wisdom explain the present state of the world.

This hymn to wisdom in *1 Enoch* 42 contrasts with another hymn found in Sirach, a wisdom book. There wisdom says that she has journeyed through creation and visited every nation. God tells her, "Make your dwelling in Jacob, and in Israel receive your inheritance" (Sir 24:8). Wisdom says,

> In the holy tent I ministered before him,
>   and so I was established in Zion.
> Thus in the beloved city he gave me a resting place,
>   and in Jerusalem was my domain.
> I took root in an honored people,
>   in the portion of the Lord, his heritage. . . .
> All this is the book of the covenant of the Most High God,
>   the law that Moses commanded us
>   as an inheritance for the congregations of Jacob.
> It overflows, like the Pishon, with wisdom,
>   and like the Tigris at the time of first fruits.
> It runs over, like the Euphrates, with understanding,
>   and like the Jordan at harvest time.
> It pours forth instruction like the Nile,
>   like the Gihon at the time of vintage. (24:10-12, 23-27)

For this hymn, Torah is the source of all wisdom and is available to all. River imagery conveys the idea that Torah overflows with wisdom and understanding and fills those who open themselves to it. The contrast between *1 Enoch* 42 and Sirach 24 corresponds to the difference between sapiential and apocalyptic wisdom. In sapiential wisdom, wisdom is available to all. It can be attained by the exercise of human reason on events in the human and natural worlds. But apocalyptic wisdom comes only through direct revelation, and is known only to the elite.

Chapter 45 introduces the second parable. Again, its subject is judgment. The sinners "denied the name of the Lord of Spirits" (45:2), and they will be denied entrance to heaven and earth. The Elect One judges them.

On that day Mine Elect One shall sit on the throne of glory
And shall try their works,
And their places of rest shall be innumerable.
And their souls shall grow strong within them when they see Mine
    elect ones,
And those who have called upon My glorious name:
Then I will cause Mine Elect One to dwell among them.
And I will transform the heaven and make it an eternal blessing
    and light:
And I will transform the earth and make it a blessing:
And I will cause Mine elect ones to dwell upon it:
But the sinners and evil-doers shall not set foot thereon. (45:3-5)

A connection is made between the elect ones on earth who trust in God's name, and the Elect One in heaven who will be the judge at the endtime. Sinners are excluded from the new heaven and earth.

Chapter 46 is important for understanding the roots of the figure of the Elect One, the Son of Man, and for appreciating his function.

And there I saw One who had a head of days,
And His head was white like wool,
And with Him was another being whose countenance had the
    appearance of a man,
And his face was full of graciousness, like one of the holy
    angels.
And I asked the angel who went with me and showed me all the hidden things
concerning that Son of Man, who he was, and whence he was, and why he went
with the Head of Days? And he answered and said unto me:
This is the Son of Man who hath righteousness,
With whom dwelleth righteousness,
And who revealeth all the treasures of that which is hidden,
Because the Lord of Spirits hath chosen him,
And whose lot hath the pre-eminence before the Lord of Spirits in
    uprightness for ever. (46:1-3)

The passage depends on Daniel 7. The "Head of Days" is God and corresponds to the "Ancient of Days" in Daniel (RSV). In both cases God's hair is as white as wool, signifying extreme age, wisdom, and dignity. Both passages feature one in God's presence who resembles a "son of man," a human. In Daniel 7 the Son of Man is Israel's angelic patron. In the *Similitudes* the Son of Man is compared to the angels and is the heavenly patron of the elect on earth, a group not inclusive of all of Israel. The visionary behind chapter 46 saw Daniel 7 as the key to the solution of the oppression of the righteous. Their heavenly representative, hidden in God's presence and unknown by the oppressors, would come at the end of time to vindicate them. The Son of Man epitomizes righteousness, and so he is close to God. He is "chosen" by God and so is "elect." He knows all secret wisdom, and is able to disclose that the powerful of the earth will meet a dismal end and the righteous of the earth will be glorified. This is the hidden secret that only the righteous know because Enoch has revealed it to them.

The rest of the passage portrays the sinners as the powerful.

> And this Son of Man whom thou hast seen
> Shall raise up the kings and the mighty from their seats,
> And the strong from their thrones
> And shall loosen the reins of the strong,
> And break the teeth of the sinners.
> And he shall put down the kings from their thrones and kingdoms
> Because they do not extol and praise Him,
> Nor humbly acknowledge whence the kingdom was bestowed upon them.
> And he shall put down the countenance of the strong,
> And shall fill them with shame.
> And darkness shall be their dwelling,
> And worms shall be their bed,
> And they shall have no hope of rising from their beds,
> Because they do not extol the name of the Lord of Spirits.
> And these are they who judge the stars of heaven,
> And raise their hands against the Most High,
> And tread upon the earth and dwell upon it.
> And all their deeds manifest unrighteousness,
> And their power rests upon their riches,
> And their faith is in the gods which they have made with their hands,
> And they deny the name of the Lord of Spirits,
> And they persecute the houses of His congregations,
> And the faithful who hang upon the name of the Lord of Spirits. (46:4-8)

The community behind the *Similitudes* sees itself as persecuted by the powerful. The powerful do not acknowledge that their power derives from the Lord of Spirits. Instead, they trust in their own wealth and might, and create idols for themselves. Their conduct is seen as an assault on the stars (angels) and God (*see* Daniel 8 and 11).

"And in those days shall have ascended the prayer of the righteous, and the blood of the righteous from the earth before the Lord of Spirits" (47:1). The next verse says that the holy ones in the heavens will pray "on behalf of the blood of the righteous which has been shed." Members of the community of the righteous have actually shed their blood, and their blood now calls to the Lord for vengeance. Then comes a judgment scene:

In those days I saw the Head of Days when He seated himself upon
   the throne of His glory,
And the books of the living were opened before Him:
And all His host which is in heaven above and His counsellors
   stood before Him,
And the hearts of the holy were filled with joy;
Because the number of the righteous had been offered,
And the prayer of the righteous had been heard,
And the blood of the righteous been required before the Lord of
   Spirits. (47:3-4)

The scene recalls the judgment scene of Daniel 7. There the Ancient of Days takes his seat in the heavenly court, and "the books" are opened. The books are heavenly records of human deeds. They will be used in the final judgment, an idea common in the ancient Near East and in apocalypticism. Another idea common in apocalypticism is that a certain number of righteous must be martyred before the eschaton can come. In this passage the holy ones rejoice because the number has been reached.

The Son of Man makes another appearance in the next chapter.

And in that place I saw the fountain of righteousness
Which was inexhaustible:
And around it were many fountains of wisdom:
And all the thirsty drank of them,
And were filled with wisdom,
And their dwellings were with the righteous and holy and elect.
And at that hour that Son of Man was named
In the presence of the Lord of Spirits,
And his name before the Head of Days. (48:1-2)

Enoch is still in heaven. Although wisdom is scarce on earth, it is abundant in heaven. Wisdom and righteousness are closely associated, because righteousness, being in the proper relationship with God, is possible only to those who really know how things are, the wise. In this scene the identity of the Son of Man is made public, at least in heaven. The next verse says that the Son of Man was named before the Lord even before the sun and moon were created. God has planned all in advance, even before creation.

And for this reason hath he [the Son of Man] been chosen and hid-
   den before Him,
Before the creation of the world and for evermore.
And the wisdom of the Lord of Spirits hath revealed him to the
   holy and righteous;
For he hath preserved the lot of the righteous,

Because they have hated and despised this world of unrighteous-
ness,
And have hated all its works and ways in the name of the Lord of
Spirits:
For in his name they are saved,
And according to his good pleasure hath it been in regard to their
life. (48:6-7)

The community of the righteous on earth is truly alone in the world. They alone know about the Son of Man and his coming judgment. They have rejected this world and believed in the Lord of Spirits. Only they will be saved.

The next part of the chapter tells of the fate of the sinners.

In these days downcast in countenance shall the kings of the earth
have become,
And the strong who possess the land because of the works of their
hands,
For on the day of their anguish and affliction they shall not be
able to save themselves
And I will give them over into the hands of Mine elect:
As straw in the fire so shall they burn before the face of the
holy:
As lead in the water shall they sink before the face of the
righteous,
And no trace of them shall any more be found.
And on the day of their affliction there shall be rest on the earth,
And before them they shall fall and not rise again:
And there shall be no one to take them with his hands and raise
them:
For they have denied the Lord of Spirits and His Anointed. (48:8-10)

The sinners are the powerful of the earth—kings and large landowners. Their present strength means nothing in the end. They will be handed over to the righteous for punishment. The community is given its full characterization— elect, holy, righteous. Those who have opposed the community have denied the name of the Lord and the Lord's Messiah (Anointed). The Messiah is undoubtedly the same as the Elect One and the Son of Man. Chapter 49 is a hymn of praise to the Elect One with whom resides all wisdom, insight, might, understanding, and to whom it has been given to judge the "secret things."

Chapters 50 and 51 are jubilant accounts of the fate of the righteous. They will be raised from the dead, glorified. They will be saved through the name of the Lord of Spirits, who will have compassion on them. The Elect One will arise and "chose the righteous and holy from among them" (51:2), an act of judgment. God says, "And the Elect One shall in those days sit on My throne, and his mouth shall pour forth all the secrets of wisdom and counsel'' (51:3), indicating that the Elect One possesses divine authority.

Enoch is now carried by a whirlwind to the far west of the universe where he observes mountains of iron, copper, silver, gold, soft metal, and lead. He learns that the mountains are there to show the power of the Messiah when he comes, for they will melt in his presence. That will demonstrate that at the coming of the Elect One, ''None shall be saved, either by gold or by silver, and none be able to escape. And there shall be no iron for war, nor shall one clothe oneself with a breastplate'' (52:7-8). Those who are presently powerful, who possess wealth and military strength, will be powerless.

In chapter 53, Enoch views the valley of judgment where the wicked will be brought. He sees the ''angels of punishment abiding (there) and preparing all the instruments of Satan'' (53:3). The wicked are identified as the ''kings and the mighty of this earth'' (53:5). Enoch learns that when the sinners are destroyed, ''The Righteous and Elect One shall cause the house of his congregation to appear'' (53:6). In the next chapter he sees a fiery valley being prepared for the punishment of the evil angels who led humanity astray. The second parable ends with Enoch's vision of the return of Israel's exiles.

Chapter 58 introduces the last parable. It predicts glory, eternal life, and peace for the righteous. The next few chapters show Enoch seeing more of the secrets of the universe. The theme of eschatological judgment is prominent. God appears as judge on the divine throne in 60:2 and 61:1. Chapters 62 and 63 are an extended judgment scene in which the kings and the mighty are judged by the Son of Man.

> And they [the kings and mighty] shall be downcast of countenance,
> And pain shall seize them,
> When they see that Son of Man
> Sitting on the throne of his glory.
> And the kings and the mighty and all who possess the earth shall
> bless and glorify and extol him who rules over all, who was
> hidden.
> For from the beginning the Son of Man was hidden,
> And the Most High preserved him in the presence of His might,
> And revealed him to the elect.
> And the congregation of the elect and holy shall be sown,
> And all the elect shall stand before him on that day. (62:5-8)

The powerful of the earth do not know God, nor do they understand that the community behind the *Similitudes* is the community of the elect, holy and righteous. Similarly, the Son of Man is hidden, and is revealed only to the elect until the judgment. At the judgment he will be revealed to all as judge. The ideal situation for the righteous, realized at the end of time, is to be with the Son of

Man forever: "And the Lord of Spirits will abide over them, and with that Son of Man shall they eat and lie down and rise up for ever and ever" (62:14).

The once-powerful sinners beg for the chance to mend their ways and to worship God. They confess, "We have not believed before Him nor glorified the name of the Lord of Spirits, nor glorified our Lord but our hope was in the sceptre of our kingdom, and in our glory" (63:7). They are refused any opportunity to repent, because it is too late. Their last words are, "Our souls are full of unrighteous gain, but it does not prevent us from descending from the midst thereof into the burden of Sheol" (63:10). They are then driven from the Son of Man's presence.

The formal end of the third parable is 69:26-29. The righteous rejoice that the name of the Son of Man was revealed to them. The parable ends with the picture of the Son of Man sitting on his glorious throne, judging the sinners, acting for the Lord of Spirits.

The *Similitudes of Enoch* have two endings. Chapter 70 is probably the original ending, and chapter 71 was added later. Chapter 70 begins,

> And it came to pass after this that his [Enoch's] name during his lifetime was raised aloft to that Son of Man and to the Lord of Spirits from amongst those who dwell on the earth. And he was raised aloft on the chariots of the spirit and his name vanished among them. (70:1-2)

This reflects the mysterious end of the biblical Enoch where God simply takes him (Gen 5:24). The mysterious end of Enoch combined with his legendary righteousness made him an apt patron for the Enoch traditions.

Chapter 71 is a much longer ending and recapitulates Enoch's visions of heaven. Most interesting is an interchange between Enoch and an angel: "And he . . . came to me and greeted me with His voice, and said unto me: 'You are the Son of Man who is born unto righteousness'" (71:14). The identification of Enoch with the Son of Man is startling.[9] Of course, Enoch embodies righteousness and holiness and the elect status that the community shares with the Son of Man. But nothing in the book prepares for the complete identification of Enoch with the Son of Man. It has been suggested that when Christians identified Jesus as the Son of Man on the basis of Daniel 7, Jews did the same with Enoch to counter Christian claims. Others find it unlikely that Jews would imitate Christians in this way.

Whatever the reason for the identification of Enoch with the Son of Man, the *Similitudes of Enoch* provide some remarkable parallels with Christianity. Although the *Similitudes* do not oppose Torah, Torah receives almost no attention in the book. Instead, salvation depends on rejection of this world and belief in a hidden world where God controls all. God works through an agent called the Son of Man in whom the elect must have faith. The focus is on the Son

271

of Man, also called the Elect One, the Righteous One, and the Messiah. The Messiah in the *Similitudes* is a supernatural figure, something which has not been seen before in this study, but which is found in later Jewish works. All of this is similar to how early Christianity looks upon Jesus. Jesus is a supernatural person in whom one must have faith to be saved. Further, the titles borne by Enoch's Son of Man—Messiah, Righteous One, Elect One—are applied to Jesus in Christian traditions.

The similarities between the *Similitudes* and Christianity do not prove dependence in either direction. The importance of the *Similitudes* has often been thought to depend upon whether they could be shown to be the origin of Christian portrayals of Jesus as Son of Man. Such an approach is too narrow. Collins redirects the discussion to a more fruitful path: "It is apparent that Jewish conceptions of savior figures in this period were variable, but the Similitudes illustrate the *kind* of speculation that was also at work in the New Testament development of christological titles" (*AI*, 154).

EXCURSUS: THE SYNAGOGUE

The word "synagogue" comes from the Greek *synagōgē* meaning "gathering" or "assembly." A synagogue is a gathering for reading and interpretation of Torah, for teaching, and for prayer. Evidence for the existence of synagogues is plentiful in the New Testament, Josephus, and Philo, but the origins of the institution are obscure. The fact that synagogues were so widespread in the first century CE makes it likely that they existed in some form before then. Many scholars have thought that some institution like the synagogue must have been created by the exiled Jews in Babylon to compensate for their loss of the Temple and the holy land. As true as that may be in theory, there is little direct evidence for it. Reference is made to "places of prayer" (Greek: *proseuchē*) in third-century BCE Egypt. The term is also used by Josephus and Acts of the Apostles. The relation of the places of prayer to synagogues is unclear. Archeology does not help much, since there is no building predating the first century that can claim to be a synagogue. Of course, there may have been synagogues, "gatherings," in private homes or in buildings built for some other purpose. One cannot really be much more specific than to say that the synagogue most probably predates the first century, but that little is known about it.

Josephus stresses the teaching function of the synagogue on the sabbath.

He [Moses] appointed the Law to be the most excellent and necessary form of instruction, ordaining, not that it should be heard once for all or twice or on several occasions, but that every week men should desert their other occupations and assemble to listen to the Law and to obtain a thorough and accurate knowledge of it.

(*Against Apion* 2.17 § 175)

Josephus' observations about the importance of weekly reading and interpretation of the Law is supported by Philo (*Life of Moses* 2.39 § 216), and by numerous references in the New Testament. To the extent that Torah was central in Jewish life, the institution of the synagogue was crucial. When the Temple was destroyed, Torah and synagogue became still more important.

Jesus' appearance in the synagogue of Nazareth in Luke 4 shows what Luke thought would happen in a synagogue. It begins, "When he came to Nazareth, where he had been brought up, he went to the synagogue on the sabbath day, as was his custom. He stood up to read, and the scroll of the prophet Isaiah was given to him" (Luke 4:16-17). Jesus finds a passage and reads it. After reading the passage, Jesus "rolled up the scroll, gave it back to the attendant" (Luke 4:20). The "attendant" is presumably some sort of helper in the synagogue. Jesus then explains the passage. Rabbinic documents show that at a later date the synagogue service consisted of prayer, readings from the Torah and the Prophets with translation, a sermon, and a blessing (*m. Megilla* 4:3). Translation was necessary because Hebrew was no longer the vernacular of either Palestinian or Diaspora Jews. The number of those able to read the Hebrew text was limited, as was the number of those qualified to expound it.

In Acts, Paul and his companions arrive in a place called Antioch in Asia Minor. "And on the sabbath day they went into the synagogue and sat down. After the reading of the law and the prophets, the officials of the synagogue sent them a message, saying, 'Brothers, if you have any word of exhortation for the people, give it'" (Acts 13:14-15). Here readings from the Torah and the prophets are attested, as is an explanation of the readings. Later in Acts Paul claims to be a Pharisee (23:6), so that may explain why he is asked to deliver the sermon. This passage claims that the synagogue had "officials," a somewhat vague term. Perhaps the officials were the prominent, educated members of the Jewish community.

CONCLUSION

The independent Jewish kingdom of the Hasmoneans was cut short by the arrival of the Romans in the person of Pompey and his army. Pompey was invited by the brothers Hyrcanus II and Aristobulus II to intervene in their power dispute. Pompey did so and subjugated Palestine to Roman rule. Just over two decades of Roman rule through the Hasmoneans and the aristocracy was disturbed by Roman civil struggles. Partly as a result of those struggles, Herod the Great became king. His rule was oppressive. At his death in 4 BCE, his kingdom was divided among his sons Archelaus, Herod Antipas, and Philip. Archelaus lasted only ten years, at which time the Romans deposed him and instituted direct Roman rule through procurators.

The three texts examined in this chapter present three reactions to the events

273

summarized in the paragraph above. The *Psalms of Solomon* lament the defilement of the Temple by Pompey, and blame the disgrace on the behavior of the Hasmoneans and their supporters among the upper classes of Jerusalem. They yearn for a Davidic Messiah who will lead a purified Israel in perfect obedience to God. The *Testament of Moses* is a work with apocalyptic elements. It was probably originally written to address the circumstances of the persecution under Antiochus IV, but was adapted to apply to the rule of Herod. It has a low opinion of the Hasmoneans and of Herod. It anticipates the coming of God as warrior in the midst of cosmic disturbances to destroy idolatry, and to exalt those faithful to God to the stars. The *Similitudes of Enoch* do not contain historical references as clear as those of the other two works, but most scholars date it to the first century CE. It complains about the abuses of the powerful and accuses them of not recognizing that their power comes from God. It awaits a supernatural figure called the Son of Man, the Elect One, and the Righteous One, who will judge all people, punishing the powerful and exalting the suffering righteous.

SELECT BIBLIOGRAPHY

Avi-Yonah, Michael, and Zvi Baras, eds. *The World History of the Jewish People*, vol. 7, *The Herodian Period*. New Brunswick, N.J.: Rutgers University Press, 1975.

Collins, John J. "The Heavenly Representative: The 'Son of Man' in the Similitudes of Enoch," in *IFAJ*, 111-33.

──────. "The Similitudes of Enoch," in *AI*, chap. 6.

Garnsey, Peter, and Richard Saller, *The Roman Empire: Economy, Society, and Culture*. Berkeley: University of California Press, 1987.

Goodman, Martin. *The Ruling Class of Judaea: The Origins of the Jewish Revolt Against Rome A.D. 66–70*. Cambridge: Cambridge University Press, 1987.

Grant, Michael. *The Jews in the Roman World*. New York: Scribner's, 1973.

Leaney, A. R. C. *The Jewish and Christian World: 200 BC to AD 200*. Cambridge: Cambridge University Press, 1984.

Nickelsburg, George. "The Romans and the House of Herod," in *JLBBM*, chap. 6.

──────, ed. *Studies on the Testament of Moses*. Cambridge, Mass.: Society of Biblical Literature, 1973.

Saldarini, Anthony J. *Pharisees, Scribes, and Sadducees in Palestinian Society: A Sociological Approach*. Wilmington, Del.: Michael Glazier, 1988.

Sandmel, Samuel. *Herod: Portrait of a Tyrant*. Philadelphia: Lippincott, 1967.

Schalit, Abraham. "Herod and His Successors," in *JHT*, 36-46.

Sherwin-White, A. N. *Roman Society and Roman Law in the New Testament*. Oxford: Clarendon Press, 1963.

Smallwood, E. Mary. *The Jews Under Roman Rule: From Pompey to Diocletian: A Study in Political Relations*. Leiden: Brill, 1981.

Suter, D. W. *Tradition and Composition in the Parables of Enoch*, SBLDS 47. Missoula, Mont.: Scholars Press, 1979.

_____. "Weighed in the Balance: The Similitudes of Enoch in Recent Discussion," *RelSRev* 7 (1981): 217-21.

CHAPTER TEN

Jewish Palestine Under Rome

Primary Sources: Josephus' Jewish War and Jewish Antiquities
18–20

This chapter covers the time from the death of Herod the Great to the beginning of the Jewish revolt against the Romans.[1] The period is important to Jews because it immediately precedes the destruction of Jerusalem and its Temple, events that led to the formation of rabbinic Judaism. It is important to Christians because it encompasses the ministry of Jesus and the beginnings of Christianity. Of special interest is the interplay between politics, economics, and religion in the events and movements of the time.

PRELIMINARY TOPICS

Josephus

Since Josephus lived in Palestine and Rome in the first century CE, it is appropriate to discuss him here at greater length than has been done before. Josephus is not unbiased, so it is helpful to understand his biases when using his writings. Josephus was born into Jerusalem's priestly aristocracy in 37 CE and died around 100 CE. He claims to be descended from the Hasmoneans through his mother. Josephus was familiar with the Romans. At age twenty-six he traveled to Rome to defend some fellow priests against an unspecified charge. While there he won the friendship of Nero's wife, Poppaea. He returned to Palestine in 66 CE as the Jews were about to revolt against Rome. He says that he initially tried to stop the revolt, but when that proved impossible, he went along with it, hoping to keep things under control and to take advantage of opportunities to stop the rebellion. His viewpoint probably coincided with that of much of Jerusalem's aristocracy.

Josephus was appointed general of Galilee by the rebel government in Jerusalem, which was composed of people of his own class. Despite some difficulty in consolidating his control over Galilee—a certain John of Gischala being his chief rival—he was in command of the area when the Romans retook it. Josephus was captured, but won the favor of the Roman general Vespasian by prophesying that he would be named emperor. When that happened in 69 CE,

277

Josephus was freed from his chains and became the guide and interpreter for Vespasian's son, Titus, who took over his father's command. After the war Josephus went to Rome. Vespasian's family, the Flavians, became his patrons.

Josephus wrote four works still extant. The *Jewish War* was written in the late seventies to explain the war to Diaspora Jews. It takes the view that God was displeased with the Jewish rebels and so was on the Romans' side. Josephus asserts that the war began because of a few hotheads with bad intentions who deceived the rest of the population. In the nineties Josephus wrote the *Jewish Antiquities,* a work retelling Jewish history from creation to the beginning of the Jewish revolt. It attempts to make Judaism understandable to a non-Jewish audience. His *Life* concentrates on his rivals in Galilee during his command. Finally, Josephus wrote *Against Apion,* a work defending Judaism against the anti-Semitic slurs of an Egyptian named Apion. Both the *Life* and *Against Apion* were written after the *Antiquities.*

The Samaritans

Since several incidents in the first century involve Samaritans, they will be briefly examined here. Only the Samaritans' impact on Jewish history will be considered.

In the late Second Temple period the Samaritans lived in the area between Judea and Galilee, which had been the capital and surrounding lands of the northern kingdom of Israel. In 722 BCE the Assyrians conquered the northern kingdom and exiled many of its people. The following passage is a Judahite, that is, a southern, perspective on what then happened.

> The king of Assyria brought people from Babylon, Cuthah, Avva, Hamath, and Sepharvaim, and placed them in the cities of Samaria in place of the people of Israel; they took possession of Samaria, and settled in its cities. When they first settled there, they did not worship the LORD; therefore the LORD sent lions among them, which killed some of them. So the king of Assyria was told, ''The nations that you have carried away and placed in the cities of Samaria do not know the law of the god of the land; therefore he has sent lions among them; they are killing them, because they do not know the law of the god of the land.'' Then the king of Assyria commanded, ''Send there one of the priests whom you carried away from there; let him go and live there, and teach them the law of the god of the land.'' So one of the priests whom they had carried away from Samaria came and lived in Bethel; he taught them how they should worship the LORD. (2 Kgs 17:24-28)

This passage explains how it could be that the Samaritans had a version of the Torah, but were not really members of Israel. It also explains how God allowed them to live in the land, even though they were not really the chosen people. The passage says that although the nations brought to Samaria worshiped God, they also brought along their own gods whom they continued to worship. The passage ends with the condemning comment, "So these nations worshiped the Lord, but also served their carved images; to this day their children and their children's children continue to do as their ancestors did" (2 Kgs 17:41). This last verse is thought to be a late editorial comment demonstrating the anti-Samaritan attitude of exilic or postexilic Jews.

The books of Ezra and Nehemiah are also anti-Samaritan. In Ezra 4 the Samaritans, among others, come to the returned exiles who are about to rebuild the Temple and ask to be allowed to join in the rebuilding. "Let us build with you, for we worship your God as you do, and we have been sacrificing to him ever since the days of King Esarhaddon of Assyria who brought us here" (Ezra 4:2). The returned exiles spurn the Samaritans' offer. The rest of the chapter shows the Samaritans trying to subvert the building of the Temple. This passage shows Jewish awareness that the Samaritans claimed to worship the same God they did, but that the Jews did not see the Samaritans as true members of their religion.

In 331 BCE Alexander the Great destroyed the city of Samaria because of its resistance to his conquest of the area. The ancient city of Shechem then became the main city of the area, and the Samaritans built a temple on Mount Gerizim at Shechem. John Hyrcanus destroyed the Samaritan temple in 128 BCE when he conquered the area. That act undoubtedly stuck in Samaritan memory. Tension between Jews and Samaritans on the proper place to worship emerges in the dialogue between Jesus and the Samaritan woman in John 4. Jesus meets the woman at a well near Mount Gerizim and asks for water. The woman replies, "How is it that you, a Jew, ask a drink of me, a woman of Samaria?" The narrator explains, "Jews do not share things in common with Samaritans" (4:9). Later, the woman perceives that Jesus is a prophet and says, "Our ancestors worshiped on this mountain, but you say that the place where people must worship is in Jerusalem" (4:20).

The poor relations between Samaritans and Jews in the first century CE are demonstrated by incidents during the administration of Pontius Pilate and Cumanus examined later in this chapter. Another such incident is found in the Gospel of Luke, when Jesus and his followers are going to Jerusalem.

When the days drew near for him to be taken up, he set his face to go to Jerusalem. And he sent messengers ahead of him. On their way they entered a village of the Samaritans to make ready for him; but they did not receive him, because his face was set toward Jerusalem. When his disciples James and John saw it, they said, "Lord, do you want us to command fire to come down from heaven and consume them?" But he turned and rebuked them. Then they went on to another village.
(9:51-56)

The Samaritans were inhospitable because Jesus was a Jewish pilgrim on his way to Jerusalem. It is likely that many Galilean pilgrims went out of their way to avoid Samaritan territory on their way to Jerusalem.

Another incident illustrating the hostility of the Samaritans to Jerusalem took place under the procurator Coponius (6–8 CE).

> When the Festival of Unleavened Bread, which we call Passover, was going on, the priests were accustomed to throw open the gates of the temple after midnight. This time, when the gates were first opened, some Samaritans, who had secretly entered Jerusalem, began to scatter human bones in the porticoes and throughout the temple. (*Ant.* 18.2.2 §§ 29–30)

Human bones were ritually impure, and so would defile the Temple. The Samaritans' act was clearly hostile to the Jerusalem cult and to the Jews.

Jewish hostility toward Samaritans is also attested in the parable of the Good Samaritan (Luke 10:30-35), where the point of the story is the realization that a Samaritan can indeed be good, an unwelcome idea in Jewish circles. It is also present in the story of the ten lepers cured by Jesus, only one of whom, a Samaritan, returned to give him thanks (Luke 17:11-19).

The Samaritans were monotheists who thought themselves to be within the Mosaic covenant. They were conservative in their choice of Scripture, for, like the Sadducees, they accepted only the five books of Moses as authoritative. Their sacred books were a version of the five books of Moses. Some of the differences between the Jewish and the Samaritan Pentateuchs involve specifically Samaritan beliefs, such as the conviction that God's sacred mountain is Gerizim in Samaria and not Zion in Jerusalem. Also like the Sadducees, the Samaritans did not accept the idea of resurrection from the dead. Priests were dominant in Samaritanism. Their eschatological expectation involved the coming of a prophet like Moses, called the *Taheb,* "Restorer," a hope based on Deuteronomy 18.

It is not surprising that the Jews and the Samaritans were enemies. They both claimed to worship the same God, but each denigrated the worship of the other. Indeed, religious groups that have much in common can become the bitterest enemies, because they fight for control of many of the same symbols.

Peasants and Artisans

First-century peasants and artisans did not write books. They were not even literate for the most part. Consequently, their side of history is often ignored for lack of evidence. However, close attention to Josephus' writings in combination with insights about peasant societies generally makes possible a reconstruction of the activities and attitudes of first-century Jewish peasants.

Peasants lived a restricted life dictated by the need to survive. Material goods were scarce. The family was the basic unit of production and consumption. Local villages and local markets were as far as most peasants traveled in the course of their lives. In Jewish Palestine, pilgrimages to Jerusalem might also have been common, but one should not assume that the trip was easy or made frequently. In general, peasants were born, grew up, and died in a very small area. Their knowledge of the wider world was limited, and they probably came into contact with it primarily through tax collectors and invading armies. Peasants tended to be conservative socially and religiously.

Peasants were often under economic pressure. Because agriculture was the basis of most ancient empires, the peasants paid for wars, royal courts, bureaucracies, and religious establishments. Jewish peasants fed their families, helped maintain the Temple establishment, supported the local nobility, and helped pay taxes to the ruling empire. Famines could be disastrous under such pressures. Hard years may have led to foreclosures and loss of land to the upper classes. The gospels attest to peasants resorting to day labor (Matt 20:1-16), and to tenant farmers working for absentee landlords (Mark 12:1-9).

Artisans are skilled craftsmen, such as potters, stone carvers, or makers of clothing. In the modern world, artisans are often economically middle class. In the ancient world, they were for the most part of the lower classes. They were probably found mostly in villages and urban areas. Urban workers may have had a bit more political power than the peasants, since they could mount demonstrations or even riots in the very places where the upper classes lived, and so exert direct pressure on the ruling class.

Bandits

A category of analysis important for the first century is that of "bandit" (Greek: *lēstēs*). Josephus employs the term in a derogatory way, claiming that Palestine's bandits were simple robbers, having only the basest motives. But he speaks from the point of view of the priestly aristocracy, which had the most to lose by confrontation with Rome. Recent research has highlighted the social and political sides of banditry. Bandits live in groups and make their living by robbery, at times with the support of the peasantry. Banditry is most likely to occur when the peasants are oppressed and are economically vulnerable, and when governments are ineffective. When peasants are pressed by the difficulty of farming, social oppression, taxation, and coercion by the government, sometimes their only option is to leave their land and live outside the law. This is a kind of prepolitical rebellion. Such bandits opt out of the political and economic system, but do not yet oppose the system itself. Their activity aims at survival, and sometimes at righting specific wrongs, not at overthrowing political authorities. If things get bad enough, and the bandit groups numerous and large enough, widespread banditry can develop into full-scale revolt.

Conditions in Palestine were ripe for banditry at various points in the first century CE. Under the Herods, the people paid taxes supporting the Herodian establishment, the Temple, and the Roman Empire. The Herodian rulers and then Roman procurators were at times oppressive and ineffective in controlling the population. When a difficult political situation was combined with a natural disaster such as a drought, the situation could become critical. When religious symbols and systems, which were often the only thing the people had left to give their lives meaning and to maintain self-respect, were trampled on, the situation could become volatile.

While administering Galilee, Herod the Great captured and executed the most notorious bandit chief in the area, a man named Hezekiah. Hezekiah was no ordinary robber, as is suggested by the fact that his execution was protested by a Galilean contingent that traveled to the Sanhedrin in Jerusalem. It is likely that Herod's execution of Hezekiah was not just law enforcement, but was the suppression of resistance to the oppressive rule of the Romans and their local representatives, native aristocrats. The support shown for Hezekiah shows that bandits could command the respect and support of other segments of society.

The "Zealots"

For many years there has been a misleading theory that there was organized, continuous Jewish resistance to Roman rule throughout the first century, the goal of which was the ouster of the Romans. Josephus mentions a certain Judas the Galilean who in 6 CE founded a "fourth sect" (in addition to Pharisees, Sadducees, and Essenes). The aim of the fourth sect, allegedly later called the "Zealots," was freedom. Only God could be master of Israel. Foreign domination was unacceptable. The theory holds that this "sect" advocated violence to achieve its aims. Its efforts culminated in revolt against the Romans in 66 CE.

The evidence upon which the Zealot theory is based is minimal and ambiguous, and there is much that speaks against it, as will be shown. Over the years it has served Christian interests to see first-century Jewish society as dominated either by legalistic hypocrites (Pharisees), or by violent revolutionaries (Zealots). Prejudices against the Pharisees were addressed in chapter 8. If it is true that the Zealot theory also is faulty, then the other side of the stereotyped picture of Judaism in the time of Jesus also collapses.

The Spiral of Violence

Horsley uses a model of how colonial powers interact with subject peoples that is helpful for understanding first-century Palestine. It is called the "spiral of violence." When injustice perpetrated on a subject people becomes burdensome enough, they may resist it. Initial resistance is often nonviolent and aims simply to remove the injustice. The ruling power may respond with repression. If so, the subjects can be driven to revolution. The spiral of violence thus has four stages (a) injustice; (b) resistance; (c) repression; (d) revolt. Of course, the stages are not always neatly separated, but frequently there is a definite progression over time. The language used by various observers and participants in this spiral encodes value judgments about what is happening. For example, the act of killing someone might be called "terrorism" if done by revolutionaries, but "legitimate use of force" if done by the occupying power. Even the term "violence" itself usually carries negative connotations, and is more likely to be used when describing actions with which one disagrees, whereas "force" might be used to describe the same action if one agrees with it. Keeping these distinctions in mind will help in assessing Josephus' judgments about resisters to Roman rule.

THE HISTORY OF FIRST-CENTURY JEWISH PALESTINE

The Eagle Incident

In 4 BCE, Herod the Great was desperately ill. A large portion of the populace waited eagerly for his death, hoping that it would bring improved conditions for Jews in Palestine. Then the following incident occurred.

> To his other troubles was now added an insurrection of the populace. There were in the capital two doctors with a reputation as profound experts in the laws of their country, who consequently enjoyed the highest esteem of the whole nation; their names were Judas, son of Sepphoraeus, and Matthias, son of Margalus. Their lectures on the laws were attended by a large youthful audience, and day after day they drew together quite an army of men in their prime. Hearing now that the king was gradually sinking under despondency and disease, these doctors threw out hints to their friends that this was the fitting moment to avenge God's honour and to pull down those structures which had been erected in defiance of their fathers' laws. It was, in fact, unlawful to place in the temple either images or busts or any representation whatsoever of a living creature; notwithstanding this, the king had erected over the great gate a golden eagle. This it was which these doctors now exhorted their disciples to cut down, telling them that, even if the action proved hazardous, it was a noble deed to die for the law of one's country; for the souls of those who came to such an end attained immortality and an eternally abiding sense of felicity; it was the ignoble, uninitiated in their philosophy, who clung in their ignorance to life and preferred death on a sick-bed to that of a hero.
>
> While they were discoursing in this strain, a rumour spread that the king was dying; the news caused the young men to throw themselves more boldly into the enterprise. At mid-day, accordingly, when numbers of people were perambulating the temple, they let themselves down from the roof by stout cords and began chopping off the golden eagle with hatchets. The king's captain, to whom the matter was immediately reported, hastened to the scene with a considerable force, arrested about forty of the young men and conducted them to the king. Herod first

asked them whether they had dared to cut down the golden eagle; they admitted it. "Who ordered you to do so?" he continued. "The law of our fathers." "And why so exultant, when you will shortly be put to death?" "Because, after our death, we shall enjoy greater felicity." (*War* 1.33.2-3 §§ 648–53)

The young men and their teachers were burned alive as punishment.

One of Herod's most notable achievements was the rebuilding of Jerusalem's Temple. He may have wanted to gain the support of his Jewish subjects by rebuilding their cultic place, but he showed his disregard for Jewish sensitivities by placing on the Temple a golden eagle, symbol of the Roman Empire. The prohibition of images was enshrined in the ten commandments (Exod 20:4-6; Deut 5:8-10).

The decision to remove the eagle was made by two teachers of Torah who were renowned for their adherence to Torah. They are not characterized as revolutionaries.[2] They showed no desire to change the political system or to take power. They wanted only to put an end to a violation of Torah that defiled the Temple. They persuaded forty of their students to undertake the task. No provisions were made for their safety or for armed resistance. They knew that they endangered their lives, but the students cut down the eagle in broad daylight, when the Temple was full of people. They probably wanted maximum exposure for their deed so as to win popular support.

Disturbances in 4 BCE

When Herod died, Augustus Caesar divided his kingdom among his three sons. Archelaus took charge of Judea. At first the people hoped that he would be a more just ruler than his father. Archelaus at first listened sympathetically to some of their requests, such as lower taxes and freedom for some of Herod's political prisoners. But then the people went so far as to ask that the high priest appointed by Herod be deposed so that Archelaus might "choose another man who would serve as high priest more in accordance with the law and ritual purity" (*Ant.* 17.9.1 § 207). Some went farther still, and demanded punishment for the executioners of those who cut down the eagle. This touched a sensitive area, because it would mean that Herod's officers and members of the ruling class would be punished for suppressing a challenge to Herodian and Roman rule.

Josephus says that the Jews who made this final request did so out of a desire for innovation (*Ant.* 17.9.1 § 206). The charge assumes that Josephus' audience will see innovation as negative. In fact, the Greek word *neōtera,* taken here as "innovation," can also mean "revolution." In traditional societies, where the weight of custom is heavy and things are perceived as basically static, change can appear to be negative. Such societies contrast markedly with that of the United States, for example, in which change is often seen as progress. Again, the words chosen to describe certain activities imply value judgments on those activities. Whether or not something is an innovation depends on one's frame of reference. Josephus sees the request of the protesters as challenging the established order, and so as an innovation. The protesters probably saw Herod's aristocracy as an unwanted innovation that led to the violation of Torah, Israel's ancient law.

Soon after Archelaus' accession the feast of Passover arrived. During feasts tremendous crowds of pilgrims poured into Jerusalem, creating a problematic situation for the authorities. Passover's danger lay not only in the concentration of people, but also in that Passover traditions recalled the liberation of Israel from its Egyptian oppressors. Fearing trouble, Archelaus sent armed soldiers to the Temple. Some of the people threw stones at the soldiers. Archelaus then sent in the cavalry and killed a large number of people. The carnage persuaded the crowds to leave Jerusalem and return home.

Then Archelaus sailed for Rome to persuade Augustus to grant him the title of king. Other segments of the Herodian family also went to Rome to plead their case. They were followed by another Jewish embassy, which Josephus defines only by their opposition to Archelaus (*Ant.* 17.11.1-3 §§ 299–316). They told Augustus of Herod's tyranny. It is likely that they were people of means, and prominent in Jewish society. That likelihood is confirmed by the nature of their complaints. Among other things, they complained that Herod killed members of the nobility and confiscated their estates. He also showed little regard for the integrity of the Jewish family system and wreaked havoc with marriage rules and rules for sexual conduct. The embassy says that they had initially welcomed Archelaus as leader of the nation, hoping that he would not follow his father's example. His slaughter of the worshipers showed that to be an empty hope. They petitioned Augustus to annex Judea to Syria, asking only that they be allowed to follow Torah. They said that their conduct would prove them uninterested in overthrowing Roman rule.

The Jewish embassy seems to have represented the viewpoint of a sizable portion of the nobility and retainer class of Judea, who had suffered under Herod. They saw no reason they could not live peacefully and submissively under Roman rule, if only they were not oppressed and were allowed to live according to their own customs. In the end they lost their cause, for Augustus allowed Archelaus to continue in charge of Judea.

When Archelaus went to Rome, revolt broke out in all sectors of Palestine (*Ant.* 17.10 §§ 250–98). The Roman Sabinus had been left in charge as procurator in Judea. Sabinus "greatly harassed the rebels, being confident that he would overcome them with the army that had been left behind and with a large number of his own slaves, for he had armed many of these and used them as terrorists, thereby goading and disturbing the Jews to the point of rebellion" (*Ant.* 17.10.1 §§ 252-53). Josephus accuses the procurator of acting from greed. In this instance, Josephus blames both the Jews and the Roman official for the outbreak of hostilities. However, it seems that the "innovation" for which Josephus castigates the Jews is really a desire for justice. Given Josephus' pro-Roman agenda, his criticism of the Roman official's provocation of the people must be taken seriously. It is easy to trace the pattern of injustice, resistance, repression, and revolt in Josephus' narrative. Herod's injustice in the eagle incident, as well as his other political, economic, and religious injustices, was protested before Archelaus. Archelaus initially appeared sympathetic, but then reacted repressively. Continued resistance under Sabinus met with repression.

At the feast of Pentecost (Weeks), fifty days after Passover, a large number of pilgrims converged on Jerusalem. Josephus says they came not only to celebrate the feast, but also to attack Sabinus. There follows an extensive description of conflicts between Roman soldiers and Jews in which both sides suffered substantial casualties. Battles then erupted throughout Judea between Jews and Gentiles.

Next Josephus tells the story of Judah son of Hezekiah the bandit.

> Then there was Judas, the son of the brigand chief Ezekias,[3] who had been a man of great power and had been captured by Herod only with great difficulty. This Judas got together a large number of desperate men at Sepphoris in Galilee and there made an assault on the royal palace, and having seized all the arms that were stored there, he armed every single one of his men and made off with all the property that had been seized there. He became an object of terror to all men by plundering those he came across in his desire for great possessions and his ambition for royal rank, a prize that he expected to obtain not through the practice of virtue but through excessive ill-treatment of others. (*Ant.* 17.10.5 §§ 271–72)

Josephus recalls what a formidable foe Hezekiah had been for Herod in Galilee. Resistance to the ruling class extended to Hezekiah's son, Judah. Taking advantage of the disorder in Jerusalem he broke into the armory of the Galilean city of Sepphoris. Sepphoris was capital of Galilee and so contained weapons and wealth. Josephus accuses Judah of wanting power and aspiring to royal rank.

Next comes the story of Simon.

> There was also Simon, a slave of King Herod but a handsome man, who took pre-eminence by size and bodily strength, and was expected to go farther. Elated by the unsettled condition of affairs, he was bold enough to place the diadem on his head, and having got together a body of men, he was himself also proclaimed king by them in their madness, and he rated himself worthy of this beyond anyone else. After burning the royal palace in Jericho, he plundered and carried off the things that had been seized there. He also set fire to many other royal residences in many parts of the country and utterly destroyed them after permitting his fellow-rebels to take as booty whatever had been left in them. . . . Such was the great madness

that settled upon the nation because they had no king of their own to restrain the populace by his preeminence, and because of the foreigners who came among them to suppress the rebellion were themselves a cause of provocation through their arrogance and their greed. (*Ant.* 17.10.6 §§ 273–77)

Simon was active in the neighborhood of the Jordan River. He put on a crown and declared himself king. He was a member of Herod's entourage, and so was a servant of the ruling class who saw an opportunity to take power. Josephus emphasizes Simon's strength and size. At the end of this story, Josephus editorializes that the disturbances were due to the lack of a king to keep order, and to the brutal oppression by "foreigners."

Now Josephus recounts the history of Athronges.

Then there was a certain Athronges, a man distinguished neither for the position of his ancestors nor by the excellence of his character, nor for any abundance of means but merely a shepherd completely unknown to everybody although he was remarkable for his great stature and feats of strength. This man had the temerity to aspire to the kingship, thinking that if he obtained it he would enjoy freedom to act more outrageously; as for meeting death, he did not attach much importance to the loss of his life under such circumstances. He also had four brothers, and they too were tall men and confident of being very successful through their feats of strength, and he believed them to be a strong point in his bid for the kingdom. Each of them commanded an armed band, for a large number of people had gathered round them. Though they were commanders, they acted under his orders whenever they went on raids and fought by themselves. Athronges himself put on the diadem and held a council to discuss what things were to be done, but everything depended upon his own decision. This man kept his power for a long time, for he had the title of king and nothing to prevent him from doing as he wished. He and his brothers also applied themselves vigorously to slaughtering the Romans and the king's men, toward both of whom they acted with a similar hatred, toward the latter because of the arrogance that they had shown during the reign of Herod, and toward the Romans because of the injuries that they were held to have inflicted at the present time. (*Ant.* 17.10.7 §§ 278–81)

Athronges was not from the nobility, nor was he a person of wealth. He was a shepherd. As he did in the case of Simon, Josephus stresses his size and strength. His area of activity seems to have been Judea. Josephus ascribes low motives to Athronges. Even when Athronges operated in a rather democratic fashion, Josephus insists that he was really reserving all power for himself. Athronges explicitly claimed kingship, and managed to survive for a long time. Although Josephus calls Athronges' motive "wantonness," he admits that he attacked Roman and Herodian troops because of the wrongs they committed.

Josephus ends this section with a generalization about the nature of the disturbances:

And so Judaea was filled with brigandage. Anyone might make himself king as the head of a band of rebels whom he fell in with, and then would press on to the destruction of the community, causing trouble to few Romans and then only to a small degree but bringing the greatest slaughter upon their own people.

(Ant. 17.10.8 § 285)

There is no evidence that these bands of rebels had anything to do with each other. Since Josephus presents rebellions against Rome as conspiracies of a minority of the Jews with low motives, it is significant that he does not assert that Judah, Simon, or Athronges were in contact with each other or with any other of the "gangs of bandits." He does claim that the bandits were interested in establishing a new monarchy, which of course implies the overthrow of Roman and Herodian hegemony. Josephus points out that they did far more damage to their countrymen than to the Romans. This may not be accidental. The injustices suffered by the lower classes of Jewish Palestine were inflicted not only by the Romans. There were probably relatively few Romans in Palestine. As elsewhere, the Romans exercised their rule through the local aristocracy. Their rule was oppressive to common people and to large segments of the nobility. It is no accident that the rebels attacked Herodian troops. Further, they could not have "plundered" the nobility, whose estates had already been confiscated by Herod and his constituents. They were probably raiding the properties of those who profited from Herod's rule at the expense of other parts of Jewish society—peasants, disenfranchised nobility, disaffected scribes, Pharisees, and others.

Varus, the governor of Syria, went to Galilee and Judea to put down the rebellion. Sepphoris he burned to the ground, enslaving its inhabitants. Other villages involved in the revolt were punished similarly. Varus arrived in Jerusalem and was told by its inhabitants that they had not favored rebellion, but that the crowds of pilgrims for the feast of Weeks were responsible for the trouble. Varus treated those who claimed to have had nothing to do with the revolt leniently, but carried on mopping up operations in the countryside. Most participants in the revolt were severely punished. Josephus claims that Varus crucified two thousand rebels. Crucifixion was a horrible Roman punishment reserved for political offenders, slaves, and hardened criminals. It not only punished the guilty, but also graphically warned others.

Judah, Simon, and Athronges are each said to aspire to royal rank. Various forms of official ideology restricted kingship to those with Davidic lineage, or Hasmonean blood, and so on. The common people probably had their own versions of Israel's sacred traditions. The establishment's control of sacred traditions was a form of social control, but it could not have been completely successful. Groups and individuals not in power could read the traditions differently from how the elite did. It would be natural for the ruling class to read the traditions so as to reinforce their own power, whereas groups not in power might have emphasized aspects of the tradition that challenged the rulers. That might be what happened in the popular uprisings.

Horsley assembles evidence from Jewish literature for a notion of popular kingship. That notion did not stress lineage, but rather saw kingship as conferred by God for the good of the people. God sometimes chose a king who would be popularly acclaimed. The king was not absolute, but was under God's Law. His rule would result not in an oppressively hierarchical society, but would preserve the dignity and importance of all Israelites. Such a kingship could be revolutionary, overthrowing existing structures. Such kings were often praised for their military prowess or their physical attractiveness. David and Saul are prototypes of such kings. Another example is Jeroboam. After the death of Solomon, God raised up Jeroboam to throw off the oppression of the Jerusalem monarchy and to found the northern kingdom of Israel. Later, Jehu was instructed by God to lead a successful revolt against a northern dynasty that had incurred God's displeasure.

Elements of Israel's traditional popular kingship can be discerned in Josephus's narrative. Simon's strength and size are mentioned, and he attacks the Herodian establishment. Athronges, like David, starts as a shepherd, and is known for his stature and strong deeds. His rule is somewhat democratic, and he is said to fight Roman and Herodian injustice. One might imagine that segments of the population saw such figures as God-sent liberators.

Josephus characterizes Archelaus' ten-year rule as tyrannical. The prominent men of Judea and Samaria finally appealed to Augustus in 6 CE, and he banished Archelaus to Gaul.

The Tax Revolt of Judas the Galilean (6 CE)

Augustus did not appoint another Herodian in Judea. He appointed a Roman procurator who was subordinate to the Roman governor of Syria. The procurator had a small body of troops, but relied on the governor of Syria for help should there be large-scale disturbances. The procurator resided in the coastal city of Caesarea, the town of mixed (Jewish and Gentile) population that Herod the Great rebuilt and renamed in honor of Augustus Caesar. The procurators traveled to Jerusalem for the Jewish festivals because of the potential for trouble, and while there, occupied the fortress Antonia (named after Marc Antony) overlooking the Temple. A permanent garrison of two hundred men was maintained at Antonia.

The procurator was primarily interested in keeping the peace and in ensuring that taxes were paid, but he had general oversight of all that happened in Judea. He was of the equestrian order of Roman society. That meant that he was not of the Roman nobility, the senatorial order. Members of the equestrian order had some military ability, and had to have a certain minimal income. Although it was expected that the procurator would make a profit for himself from his tenure, he was answerable to Rome, which expected him to keep peace. That usually prevented gross abuses of the office. However, procurators were sometimes insensitive to Jewish concerns, a situation that led to unrest.

As before, the aristocracy played a strong role in the daily running of Judea. The difference was that the Herodians were no longer in charge, and the high priest was the leading Jewish authority under the procurator. Herod had established the practice of deposing and appointing high priests as he saw fit. The Romans continued the policy, so the identity of the high priest was now dependent on the decision of the procurator. The Sanhedrin was more powerful than under Herod.

In 6 CE, Augustus sent Quirinius to Syria to conduct a census for purposes of taxation. Since Judea was now part of the province of Syria, Quirinius accompanied the new procurator, Coponius, to deal with matters related to the census. At first the Jews resisted the census, but their high priest, Joazar son of Boethus, persuaded them not to make trouble. Not all went along with the plan, however.[4]

Although the Jews were at first shocked to hear of the registration of property, they gradually condescended, yielding to the arguments of the high priest Joazar, the son of Boethus, to go no further in opposition. So those who were convinced by him declared, without shilly-shallying, the value of their property. But a certain Judas, a Gaulanite from a city named Gamala, who had enlisted the aid of Saddok, a Pharisee, threw himself into the cause of rebellion. They said that the assessment carried with it a status amounting to downright slavery, no less, and appealed to the nation to make a bid for independence. They urged that in case of success the Jews would have laid the foundation of prosperity, while if they failed to obtain any such boon, they would win honour and renown for their lofty aim; and that Heaven would be their zealous helper to no lesser end than the furthering of their enterprise until it succeeded—all the more if with high devotion in their hearts they stood firm and did not shrink from the bloodshed that might be necessary. Since the populace, when they heard their appeals, responded gladly, the plot to strike boldly made serious progress; and so these men sowed the seed of every kind of misery, which so afflicted the nation that words are inadequate. When wars are set afoot that are bound to rage beyond control, and when friends are done away with who might have alleviated the suffering, when raids are made by great hordes of brigands [bandits] and men of the highest standing are assassinated, it is supposed to be the common welfare that is upheld, but the truth is that in such cases the motive is private gain. They sowed the seed from which sprang strife between factions and the slaughter of fellow citizens. Some were slain in civil strife, for these men madly had recourse to butchery of each other and of themselves from a longing not to be outdone by their opponents; others were slain by the enemy in war. Then came famine, reserved to exhibit the last degree of shamelessness, followed by the storming and razing of cities until at last the very temple of God was ravaged by the enemy's fire through this revolt. Here is a lesson that an innovation and reform in ancestral traditions weighs heavily in the scale in leading to the destruction of the congregation of the people. In this case certainly, Judas and Saddok started among us an intrusive fourth school of philosophy; and when they had won an abundance of devotees, they filled the body politic with tumult, also planting the seeds of those troubles which subsequently overtook it, all because of the novelty of this hitherto unknown philosophy that I shall now describe. My reason for giving this brief account of it is chiefly that the zeal which Judas and Saddok inspired in the younger element meant the ruin of our cause. (*Ant.* 18.1.1 §§ 3–10)

As for the fourth of the philosophies, Judas the Galilaean set himself up as leader of it. This school agrees in all other respects with the opinions of the Pharisees, except that they have a passion for liberty that is almost unconquerable, since they are convinced that God alone is their leader and master. (*Ant.* 18.1.6 § 23)

The territory of Archelaus was now reduced to a province, and Coponius, a Roman of the equestrian order, was sent out as procurator, entrusted by Augustus with full powers, including the infliction of capital punishment. Under his administration, a Galilaean, named Judas, incited his countrymen to revolt, upbraiding them as cowards for consenting to pay tribute to the Romans and tolerating mortal masters, after having God for their lord. This man was a sophist who founded a sect of his own, having nothing in common with the others. (*War* 2.8.1 §§ 117–18)

The passages above are the only evidence for a sect founded by Judas the Galilean. They state that Judas founded a fourth school (or sect) of Jewish philosophy in addition to the Pharisees, Essenes, and Sadducees. In *Antiquities* 18.1.1 § 9 and 18.1.6 § 25, Josephus blames the school for all subsequent troubles, right up to 66 CE when the Jewish revolt erupted. In *Antiquities* 18, Josephus claims that the school was "intrusive," caused tumult among the people, and planted the seeds of Israel's future woes. Josephus adduces a long list of the occurrences of the first century including civil strife, assassinations, and even famine. All is laid at the doorstep of this new "Fourth Philosophy."

The Zealot theory of Jewish resistance to Roman rule in the first century is based primarily on this evidence. In the Roman war, a Jewish party called the "Zealots" is prominent. Some scholars have argued that the Zealots of the war are the same as Judas' group, but active several decades later. Because of repression, they supposedly went underground until the sixties of the first century, but were always present, stirring up resistance to Roman rule, assassinating Jewish collaborators, and waiting for a chance to realize their nationalistic program.

There are serious problems with the Zealot theory. *War* 2, written shortly after the end of the Jewish revolt, does not claim that Judas' group was responsible for all subsequent problems in Jewish Palestine in the first century. In fact, the group is not mentioned anywhere else in *War,* a work whose purpose is to explain the causes of the revolt. It would be strange indeed if Josephus had neglected to describe the actions of Judas' group after 6 CE, if that group was really behind resistance to Roman rule. Further, nowhere does Josephus label Judas' group "the Zealots." It is true that both Judas' group and the Zealots wanted freedom from Roman rule, but that is hardly enough to identify them as the same group. When Josephus summarizes the things for which Judas' group is allegedly responsible, he includes almost every type of conflict and act of resistance of the first century. Even if Judas' group did exist in an organized form throughout the first century, which is unlikely, it could hardly have been responsible for all that Josephus attributes to it, nor would it be the only segment of the population responsible for the war.

When Josephus wrote the *Antiquities* in the nineties, he blamed all of the troubles of the first century on a single group that he could categorize as a minority of the population. He did not want his own people to seem anti-Roman or troublesome to the empire in any way. The philosophy of Judas' group was portrayed as alien to Judaism, and an innovation. A close look at Josephus' language shows that he does not really claim that Judas' group *did* all the things he lists. He says only that they were in some way *responsible* for them. What Josephus is really saying is that their introduction of the idea of freedom into the Palestinian equation led to the troubles of the first century. That is quite a different thing from claiming that the group continued in an organized way and that its members were engaged in revolutionary acts throughout the first century.

Judas is not portrayed as initiating full-scale rebellion. Rather, his actions have the nature of a tax revolt. Nowhere is it claimed that he took up arms. He merely refused to cooperate with the census and so refused to pay taxes and urged his countrymen to do the same. Judas knew that the Romans would not take his position lightly. He realized that the Romans would respond with repression, and exhorted his followers to be ready to shed their own blood for the cause, confident that God would be on their side. God might even use their actions as an opportunity to reinstate Jewish independence.

Belief that God was Israel's only master was not new in Jewish thought. However, Israel had lived for centuries under foreign rule. Jews had learned to reconcile devotion to God with submission to colonial powers. What was relatively new was Judas' insistence that one could not serve God and the Romans simultaneously. But Jews had been playing taxes to the Romans for almost seven decades by the time Judas refused to do so. What was the new factor that made 6 CE the time to see paying taxes as slavery? The most plausible answer is that in 6 CE the Romans undertook for the first time to rule Palestine directly. The shock of direct Roman rule generated resistance, and the census for the purposes of taxation made direct Roman rule obvious.

Josephus provides no evidence of widespread resistance under Judas. The high priest persuaded the populace to cooperate with the Romans. Perhaps the memory of the repression of Varus ten years earlier dissuaded the people from defiance. Judas' action deserved mention, but did not require further comment. Josephus says nothing about a Roman reaction, and gives no details of exactly what happened to Judas and his group. It can hardly have been a large rebellion, and it seems to have been nonviolent.

Pontius Pilate (26–36 CE)

Josephus mentions no significant disturbance in Jewish Palestine between 6 CE and the coming of Pontius Pilate as procurator of Judea. Far from fanning the flames of rebellion, Judas' tax resistance ushered in a peaceful period in Judea. Nor does Josephus castigate any of the procurators of those twenty years for trampling on Jewish sensitivities. That was to change with the coming to office of Pontius Pilate. He stirred the Jews to protest several times. The first incident came early in Pilate's administration.

> Pilate, being sent by Tiberius as procurator to Judaea, introduced into Jerusalem by night and under cover the effigies of Caesar which are called standards. This proceeding, when day broke, aroused immense excitement among the Jews; those on the spot were in consternation, considering their laws to have been trampled under foot, as those laws permit no image to be erected in the city; while the indignation of the townspeople stirred the country-folk, who flocked together in crowds. Hastening after Pilate in Caesarea, the Jews implored him to remove the standards from Jerusalem and to uphold the laws of their ancestors. When Pilate refused, they fell prostrate around his house and for five whole days remained motionless in that position.
>
> On the ensuing day Pilate took his seat on his tribunal in the great stadium and summoning the multitude, with the apparent intention of answering them, gave the arranged signal to his armed soldiers to surround the Jews. Finding themselves in a ring of troops, three deep, the Jews were struck dumb at this unexpected sight. Pilate, after threatening to cut them down, if they refused to admit Caesar's images, signalled to the soldiers to draw their swords. Thereupon the Jews, as by concerted action, flung themselves in a body on the ground, extended their necks, and exclaimed that they were ready rather to die than to transgress the law. Overcome with astonishment at such intense religious zeal, Pilate gave orders for the immediate removal of the standards from Jerusalem. (*War* 2.9.2-3 §§ 169–74)

Thirty years after the incident of Herod's golden eagle, Pilate again tested Jewish concern for the divine command against images. The images were on the standards carried by the Roman army. That Pilate was aware of the Jewish prohibition is suggested by the fact that he introduced the images of Caesar into Jerusalem at night. Daybreak brought discovery of the defilement. News spread to the countryside. This was an issue that united both city-dweller and peasant. Since Pilate resided at Caesarea, a large crowd went there. That also attests to the seriousness of the protest. A trip from Jerusalem to Caesarea involving a lengthy stay in the city and absence from one's work was a hardship. Pilate's first instinct was to intimidate the crowd. One might imagine that he did not want to start his term of office on the wrong foot. To show weakness early might mean difficulty later. Using pretense to get the protesters to the stadium, he revealed his true intentions when the soldiers drew their swords. The reaction of the crowd surprised Pilate. He must have presumed that they would recognize the hopelessness of their position and simply yield to his will. Instead they showed themselves willing to die rather than accept such gross violation of Torah. The great size of the protest is intimated by Pilate's giving in to it.

This incident indicates something significant about the mood of the majority of Jews in 26 CE. Far from being hotheaded, thirsting for revolt, and unruly, they resorted to nonviolent protest to deal with Roman injustice. Their nonviolence was not due to apathy. They were willing to die for Torah. The overthrow of Roman rule was not their aim. They did not appear "nationalistic," but they would not allow a colonial power to defile Jerusalem. Events did not progress to the next step in the spiral of violence—repression. Even Pilate saw that such a step would be disastrous.

A similar story is told by the Jewish philosopher Philo of Alexandria (*Embassy to Gaius* 38 §§ 299–305). Pilate put some golden shields dedicated to the emperor Tiberius in Herod's palace in Jerusalem. The residents of Jerusalem objected to the shields as violating their sacred customs. Pilate refused to remove the shields. The Jewish leaders appealed to Tiberius, who ordered the shields to be removed.

Later in his administration Pilate again aroused the people.

On a later occasion he provoked a fresh uproar by expending upon the construction of an aqueduct the sacred treasure known as *Corbonas;*[5] the water was brought from a distance of 400 furlongs. Indignant at this proceeding, the populace formed a ring round the tribunal of Pilate, then on a visit to Jerusalem, and besieged him with angry clamor. He, foreseeing the tumult, had interspersed among the crowd a troop of his soldiers, armed but disguised in civilian dress, with orders not to use their swords, but to beat any rioters with cudgels. He now from his tribunal gave the agreed signal. Large numbers of the Jews perished, some from the blows which they received, others trodden to death by their companions in the ensuing flight. Cowed by the fate of the victims, the multitude was reduced to silence. (*War* 2.9.4 §§ 175–77; cf. *Ant.* 18.3.2 §§ 60–62)

The account in *Antiquities* is kinder to Pilate. It says that his action was caused by abuse hurled at him by the crowd, and that the soldiers got carried away and beat people harder than Pilate intended. Josephus may have softened his picture of the

Roman procurator for his Roman audience in the nineties. The account in *War* states that Pilate knew what was going to happen, and planned to beat the protesters as an example to those who would question his decisions. His strategy worked. Josephus relates one more episode involving Pilate.

> The Samaritan nation too was not exempt from disturbance. For a man who made light of mendacity and in all his designs catered to the mob, rallied them, bidding them go in a body with him to Mount Gerizim, which in their belief is the most sacred of mountains. He assured them that on their arrival he would show them the sacred vessels which were buried there, where Moses had deposited them. His hearers, viewing this tale as plausible, appeared in arms. They posted themselves in a certain village named Tirathana, and, as they planned to climb the mountain in a great multitude, they welcomed to their ranks the new arrivals who kept coming. But before they could ascend, Pilate blocked their projected route up the mountain with a detachment of cavalry and heavy-armed infantry, who in an encounter with the firstcomers in the village slew some in a pitched battle and put the others to flight. Many prisoners were taken, of whom Pilate put to death the principal leaders and those who were most influential among the fugitives. When the uprising had been quelled, the council of the Samaritans went to Vitellius, a man of consular rank who was governor of Syria, and charged Pilate with the slaughter of the victims. For, they said, it was not as rebels against the Romans but as refugees from the persecution of Pilate that they had met in Tirathana. Vitellius thereupon dispatched Marcellus, one of his friends, to take charge of the administration of Judaea, and ordered Pilate to return to Rome to give the emperor his account of the matters with which he was charged by the Samaritans.
>
> (*Ant.* 18.4.1-2 §§ 85–89)

On the basis of Deuteronomy 18:15-19, the Samaritans believed that the eschatological figure would be of the tribe of Levi, and a prophet like Moses. That prophet would restore the Samaritan nation. The events in this passage seem related to that belief. The finding of the sacred vessels hidden by Moses would signal the beginning of the eschatological age. Pilate saw the people's eschatological fervor as a threat to public order, so he reacted brutally. The incident illustrates once again the close connection between politics and religion in first-century Palestine. Vitellius' action implies that he found the Samaritans' charges of injustice on the part of Pilate plausible. Vitellius, as Pilate's Roman superior, sent him to Rome to answer to Tiberius. Pilate's time of office ended because of his own ruthlessness.

Having dispatched Pilate, Vitellius visited Jerusalem. It was Passover, so the city was again filled with pilgrims. Vitellius was received warmly by the crowd. He remitted sales taxes on agricultural produce and awarded custody of the high priestly vestments to the priests. Custody of the vestments was an important symbol. Herod had taken the vestments away from the priests and allowed them to be used only at the festivals. The vestments had to be worn at specified times according to sacred law, so by taking custody of them Herod was able to control aspects of the high priest's activity and Temple liturgy. Since the festivals were volatile times, control of the vestments meant some command of the situation at those times. Until Vitellius, the procurators followed Herod's practice. Before leaving Jerusalem, Vitellius deposed the high priest Caiaphas, a friend of Pilate who had ruled 18–36 CE.

Philo of Alexandria, a contemporary of Pilate who was a Jew of Alexandria, said that Pilate wanted to hide from the emperor "the briberies, the insults, the robberies, the outrages and wanton injuries, the executions without trial constantly repeated, the ceaseless and supremely grievous cruelty" that characterized his administration (*Embassy to Gaius* 38 § 302). It may be that Pilate was influenced by his friend in Rome, a certain Sejanus who was an advisor to the emperor Tiberius and who was known for his anti-Jewish sentiments. It is remarkable that most Jewish protest against Pilate's abuses was nonviolent. It is possible that there was some armed resistance to Pilate, however. The gospels imply such resistance: "Now a man called Barabbas was in prison with the rebels who had committed murder during the insurrection" (Mark 15:7). Furthermore, Jesus is crucified between two "bandits," who were perhaps political resisters. Nonetheless, there is no solid evidence for any widespread violent resistance during Pilate's administration.

John the Baptist

Two figures of considerable importance for Christians—John the Baptist and Jesus Christ—carried on their public ministries during the time of Pilate. It is generally thought that Josephus' account of Jesus was extensively rewritten by Christians. Because of the difficulty of deciding what if anything comes from Josephus' hand, it will not be considered here. Josephus' report on John the Baptist seems free of Christian redaction. He tells of John in the context of a story about Herod Antipas. Antipas had been married to the daughter of King Aretas of the Nabateans in a political marriage. He then rejected her for Herodias, his half-brother's wife. There were also boundary disputes between Herod Antipas and Aretas. War broke out between the two, and Herod suffered a defeat. In the gospels, John castigates Herod for his unlawful taking of his brother's wife, and so is beheaded.[6] Josephus puts the story in a political light, connecting the events concerning Aretas to John's death.

But to some of the Jews the destruction of Herod's army seemed to be divine vengeance, and certainly a just vengeance, for his treatment of John, surnamed the Baptist. For Herod had put him to death, though he was a good man and had exhorted the Jews to lead righteous lives, to practice justice towards their fellows and piety towards God, and so doing to join in baptism. In his view this was a necessary preliminary if baptism was to be acceptable to God. They must not employ it to gain pardon for whatever sins they committed, but as a consecration of the body implying that the soul was already thoroughly cleansed by right behaviour. When others too joined the crowds about him, because they were aroused to the highest degree by his sermons, Herod became alarmed. Eloquence that had so great an effect on mankind might lead to some form of sedition, for it looked as if they would be guided by John in everything that they did. Herod decided therefore that it would be much better to strike first and be rid of him before his work led to an uprising, than to wait for an upheaval, get involved in a difficult situation and see his mistake. (*Ant.* 18.5.2 §§ 116–18)

There may be three factors in why John was seen as a threat by Herod. First, behavior toward God and humans is laid out in Torah, and John's reading of that Torah did not coincide with Herod's. Disagreement over Torah could mean social, legal, economic, and political conflict. Second, John drew a large following, and the crowds were enough to make Herod nervous. Finally, John's preaching consisted of more than morality; it also had an eschatological content. Josephus does not make the eschatological nature of John's message explicit, but it is evident in the gospels. John's baptism prepared a person for the intervention of God in history.[7] One cannot be sure that John's exact words are preserved by the gospels, but it is likely that the following is true to the tone of John's message.

You brood of vipers! Who warned you to flee from the wrath to come? Bear fruit worthy of repentance. Do not presume to say to yourselves, "We have Abraham as our ancestor"; for I tell you, God is able from these stones to raise up children to Abraham. Even now the ax is lying at the root of the trees; every tree therefore that does not bear good fruit is cut down and thrown into the fire. I baptize you with water for repentance, but one who is more powerful than I is coming after me; I am not worthy to carry his sandals. He will baptize you with the Holy Spirit and fire. His winnowing fork is in his hand, and he will clear his threshing floor and will gather his wheat into the granary; but the chaff he will burn with unquenchable fire.

(Matt 3:7-12)

John urged people to baptism in the face of the wrath to come. "Wrath" is a technical term in apocalypticism and refers to God's anger at sin, soon to be manifest in the destruction of evil. John was an apocalyptic preacher whose message was attractive to many, and who paid the price when Herod realized the political potential of his movement. John did not plan armed rebellion, but he was convinced that God would soon come to change the world. His message challenged the establishment, and Herod was aware of that.

37 to 44 CE

Gaius (Caligula) was Roman emperor from 37 to 41 CE. During his rule there was a dispute between the Jews and the Gentiles of Alexandria in Egypt, where there was a sizable Jewish population. The Gentile Alexandrians charged the Jews with being unwilling to set up and worship statues of Gaius, and told the emperor that this demonstrated Jewish disloyalty. Gaius ordered the governor of Syria, Petronius, to march to Jerusalem and set up a statue of the emperor in the Temple. Such a desecration of the Temple had not taken place since Antiochus IV set up a statue of Zeus there.

Petronius brought his army to Ptolemais, a city on the coast west of Galilee, to winter there. Tens of thousands of Jews gathered to him and begged him to desist. When he told them that he had no choice, they replied, "In order to preserve our ancestral code, we shall patiently endure what may be in store for us, with the assurance that for those who are determined to take the risk there is hope even of prevailing; for God will stand by us if we welcome danger for His glory" (*Ant.* 18.8.2 § 267). Petronius recognized that the Jews would not back down, so he withdrew to Tiberias by the Sea of Galilee. Another crowd gathered. Petronius asked whether they were willing to go to war over the issue.

> "On no account would we fight," they said, "but we will die sooner than violate our laws." And falling on their faces and baring their throats, they declared that they were ready to be slain. They continued to make these supplications for forty days. Furthermore, they neglected their fields, and that, too, though it was time to sow the seed. For they showed a stubborn determination and readiness to die rather than to see the image erected. (*Ant.* 18.8.3 §§ 271–72)

The protesters did not bear arms or intend to fight. Since their absence from their fields meant that the fields would not be sown, they must have been peasants, at least in large part. Their abandonment of their fields amounted to a peasant strike, a strike that would have been costly to them, to the rich landowners, and to the Romans. It could mean disaster all around.

The native aristocracy intervened, asking Petronius to inform Gaius of the people's resolve. Part of their argument stressed the economic factor: "Let him point out that, since the land was unsown, there would be a harvest of banditry, because the requirement of tribute could not be met" (*Ant.* 18.8.4 § 274). This sentence connects banditry with peasants being caught between no crops and the demands of taxation. In this case the lack of crops would be owing to the peasant strike. Petronius saw the force of the argument and appealed to Gaius. Meanwhile Agrippa I, grandson of Herod the Great, was in Rome, and had become the friend of Gaius. He persuaded Gaius to rescind his order. The incident demonstrates the Jews' willingness to live in peace under Roman rule, but their refusal to see their Temple and the Torah violated. It also shows the importance of economic factors, and the extent to which these are tied up with religion and politics. Finally, it is another example of the alliance between the Herodian family and the Romans.

In 37 CE, Gaius made Agrippa I king of the territory of Herod's son Philip, who had died. In 41 CE a new emperor, Claudius, made him king of Judea, Galilee, and Perea. (Perea was an area east of the Jordan.) Josephus records no disturbances during the rule of Agrippa I. The lack of disturbances may be owing to Agrippa's sympathetic attitude to the Jews. His Gentile subjects may not have enjoyed his rule, however. The cities of Caesarea and Sebaste celebrated the news of his death in 44 (*Ant.* 19.9.1 §§ 356–57). Agrippa I seems to have desired to strengthen his own kingdom and influence. He undertook to refortify Jerusalem and to call an unauthorized meeting of regional rulers, but the governor of Syria ended those endeavors. Agrippa I died of natural causes, and Rome turned his kingdom over to a procurator. This was a return to a previous status for Judea, but it was the first time that Galilee came under direct Roman rule.

Between 4 BCE and 44 CE there is no evidence for sustained, organized Jewish resistance to Roman rule. On the contrary, except for the incident involving the tax revolt of Judas the Galilean, evidence indicates a willingness to accept Roman rule. The people would not do so, however, at the price of gross violation of divine laws. The reaction of the Jews to such violations was peaceful protest. The few prophets who pointed to God's imminent intervention did not encourage military preparation for the event. God would do it all. The picture in Josephus contrasts starkly with what has been a common view that the Jews were "nationalistic," and were spoiling for a fight with the Romans so as to put an end to Roman rule. That picture furnished a convenient foil for a peaceful Jesus who taught love of enemies, but it does not survive close scrutiny.

Fadus and Tiberius Alexander (44–48 CE)

Fadus was procurator from 44 to 46 CE. He tried to regain control of the priestly vestments, but was overruled by the emperor, who awarded them and the power to appoint high priests to Herod of Chalcis, a member of the Herodian family who ruled the small territory of Chalcis north of Galilee. Fadus captured a bandit named Tholomaeus who operated in Idumea and in Arab territory, but nothing specific is known of Tholomaeus or his motivations. There was one other noteworthy occurrence during Fadus' administration.

During the period when Fadus was procurator of Judaea, a certain impostor named Theudas persuaded the majority of the masses to take up their possessions and to follow him to the Jordan River. He stated that he was a prophet and that at his command the river would be parted and would provide them an easy passage. With this talk he deceived many. Fadus, however, did not permit them to reap the fruit of their folly, but sent against them a squadron of cavalry. These fell upon them unexpectedly, slew many of them and took many prisoners. Theudas himself was captured, whereupon they cut off his head and brought it to Jerusalem.

(*Ant.* 20.5.1 §§ 97–98)

The word translated "impostor" here is the Greek word *goēs*. It means "wizard," "sorcerer," "enchanter." It is a pejorative term and has the connotation of "con man" in colloquial American. Josephus applies it to those he thinks mislead the people with false promises of miracles, liberation, and God's intervention. Theudas undoubtedly thought of himself as a real prophet, as his actions prove. He did not advocate armed resistance, but depended upon God's miraculous action. He showed remarkable trust in God. Theudas knew Israel's traditions, and remembered that when the people were liberated from Egypt, God split the Reed Sea. When Joshua led the people into the promised land across the Jordan, God split the Jordan so that they could cross on foot. Theudas believed that as God had come to Israel's aid in Joshua's time and given them the land, so now God would do the same. Divine action in the past was the model for present and future divine action. Fadus understood. He moved quickly and brutally.

The next procurator was Tiberius Alexander (46–48). He was from the Jewish community at Alexandria, and was the nephew of the Jewish philosopher Philo of Alexandria. He had given up Judaism and was thoroughly Hellenized.

> It was in the administration of Tiberius Alexander that the great famine occurred in Judaea, during which Queen Helena bought grain from Egypt for large sums and distributed it to the needy, as I have stated above. Besides this James and Simon, the sons of Judas the Galilaean, were brought up for trial and, at the order of Alexander, were crucified. This was the Judas who, as I have explained above, had aroused the people to revolt against the Romans while Quirinius was taking the census in Judaea. (*Ant.* 20.5.2 §§ 101–2)

Queen Helena was a convert to Judaism and ruled a kingdom called Adiabene. The information that there was a great famine at this time means that there was increased economic pressure on Jewish society, especially peasants. That pressure may have had something to do with the crucifixion of James and Simon. Famine often led to banditry. It is possible that James and Simon were involved in anti-Roman or at least anti–ruling class activity, since crucifixion was the punishment for such crimes. Anti-Roman activity seems to have run in the family of Judas the Galilean.

Cumanus (48–52 CE)

As procurator of the rest of the province (Tiberius) Alexander was succeeded by Cumanus; under his administration disturbances broke out, resulting in another large loss of Jewish lives. The usual crowd had assembled at Jerusalem for the feast of unleavened bread, and the Roman cohort had taken up its position on the roof of the portico of the temple; for a body of men in arms invariably mounts guard at the feasts, to prevent disorders arising from such a concourse of people. Thereupon one of the soldiers, raising his robe, stooped in an indecent attitude, so as to turn his backside to the Jews, and made a noise in keeping with his posture. Enraged at this insult, the whole multitude with loud cries called upon Cumanus to punish the soldier; some of the more hot-headed young men and seditious persons in the crowd started a fight, and, picking up stones, hurled them at the troops. Cumanus, fearing a general attack upon himself, sent for reinforcements. These troops pouring into the porticoes, the Jews were seized with irresistible panic and turned to fly from the temple and make their escape into the town. But such violence was used as they pressed round the exits that they were trodden under foot and crushed to death by one another; upwards of thirty thousand perished, and the feast was turned into mourning for the whole nation and for every household into lamentation. (*War* 2.12.1 §§ 223–27)

Feasts were dangerous times for the authorities, but Passover (celebrated with the feast of Unleavened Bread) was especially volatile. The contempt shown by the soldier was the more heinous since it occurred at the Temple itself. In the holiest place in Judaism, at one of the holiest times of the year, at a feast celebrating the liberation of Israel from foreign oppression, the pilgrims were subjected to a painful reminder of their subordinate position. Josephus blames the crowd for its hostile response. Cumanus reacts with force, and the result is disaster.

This calamity was followed by other disorders, originating with brigands. On the public road leading up to Bethhoron some brigands attacked one Stephen, a slave of Caesar, and robbed him of his baggage. Cumanus, thereupon, sent troops round the neighboring villages, with orders to bring up the inhabitants to him in chains, reprimanding them for not having pursued and arrested the robbers. On this occasion a soldier, finding in one village a copy of the sacred law, tore the book in pieces and flung it into the fire. At that the Jews were roused as though it were their whole country which had been consumed in the flames; and, their religion acting like some instrument to draw them together, all on the first announcement of the news hurried in a body to Cumanus at Caesarea, and implored him not to leave unpunished the author of such an outrage on God and on their law. The procurator, seeing that the multitude would not be pacified unless they obtained satisfaction, thought it fit to call out the soldier and ordered him to be led to execution through the ranks of his accusers. On this the Jews withdrew. (*War* 2.12.2 §§ 228–31)

The attack on the caravan of Caesar's servant came from bandits. How politically motivated they were is unknown. The existence of the bandits might well have been the result of the earlier famine, or of Roman repression, as in the Temple incident under Cumanus. In any case, Cumanus suspected the villagers of being in league with the bandits. The hostility of the procurator's soldiers is evident in the contemptuous destruction of a Torah scroll. Cumanus was pressured into executing the perpetrator. The Jews were satisfied with righting the wrong and did not rebel.

The next incident under Cumanus involved the Samaritans (*War* 2.12.3-7 §§ 232–46). A Galilean was murdered while passing through Samaria on the way to Jerusalem for a feast. Cumanus refused to give the incident any attention. Jewish bandits, supported by a crowd of Jews, decided to take justice into their own hands. This is an example of bandits effecting the justice that the government will not. Cumanus intervened to prevent war between the Jews and the Samaritans. He killed many of the bandits. Jewish aristocrats pleaded with the rest of the people to return home. Most did so, but Jewish bandits continued their fight. Samaritan and Jewish notables appealed to the Syrian governor, the Jews blaming Cumanus for his failure to attend to his duties. This was one case in which the Jewish aristocrats sided with the people. The governor went to Caesarea and crucified those Cumanus had taken prisoner. He then sent Jewish and Samaritan nobles, as well as Cumanus and another Roman official, to Rome for a hearing. The emperor heard the case in the presence of Agrippa II, son of Agrippa I. Agrippa II had received the kingdom of Chalcis when Herod of Chalcis died in 48 CE. He did not rule over Jewish Palestine directly, but as a Jewish king he had some influence over it. He also exerted some legal power because he inherited authority over the priestly vestments, and authority to appoint the high priest.

Claudius banished Cumanus and condemned the other Roman, thus acknowledging Roman responsibility. He then found fault with the Samaritans and executed three of them. Claudius' judgment makes it clear that he did not see Jewish actions as unwarranted or seditious. That the Jews had no revolutionary intent is corroborated by the fact that when the governor of Syria went from Caesarea to Jerusalem, he found the people "peacefully celebrating the feast of unleavened bread" (*War* 2.12.6 § 244), and so returned to Antioch.

War Approaches

Felix was procurator of Judea, Samaria, Galilee, and Perea from 52 to 60 CE. He was a freed slave, and not even a member of the equestrian order. Such an appointment was unprecedented. His corrupt administration aggravated the already troubled situation in Jewish Palestine.

Felix first took on the problem of banditry.

> Felix took prisoner Eleazar, the brigand chief, who for twenty years had ravaged the country, with many of his associates, and sent them for trial to Rome. Of the brigands whom he crucified, and of the common people who were convicted of complicity with them and punished by him, the number was incalculable.
> (*War* 2.13.2 § 253)

Again there is evidence of peasant support for banditry. Eleazar had managed to operate with impunity for twenty years.

The procuratorship of Felix saw the emergence of a new form of Jewish resistance to oppressive rule.

> But while the country was thus cleared of these pests, a new species of banditti was springing up in Jerusalem, the so-called *sicarii*, who committed murders in broad daylight in the heart of the city. The festivals were their special seasons, when they would mingle with the crowd, carrying short daggers concealed under their clothing, with which they stabbed their enemies. Then, when they fell, the murderers joined in the cries of indignation and, through this plausible behaviour, were never discovered. The first to be assassinated by them was Jonathan the high-priest; after his death there were numerous daily murders. The panic created was more alarming than the calamity itself; every one, as on the battlefield, hourly expecting death. Men kept watch at a distance on their enemies and would not trust even their friends when they approached. Yet, even while their suspicions were aroused and they were on their guard, they fell; so swift were the conspirators and so crafty in eluding detection. (*War* 2.13.3 §§ 254–57)

The Sicarii took their name from the weapon they used, the dagger (Latin: *sica*). Although Josephus calls them another kind of bandit, they do not resemble other bandits he describes. Bandits operated in the countryside, whereas the Sicarii operated in the city. Bandits lived by raiding. Frequently, they did not kill unless forced to fight. The Sicarii's whole program was assassination and terrorism. Whereas bandits were often well known to peasants and to authorities who tried to catch them, the identities of the Sicarii were secret.

Judging from their tactics, the Sicarii had a specific political program. Their targets were not Romans, but the Jewish upper classes that collaborated with the Romans. The high priest was their first victim. The assassinations caused panic among the aristocrats. Members of the ruling class began to distrust one another. There was a breakdown of social structure in Jerusalem, and the aristocracy's hold on the people was weakened. The political program of the Sicarii went beyond righting specific wrongs. It extended to the destabilization of the ruling structure of Jerusalem. They went farther than rural bandits in political awareness, organization, and goals.

The procurator Albinus (62–64 CE) managed to capture some Sicarii. The group evolved a new tactic to deal with this development.

Once more the *sicarii* at the festival, for it was now going on, entered the city by night and kidnapped the secretary of the captain Eleazar—he was the son of Ananias the high priest—and led him off in bonds. They then sent to Ananias saying that they would release the secretary to him if he would induce Albinus to release ten of their number who had been taken prisoner. Ananias under this constraint persuaded Albinus and obtained this request. This was the beginning of greater troubles; for the brigands contrived by one means or another to kidnap some of Ananias' staff and would hold them in continuous confinement and refuse to release them until they had received in exchange some of the *sicarii*.

(*Ant.* 20.9.3 §§ 208–10)

This passage shows that the Sicarii were an organized group capable of devising a program and putting it into effect. It also shows that the priestly aristocracy was caught between the Sicarii and the Romans.

During the term of Felix troubles were rife: "In Judaea matters were constantly going from bad to worse. For the country was again infested with bands of brigands and impostors who deceived the mob. Not a day passed, however, but that Felix captured and put to death many of these impostors and brigands" (*Ant.* 20.8.5 §§ 160–61). Josephus goes on to describe the deeds of the Sicarii, calling them simply "brigands" in this passage. He accuses Felix of bribing them to kill the high priest Jonathan because Jonathan was constantly trying to get Felix to rule more justly. Josephus says that the blood shed by the resisters within the holy city and even in the Temple precincts was a desecration that turned God against them and their cause.

At this point, Sicarii, prophets, and bandits were active.

With such pollution did the deeds of the brigands infect the city. Moreover, impostors and deceivers called upon the mob to follow them into the desert. For they said that they would show them unmistakable marvels and signs that would be wrought in harmony with God's design. Many were, in fact, persuaded and paid the penalty for their folly; for they were brought before Felix and he punished them. At this time there came to Jerusalem from Egypt a man who declared that he was a prophet and advised the masses of the common people to go out with him to the mountain called the Mount of Olives, which lies opposite the city at a distance of five furlongs. For he asserted that he wished to demonstrate from there that at his command Jerusalem's walls would fall down, through which he promised to provide them an entrance into the city. When Felix heard of this he ordered his soldiers to take up their arms. Setting out from Jerusalem with a large force of cavalry and infantry, he fell upon the Egyptian and his followers, slaying four hundred of them and taking two hundred prisoners. The Egyptian himself escaped from the battle and disappeared. And now the brigands once more incited the populace to war with Rome, telling them not to obey them. They also fired and pillaged the villages of those who refused to comply. (*Ant.* 20.8.6 §§ 167–72)

The specific example of an ''impostor'' (eschatological prophet) that Josephus gives, that of the Egyptian, shows that those who advocated overthrowing Roman rule did not expect to do so alone. They thought that God would fight on their side. The hope that the walls of Jerusalem would fall recalls the battle of Jericho in Joshua 6.

The Egyptian's efforts were aimed at defeating the Roman garrison in Jerusalem, as is clear from the version of this episode in the *Jewish War:* ''From there [Mount of Olives] he proposed to force an entrance into Jerusalem and, after overpowering the Roman garrison, to set himself up as tyrant of the people, employing those who poured in with him as his bodyguard'' (*War* 2.13.5 § 262). Felix did not wait to see if the Egyptian's prediction would come to pass. He reacted with harsh repression. Rather than quell the Jews' rebellious attitude, Felix's measures increased it.

> No sooner were these disorders reduced than the inflammation, as in a sick man's body, broke out again in another quarter. The impostors and brigands, banding together, incited numbers to revolt, exhorting them to assert their independence, and threatening to kill any who submitted to Roman domination and forcibly to suppress those who voluntarily accepted servitude. Distributing themselves in companies throughout the country, they looted the houses of the wealthy, murdered their owners, and set the villages on fire. The effects of their frenzy were thus felt throughout all Judaea, and every day saw this war being fanned into fiercer flame. (*War* 2.13.6 §§ 264–65)

In the course of the fifties, resistance to Roman rule became more widespread and better organized. Violence was directed more at fellow Jews than at Romans. In colonial situations native collaborators were accessible targets. Attacking them could have a strong effect on the empire, since the empire needed the native aristocracy. The wealthy in particular were singled out.

The priests among the wealthy aristocracy were not the only priests in Jewish society. Priesthood was hereditary in Judaism, but only the leading priestly families belonged to the ruling class. Toward the end of the rule of Felix there was a clash in Jerusalem that pitted priest against priest.

> At this time King Agrippa [II] conferred the high priesthood upon Ishmael, the son of Phabi. There now was enkindled mutual enmity and class warfare between the high priests, on the one hand, and the priests and the leaders of the populace of Jerusalem, on the other. Each of the factions formed and collected for itself a band of the most reckless revolutionaries and acted as their leader. And when they clashed, they used abusive language and pelted each other with stones. And there was not even one person to rebuke them. No, it was as if there was no one in charge of the city, so that they acted as they did with full license. Such was the shamelessness and effrontery which possessed the high priests that they actually

were so brazen as to send slaves to the threshing floors to receive the tithes that were due to the priests, with the result that the poorer priests starved to death. Thus did the violence of the contending factions suppress all justice.

(*Ant.* 20.8.8 §§ 179–81)

Class conflict divided priest from priest. Poor priests had more in common with the workers of the city than with the ruling priests. The unrest and disorder in the city was not addressed by Felix, who did not live there.

Felix did live in Caesarea, and that city was not immune from the disturbances shaking the country. The discord in Caesarea was different in kind from that in Jerusalem. In Jerusalem, it was Jew against Jew. In Caesarea it was Jew against Gentile. Caesarea was a mixed city, and each group aspired to dominance in terms of civic rights and privileges. Clashes between the groups grew more and more violent. Felix finally sent in the troops, who killed many Jews, captured others, and plundered their houses. He then sent representatives from the Jewish and Gentile segments of Caesarea to Rome to argue their cases before Nero. The Jews sent to Rome by Felix used this opportunity to accuse Felix of maladministration. Nero gave the Jews no satisfaction.

In 60 CE, Felix was replaced by Festus who ruled until 62. Festus devoted his time in office to campaigning against the bandits in the countryside, and Josephus credits him with some success. Festus died in office, and Nero sent Albinus (62–64) to replace him. Meanwhile, Agrippa II appointed Ananus, son of the earlier high priest Ananus, as high priest.

The younger Ananus, who, as we have said, had been appointed to the high priesthood, was rash in his temper and unusually daring. He followed the school of the Sadducees, who are indeed more heartless than any of the other Jews, as I have already explained, when they sit in judgment. Possessed of such a character, Ananus thought that he had a favorable opportunity because Festus was dead and Albinus was still on the way. And so he convened the judges of the Sanhedrin and brought before them a man named James, the brother of Jesus who was called the Christ, and certain others. He accused them of having transgressed the law and delivered them up to be stoned. Those of the inhabitants of the city who were considered the most fair-minded and who were strict in observance of the law were offended at this. They therefore secretly sent to King Agrippa urging him, for Ananus had not even been correct in his first step, to order him to desist from any further such actions. Certain of them even went to meet Albinus, who was on his way from Alexandria, and informed him that Ananus had no authority to convene the Sanhedrin without his consent. Convinced by these words, Albinus angrily wrote to Ananus threatening to take vengeance upon him. King Agrippa [II], because of Ananus' action, deposed him from the high priesthood which he had held for three months and replaced him with Jesus the son of Damnaeus.

(*Ant.* 20.9.1 §§ 199–203)

Ananus' deed did not have the support of all members of the Jerusalem aristocracy. In fact, their indignation at his high-handedness and disregard for legal proceedings led them to protest to both Agrippa and Albinus. Ananus' prosecution of James and the others led to his downfall.

Under Albinus conflicts between the upper and lower echelons of the priesthood continued (*Ant.* 20.9.2 §§ 206–7). Power struggles within the aristocracy sank to the level of street fights between factions (*Ant.* 20.9.4 §§ 213–14). Things were deteriorating in Jerusalem. Josephus' summary of Albinus' term of office is scathing.

> The administration of Albinus, who followed Festus, was of another order; there was no form of villainy which he omitted to practise. Not only did he, in his official capacity, steal and plunder private property and burden the whole nation with extraordinary taxes, but he accepted ransoms from their relatives on behalf of those who had been imprisoned for robbery [banditry] by the local councils or by former procurators; and the only persons left in gaol as malefactors were those who failed to pay the price. Now, too, the audacity of the revolutionary party in Jerusalem was stimulated; the influential men among their number secured from Albinus, by means of bribes, immunity from their seditious practices. (*War* 2.14.1 §§ 272–74)

The result of Albinus' actions was that "The prison was cleared of inmates and the land was infested with brigands" (*Ant.* 20.9.5 § 215). Albinus' corruption pushed the country farther toward war.

Albinus was succeeded by Gessius Florus (64–66 CE). It was his rule that finally pushed the Jews to revolt: "It was Florus who constrained us to take up war with the Romans, for we preferred to perish together rather than by degrees" (*Ant.* 20.11.1 § 257). Around the time of the beginning of his term, the rebuilding of the Temple begun by Herod the Great was completed, throwing 18,000 workers (according to Josephus' count) out of work. To employ them and to prevent Temple funds being diverted into Roman hands, Agrippa II approved plans to pave Jerusalem with white stone. Before that could happen, the city was destroyed.

Josephus condemns Florus for being in league with the bandits. They had a free hand during Florus' term, as long as they were willing to pay him bribes. Josephus charges him with despoiling individuals, villages, and cities on a grand scale. The Jews appealed to the governor of Syria to no avail (*War* 2.14.3 §§ 280–83). Josephus even accuses Florus of deliberately provoking the Jewish revolt in order to camouflage his own crimes.

During Florus' term, Nero resolved the dispute between the Jews and the Gentiles of Caesarea in favor of the Gentiles. The Jews lost equal citizenship. This exacerbated already tense relations between the two groups. Things escalated when some Gentiles performed sacrifices near the synagogue to provoke the Jews. When the Jews turned to Florus, he treated them with disdain. Then Florus decided to take money from the Temple treasury, perhaps to pay tribute to Rome. The Jews protested. One protest involved taking up a mock collection for the "poor" Florus. Florus went to Jerusalem with troops. When some Jews came out of the city to greet him, he dispersed them with cavalry. His troops then plundered parts of the city, and scourged and crucified some citizens. The city crowd was ready to go to war with Florus, but their prominent citizens urged caution. The ruling priests in particular were concerned to check the emotions of the crowd. Florus made that difficult when he forced the Jews to go to greet a new contingent of Roman soldiers coming from Caesarea, and then had the troops attack them. The Jews began to fight back, and would not allow Florus and his men to reach the Temple or the fortress of Antonia adjoining it. He then left the city, leaving a cohort of troops under the command of the chief priests.

Agrippa II now entered the scene. He went to Jerusalem and tried to persuade the people to remain peaceful. He induced them to collect the taxes that were in arrears, but when he counseled them to submit to Florus until a new procurator could be sent out, they drove him out of the city. He withdrew to his own kingdom to the north. Some insurgents now captured the fortress of Masada. Eleazar, the Temple captain and son of the former high priest Ananias, persuaded the priests to cease the daily Temple sacrifice for Rome and emperor. Cessation of sacrifices was a declaration of independence.

CONCLUSION

Jewish Palestine suffered much under the oppression of Herod the Great. When it became obvious that it would get no relief under his sons, revolts erupted in Judea, Perea, and Galilee. The revolts had the character of popular uprisings, and may have drawn their ideological support from Israel's ancient traditions of popular kingship. Varus, governor of Syria, crushed the revolts, and the Jews of Judea endured ten years of Archelaus' cruelty. Eventually even the Romans had to admit Archelaus' failure, and they began to rule Judea directly through procurators.

The transition to direct rule was marked by the tax revolt under Judas the Galilean, but there is little evidence that it was an armed revolt or that it was widespread. The next forty years were marked by a sustained effort by all segments of the population to live in peace with the Roman occupiers. Crises were causes by the Romans, Pilate, and Gaius especially, and the Jews in each case reacted with nonviolent protest. The fact that Pilate and Cumanus were sent to Rome to answer for their behavior shows that the emperor was not entirely unconcerned about the conduct of his representatives, but in general the procurators were allowed fairly free reign.

To counter Roman abuses, the Jews resorted to direct appeal to the procurator, the governor of Syria, or the emperor. During the crisis over the statue of Gaius, they effectively conducted a peasant strike. John the Baptist and the Samaritan prophet are examples of prophets critical of the ruling aristocracy, expecting imminent eschatological relief. The famine of the mid-forties increased economic pressure on the peasants and their landlords, and may have led to an increase in banditry. Eschatological prophets preached imminent liberation through divine action. The errors of Cumanus further aggravated the situation. Organized, politically aware resistance emerged in the Sicarii movement, aimed at terrorizing and rendering ineffective the local aristocracy. Growing Roman corruption and incompetence under Felix, Festus, Albinus, and Florus brought things to the boiling point. Florus' ruthless repression finally caused the eruption of open revolt.

In the broad sweep of the events of the first century, one can discern the fourfold pattern of injustice, protest, repression, and revolt. As injustices multiplied, so did protests, at first nonviolent, then violent. As protests grew stronger, so did repression. As repression reached its peak under Florus, the people finally resorted to complete renunciation of Roman rule and violent revolt.

SELECT BIBLIOGRAPHY

Applebaum, S. "Judea as a Roman Province: The Countryside as a Political and Economic Factor," in *ANRW* II, 8, 355-96.

Attridge, Harold. "Jewish Historiography," in *EJMI,* 311-43.

Bowman, John. *The Samaritan Problem: Studies in the Relationship of Samaritanism, Judaism, and Early Christianity.* Pittsburgh: Pickwick, 1975.

Feldman, Louis H., and Gohei Hata, eds. *Josephus, Judaism, and Christianity.* Detroit: Wayne State University Press, 1987.

Grant, Michael. *The Jews in the Roman World.* New York: Scribner's, 1973.

Hobsbawn, E. J. "Social Banditry," in *Rural Protest: Peasant Movements and Social Change,* ed. H. A. Landsberger. New York: Macmillan, 1974.

_____. *Bandits,* rev. ed. New York: Pantheon Books, 1981.

_____. *Primitive Rebels.* New York: W. W. Norton & Co., 1965.

Horsley, Richard A. *Jesus and the Spiral of Violence: Popular Jewish Resistance in Roman Palestine.* San Francisco: Harper and Row, 1987.

Horsley, Richard A., and John S. Hanson. *Bandits, Prophets, and Messiahs: Popular Movements at the Time of Jesus.* Minneapolis: Winston, 1985.

Jeremias, Joachim. *Jerusalem in the Time of Jesus.* Philadelphia: Fortress Press, 1969.

Purvis, James D. "The Samaritans and Judaism," in *EJMI,* 81-98.

Rajak, Tessa. *Josephus: The Historian and His Society.* Philadelphia: Fortress Press, 1983.

Rhoads, David M. *Israel in Revolution: A Political History Based on the Writings of Josephus*. Philadelphia: Fortress Press, 1976.

Safrai, S., and M. Stern, eds. *The Jewish People in the First Century: Historical Geography, Political History, Social, Cultural, and Religious Life and Institutions*, 2 vols. Philadelphia: Fortress Press, 1974, 1976.

Saldarini, Anthony J. "Reconstructions of Rabbinic Judaism," in *EJMI*, 437-77.

Schürer, Emil. *The Jewish People in the Age of Jesus Christ*, 3 vols., rev. Geza Vermes, Fergus Millar, Matthew Black. Edinburgh: T. & T. Clark, Ltd., 1973–87.

Sherwin-White, A. N. *Roman Society and Roman Law in the New Testament*. Oxford: Clarendon Press, 1963.

Smallwood, E. Mary. "High Priests and Politics in Roman Palestine," *JTS* 13 (1962): 17-37.

———. *The Jews Under Roman Rule from Pompey to Diocletian: A Study in Political Relations*. Leiden: Brill, 1981.

Smith, Morton. "Zealots and Sicarii, Their Origins and Relation," *HTR* 64 (1971): 1-19.

CHAPTER ELEVEN

Jesus, a Jew of First-Century Palestine

Primary Readings: Matthew, Mark, Luke, John

THE QUEST FOR THE HISTORICAL JESUS

The historical Jesus lived and worked in Jewish Palestine during the first thirty years or so of the first century CE, and so he lived under the circumstances described in the preceding chapter. Since he lived before the revolt against the Romans, it is appropriate to study him here, before treating the revolt, rather than to discuss him as an appendix to the study of first-century Jewish society.

This chapter is not a full treatment of the historical Jesus. Its purpose is to illustrate the Jewishness of Jesus. The focus is on the *humanity* of Jesus, prescinding from the question of Christian belief about his divinity. Even when Christians try to take the humanity of Jesus fully into account, there has traditionally been a reluctance to make him too much of a Jew. Rather, it is his uniqueness that has been emphasized. How he differed from his fellow Jews has been stressed, not how he was the same. The result is that the Jewishness of Jesus has faded. He becomes a universal, a person without a homeland, native language, traditional religion. The trend begins as early as the New Testament. For example, Jesus is often portrayed as speaking with "the Jews." That is indeed a strange way to talk, given that Jesus is a Jew. This way of talking sets Jesus apart from the Jews, almost denying that he is one of them. To ask how Jesus related to the Jews of his day makes about as much sense as asking how a modern American college student relates to "the Americans."

The Historical Jesus

Several terms are useful in discussing the historical Jesus: "historical Jesus," "historic Jesus," "Christ of faith," and the "real" Jesus. The historical Jesus is simply that Jesus who walked and spoke in Palestine of the first century CE. What is "historical" is what "actually happened," what could have been observed by an eyewitness.

The Historic Jesus

Not everything that is historical about Jesus is significant for later generations. Aspects of a person whose significance transcends his or her own lifetime are "historic." Jesus is a historic figure, even for non-Christians. His effect on world history is undeniable.

311

The Christ of Faith

The "Christ of faith" is the object of Christian worship. "Christ" comes from the Greek *christos* meaning "anointed one." *Christos* is the Greek equivalent of the Hebrew "messiah." Many things are claimed for the Christ of faith (for example, that he is divine) that cannot be proved or disproved by historical method.

The "Real" Jesus

The "real" Jesus is an elusive concept. There is a certain "common sense" quality to the desire to know the "real" Jesus, but if that means to comprehend the totality of his being, it would seem to be an impossible task. How well can one know the "reality" even of one's friends, much less of someone who lived two millennia ago? If one says that Jesus lives and that believers have a personal relationship with him, and that is the real Jesus, then one is back to the sphere of the Christ of faith. The dialogue between one inside that sphere of faith and one outside it is limited, since their definitions of the "real" Jesus may be quite different.

The Sources

This chapter limits itself to the historical Jesus. But even this circumscribed area is not without problems. The most fruitful sources for the historical Jesus are the canonical gospels, Matthew, Mark, Luke, and John. The first three are called the "synoptic gospels." Because of the large amount of material they have in common, they can be "seen together," the root meaning of the Greek *synopsis*. The gospels are not unbiased sources. They are selective in what they report. Their aim is neither to be exhaustive, nor to be "objective history" in any modern sense. They are expressions of faith meant to encourage and support belief. There is historical information in the gospels, but the gospels are not themselves histories. One might accurately call them long sermons in narrative form. A modern preacher might retell a biblical story to make a point; the gospel writers do something similar. They add, subtract, and rewrite material in order to present their own views.

The historian must disentangle the historical from the nonhistorical within the gospels, and then put the "facts" into a comprehensible historical framework. The job is difficult, some would say impossible. The problem with giving up is that one may well have an implicit view of the historical Jesus that colors what one thinks about him. Even if no definitive answers to the historical questions are forthcoming, the task of asking the questions is important so as to make explicit one's implicit picture of the historical Jesus, and to examine its historical bases critically.

Mark was the first gospel written (ca. 70 CE). It used oral and written sources, but they no longer exist. The materials Mark used had been shaped by the church's needs for about forty years. Matthew and Luke used Mark, but they also most probably had in common another source, which has been called "Q," consisting primarily of the sayings of Jesus.[1] Q no longer exists, but reasonable reconstructions of it are possible based on comparisons of Matthew and Luke. Matthew and Luke each have material peculiar to themselves that may come from a variety of sources. The Gospel of John is independent of the synoptics and used other, no longer extant, sources.

Scholars have devised criteria by which to judge the historicity of a given saying or deed of Jesus.[2] (1) *Dissimilarity*. Something may be considered "authentic" (going back to Jesus himself) if it is contrary to typical emphases of first-century Judaism and of early Christianity. The problem with such a criterion is that it excludes material that would make Jesus a Jew of his time, as well as material that provides a continuity between Jesus and the church. Another difficulty is that knowledge about first-century Judaism and the early church is fragmentary, so that although something might seem to be unique to Jesus, that may be only because extant sources for first-century Judaism or early Christianity did not preserve it. (2) *Embarrassment*. There are certain things in the gospels that are unlikely to have been invented by the church, because it found them embarrassing. (3) *Multiple Attestation*. Some things are found in more than one literary form, or more than one source. A characteristic of Jesus found in parables, sayings, and other sorts of narratives, as well as in Mark, Q, and John, for example, would have a claim to authenticity. (4) *Coherence*. Once a core of material has been established by the preceding criteria, one might include other material that does not pass the stricter tests of authenticity, but which coheres with the core of material that does pass those tests. (5) *Linguistic and Environmental Context*. This criterion is used to reject material that does not fit the environment of first-century Palestine. (6) *Rejection and Execution*. Because Jesus was rejected by the Jerusalem establishment and executed by the Romans, any reconstruction of his life and work that portrays him as a politically harmless teacher would be inadequate. The foregoing criteria have provided ways to discuss the authenticity of Jesus material, but numerous reconstructions of the historical Jesus are still possible even using those criteria.

Some scholars have examined primarily the "facts" about Jesus, while others have concentrated on his teaching. This chapter combines both approaches. What follows is a fairly mainstream interpretation, yet owing to limited knowledge, many of its aspects can be debated.

THE "FACTS" ABOUT JESUS

Sanders' list of "indisputable facts" provides a useful framework for the discussion in this section.

1. Jesus was baptized by John the Baptist.
2. Jesus was a Galilean who preached and healed.
3. Jesus called disciples and spoke of there being twelve.
4. Jesus confined his activity to Israel.
5. Jesus engaged in a controversy about the temple.
6. Jesus was crucified outside Jerusalem by the Roman authorities.
7. After his death Jesus' followers continued as an identifiable movement.
8. At least some Jews persecuted at least parts of the new movement (Gal. 1.13, 22; Phil. 3.6), and it appears that this persecution endured at least to a time near the end of Paul's career (II Cor. 11.24; Gal. 5.11; 6.12; cf. Matt. 23.34; 10:17).[3]

1. Baptized by John the Baptist

In chapter 10, John the Baptist was discussed in the context of first-century prophetic movements. Herod Antipas eliminated John because his message was attractive to the masses. John's apocalyptic message is summarized in Matthew 3:7-12. He preached that the eschaton was coming soon, at which time the wrath of God would descend upon sinners. He urged repentance and baptized those who accepted his message. John believed that baptism would protect against God's wrath if accompanied by genuine repentance.

Jesus begins his ministry by being baptized by John. Jesus accepted John's message and submitted to a baptism of repentance. That embarrassed early Christians. A story unique to Matthew tries to come to terms with it.

> Then Jesus came from Galilee to John at the Jordan, to be baptized by him. John would have prevented him, saying, "I need to be baptized by you, and do you come to me?" But Jesus answered him, "Let it be so now; for it is proper for us in this way to fulfill all righteousness." Then he consented. (3:13-15)

John recognizes that the greater baptizes the lesser. Jesus' explanation, that righteousness must be fulfilled, responds to this concern, maintaining that God's plans must be fulfilled. "Now" seems to indicate that John's superiority is temporary. What is significant is that such an explanation is needed. Luke deals with the issue by assuming that Jesus was baptized by John, but by avoiding a direct description of the baptism. The Gospel of John avoids the issue altogether by omitting the baptism.

The Gospel of John is especially insistent on Jesus' superiority to John the Baptist. When members of the Jerusalem establishment come to ask John why he baptizes, "He confessed and did not deny it, but confessed, 'I am not the

314

Messiah'" (1:20). John's emphatic denial suggests that some did think that John was the messiah. Rivalry between John and Jesus is also suggested by the following passages.

> They came to John and said to him, "Rabbi, the one who was with you across the Jordan, to whom you testified, here he is baptizing, and all are going to him." John answered, "No one can receive anything except what has been given from heaven. You yourselves are my witnesses that I said, 'I am not the Messiah, but I have been sent ahead of him.'" (3:26-28)

> Jesus learned that the Pharisees had heard, "Jesus is making and baptizing more disciples than John"—although it was not Jesus himself but his disciples who baptized. (4:1-2)

These verses conflict with the synoptic contention that Jesus began his ministry only after John ended his. Here Jesus and John carry on simultaneous ministries. Since the gospels claim that the Baptist was merely the forerunner of Jesus, it is more likely that the synoptics came up with the neat succession of ministries, rather than that the fourth gospel made them simultaneous. In John's gospel the disciples of the Baptist are confused because Jesus carries on an independent ministry, and are distressed that he is more successful than their master. In John 1, Jesus draws his first disciples from among John's followers. It is plausible that Jesus began his public life as a disciple of John the Baptist, but then began his own ministry, followed by some other disciples of John. The confusion over whether or not Jesus himself baptized may be due to the embarrassment of the relation between John and Jesus. Early Christians may have wanted to avoid any appearance that Jesus was merely copying the Baptist. Thus, although John 3:26 and 4:1 state that Jesus was baptizing, 4:2 denies it.

The question arises whether the Baptist ever recognized Jesus as the one for whom he was preparing Israel. Many scholars think that John expected the impending advent of God, not of a messiah. John says that he comes to prepare the way of the Lord, but those words occur in a quotation from Isaiah in which "Lord" means God (Mark 1:3). Even if John did expect a messiah, there is some evidence that he was doubtful whether Jesus was that messiah. Matthew and Luke claim that well into Jesus' ministry John sent his own disciples to Jesus asking, "Are you the one who is to come, or are we to wait for another?" (Matt 11:3; see also Luke 7:19). If John had recognized Jesus as messiah, it would be strange that this story would circulate in Christian circles.

There is a saying of Jesus contrasting John and Jesus that preserves historical information about the two figures: "John came neither eating nor drinking, and they say, 'He has a demon'; the Son of Man came eating and drinking, and they

say, 'Look, a glutton and a drunkard, a friend of tax collectors and sinners!' ''
(Matt 11:18-19; *see also* Luke 7:33-34). This saying is probably authentic, for it
is hard to believe that the early church would have made up charges against Jesus
of being a glutton and a drunkard. Throughout the gospels, Jesus is depicted as
participating in dinner parties. The Baptist was an ascetic, but Jesus was not. His
attitude toward food and drink, which differs from that of John the Baptist,
probably has something to do with his preaching of the kingdom of God, to be
discussed below.

2. A Galilean Who Preached and Healed

Jesus was born at the end of the reign of Herod the Great (4 BCE; Matt 2:1; Luke
1:5). Luke 2:1-2 says that he was born when Quirinius was governor of Syria and
the census was taken (6 CE), but the earlier date, attested to independently by
Matthew and Luke, is more likely. Jesus was from the Galilean town of
Nazareth, in the hills just north of the valley separating Galilee from Samaria.
Nazareth was about three miles southeast of the Hellenistic city of Sepphoris,
which served as an administrative center for Galilee under Herod Antipas (ruled
4 BCE–39 CE). The gospels never say that Jesus entered Sepphoris. He spent most
of his time in the small villages of Galilee. If the tradition about his being a
carpenter is correct, he was a rural artisan, and so a member of the lower classes.
His native language was Aramaic.

Herod Antipas ruled Galilee during Jesus' life, and Judea was under a different
jurisdiction. It is not clear how much power the Jerusalem establishment had
over Galilee, probably only as much as Herod allowed. The synoptics leave the
impression that Jesus spent most of his time in Galilee, and went to Jerusalem
only at the end of his life. John has Jesus making at least three trips to Jerusalem.
Even if Jesus did go to Jerusalem for feasts more than once, most of his active
ministry was probably in Galilee. In that case, the ''scribes'' with whom he
interacts would be Herodian officials, or Galilean village scribes. There may
have been some Pharisees there, but their presence was not strong. When Jesus
went to Jerusalem, he came into direct conflict with the Temple priests and
scribes, and with Jerusalem's elders—leading citizens. It was Jesus' clash with
the Temple establishment that caused his death.

Differences between Judea and Galilee sometimes form the backdrop for
analyses of Jesus the Jew. Galilee is sometimes depicted as a hotbed of
revolutionary activity. This is offered as an explanation of Jesus' independent
attitude toward Jerusalem and its priestly and scribal establishment. However,
close examination of the sources does not make Galilee appear any more
revolutionary than Judea, at least not before 44 CE when the procurators added it
to their jurisdiction and Galilee came under direct Roman rule for the first time.

Galilean religion, especially that of the lower classes to which Jesus belonged, is sometimes presented as charismatic, that is, loosely organized and open to spontaneous developments, as opposed to the more established and structured religion of Judea and Jerusalem. Jesus is depicted as a charismatic wonder-worker whose popularity aroused the resentment of the establishment, which did not enjoy popular support. Galilee differed from Judea, but to what degree is uncertain. The Temple establishment had less control in Galilee than in Judea. Jesus' attitude toward the establishment may have been part of a broader Galilean attitude, but that is not known for sure. Any suggestions of Galilean independence from the Jerusalem establishment must be balanced against the evidence for Galilean devotion to the Temple, made evident by festival pilgrimages by natives of Galilee to the holy city. At the same time, previous chapters have shown that devotion to the Temple was not incompatible with a critical attitude toward Temple personnel, and this may have been the position taken by Jesus.

Few question that Jesus was known to his contemporaries as a healer and an exorcist. Even Jesus' enemies admitted his powers. The issue was not whether Jesus could do healings and exorcisms, but why he could do them. The following passage shows the debate.

> And the scribes who came down from Jerusalem said, ''He has Beelzebul, and by the ruler of the demons he casts out demons.'' And he called them to him, and spoke to them in parables, ''How can Satan cast out Satan? If a kingdom is divided against itself, that kingdom cannot stand. And if a house is divided against itself, that house will not be able to stand. And if Satan has risen up against himself and is divided, he cannot stand, but his end has come. But no one can enter a strong man's house and plunder his property without first tying up the strong man; then indeed the house can be plundered.'' (Mark 3:22-27)

Beelzebul is another name for the leader of the demons, otherwise known as Satan. Christians would not have invented a charge of collaboration with Satan. The charge means that the accusers believed that Jesus had special powers, but thought that he was in league with the devil. Jesus' answer discloses his own (according to Mark) interpretation of his exorcisms. To cast out demons is to cast out Satan. Exorcisms are identified with tying Satan up and plundering his house. This is comprehensible within an apocalyptic world view. The world is controlled by Satan, and God will soon intervene to defeat Satan and recapture the world. Jesus claims that God's intervention begins with his exorcisms. To liberate people from the power of Satan is to plunder Satan's house.

The eschatological element in Jesus' wonder working sets him apart from other figures of the time with whom he has been compared. Vermes suggests comparison of Jesus with two Jewish holy men.[4] Honi the Circle-Drawer lived in

317

the first century BCE. His prayers ended a drought, according to Josephus and rabbinic sources. The rabbinic story compares his behavior toward God to that of a son toward his father. The other holy man was Hanina ben Dosa, from a Galilean village ten miles north of Nazareth, who is said to have been a pupil of the Pharisaic master Yohanan ben Zakkai, who helped to reconstitute Judaism after the revolt of 66–70 CE. Like Jesus, Hanina cured people from a distance, controlled nature, and performed exorcisms. He showed little interest in ritual matters, but focused on moral issues. The parallels with Jesus are clear, especially in the case of Hanina ben Dosa. But neither man is said to preach the eschatological message attributed to Jesus.

3. The Twelve

There is little reason to doubt that Jesus chose twelve disciples. In 1 Corinthians 15:5 (written ca. 54 CE), Paul quotes a tradition to the effect that Jesus appeared to "the twelve" after appearing to Peter. It is the number twelve, rather than the individuals involved, that is important here, as is demonstrated by the fact that the different gospels contain different lists of the twelve. If the idea of the twelve specially chosen disciples had been an invention of the early church, the church would not have included Judas, Jesus' betrayer, among their number.

The most obvious explanation for the number twelve is that there were twelve tribes of Israel. Jesus' words support such an interpretation: "Truly I tell you, at the renewal of all things, when the Son of Man is seated on the throne of his glory, you who have followed me will also sit on twelve thrones, judging the twelve tribes of Israel" (Matt 19:28). An argument for the authenticity of the second half of this verse is that since Jesus utters these words during his ministry, Matthew includes Judas among the twelve. The church would not have created a saying of Jesus promising a throne to Judas.

It is not entirely clear what "judging" means in this context. Eschatological judgment is suggested by the connection of the thrones of the twelve with the throne of the Son of Man. The Son of Man sits on a throne at the final judgment in Matthew 25:31-46 and *1 Enoch* 62:5-8. But some scholars think that the reference to the Son of Man was added to this saying by the early church. Another possibility is that the verb "to judge" is to be read in the context of the activity of the pre-monarchical judges of Israel.[5] If so, Jesus may envision a noneschatological restoration of Israel along the lines of the more egalitarian model of society prevalent at the time of the judges' rule. To judge the twelve tribes of Israel would then mean to rule Israel in conformity with the righteousness and social justice demanded by ancient covenantal traditions. In any case, the fact that Jesus thinks in terms of the twelve tribes suggests that he expects Israel's restoration, not its annihilation.

4. Jesus Confined His Ministry to Israel

Jesus had little to do with Gentiles. Despite the fact that the gospels favor the Gentile mission of the Christian church, they preserve material that opposes it. When Jesus sends the twelve on a mission in Matthew 10:5-6, he says, "Go nowhere among the Gentiles, and enter no town of the Samaritans, but go rather to the lost sheep of the house of Israel." Later in the same chapter he says, "When they persecute you in one town, flee to the next; for truly I tell you, you will not have gone through all the towns of Israel before the Son of Man comes" (10:23).

Jesus does minister to the daughter of a Gentile woman.

> Jesus left that place and went away to the district of Tyre and Sidon. Just then a Canaanite woman from that region came out and started shouting, "Have mercy on me, Lord, Son of David; my daughter is tormented by a demon." But he did not answer her at all. And his disciples came and urged him, saying, "Send her away, for she keeps shouting after us." He answered, "I was sent only to the lost sheep of the house of Israel." But she came and knelt before him, saying, "Lord, help me." He answered, "It is not fair to take the children's food and throw it to the dogs." She said, "Yes, Lord, yet even the dogs eat the crumbs that fall from their masters' table." Then Jesus answered her, "Woman, great is your faith! Let it be done for you as you wish." And her daughter was healed instantly.
>
> (Matt 15:21-28; *see* Mark 7:24-30)

Jesus' reluctance to have anything to do with the Gentile woman is striking. The explanation that he was testing her faith is pure speculation and not grounded in the text. The contrast of Jews and Gentiles as "children" and "dogs" is startling in its harshness. The healing itself is done from a distance. There is another story where Jesus heals a Gentile, this time the servant of a centurion, who is also healed from a distance (Matt 8:5-13; Luke 7:1-10). There Jesus does not approach the Gentiles; the Roman approaches him. Jesus is amazed to find such faith outside Israel.

The gospels see Jesus acting almost exclusively among Jews. Even if the anti-Gentile stories and sayings are unauthentic, it is hard to see how they could have been invented if Jesus pursued a mission to the Gentiles. Whether Jesus anticipated a mission to the Gentiles after his death is debatable, but there is little evidence for it. Acts of the Apostles and the letters of Paul attest to a lively debate over the issue of preaching to the Gentiles. That debate implies that Jesus had not settled the question. He may have thought that the Gentiles would come to worship the God of the Jews at the eschatological restoration of Israel. Such an expectation would be fully consonant with Jewish belief, especially that centered on Zion. It would be the kind of universalism that preserves the centrality of Israel as God's chosen people and true worshipers.

5. *Jesus and the Temple*

In each of the gospels there is a scene in which Jesus enters the Temple and disrupts it. The incident may have been a precipitating factor in his death.

> Then they came to Jerusalem. And he entered the temple and began to drive out those who were selling and those who were buying in the temple, and he overturned the tables of the money changers and the seats of those who sold doves; and he would not allow anyone to carry anything through the temple. He was teaching and saying, ''Is it not written, 'My house shall be called a house of prayer for all the nations'? But you have made it a den of robbers.'' And when the chief priests and the scribes heard it, they kept looking for a way to kill him; for they were afraid of him, because the whole crowd was spellbound by his teaching. (Mark 11:15-18)

The next day the chief priests, scribes, and elders confront Jesus and demand to know by what authority he acted (Mark 11:27-33).

The Temple was a very large place, and on Passover it would have been filled with thousands of people. During the principal feasts it was well policed. In addition, the procurator came to Jerusalem for the feast with his soldiers. To disrupt Temple activity substantially, Jesus would have needed a small army. If Jesus had interfered with Temple services, he would have been arrested immediately, as Roman responses to other disturbances at feasts amply demonstrate.

Jesus' action in the Temple may have been a ''symbolic action.'' Israel's prophets often performed public acts symbolizing their message. For example, in Jeremiah 19 the prophet breaks a pottery flask to symbolize the imminent destruction of Jerusalem. The act did not simply predict an event. It helped to accomplish it, since prophetic words and actions were divine oracles which brought about what they said or enacted. The synoptic gospels take Jesus' action as symbolic of cleansing the Temple from commercial activity. But to bring all commercial activity in the Temple to a halt would have undermined the Temple itself by making it difficult to pay the Temple tax, contribute to the Temple, or make sacrifices. However, there is little evidence that Jesus opposed the sacrificial system as such. Nor was he anti-Temple in general. He taught there, seems to have considered it central to Judaism, and in this passage calls it his father's house. That early Christians could attribute such a positive attitude toward the Temple to Jesus makes it unlikely that he opposed the Temple as such.

The key to Jesus' action may lie in the overturning of the tables.[6] The overturning may symbolize the coming destruction of the Temple. The Temple would be destroyed to make way for a new Temple in a restored Israel. An alternative view is that Jesus opposed the social structure implied by the Temple and its hierarchy.[7] In that case the Temple would be destroyed because it was an obstacle to the egalitarian society God wanted. In either case, Temple authorities would not appreciate Jesus' action. Mark says Jesus' act made them decide to destroy him. Since Jesus was turned over to Pilate by the Jerusalem leaders, they clearly saw him as a threat.

There is extensive evidence that Jesus predicted a destruction of the Temple. In Mark 13:2, Jesus tells his disciples, "Do you see these great buildings? Not one stone will be left here upon another; all will be thrown down." In Jesus' trial, Mark accuses false witnesses of saying, "We heard him say, 'I will destroy this temple that is made with hands, and in three days I will build another, not made with hands'" (14:58). In Matthew "false witnesses" say, "This fellow said, 'I am able to destroy the temple of God and to build it in three days'" (26:61). Luke omits the charge in the trial scene, but in Acts of the Apostles, the second volume of his work, Stephen proclaims, "This Jesus of Nazareth will destroy this place [the temple]" (6:14). The crowds at the cross say that Jesus said he "would destroy the temple and build it in three days" (Mark 15:29; *see also* Matt 27:40). John combines the "cleansing" of the Temple with a Temple saying of Jesus: "Destroy this temple, and in three days I will raise it up" (2:19). The widespread nature of the Temple sayings makes it likely that Jesus made some such statement about the Temple, but neither the original words of Jesus nor their context can be recovered. Statements critical of the Temple or its personnel spoken by someone with a popular following would threaten the Temple authorities.

6. Crucified Outside Jerusalem by Roman Authorities

Jesus was crucified outside the walls of Jerusalem near the feast of Passover. Passover brought together the Romans, the Jewish governing class and their retainers, the population of Jerusalem, and Jewish pilgrims from the Judean countryside, Galilee, and elsewhere. The combination of large crowds with the feast of liberation was volatile. The gospels claim that Jesus had a large following, and so he would have attracted the attention of the authorities.

On the day before Passover, Jesus was arrested by Jewish authorities. Exactly what happened over the next twenty-four hours is disputed. The nature of the deliberations of the Jewish authorities is unclear. There are three possibilities: (1) a night trial before the entire Sanhedrin with the high priest presiding; (2) an early morning meeting of the Sanhedrin; (3) an informal hearing on the night of the arrest before the high priest and several other notables. Whichever of these hypotheses is correct, the Jerusalem establishment saw Jesus as a threat and decided to eliminate him. The Romans would not tolerate civil unrest.

The rulers' deliberations as reported by the Gospel of John capture what may have been their reasoning.

So the chief priests and the Pharisees called a meeting of the council, and said, "What are we to do? This man is performing many signs. If we let him go on like this, everyone will believe in him, and the Romans will come and destroy both our holy place and our nation." But one of them, Caiaphas, who was high priest that year, said to them, "You know nothing at all! You do not understand that it is better for you to have one man die for the people than to have the whole nation destroyed." He did not say this on his own, but being high priest that year he prophesied that Jesus was about to die for the nation, and not for the nation only, but to gather into one the dispersed children of God. (11:47-52)

The inclusion of the Pharisees typifies John's tendency to make them more prominent than they are. None of the other gospels involves them in the final deliberations of the Jewish rulers in Jerusalem. John's gospel says that Caiaphas possessed prophetic ability because of his high priestly status. As is characteristic of John, the passage operates on at least two levels. Caiaphas thinks that he is making a shrewd political judgment in letting Jesus die so that Roman wrath does not destroy the nation. Ironically, he does not realize that God intends for Jesus to die for all people. This is John's theological interpretation, but it shows how theology builds on political events.

In searching for the reasons for Jesus' death, two facts must be kept firmly in mind: (1) he was executed by the Romans by crucifixion; (2) the charge the Romans put on the cross read "King of the Jews." Crucifixion was a Roman punishment reserved for political offenders, hardened criminals, and slaves. Jesus does not fit either of the last two categories. The charge on the cross makes his crime a political one. Jesus' confrontations with scribes, Pharisees, and others may have alienated those groups, but they were not the proximate causes of his death. Jesus' actions and words concerning the Temple establishment were a serious political threat, serious enough to be addressed by the Romans.

7. The Jesus Movement

The fact that the Jesus movement continued to exist and to grow after his death says something about what it must have been during his life. Jesus probably intended to build a lasting movement. Some foundations must have been laid to enable the movement to survive his death. That is not to say that Jesus intended to begin a religion different from Judaism. He seems to have wished to restore Israel to its proper state and relation with God. The twelve would form the nucleus of the restored Israel.

8. Jewish Persecution of the Movement

There is substantial evidence of Jewish-Christian conflict from earliest times. After 70 CE Judaism was being reconstituted according to rabbinic principles, and Christianity was becoming an important religion. Both claimed the same Scriptures and traditions. From the Jewish point of view, Christians were using

Jewish Scripture and tradition against Judaism. From the Christian point of view, Judaism had "missed the boat" by not recognizing Jesus as the messiah.

THE TEACHING OF JESUS

The Kingdom of God

The coming of the kingdom of God is an important symbol in Jesus' preaching.[8] His use of the symbol depends on his Jewish matrix. In Israel, God was frequently called king (Hebrew: *melek*), or said to reign (*mālak*). At times the kingdom of God was identified with the existing Israelite kingdom, as in 1 Chronicles 28:5. More often the notion of God's rule was not a geographical place, but denoted God's activity in ruling Israel and the world. The following passage illustrates this notion of divine rule.

> They shall speak of the glory of your kingdom,
> and tell of your power,
> to make known to all people your mighty deeds,
> and the glorious splendor of your kingdom.
> Your kingdom is an everlasting kingdom,
> and your dominion endures throughout all generations.
> (Ps 145:11-13)

During most of the Second Temple period, Israel lived under foreign domination. Under such circumstances, it was difficult to believe that God actually ruled the world. Some circles hoped for a future restoration of God's rule. That hope might be apocalyptic, but it could also be fostered by those expecting a purely historical transformation. The following sayings of Jesus should be read in the context of an expectation of the reassertion of God's rule.

The kingdom of God is not coming with things that can be observed; nor will they say, "Look, here it is!" or "There it is!" For, in fact, the kingdom of God is among you. (Luke 17:20-21)

From the days of John the Baptist until now the kingdom of heaven has suffered violence, and the violent take it by force. (Matt 11:12)

But if it is by the finger of God that I cast out the demons, then the kingdom of God has come to you. (Luke 11:20)

Many apocalypses lay out timetables for the eschaton and events leading up to it. There are signs to be observed that the wise can read. The first saying may mean that the kingdom will come too suddenly to be predicted. Some scholars go farther and say that Jesus did not expect a literal coming of the kingdom of God as a historical event. Few still defend the position that interprets this saying as meaning that Jesus thought the kingdom was an inner reality, a matter only of the heart. Jesus expected societal changes, too. His rejection of the seeking of signs is reflected in another saying: "Why does this generation ask for a sign? Truly I tell you, no sign will be given to this generation" (Mark 8:12). Early Christians were not content with the refusal of a sign, and in Matthew and Luke the text is elaborated by speaking of Jesus as a sign like the prophet Jonah (Matt 12:38-42; 16:4; Luke 11:29-32).

The second saying seems to interpret the fate of John the Baptist, and of Jesus and his followers. There is a war going on between God and Satan, and wars involve casualties. John is one of those casualties, Jesus another. The third saying recalls Mark 3. "Finger of God' alludes to Exodus 8:19, where the Egyptians who have witnessed the plagues sent through Moses say, "This is the finger of God." This implies that God acts through Jesus, as through Moses. In Jesus' exorcisms God casts out Satan.

The Parables

In this section, "parable" denotes the kind of short story exemplified by the God Samaritan, the Prodigal Son, and the Good Shepherd. Similar sorts of stories were used by the rabbis, and before them by Israel's wisdom tradition, to teach lessons. Jesus uses parables to proclaim the coming of God's kingdom. They even help to bring it about by causing a shift of world view among the hearers so that they begin to see things as God does. This use of parables is considered unique to Jesus.

The early church allegorized the parables to apply them to its own situation. Allegorization means interpreting the details of the parable so that they correspond to realities outside the story itself and teach a lesson. A good example is that of the Sower (Mark 4:3-8, allegorized in 4:14-20). Most scholars consider the allegorization to be the product of the early church and not part of the original parable.

Jesus intended that his parables accomplish a shift in world view in his hearers. An example is the Good Samaritan.

A man was going down from Jerusalem to Jericho, and fell into the hands of robbers, who stripped him, beat him, and went away, leaving him half dead. Now by chance a priest was going down that road; and when he saw him, he passed by on the other side. So likewise a Levite, when he came to the place and saw him, passed by on the other side. But a Samaritan while traveling came near him; and when he saw him, he was moved with pity. He went to him and bandaged his wounds, having poured oil and wine on them. Then he put him on his own animal, brought him to an inn, and took care of him. The next day he took out two denarii, gave them to the innkeeper, and said, "Take care of him; and when I come back, I will repay you whatever more you spend." (Luke 10:30-35)

Jesus is a Jew telling a story to Jews in Jewish Palestine. The parable has an anticlerical bent in that the "bad guys" are a priest and a Levite. Jesus may have expected his hearers to impute motives to the priest and the Levite, such as that they assumed the man was dead, and saw no reason to defile themselves so that they could not take part in Temple services. Giving priority to human needs over other types of duties seems characteristic of Jesus.

If Jesus had simply introduced a pious Jewish layperson here, the anticlerical strain would be clearer and might well win the sympathy of his audience. The shock of the story for the Jewish listeners comes when the Samaritan appears. The animosity between Jews and Samaritans arose partly because of religious reasons. Both groups considered themselves the true followers of Mosaic Torah. The contrast of a heretical Samaritan not only with a Jew, but also with the Jewish religious establishment, would scandalize Jesus' audience.

The parable of the Good Samaritan demonstrates how Jesus uses parables to shock his hearers and to wake them up to a new way of seeing things. The basic message is that society's way of seeing is not God's way of seeing. Such a message is not unique to Jesus, of course. It is characteristic of Israel's prophets, and is found in other types of Jewish literature, too. In relation to Jesus' teaching and actions as a whole, the parables were meant to bring the kingdom into existence among his hearers. To enter into the world of the parable and accept it implies giving up one's own presuppositions insofar as they conflict with God's will.

Another example of how Jesus' parables challenge the presuppositions of their hearers is in the parable of the Day Laborers (Matt 20:1-15). There a man hires workers at various times during the day. At the end of the day he pays them each the same amount, although some worked the entire day, and others only an hour. Hearers of the story probably identify with the workers who complain about working the longest but getting paid only what the late workers were paid. The point is that God's justice is not human justice. Divine generosity cannot be limited by human boundaries. Another example of a parable challenging human preconceptions is that of the Rich Man and Lazarus (Luke 16:19-23). The rich man lives luxuriously during his life, and goes to hell after his death. The poor man, Lazarus, lies suffering at the rich man's gate, and after his death he goes to heaven. There is a reversal of fates in view here. The parable expresses God's judgment on a society in which there is a tremendous gap between rich and poor. The reversal theme is typical of apocalypticism.

The theme of God's generosity evident in the parable of the Day Laborers also expresses itself as an emphasis on God's forgiveness. The parable of the Prodigal Son embodies that theme (Luke 15:11-32). A son takes his inheritance from his father while the father still lives. The son then goes to a foreign land where he squanders the inheritance. Reduced to abject poverty, he returns home, asking only that he be treated as a servant. The father receives him joyously, sweeps aside the son's request to be treated as a servant, and holds a feast to celebrate his return. This is a graphic portrayal of forgiveness.

The two parables preceding the Prodigal Son in Luke 15 have a similar theme. The good shepherd seeks the lost sheep and rejoices when it is found, and the housewife searches for the lost coin and rejoices when she discovers it. Luke 15 interprets this as God's concern for sinners. The chapter begins, "The Pharisees and the scribes were grumbling and saying, 'This fellow welcomes sinners and eats with them'" (Luke 15:2). The context is contrived by the evangelist, but it might well be true to the ministry of Jesus. His association with those whom the religious elite considered sinners is well established in the tradition. Jesus' preaching of the kingdom of God emphasized the forgiveness of God, who approached people through him.

The theme of reversal is evident once again in the parable of the Prodigal Son. At the end of the parable the sinful son is within the house at a feast. The dutiful son stays outside, resentful of his father's generosity toward his wayward brother. The theme appears again in the parable of the Great Dinner (Luke 14:15-24), where present at the feast are the unlikeliest of guests, while the invited ones are absent. When one finally enters the kingdom, symbolized by a banquet, those whom one expected to find there will not be present, and the ones whom one least expected to find will be there.

Proverbial Sayings

The first short saying to be examined here is quoted within the narrative context that elicited it. "Another of his disciples said to him, 'Lord, first let me go and bury my father.' But Jesus said to him, 'Follow me, and let the dead bury their own dead'" (Matt 8:21-22). The saying, "Let the dead bury their own dead," is probably authentic because it does not fit the ethics of Jesus' Jewish matrix, nor is it part of early Christian teaching. Jesus demands something in contradiction to the commandment to honor one's father and mother. Refusal to bury one's parent would be the height of dishonor in ancient society. Whether Jesus considered his demand to be a violation of Torah will be taken up below. The least that can be said is that Jesus demanded that his hearers make a radical break with their former ways of thinking. Jesus insisted that following him took precedence over all other obligations, even the most sacred. Such a demand makes sense in the social milieu of Jesus' itinerant preaching. To follow him would seem to entail some sort of break with one's former life, occupation, kin, acquaintances, and so on. Other sayings in the gospels support this interpretation.

326

Another saying also reveals the extent to which accepting Jesus means changing one's ways of thinking: "If any one strikes you on the right cheek, turn the other also; and if anyone wants to sue you and take your coat, give your cloak as well; and if anyone forces you to go one mile, go also the second mile" (Matt 5:39-41). The meaning of this saying is not self-evident. Did Jesus mean it literally? Was he speaking of how Jews should relate to occupying powers, such as the Romans, who pressed people into forced service or confiscated their goods? Was he encouraging pacifism? Was he speaking of how peasants should relate to one another within their villages? In the history of Christianity, this saying has been given widely varying interpretations. At the very least, Jesus is asserting that accepting his message means undermining one's former way of looking at the world, and so means radical change in one's life. Such sayings have been called "focal instances," because they try to bring about a shift in attitude by focusing in on a very concrete and particular instance.[9] Their implication goes beyond the specific instance addressed in the saying. For example, the saying about being slapped on the cheek does not just give a legal prescription for dealing with that particular situation, but is meant to change one's attitude about a whole range of human interactions.

A well-attested theme in the teaching of Jesus is that of eschatological reversal as found in the following sayings.

> For those who want to save their life will lose it, and those who lose their life for my sake, and for the sake of the gospel, will save it. (Mark 8:35)

> How hard it will be for those who have wealth to enter the kingdom of God! . . . It is easier for a camel to go through the eye of a needle than for someone who is rich to enter the kingdom of God. (Mark 10:23b, 25)

> But many who are first will be last, and the last will be first. (Mark 10:31)

> For all who exalt themselves will be humbled, and those who humble themselves will be exalted. (Luke 14:11)

The first saying continues the theme of the radicality of the demands made by the kingdom. The second saying introduces an economic factor, wealth. Jesus thinks that the eschatological reversal to take effect will mean that few if any rich will be saved. The third saying is a general principle that things will be reversed at the eschaton. It reflects the apocalyptic belief that the present world is dominated by Satan, and that social structure mirrors that circumstance in that it is unjust. God's intervention will change that. Jesus' own practice manifests the kingdom in that he has a special concern for sinners and the poor, the marginal of society. The final saying shows that one's fate depends on oneself, and that striving for success according to the norms of this world will result in being humbled.

The transformation of self and society that Jesus' proclamation commands is not an easy one, as is demonstrated by this collection of sayings.

No one who puts a hand to the plow and looks back is fit for the kingdom of God.
(Luke 9:62)

Enter through the narrow gate; for the gate is wide and the road is easy that leads to destruction, and there are many who take it. For the gate is narrow and the road is hard that leads to life, and there are few who find it. (Matt 7:13-14)

Truly I tell you, whoever does not receive the kingdom of God as a little child will never enter it. (Mark 10:15)

But I say to you, Love your enemies and pray for those who persecute you, so that you may be children of your Father in heaven; for he makes his sun rise on the evil and on the good, and sends rain on the righteous and on the unrighteous. For if you love those who love you, what reward do you have? Do not even the tax collectors do the same? And if you greet only your brothers and sisters, what more are you doing than others? Do not even the Gentiles do the same? Be perfect, therefore, as your heavenly Father is perfect. (Matt 5:44-48)

The precise meaning of each saying depends on the context in which it is read. As a group they reinforce the conclusions already drawn about the profound change in attitude and society that the kingdom requires. The saying about entering the kingdom like a child probably refers to entering it without the fixed assumptions typical of adults. The absolute commitment to the new way of life symbolized by the kingdom means that one cannot look back, as Luke 9:62 makes clear. The difficulty of entering the kingdom is likened to going through a narrow gate.[10]

The importance of context for interpretation is illustrated by Matthew 5:44-48. What Jesus meant by the command to love one's enemies is uncertain. Were the "enemies" everyone with whom one had negative relations? Did Jesus mean political enemies, such as the Romans, or perhaps the Jerusalem hierarchy, or just personal enemies? Was he speaking to peasants about their squabbles among themselves? Does "love" imply pacifism, or can one love someone whom one finds it necessary to kill, such as an enemy in war?

The Lord's Prayer

The Lord's prayer, otherwise known as "Our Father," is central to Christian worship and piety. The prayer exists in a shorter form in Luke and a longer one in Matthew. Most scholars accept the Lukan form as closer to the original. The prayer resembles one still said by Jews called the "Kaddish." Perrin supplies an English version of its ancient form.[11]

Magnified and sanctified be his great name in the world that he has created according to his will. May he establish his kingdom in your lifetime and in your days and in the lifetime of all the house of Israel, even speedily and at a near time.

Jesus' prayer echoes the Kaddish, and may be his adaptation of it.

Father, hallowed be your name. Your kingdom come. Give us each day our daily bread. And forgive us our sins, for we ourselves forgive everyone indebted to us. And do not bring us to the time of trial. (Luke 11:2-4)

"Hallowed" and "sanctified" mean "to make holy." Central to both prayers is the hope that God's name might be treated as holy in the world. In both prayers the coming of God's kingdom is the object of prayer. Jesus asks for daily sustenance, a petition that would have been meaningful to peasants struggling to survive. The next petition is for forgiveness, but it makes forgiveness contingent on how one treats other people. The same point is made in the parable of the Unforgiving Servant in Matthew 18:23-35. In particular, forgiveness is dependent upon one forgiving *debts,* an economic term that, if taken literally, would mean that Jesus was in favor of releasing people from debts.[12] The final petition speaks of "trial," a term found in eschatological contexts to denote the troubles of the endtime and the potential for apostasy that they represent. The Lord's prayer is deeply rooted in a Jewish milieu. It is concerned with daily existence and with the way people treat one another economically, but it also carries an eschatological outlook.

The Beatitudes

The word "beatitude" comes from the Latin *beatus* meaning "blessed" or "happy." The beatitude is a form common to the wisdom tradition. The gospel beatitudes exist in two versions, Matthew 5:3-12 and Luke 6:20-23. Luke follows the beatitudes with a series of woes. The theme of eschatological reversal is embodied in the beatitudes, so by the principle of coherence they might be included in a portrait of the historical Jesus. Matthew's version of the beatitudes softens the eschatological harshness of Luke's version, so Luke's beatitudes may be closer to the original form:

Blessed are you who are poor, for yours is the kingdom of God.
Blessed are you who are hungry now, for you will be filled.
Blessed are you who weep now, for you will laugh.
Blessed are you when people hate you, and when they exclude you, revile you, and

329

defame you on account of the Son of Man. Rejoice in that day and leap for joy, for surely your reward is great in heaven; for that is what their ancestors did to the prophets. (6:20-23)

Luke then adds woes that continue the theme of reversal, this time addressing the well-to-do of society. They begin, "Woe to you who are rich, for you have received your consolation" (6:24). The eschatological reversal demanded by God's justice is quite concrete, and has to do with wealth, food and drink, and human relations.

JESUS AND THE TORAH

The vast majority of Jews shared a respect for the centrality of Torah in Jewish life.[13] But different groups disagreed on how to interpret Torah. New Testament materials encompass a wide range of attitudes toward the Law. Paul thought that belief in Christ excluded Torah as a way of salvation and a religious system. Speaking to Peter he says,

> We ourselves are Jews by birth and not Gentile sinners; yet we know that a person is justified not by the works of the law but through faith in Jesus Christ. And we have come to believe in Christ Jesus, so that we might be justified by faith in Christ, and not by doing the works of the law, because no one will be justified by the works of the law. (Gal 2:15-16)

Paul never attributes his own attitude to Torah to Jesus, but he is convinced that such an attitude is implied by belief in Christ.

On the other side, among Paul's opponents is a group of Jewish Christians in Jerusalem called the "Circumcision Party" because of their insistence on circumcision and on obedience to Torah (Galatians 2). Paul's letter to the Galatians is occasioned by the arrival of Christian missionaries in Galatia who claim that obedience to at least some of the Torah's provisions is necessary for salvation. Some traditions in Matthew attribute the command to obey Torah to Jesus. Jesus says,

> Do not think that I have come to abolish the law or the prophets; I have come not to abolish but to fulfill. For truly I tell you, until heaven and earth pass away, not one letter, not one stroke of a letter, will pass from the law until all is accomplished. Therefore, whoever breaks one of the least of these commandments, and teaches others to do the same, will be called least in the kingdom of heaven; but whoever does them and teaches them will be called great in the kingdom of heaven. For I tell you, unless your righteousness exceeds that of the scribes and Pharisees, you will never enter the kingdom of heaven. (Matt 5:17-20)

330

Matthew 23 begins by having Jesus tell his disciples to obey the scribes and Pharisees because they have the authority of Moses and so can interpret Torah. Matthew 23:23 has Jesus say that the Pharisees' rules about tithing spices, often seen as examples of Pharisaic legalism, are quite proper and should be obeyed, as long as the more important aspects of the Law are not neglected.

It is clear that there were early Christians who thought that obedience to Torah was necessary, and others who thought the opposite. That is to say, there were Christians who thought that Christianity was not a religion different from Judaism, and others who thought that it was. The early church's diametrically opposed positions on this key issue would be hard to explain if Jesus had already decided it. Since the gospels portray Jesus as concerned about Israel and Torah, it is hardly likely that he saw himself as abrogating the Torah. If Jesus thought that he was nullifying Torah, he certainly would have seen fit to mention it.

Further examination of specific occasions on which Jesus is said to have violated or abrogated Torah will be useful here. Sabbath observance and food laws were live issues in the early church. Much of the first half of Acts, for example, deals with whether or not one can eat food declared unclean by Torah. These issues of Torah observance occupy Paul, too (Galatians, Romans, 1 Corinthians). Such concerns would be strange indeed if these issues had already been resolved by Jesus.

Sabbath Observance

Mark tells the following story.

> One sabbath he was going through the grainfields; and as they made their way his disciples began to pluck heads of grain. The Pharisees said to him, "Look, why are they doing what is not lawful on the sabbath?" And he said to them, "Have you never read what David did when he and his companions were hungry and in need of food? He entered the house of God, when Abiathar was high priest, and ate the bread of the Presence, which it is not lawful for any but the priests to eat, and he gave some to his companions. Then he said to them, "The sabbath was made for humankind, and not humankind for the sabbath; so the Son of Man is lord even of the sabbath." (Mark 2:23-28)

It appears likely that Jerusalem was the Pharisees' center, and that there were few if any in Galilee. Whether that is so or not, it is improbable that Pharisees passed their sabbaths in Galilean grainfields waiting to catch violators of sabbath regulations. The form of this story is that of a "pronouncement story," a story in which the narrative serves only to frame a saying of Jesus. Therefore the narrative surrounding Jesus' sayings has no independent historical value. It is

331

interesting that in this story it is not Jesus who is accused of breaking the sabbath, but his disciples. This implies that whoever made up the narrative framework thought that sabbath work was an issue for the early church, not for Jesus.

Jesus' sayings at the end of the narrative respond to the challenge that his disciples are violating Torah. The sayings supply several different solutions to the problem of the disciples' action. In the first, Jesus defends his disciples on the basis of Scripture. His point is that there is no violation of sabbath, because there is legal precedent in Scripture for breaking regulations because of human need (hunger). The next sayings are introduced with a new narrative beginning, "And he said to them." It is typical of Mark to insert this phrase when introducing new material to a story. That means that the sayings which follow were not originally part of the story but were brought to their present position by Mark. The saying about the sabbath being made for humans has potentially radical consequences for religious institutions, but it would not necessarily imply an abrogation of Torah. In rabbinic literature love of God and neighbor was seen as the essence of Torah, and there are instances of humanitarian concerns overriding sabbath regulations. The final saying, "The Son of Man is lord even of the sabbath," implies that Jesus has the authority to override sabbath rules, but it does not state that any violation of Torah has occurred. In any case, the saying is considered by most scholars to be a faith statement characteristic of early Christianity.

Matthew is even more concerned than Mark to prove that Jesus did not violate Torah in the incident of the disciples' picking grain in the fields. The gospel tries to construct a legal case that is unassailable. It adds to the story the explicit statement that the disciples "were hungry" and makes clear that they *ate* the grain (12:1). Thus Matthew makes a better legal case, since the motivation for the disciples' action is unambiguous. Matthew adds further legal arguments as well. It says that priests work on the sabbath, because they serve the Temple. Jesus is greater than the Temple, so his servants are allowed to work (12:5-6). Then Matthew quotes from the prophet Hosea to prove that mercy is more important to God than sacrifice (12:7). Matthew strengthens the case by the omission of Mark's statement, "The sabbath was made for humankind, not humankind for the sabbath." Perhaps the saying sounded too radical to the evangelist, who seems to have been a Jew who took a more conservative view of Jesus' relation to Torah than did Mark.

Mark relates another story about Jesus' sabbath activity in 3:1-6. The story gives the impression that he was breaking a law by healing a man's hand, but in fact Jesus does no work in the healing, and so no violation takes place. Speaking healing words is forbidden nowhere in Torah. Jesus' position, that it is legal to save a life on the sabbath, is attributed in rabbinic literature to one of the

Pharisaic schools (though Jesus heals only the man's hand here). In general, there is no substantial evidence that Jesus broke the sabbath.

Food Laws

Food laws, laws about what foods can be eaten and under what circumstances, are an important part of Torah. Mark introduces the issue of food laws into a controversy narrated in Mark 7. It begins,

> Now when the Pharisees and some of the scribes who had come from Jerusalem gathered around him, they noticed that some of his disciples were eating with defiled hands, that is, without washing them. (For the Pharisees, and all the Jews, do not eat unless they thoroughly wash their hands, thus observing the tradition of the elders; and they do not eat anything from the market unless they wash it; and there are also many other traditions that they observe, the washing of cups, pots, and bronze kettles.) So the Pharisees and the scribes asked him, "Why do your disciples not live according to the tradition of the elders, but eat with defiled hands?" (Mark 7:1-5)

The opponents are scribes and Pharisees. Significantly, they are seen as coming from Jerusalem into Galilee. Mark explains Jewish customs to its audience, so it is likely that they were Gentiles. The assertion that all Jews follow the strict purity rules of the Pharisees is dubious. The question posed by the Pharisees and scribes focuses on washing of hands, yet washing of hands is not covered by Torah, but is, rather, a Pharisaic rule. Jesus responds to the accusers by quoting Scripture (Isa 29:13), and asserting that his opponents are worried about human rules and do not pay attention to God's will. He proves it by quoting a section of Torah, arguing that their traditions nullify Torah. He then adds another example of human tradition interfering with God's Law, the case of gifts to God (corban) leading to neglect of parents.

Jesus continues his teaching with the claim that nothing going into a person can defile him or her. Only what comes out of a person (evil thoughts, wickedness, etc.) can defile. Mark concludes, "Thus he declared all foods clean" (7:19). Verse nineteen is not presented as words of Jesus, but is editorial, so Mark is applying Jesus' words to the kosher laws. Matthew, on the other hand, keeps the focus on unwashed hands. He omits Mark 7:19, and so does not apply Jesus' statements to kosher laws. After listing the inner things that defile, Matthew summarizes, "These are what defile a person, but to eat with unwashed hands does not defile" (Matt 15:20). Matthew does not agree that Jesus abrogated Jewish food laws. Again there is strong disagreement in the Christian sources, making it implausible that Jesus abrogated the food laws. That he may have done so is hard to explain in view of the dispute within the early church over whether Christians should observe them.

Divorce

Paul and the gospels both state that Jesus forbade divorce (Matt 5:31-32; 19:3-9; Mark 10:2-12; Luke 16:18; 1 Cor 7:10-11). By the principle of multiple attestation, one can conclude that Jesus probably did so. It is more difficult to decide whether or not he made an exception in the case of unchastity, as in Matthew 5:32 and 19:9. "Unchastity" would mean sexual misconduct on the part of one's spouse. Jesus' prohibition of divorce is based on a scriptural argument, according to Mark 10. When some Pharisees ask him why Moses permitted divorce, he says,

> Because of your hardness of heart he wrote this commandment for you. But from the beginning of creation, "God made them male and female" [Gen 1:27; 5:2]. "For this reason a man shall leave his father and mother and be joined to his wife, and the two shall become one flesh" [Gen 2:24]. So they are no longer two, but one flesh. Therefore what God has joined together, let no one separate. (Mark 10:5-9)

Jesus does not merely pronounce on divorce based on his own authority, but he uses Torah to prove his position. Matthew follows Mark in having Jesus base himself on Scripture in 19:3-9, but Matthew's Sermon on the Mount (Matthew 5–7) stresses the absolute authority of Jesus himself, and does not include the argument from Scripture (5:31-32). Luke does not contain the scriptural argument (16:18). Since the authority of Jesus increases as Christian tradition progresses, it is more likely that Jesus used a scriptural argument and that some traditions dropped it, than that he did not use such an argument and some versions added it.

There is a parallel to Jesus' argument concerning divorce in the fourth column of the *Damascus Document*. In that passage, the followers of the "Spouter" of lies "shall be caught in fornication twice by taking a second wife while the first is alive, whereas the principle of creation is, *Male and female he created them* (Gen i, 27)." The parallel with Jesus consists in the use of Genesis 1:27 to argue for restrictions in marriage practices. Although Moses allowed divorce, Jesus did not negate Torah by his prohibition of divorce. It is not a negation of Torah to be stricter than Torah itself.

Association with Sinners

The gospels portray Jesus as associating with sinners. In particular, he is seen eating with them, an act said to shock the pious who observed it. A number of traditions indicate that Jesus saw his table-fellowship as an anticipation of the "messianic banquet," a joyful feast symbolizing destruction of evil and restoration of humanity's intended relationship with God.[14] That Jesus's disciples did not fast before his death but did so afterward might be connected with the idea that table-fellowship with him anticipated the joy of the eschatological banquet (Mark 2:18-20). When Jesus was present, fasting was inappropriate. It may have been Jesus' use of the meal as a symbol that gained him the reputation as a glutton and a drunkard (Matt 11:29). Jesus' eating with sinners probably symbolizes that they will be included in the kingdom.

There are several misconceptions to be addressed in trying to grasp what Jesus' association with sinners signified. A distinction must be drawn between sin and impurity. First-century Judaism is often stereotyped as being identical with a Pharisaism for which the essence of religion is in the observance of ritualistic rules. Jesus is then seen as combatting ritual purity rules. His opponents are seen as identifying sin with impurity in a superficial and legalistic way. But there is no evidence that the Pharisees looked upon the Jews who did not follow their purity rules (probably the vast majority) as sinners for that reason. It may be true that the Pharisees and other groups with different purity rules did not eat with each other and limited their contact with each other. However, that is not the same as considering the other Jews sinners. Even in Torah's purity rules, impurity does not necessarily result from sin, and impurity is not equated with sin. Touching a dead body, for example, was not sinful, but doing so would make one ritually impure, unable to participate in the cult. Jesus' association with sinners is not merely an association with those considered impure by the scribes and Pharisees, because that would not be association with sinners.

Another fallacy is that Jesus was willing to forgive, whereas mainstream Judaism had no place for forgiveness. God's forgiveness is an important theme in Judaism. Of course Second Temple Judaism, like Christianity after it, had specified ways of obtaining God's forgiveness. There were reparations to be made and rituals to undergo. In that, Judaism is no different from many other religions, Christianity included. What may have offended many of Jesus' contemporaries was his preaching the possibility of God's forgiveness outside of normal channels. Jesus was willing to offer forgiveness directly even to those recognized by society as sinners, on his own authority as God's agent, without insisting on the usual restitution and rituals.

The following words attributed to Jesus make it clearer who some of the "sinners" were and contrast them with "religious" people who consider themselves already in a proper relationship with God: "Truly I tell you, the tax collectors and the prostitutes are going into the kingdom of God ahead of you. For John came to you in the way of righteousness and you did not believe him, but the tax collectors and the prostitutes believed him" (Matt 21:31-32). The "tax collectors" were probably those who collected tolls at border crossings. They were not popular characters. An argument for the authenticity of this saying can be made from the principle of dissimilarity. The viewpoint of the saying conflicts with first-century Judaism, and the early church probably did not invent the shocking saying about harlots entering the kingdom.

The question arises whether or not Jesus attacked Torah in bypassing cultic institutions, for Torah required those institutions. The question should not be answered in isolation from Second Temple Judaism in general. Central though the cultic establishment was, it was not above criticism. For example, though the people of Qumran withdrew from Jerusalem altogether and devised an alternative mode for atonement, the Qumran community did not think of itself as violating Torah. Jesus' attitudes should be read in light of this. Criticizing the Temple establishment was not uncommon. There are even Jewish texts envisioning the replacement of the Second Temple by a more glorious Temple (*1 Enoch* 90:28-29; Tob 14:4-7). Jesus' attack on the Temple fits this context. He was not against the Temple *per se,* any more than were the prophets who protested cultic activity in the midst of social injustice. Rather, like the Qumran community, Jesus looked forward to a restoration of Israel that would overcome injustice and evil.

Some have suggested that Jesus' saying about leaving the dead to bury the dead (Matt 8:22) is the clearest example of his opposing Torah. True, Jesus' words seem to violate the sacred obligation to care for one's parents. But Jesus speaks the words under the circumstances of the urgency of the duty to follow him. Jewish tradition attests to the notion that one religious obligation can override another. For example, in 1 Maccabees 2:39-41 Mattathias and his allies suspend sabbath obligations so as to defend Torah against Antiochus IV.

THE TITLES OF JESUS

Gospel traditions confer several titles on Jesus—Christ (Messiah), Son of God, Son of Man, Son of David, Prophet, Rabbi, Teacher, King of Israel, and others. Much of past scholarship believed that the titles held the key to Jesus' self-identity. Years of research have shown that assumption to be misleading. All of the titles applied to Jesus are ambiguous. Some of the titles can be shown to have a wide range of meaning in Second Temple Judaism, and others are not well enough attested to be able to supply any definitive meaning.

Another problem with Jesus' titles is that none can be confidently traced back to him. There are no sayings in the synoptic gospels in which Jesus states, "I am the Messiah," or "I am the Son of God." The Gospel of John is replete with such sayings, but is suspect for precisely that reason. In the synoptics Jesus says little about himself, and spends most of his time talking about the kingdom of God, or acting to bring it about. In John, Jesus spends most of his time talking about himself, and the kingdom of God as such is almost entirely absent (except for 3:3, 5). The synoptic Jesus who proclaimed God's kingdom becomes the one proclaimed in John. That is a development within early Christianity, and says little about the historical Jesus.

Christ (Messiah)

This term was fluid in Israelite and Jewish society up to the time of the destruction of the Second Temple. "Christ" comes from the Greek *christos,* and "messiah" from the Hebrew *māšîaḥ,* both meaning "anointed." To anoint meant to pour or smear oil on someone, and was a sign of being chosen by God for a specific task. The Hebrew Bible contains examples of kings, priests, prophets, and even a foreign emperor (Cyrus) being anointed. Postbiblical Jewish literature presents an equally varied set of possibilities for defining "messiah." Qumran expected two messiahs, one priestly and one royal, in addition to an eschatological prophet. The scrolls also suggest that key interpreters of Torah were messiahs. The *Similitudes of Enoch* portray a heavenly figure who will come at the endtime to judge the powerful and the wealthy. He is called "Messiah," "Elect One," "Son of Man." The *Testament of Levi* 18 expects a priestly messiah with royal and priestly functions. The *Testament of Judah* expects two messiahs, one priestly and one royal.

It is completely misleading to speak of *the* messianic expectation of first-century Jews. A variety of expectations concerning God's impending action are attested, and there were some Jews (the Sadducees, for example) who did not expect divine intervention. There were also those who expected God to intervene in history soon, but directly, not through an intermediary. Hope for mediators of God's action, who are sometimes but not always called messiahs, assumes a multitude of forms, few of them supernatural. There is simply no consistent pattern of expectation to be found. Christians sometimes wonder how the Jews missed the fact that the messiah had arrived in the person of Jesus when Jesus so clearly fulfilled their messianic expectations, as demonstrated by the fulfillment of specific prophecies. Such Christians confidently state that first-century Jews were waiting for *the* messiah. But the portrait of the messiah Christians have in mind simply *did not exist* before Christians composed it on the basis of their experience of the risen Jesus. The full picture of messiahship as found in Christianity does not conform to any Jewish expectation. In fact, the Christian messiah contradicted some Jewish expectations, such as the restoration of the Davidic monarchy in Jerusalem, or the rebuilding of the Temple and the return of the Diaspora. The variety of messianic expectations to be found among Jews reflects the variety of ways of being Jewish in the Second Temple period. A recent study of the subject is aptly named *Judaisms and Their Messiahs* (*see* bibliography).

The accusation placed by the Romans on Jesus' cross has a strong claim to authenticity. Jesus was crucified for claiming to be "King of the Jews." Those words say less about what Jesus thought about himself than they do about how he was perceived by others. If the Romans saw Jesus as a Jewish leader who was a political threat, then their charge was accurate for their purposes. Whether or not

Jesus ever used the word "messiah" of himself, others may have done so during his lifetime. Certainly Jesus' contemporaries and even his followers could have held beliefs about him that did not necessarily conform to his own. The Gospel of Mark explicitly deals with the discrepancy between what Jesus thought and what his disciples thought about messiahship. Some even expected overt political action by Jesus based on his eschatological preaching.

Prophet

In the synoptics, the closest Jesus comes to speaking of himself as the messiah is in the Gospel of Luke.

> When he came to Nazareth, where he had been brought up, he went to the synagogue on the sabbath day, as was his custom. He stood up to read, and the scroll of the prophet Isaiah was given to him. He unrolled the scroll and found the place where it was written: "The spirit of the Lord is upon me, because he has anointed me to bring good news to the poor. He has sent me to proclaim release to the captives and recovery of sight to the blind, to let the oppressed go free, to proclaim the year of the Lord's favor" [Isa 61:1-2]. And he rolled up the scroll, gave it back to the attendant, and sat down. The eyes of all in the synagogue were fixed on him. Then he began to say to them, "Today this scripture has been fulfilled in your hearing." (Luke 4:16-21)

There are other passages in which Jesus refers to himself as a prophet.[15] He certainly acted like a prophet in his willingness to speak for God and to criticize Israel and its institutions. Many of the things he said resemble prophetic teaching. Not many scholars claim authenticity for the full scene from Luke 4, but the quotation from Isaiah fits the kinds of things Jesus did. The scene demonstrates the plausibility of assigning the title "messiah" to Jesus on the basis of his prophetic activity. In this case, whether or not that assignation was made by Jesus himself or by followers after his death is secondary. The title would only be a confirmation of the claim that Jesus himself made that he was a prophet. The eschatological dimension of Jesus' message suggests that he considered himself an eschatological prophet, a prophet whose message ushers in God's final intervention in history. If Jesus was called messiah on the basis of his prophetic activity, that might explain later developments, including the Roman charge against him. Once the title of "messiah" was applied to him, the door may have opened for other interpretations of the title to be ascribed to him.

Son of David

Jesus is never depicted as using this title. Matthew makes most frequent use of it, probably because of its peculiarly Jewish interests. Matthew associates Jesus'

338

healing activity with his being Son of David, an association that may arise from Jewish tradition, which saw Solomon as wise in the sense that he knew how to control demons and heal. In Mark the title is used in chapters 10 and 12. In Mark 10 the blind beggar Bartimaeus whom Jesus cures shouts it, and so here again it is associated with healing. Mark 12 is puzzling because it can be read as challenging the very idea that the messiah will be of the Davidic line.

> While Jesus was teaching in the temple, he said, "How can the scribes say that the Messiah is the son of David? David himself, by the Holy Spirit, declared, 'The Lord said to my Lord, "Sit at my right hand, until I put your enemies under your feet."' David himself calls him Lord; so how can he be his son?" (Mark 12:35-37)

It is unclear whether this passage denies that the messiah is son of David, or simply says that despite being his son, the messiah is greater than David. In any case, Jesus probably did not claim the title.

Son of God

Christians usually assume that this title refers to the divinity of Jesus. In a Greek context, it could well indicate divinity. But Gentiles had a more fluid idea of divinity than Jews. There were humans, gods, and beings in-between. There were figures who had divine fathers and human mothers (Dionysus and Hercules, for example). Humans could become divine, as in the case of Roman emperors voted into the Roman pantheon at their deaths by the senate. There was no firm line between humanity and divinity in the Hellenistic world. But Jews were strict monotheists. God was one, and no human being could claim divinity. Jews looked with disdain upon pretensions to divinity among Hellenistic and Roman rulers. As the title "Son of God" moved from a Jewish to a Greek setting when Christianity spread beyond its Jewish origins, it took on overtones of divinity. However, it is not likely that a Jew would have understood it that way.

The "son" saying with the strongest claim to authenticity may be Mark 13:32. Speaking of the coming of the eschaton Jesus says, "But about that day or hour no one knows, neither the angels in heaven, nor the Son, but only the Father." Its claim to authenticity lies in the argument that the early church would not have made up a saying admitting ignorance on the part of Jesus.

Much has been made of the fact that in Mark 14:36 Jesus calls God 'Abbā', an Aramaic word that is an intimate form of the word "father." Christian usage of that term is attested in Galatians 4:6 and Romans 8:15. It has been suggested that the Jews never used such an intimate form of address for God, and that the Christians soon dropped it. That argues for its authenticity. But Mark 14:36 supplies the only occurrence of the term in the gospels, and Jesus is alone when he says it. Therefore the claim to authenticity of Mark 14:36 is weak. Nonetheless, there is evidence that Jesus spoke of God as father, whether or not he used the word 'Abbā'. The evidence spans various sources and literary forms. "Father" does seem to be a way that Jesus addressed God, but it is not clear that his use of it was different from first-century Jewish usage.

It is unlikely that in a Jewish context "Son of God" could mean divinity. In 2 Samuel 7:14, God tells David that Solomon will be God's son. The title may have remained an epithet for Jewish kings. The setting of Psalm 2 seems to be the enthronement of the king-messiah where God adopts the king as son on his coronation day: "You are my son, today I have begotten you" (2:7). When Matthew applies the verse, "Out of Egypt I [God] have called my son," to Jesus in 2:15, it quotes a prophecy of Hosea (11:1), originally applied to the people of Israel as a whole. In Isaiah 1:2, the Israelites are called God's sons. In Wisdom 2:13 the righteous one calls himself a child of God, and incurs the enmity of his fellows who then plot his death. All of this evidence points to a use of the term "Son of God" in Judaism that is devoid of later Christian connotations of divinity. The apostle Paul conforms to Jewish usage when he uses the term to refer to anyone in a proper relationship with God (e.g., Gal 4:1-7; Rom 8:14-17, 29). If Jesus thought of himself as Son of God at all, it was most likely in one of the Jewish senses.

The connection between "Son of God" and "messiah," already suggested in traditions such as the one behind Psalm 2, is made in Mark 14:61. There the high priest asks Jesus, "Are you the Messiah, the Son of the Blessed One [God]?" Matthew's version of the confession of Peter reads, "You are the Messiah, the Son of the living God" (16:16). The connection of the two titles suggests that in this case, New Testament usage remains within Jewish limits.

Son of Man

Whereas most other titles discussed here are not found on the lips of Jesus, "Son of Man" is often found there. Jesus' sayings about the Son of Man are usually put into three categories. The apocalyptic Son of Man sayings refer to one who is to come at the end of time to rescue the righteous and judge the wicked. He judges people according to how they have related to Jesus. The earthly Son of Man sayings deal with the authority of the earthly Jesus to forgive sins and to rule on sabbath observance. The suffering Son of Man sayings speak of the suffering Jesus must endure.

Scholars debate the issues raised by this title at great length. Recent interpretation questions whether Jesus ever used the term as a title for himself or anyone else, arguing that he may have used it only in a generic sense of "human being," as it is used in Ezekiel (e.g., 2:1, 3, 6, 8), or more specifically as a circumlocution for "I." The early church could then have picked up on the term and interpreted it in terms of the figure of the Son of Man in Daniel 7. However, the use of "son of man" to mean "I" is not attested in the Aramaic of Jesus' day, nor would this explain why the church adopted it as an important title of Jesus.

The church probably did not initiate the use of the title Son of Man. Since it was not widespread in Judaism of Jesus' day, it is hard to explain why the early church would have adopted it as a title for Jesus. Further, in the gospels the term is found only on the lips of Jesus. No one else uses it. Nor was it a popular title for Jesus beyond New Testament times. It does not occur in the church's creeds, liturgical formulas, or summaries of teaching. However, the title is well entrenched in the tradition. It enjoys the attestation of multiple sources and literary forms. Therefore, Jesus himself probably initiated use of the term.

If Jesus did originate the use of the term "Son of Man," his reference is most likely to the apocalyptic Son of Man. Both the suffering and the earthly Son of Man sayings evolved under the influence of early Christian reflection on Jesus in the light of his death and resurrection. If Jesus was an eschatological preacher, he expected an eschaton and a judgment. He may have settled on his vision of the Son of Man through reflection on Daniel 7. Some have claimed, on the basis of his use of the third person in speaking of the Son of Man, that he expected an eschatological figure other than himself to vindicate his ministry. But others find it hard to believe that Jesus would deprive himself of a role in the judgment he predicted, and so see Jesus as referring to himself in his prediction of the Son of Man.

CONCLUSION

This chapter has sketched a plausible picture of the historical Jesus. It is certainly incomplete, both for lack of space, and because many of the issues raised here are insoluble given the present state of knowledge. However, the underlying assumption that Jesus was a Jew living in Palestine at the end of the Second Temple period is crucial. The point is not that anyone really denies that Jesus was a Jew, but that the fact of his Jewishness is sometimes rendered almost irrelevant because of an interest in *contrasting* him with his fellow Jews, to the denigration of Judaism and Jewish society. Any reconstruction that does not see Jesus within first-century Jewish society is unacceptable. Any treatment that uses the Jewish setting simply to prove that Judaism is inferior to Christianity, or to put all Jews of Jesus' time into a negative category, perpetuates Christian mistreatment of Jews. Further, any theology that does not see Jesus' humanity in relation to his Jewishness runs the risk of depriving that humanity of any but the most abstract qualities.

Seeing Jesus as a real Jew of his period is critical to undermining the theoretical basis for the anti-Judaism that has been so significant in Christian traditions, and which is still strong today. Setting Jesus off against the Jews almost as if he were not Jewish, and portraying Jesus as representing the true Israel while everyone else misses the point is a course of action well attested in the New Testament itself. This tendency facilitates false and dangerous stereotyping of Jews and their religion. The reader should now be sensitive to the countless indications that Jesus, his followers, and his opponents were Jews, living in first-century Jewish Palestine. To speak of "the Jews" as a monolithic block, and as condemned as a group by opposition to Jesus, is to ignore that fact.

This chapter fits Jesus into his own milieu, first-century Jewish society. But a sense of closure is missing. There is too much that is unknown about the Judaism of Jesus' day, about Jesus himself, and about the early church. Yet the lack of full information should not dissuade us from raising and attempting to answer questions. Such an inquiry can help us to be critical of our own presuppositions and reconstructions and open to alternative explanations. Even more, it can bring us closer to the historical foundations of the Christian religion, at the same time correcting destructive misapprehensions about Judaism.

SELECT BIBLIOGRAPHY

Borg, Marcus J. *Conflict, Holiness, and Politics in the Teachings of Jesus.* Lewiston, N.Y.: Edwin Mellen, 1984.

Bornkamm, Günther. *Jesus of Nazareth.* London: Hodder and Stoughton, 1960.

Bultmann, Rudolf. *The History of the Synoptic Tradition.* New York: Harper and Row, 1963.

Charlesworth, James H. *Jesus Within Judaism: New Light from Exciting Archaeological Discoveries.* New York: Doubleday & Co., 1988.

Collins, Adela Yarbrough. "The Origin of the Designation of Jesus as 'Son of Man,'" *HTR* 80 (1987): 391-407.

Cook, Michael J. *Mark's Treatment of the Jewish Leaders.* Leiden: Brill, 1978.

Crossan, John Dominic. *In Parables: The Challenge of the Historical Jesus.* New York: Harper and Row, 1973.

Dunn, J. D. G. *The Evidence for Jesus.* Philadelphia: Westminster Press, 1985.

Freyne, Sean. *Galilee From Alexander the Great to Hadrian: 325 B.C.E. to 135 C.E.* Wilmington, Del.: Michael Glazier, 1980.

―――. *Galilee, Jesus and the Gospels: Literary Approaches and Historical Investigations.* Philadelphia: Fortress Press, 1988.

Fuller, Reginald H. *A Critical Introduction to the New Testament.* London: Duckworth, 1966.

―――. *The Foundations of New Testament Christology.* New York: Scribner's, 1965.

Gowan, Donald E. "The Messiah," in *BBT,* 387-95.

Harrington, Daniel J. "The Jewishness of Jesus: Facing Some Problems," *CBQ* 49 (1987): 1-13.

Harvey, A. E. *Jesus and the Constraints of History*. Philadelphia: Westminster Press, 1982.

Hollenbach, Paul W. "The Conversion of Jesus: From Jesus the Baptizer to Jesus the Healer," *ANRW* 2, 25.1, 196-219.

_____. "Liberating Jesus for Social Involvement," *BTB* 15 (1985): 151-57.

Horsley, Richard A. *Jesus and the Spiral of Violence: Popular Jewish Resistance in Roman Palestine*. San Francisco: Harper and Row, 1987.

Jeremias, Joachim. *New Testament Theology: The Proclamation of Jesus*. New York: Scribner's, 1971.

_____. *The Parables of Jesus*, rev. ed. New York: Scribner's, 1963.

Lindars, Barnabas. *Jesus Son of Man: A Fresh Examination of the Son of Man Sayings in the Gospels*. Grand Rapids: Wm. B. Eerdmans Publishing Co., 1983.

Meier, John P. "Jesus," in *NJBC*, 1316-28.

Neusner, Jacob, William S. Green, Ernest Frerichs, eds. *Judaisms and Their Messiahs at the Turn of the Christian Era*. Cambridge: Cambridge University Press, 1987.

Oakman, Douglas E. *Jesus and the Economic Questions of His Day*. Lewiston, N.Y.: Edwin Mellen, 1986.

Perrin, Norman. *Jesus and the Language of the Kingdom: Symbol and Metaphor in New Testament Interpretation*. Philadelphia: Fortress Press, 1976.

_____. *Rediscovering the Teaching of Jesus*. San Francisco: Harper and Row, 1976.

_____, and Dennis Duling. "The Presupposition of the New Testament: Jesus," chap. 13 in *The New Testament: An Introduction*. New York: Harcourt Brace Jovanovich, 1982.

Reumann, John. "Jesus and Christology," in *The New Testament and Its Modern Interpreters*, ed. Eldon Jay Epp and George W. MacRae. Philadelphia: Fortress Press, 1989, 501-64.

Riches, John. *Jesus and the Transformation of Judaism*. New York: Seabury Press, 1982.

Sanders, E. P. *Jesus and Judaism*. Philadelphia: Fortress Press, 1985.

Schweitzer, Albert. *The Quest of the Historical Jesus: A Critical Study of Its Progress from Reimarus to Wrede*. New York: Macmillan, 1968.

Scott, Bernard Brandon. *Hear Then the Parable: A Commentary on the Parables of Jesus*. Philadelphia: Fortress Press, 1989.

Tannehill, Robert. "The 'Focal Instance' as a Form of New Testament Speech: A Study of Matthew 5:39*b*-42," *JR* 50 (1970): 377-82.

Tödt, Heinz Eduard. *The Son of Man in the Synoptic Tradition*. London: SCM, 1965.

Vermes, Geza. *Jesus and the World of Judaism*. Philadelphia: Fortress Press, 1984.

_____. *Jesus the Jew: A Historian's Reading of the Gospels*. Philadelphia: Fortress Press, 1973.

Westerholm, S. *Jesus and Scribal Authority*. Lund, Sweden: Gleerup, 1978.

Wilcox, M. "Jesus in the Light of His Jewish Environment," *ANRW* 2/25.1, 129-95.

CHAPTER TWELVE

The Revolt Against the Romans

Primary Readings: 4 Ezra; 2 Baruch

Chapter 10 gave an account of the first century CE in Jewish Palestine. Interactions between Jews and Romans and between Jews and Jews in the first century eventually led to the outbreak of revolution against the Romans.

CAUSES OF THE WAR

There is no absolute agreement among scholars on what caused the Jewish revolt.[1] That is partly a result of a lack of evidence. Josephus, the principal source for the period, is biased, and he leaves much unsaid. In addition, wars are complex affairs, resulting from an interplay of nations, personalities, institutions, events, economic factors, and religious elements. What follows is a brief listing of some central factors contributing to the outbreak of the Jewish-Roman war of 66–70 CE.

Roman Maladministration

Josephus details the misdeeds of the Roman procurators. Crises in Pilate's and Cumanus' administrations resulted in their being recalled, a sign that even Rome recognized their inadequacy. In the fifties and sixties the Jews suffered at the hands of corrupt and greedy Roman administrators. Anti-Semitism may have been involved, but Roman insensitivity to local populations caused revolts elsewhere in the early empire as well.

Roman Oppression

Roman rule of Palestine began with Pompey's desecration of the Temple, and was full of repression, high taxes, various forms of humiliation, enslavement and crucifixion of resisters, and even the effort of Gaius (Caligula) to force emperor worship on the Jews.

Judaism as a Religion

For centuries the Jews reconciled scriptural promises of independence and of an anointed Jewish king with the reality of colonialism. Jewish religion did not automatically produce rebellion. On the contrary, Judaism of the first century had its origins in the reconstitution of Jewish society under the Persians at the time of Ezra. But when foreign oppression grew strong, sacred traditions supplied hope. That is seen in such documents as the *Psalms of Solomon* and the *Testament of Moses,* as well as in some of the popular movements of the first century CE. The tax revolt of Judas the Galilean, for example, was based on the idea that the Jews should accept no ruler but God.

Although the Romans allowed the Jews to live by their own customs for the most part, tensions inevitably arose. Elements of foreign culture brought into Jewish Palestine aroused resentment. Such is the case with the military standards brought into Jerusalem by Pilate, Herod's golden eagle, Caligula's statue, Roman and Herodian marriage practices, confiscation of Temple funds, and other occurrences. Florus' attempt to take Temple funds was one of the precipitating causes of the war.

Class Tensions

In the *Jewish War,* Josephus lists the horrors of the war. One of his generalizations speaks of "those in power oppressing the masses, and the masses eager to destroy the powerful. These are bent on tyranny, those on violence and plundering the property of the wealthy" (*War* 7.8.1 §§ 260–61). Here class conflict is obvious. The colonial situation caught the local aristocracy between the Romans and the lower classes. Some aristocrats used that position to oppress peasants and workers, and at times the lower classes resisted.

Conflicts with Gentiles

Non-Jewish inhabitants preferred Roman to Jewish rule. Gentiles living in Greek cities in Palestine did not support the revolt against the Romans. Josephus reports violence between Jews and Gentiles, and says that the Gentiles furnished the Romans with auxiliary troops at various times in the first century. This must be balanced with the observation that Jews and Gentiles also spent a good deal of time living peacefully together. Increasing movement toward Jewish independence may have roused the Gentiles, and embittered the Jews against them.

The Ruling Class

There was factionalism and a range of attitudes toward the war among the upper classes. Herodian rule introduced new and disruptive factors into the Jewish aristocracy, and not all segments of that aristocracy benefited equally from Roman and Herodian rule. Disaffected aristocrats may have made common cause with elements of resistance in the lower classes.

THE WAR AGAINST THE ROMANS

The Beginning of the War

Chapter 10 ended with refusal by the Temple captain Eleazar and the lower priests to accept any sacrifices from foreigners.[2]

> This action laid the foundation of the war with the Romans; for the sacrifices offered on behalf of that nation and the emperor were in consequence rejected. The chief priests and the notables earnestly besought them not to abandon the customary offering for their rulers, but the priests remained obdurate.
> (*War* 2.17.2 §§ 409–10)

The rebels barricaded themselves in the Temple and did not allow the chief priests to enter. The chief priests and prominent Pharisees appealed to the people to desist from an impossible struggle with the Romans. They brought forth Torah experts who argued that it was unlawful to refuse the sacrifices of foreigners. They then sent messengers to Florus and Agrippa II asking for troops to crush the revolt. With this military aid the anti-war factions controlled the upper city, while the rebels occupied the lower city and the Temple. This was civil war, and aristocratic elements were involved on both sides of the issue.

After some days Eleazar and the rebel priests were joined by the Sicarii. With their augmented numbers they ousted the loyalists from the upper city and captured most of Jerusalem except for the Roman troops in Antonia and Herod's palace. They then proceeded to besiege the palace.

> At this period a certain Menahem, son of Judas surnamed the Galilaean—that redoubtable doctor who in old days, under Quirinius, had upbraided the Jews for recognizing the Romans as masters when they already had God—took his intimate friends off with him to Masada, where he broke into king Herod's armoury and provided arms both for his fellow-townsmen and for other brigands; then, with these men for his bodyguard, he returned like a veritable king to Jerusalem, became the leader of the revolution, and directed the seige of the palace.
> (*War* 2.17.8 §§ 433–34)

The procurator Tiberius Alexander had already crucified two sons of Judas in the mid-forties. Resistance seems to have run in Judas' family. Josephus calls Menahem a "doctor," suggesting that Menahem was a Torah teacher, and he accuses him of royal pretensions. Eleazar's followers resented Menahem: "So they laid their plans to attack him in the Temple, whither he had gone up in state to pay his devotions, arrayed in royal robes and attended by his suite of armed fanatics" (*War* 2.17.9 §§ 443–44).[3] Menahem was killed, and his surviving supporters fled to Masada. Among them were Sicarii who spent the rest of the war in Masada, leaving it only to make raids on the surrounding area (*War* 4.7.2 §§ 398–409). Shortly afterward the Romans in Herod's palace were lured out with promises of safe passage but then slaughtered.

Syria's governor advanced on Jerusalem. Deprived of a quick victory, he withdrew to Antioch, sustaining considerable casualties along the way. The rebel victory caused the anti-war factions who could to flee from Jerusalem to the Romans. A provisional government comprising the remaining aristocrats was established. It appointed generals for the Jewish forces. Josephus was given charge of Galilee, an appointment that attests to his status among Jerusalem's ruling elite. He engaged in fortifying Galilee and training its citizens for war.

Josephus in Galilee

Josephus gives two accounts of his activity in Galilee, one in *War* and the other in his autobiography, the *Life*. Both reports are filled with scathing indictments of those who opposed him. His main rival was a man named John from the city of Gischala in northern Galilee. John suspected Josephus of being pro-Roman and did not trust him (*War* 2.21.2 § 594). Much of what Josephus says lends credibility to John's suspicions. Josephus claims of himself that he was a reluctant revolutionary, and took every opportunity to leave the door open for reconciliation with the Romans. Josephus' attitude probably coincided with that of some of the Jerusalem leaders. One of the chief tasks with which he was entrusted by those leaders was the disarming of bandits in Galilee. This was probably because they could not be controlled by the ruling elite, and were perhaps too pro-revolution as well.

John was never able to oust Josephus, although he tried several times. Once John appealed to the provisional government in Jerusalem (*Life* 38 §§ 189–94). He had a friend in Jerusalem in the person of Simon son of Gamaliel, a prominent citizen and a Pharisee. Simon did not have the authority to remove Josephus, but tried to use his influence with the Sanhedrin to accomplish that. The high priest Ananus blocked the move. The incident is significant from a number of perspectives. First, John may have been a member of the ruling class since he was prominent in his town of Gischala, and had a friend of such eminence as Simon. Second, Simon was a prominent Pharisee, but that did not make him the decision-maker in this case. Ananus the high priest had the final word. Ananus' decision was a judgment between two aristocrats, Josephus and John. Third, if John was more intent on revolution than Josephus, then the high priest's decision favored moderation. The "moderate" position would mean that one prepared for the inevitable war with Rome, but hoped not so much for victory over the Romans as for a good negotiating position.

Vespasian's Advance

Nero appointed Vespasian and Vespasian's son Titus to prosecute the war. Vespasian collected a large army and in the spring of 67 CE was poised to retake Galilee. The city of Sepphoris requested a Roman garrison, which Vespasian supplied, thus regaining one of Galilee's principal cities without a battle. When the Romans advanced, Josephus' army fled. Many ended up in the fortress of Jotapata, north of Sepphoris. After a siege the fortress was taken, most of its inhabitants killed or enslaved, and Josephus captured. From then on he viewed the war from the Roman side, first as a prisoner, and later as Titus' aide. His change from prisoner to aide happened when a prediction he made to Vespasian that he would become emperor came true in 69 CE (*War* 3.8.9 §§ 399–408). Titus assumed command of the war, and Josephus became his interpreter and guide.

When Vespasian and Titus retook the rest of Galilee and environs, John of Gischala escaped to Jerusalem with his men. There he was admitted to the inner group of aristocrats running the city under Ananus the high priest. The rest of the war centered mostly on Jerusalem. As the Romans advanced in the winter of 67–68, civil strife broke out in Jerusalem between pro-war and anti-war factions. Jews from the countryside and villages were forced to withdraw before the advance of the Romans, and many ended up in Jerusalem, where they complicated the situation and added to the factionalism already present.

The Zealots

The Zealots now entered the picture. They were Jews who fled to Jerusalem before the Roman advance, and they seem to have had no existence as a group before that time. Josephus first uses the term "Zealot" of an organized party when he describes the effects of the entrance of "bandits" into Jerusalem in the winter of 67–68 (*War* 4.3.3-9 §§ 135–61). Josephus says that bandits who had been active in Judea joined forces and entered Jerusalem as a group. Those bandits were the Zealots. A lack of strong leadership in Jerusalem made resistance to their entrance impossible. Josephus describes what happened when they entered the city.

> The brigands, however, were not satisfied with having put their captives in irons, and considered it unsafe thus to keep for long in custody influential persons, with numerous families quite capable of avenging them; they feared, moreover, that the people might be moved by their outrageous action to rise against them. They accordingly decided to kill their victims. . . . For such a monstrous crime they invented as monstrous an excuse, declaring that their victims had conferred with the Romans concerning the surrender of Jerusalem and had been slain as traitors to the liberty of the state. In short, they boasted of their audacious acts as though they had been the benefactors and saviours of the city. (*War* 4.3.5 §§ 143–46)

Josephus reports the Zealots' rationale for their behavior, a rationale that is plausible. They suspected the rulers of wanting to reach an accommodation with the Romans. The Zealots may have been right about the "moderate" ruling class. They thought it advisable to do away with the "traitors" rather than take the chance that they would be rescued by their supporters or influence the people.

The Zealots then took action with respect to the priesthood.

> They actually took upon themselves the election to the high priesthood. Abrogating the claims of those families from which in turn the high priests had always been drawn, they appointed to that office ignoble and low born individuals, in order to gain accomplices in their impious crimes; for persons who had undeservedly attained to the highest dignity were bound to obey those who had conferred it. Moreover, by various devices and libellous statements, they brought the official authorities into collision with each other, finding their own opportunity in the bickerings of those who should have kept them in check; until, glutted with the wrongs which they had done to men, they transferred their insolence to the Deity and with polluted feet invaded the sanctuary.
>
> An insurrection of the populace was at length pending, instigated by Ananus, the senior of the chief priests, a man of profound sanity, who might possibly have saved the city, had he escaped the conspirators' hands. At this threat these wretches converted the temple of God into their fortress and refuge from any outbreak of popular violence, and made the Holy Place the headquarters of their tyranny. To these horrors was added a spice of mockery more galling than their actions. For, to test the abject submission of the populace and make trial of their own strength, they essayed to appoint the high priests by lot, although, as we have stated, the succession was hereditary. As pretext for this scheme they adduced ancient custom, asserting that in old days the high priesthood had been determined by lot; but in reality their action was the abrogation of established practice and a trick to make themselves supreme by getting these appointments into their own hands.
>
> They accordingly summoned one of the high priestly clans, called Eniachin, and cast lots for a high priest. By chance the lot fell to one who proved a signal illustration of their depravity; he was an individual named Phanni, son of Samuel, of the village of Aphthia, a man who not only was not descended from high priests, but was such a clown that he scarcely knew what the high priesthood meant. At any rate they dragged their reluctant victim out of the country and, dressing him up for his assumed part, as on the stage, put the sacred vestments upon him and instructed him how to act in keeping with the occasion. To them this monstrous impiety was a subject for jesting and sport, but the other priests, beholding from a distance this mockery of their law, could not restrain their tears and bemoaned the degradation of the sacred honours. (*War* 4.3.6-8 §§ 147–57)

Josephus scoffs at the Zealots' decision to use lots to choose a high priest, but the use of lots to determine God's will is well attested in Jewish tradition. Had the Zealots wanted simply to appoint someone whom they could control, they

350

probably could have found a better candidate. They used lots because that would ensure that the priest was chosen by God. The Zealots were careful to put forth candidates from one of the recognized high priestly clans, although not from the approved aristocratic families. The Zealots made the Temple their headquarters. It was both a fortress and the center of religious and political authority. It is natural that their new high priest should rule from there. Josephus was shocked that the Zealots appointed a new high priest from a family not of the Jerusalem elite. But the families that controlled the high priesthood in the first century CE were interlopers, comparatively speaking, for Herod had brought in priestly families from the Diaspora to replace the Hasmoneans. The Hasmoneans themselves were not originally of high priestly stock, for that matter. The Zealots' actions can be read as a genuine attempt to restore the priesthood by replacing unworthy priests with priests of God's own choosing.

Protest against the Zealots was led by the high priest Ananus, as might be expected, but they managed to eliminate him. Other members of the priestly elite bemoaned the new order, although Josephus claims that their internal disagreements and power struggles helped to make it possible. The leading citizens and chief priests "vehemently upbraided the people for their apathy and incited them against the Zealots; for so these miscreants called themselves, as though they were zealous in the cause of virtue and not for vice in its basest and most extravagant form" (War 4.3.9 §§ 160–61). "Zealots" was a name adopted by the group itself. In Jewish texts "zeal" usually means devotion to Torah. The name embodied the group's ideology. They came to Jerusalem from the countryside, so there may have been an element of country versus city piety and politics in their conflicts with the ruling priests. Perhaps because of that same tension, the chief priests were able to arouse the city residents against them, and they were trapped in the Temple. A contingent of Zealots occupied part of the Temple until the war's end. Josephus expresses priestly indignation that each time the Zealots came out to fight and were wounded, they went back to the inner sanctuary and defiled it with their blood. He also claims that Ananus would not attack the inner sanctuary because his men were not properly purified to enter it, although he admits that the Zealots' weapons may have had something to do with Ananus' decision.

John of Gischala, the Zealots, and the Idumeans

At this point John of Gischala entered the story again. He pretended to work for the priests, but Josephus says that he was in fact on the Zealots' side (War 4.3.13 § 209). The priests chose him as their liaison with the Zealots, but John used this position to keep the Zealots informed of the priests' plans. John told the Zealots that Ananus was about to hand Jerusalem over to the Romans, and he advised them to seek help from the Idumeans.

The Idumeans marched to Jerusalem, but the gates were closed by Ananus and the city populace. The Zealots let the Idumeans into the city, and the Idumeans killed many in it.

> Thinking their energies wasted on the common people, they went in search of the chief priests; it was for them that the main rush was made, and they were soon captured and slain. . . . I should not be wrong in saying that the capture of the city began with the death of Ananus; and that the overthrow of the walls and downfall of the Jewish state dated from the day on which the Jews beheld their high priest, the captain of their salvation, butchered in the heart of Jerusalem.
>
> (*War* 4.5.2 §§ 315–16, 318)

For Josephus, the real end of Jerusalem comes when the leader of the priestly aristocracy is killed. He suggests that God allowed the Temple to be burned to cleanse it from the Zealots' pollutions.

The Zealots and Idumeans began a bloody campaign against the ruling class of Jerusalem. Josephus says that eventually even many of the Idumeans were alienated by the excesses of the Zealots, but since he is so negative about the Zealots, this judgment is questionable. Most of the Idumeans left the city, but not before liberating many of the prisoners taken by the Zealots. At this point John of Gischala made a bid for more power among the Zealots. That produced a split of the Zealots into two sections, although there were no open battles between them. The Idumeans remaining in the city sided with John. Josephus credits those who did not join John's group as being suspicious of monarchical authority, and dedicated to an egalitarian power structure (*War* 4.7.1 §§ 393–94). The Zealots continued to control the city until the spring of 69. Meanwhile the Romans waited, having received intelligence that civil strife divided the Jews.

Simon Son of Giora

Simon was leader of one of the groups of bandits operating in Judea and Idumea. He had led his bandits against the wealthy of northeast Judea. Ananus had tried to disarm him, but Simon evaded capture. "He withdrew to the hills, where, by proclaiming liberty for slaves and rewards for the free, he gathered around him the villains from every quarter" (*War* 4.9.3 § 508). It is not clear whether Simon espoused a program of social reform, or whether his social policies were purely pragmatic. He is similar to the ancient King David, who began his rise to power by gathering a gang of bandits in the countryside composed of the disaffected of society (1 Sam 22:1-2). Like David, Simon knew how to hold people together, and gained a reputation for being a disciplined and effective leader. Simon attracted increasing numbers of people to his band as his reputation spread. They were "subservient to his command as to a king" (*War*

4.9.4 § 510). This may suggest that Simon was the sort of popular king described in chapter 10.

As the Romans reconquered Idumea and parts of Judea, Simon began to harass Jerusalem. The Idumeans still under John of Gischala's command revolted against John, forcing him and his supporters into the outer precincts of the Temple. Together with the remnants of the priestly aristocracy the Idumeans then invited Simon into the city. In the spring of 69 Simon became master of Jerusalem, and his only Jewish rivals were confined to the Temple. Simon's rule of Jerusalem was marked by frequent battles with the Zealots that destroyed much of Jerusalem's supplies, and an iron discipline featuring the death penalty for all who opposed him.

The Fall of Jerusalem

Around Passover in 70 CE, Titus began to besiege Jerusalem. Within the city, Eleazar opened the gates to the inner Temple for the festival. John smuggled his armed men into that area. They then attacked and defeated Eleazar, leaving John and Simon the only leaders in Jerusalem. The two came to terms with each other in the face of their Roman enemy. In 70 CE Jerusalem fell to the superior strength of the Romans, and John and Simon were both captured and taken to Rome. Simon was treated as the main leader by the Romans. He was paraded through Rome in the triumphal march, and then executed. John was sentenced to life imprisonment. Titus consigned Jerusalem and its Temple to the flames. The Roman soldiers planted their idolatrous standards in the ruined courts of the Temple and sacrificed to them.

Divine Signs

After narrating the fall of Jerusalem, Josephus says that there had been numerous divine signs predicting the city's doom. Those who should have been able to read the signs misled the people, giving them false hope. The following is the last of the signs he enumerates.

> At the feast which is called Pentecost, the priests on entering the inner court of the temple by night, as their custom was in the discharge of their ministrations, reported that they were conscious, first of a commotion and a din, and after that of a voice as of a host, "We are departing hence." (*War* 6.5.3 §§ 299–300)

The words "We are departing hence" recall the departure of God from the Temple in Ezekiel (Ezek 11:22-23). Jerusalem and its Temple could not be destroyed unless God abandoned them to the enemy. Josephus blames God's abandonment not on the Jews as a whole, but on the insurgents, especially the Zealots, who defiled the holy city.

There was another means by which Josephus claims that God told the Jews that they were not going to get divine support in their revolt.

> Four years before the war, when the city was enjoying profound peace and prosperity, there came to the feast at which it is the custom of all Jews to erect tabernacles to God, one Jesus, son of Ananias, a rude peasant, who, standing in the temple, suddenly began to cry out, "A voice from the east, a voice from the west, a voice from the four winds; a voice against Jerusalem and the sanctuary, a voice against the bridegroom and the bride, a voice against all the people." Day and night he went about all the alleys with this cry on his lips. Some of the leading citizens, incensed at these ill-omened words, arrested the fellow and severely chastised him. But he, without a word on his own behalf or for the private ear of those who smote him, only continued his cries as before. Thereupon, the magistrates, supposing, as was indeed the case, that the man was under some supernatural impulse, brought him before the Roman governor; there, although flayed to the bone with scourges, he neither sued for mercy nor shed a tear, but merely introducing the most mournful of variations into his ejaculation, responded to each stroke with "Woe to Jerusalem!" When Albinus, the governor, asked him who and whence he was and why he uttered these cries, he answered him never a word, but unceasingly reiterated his dirge over the city, until Albinus pronounced him a maniac and let him go. During the whole period up to the outbreak of war he neither approached nor was seen talking to any of the citizens, but daily, like a prayer that he had conned, repeated his lament, "Woe to Jerusalem!" He neither cursed any of those who beat him from day to day, nor blessed those who offered him food: to all men that melancholy presage was his one reply. His cries were the loudest at the festivals. So for seven years and five months he continued his wail, his voice never flagging nor his strength exhausted, until in the siege, having seen his presage verified, he found his rest. For, while going his round and shouting in piercing tones from the wall, "Woe once more to the city and to the people and to the temple," as he added a last word, "and woe to me also," a stone hurled from the *ballista* struck and killed him on the spot. So with those ominous words still upon his lips he passed away. (*War* 6.5.3 §§ 300–309)

There are numerous parallels between this account and traditions about Jesus Christ: the name Jesus; the message about the destruction of Jerusalem; the supernatural origins of the message; both are from the countryside and deliver their messages in the city; both are considered crazy by some; the investigation before Jewish authorities followed by the appearance before the Roman governor; the scourging; the silence before their accusers; the importance of the circumstance of a Jewish feast; imagery of bride and bridegroom. Of course, there are important differences as well. The parallels are noted only to bring home the fact that Jesus of Nazareth was a person of his own times, and is similar in some ways to various of his contemporaries.

The Fortress of Masada

Masada was not taken until 74 CE. It was occupied by the Sicarii under the command of Eleazar son of Jair, another descendant of Judas the Galilean. It held out for so long because it was built on a high hill with very steep sides and was well supplied. Before it fell its last defenders committed suicide, a fate deemed more honorable than submission to the Romans.

JEWISH PALESTINE: 74 to 135 CE

The fall of Jerusalem and its Temple in 70 CE marks the end of the Second Temple period. A brief sketch of the next sixty-five years will indicate what direction Judaism took after the destruction. The sources that date from this period are scarce and do not give much historical information.

After the war Palestine received a governor of senatorial status, and so was no longer subject to the province of Syria. The Romans recognized that the area needed more direct attention, and that rule through members of the Equestrian order had not worked. The Sanhedrin no longer existed. The city of Jerusalem had been reduced to rubble, for the most part, and became a Roman military encampment.

In 132 CE about fifteen years into Hadrian's rule, the Jews of Palestine revolted again. It is not known what started the war. It may be that Hadrian's plans to turn Jerusalem into a Greco-Roman city, complete with a temple to Jupiter (the chief Roman god) provoked the Jews. The revolt lasted until 135, and was led by Simon bar Kosiba. A pun on his name turned it into Bar Kokhba, the Aramaic for "Son of a Star." This is probably a reference to his messianic claims. There is a reference in Numbers 24:17 to a star that will arise from Jacob that was interpreted messianically at this period (*see* 4QTest from Qumran). Tradition has it that Rabbi Akiba, a prominent teacher of the period, acknowledged Bar Kokhba as messiah. One of Bar Kokhba's coins features a star over the Temple, suggesting that rebuilding of the Temple was one of his goals. Documents from the Judean desert indicate that observance of traditional religion was a priority of Bar Kokhba, once again illustrating the convergence of religion and politics.

The close of the war in 135 CE brought retribution on the Jews. Circumcision was forbidden.[4] Hadrian went ahead with his plans to build a new city on the site of Jerusalem. The city was named Aelia Capitolina—"Aelia" after Hadrian's family and "Capitolina" after Jupiter Capitolinus. Jews were forbidden under pain of death to enter the city.

THE BEGINNINGS OF RABBINIC JUDAISM

Most of the known Palestinian Jewish groups passed out of existence owing to the war.[5] The priestly elite lost its power base when Jerusalem and the Temple were destroyed. The Qumran community was attacked and destroyed by the

Romans around 68 CE. With the decrease of power, land, and wealth held by the Judean aristocracy, the Sadducees faded from view. The Jerusalem Sanhedrin no longer existed. Some of the Sicarii fled to the Diaspora where they fomented further disturbances, but they were soon eliminated (*War* 7.10.1 §§ 409–19; 7.11.1 §§ 437–40). Other groups associated with the Jewish-Roman war, such as the Zealots, are not mentioned again in the primary sources.

Before the destruction of Jerusalem, a prominent Pharisee named Yohanan ben Zakkai, a member of the anti-war faction, escaped from Jerusalem and obtained Roman permission to go to the coastal city of Jamnia (Yavneh in Hebrew) to found a school. Yohanan's school survived the war, and after the conflict he probably gathered to himself many of the leading Pharisees, scribes, and priests left in Palestine. The Pharisees dominated at Jamnia. They were poised to take the reins of leadership after the war. They had always been a political interest group, and prominent Pharisees were involved in the governing of Israel at various points in its history. Their claim to have the true interpretation of Torah was a claim to be able to implement Torah as the constitution and law of Israel.

The Pharisaic world view offered hope after the war. Yohanan taught that atonement could be attained through prayer, fasting, and good works, and so was possible without the Temple. Rules for sanctification of the Temple and of those who participated in its liturgies were widened to include everyday Jewish life, especially those areas that affected food, its production, and its consumption. That afforded the Jews a powerful symbolic system embodying the belief that they were God's chosen people and therefore holy. It also made possible the maintenance of Jewish identity in the face of the loss of a territorial nationhood. Distinctive practices would mark out the Jews as a special people, and since those practices were based on Torah, they were divinely ordained. All of Torah received close attention from the rabbis. (After the war it became customary to refer to the experts in Torah who became the authorities in Judaism as "rabbis," a term that literally means "my great one," but can be roughly translated "teacher.") Parts dealing with the Temple and cult received special attention, even though the cult was not in operation and the Temple no longer existed. There was still hope for the restoration of the Temple, of course, but even beyond that motive was the strong belief that all of Torah came directly from God and deserved detailed explanation. Increased concentration on Torah led to standardization of the list of books that were considered authoritative or "canonical." There was also a move to standardize the text of the Hebrew Bible.

Pharisaic oral traditions afforded Judaism a vehicle through which new ideas and new interpretations of Torah could enter. Over time, those interpretations assumed the authority of Torah. That authority was expressed in the notion of oral Torah. The idea was that God gave Moses both a written and an oral Torah on Sinai. The written Torah was contained in the Hebrew Bible, the oral Torah was passed down from generation to generation, and was finally written down in the rabbinic documents called the Mishnah (ca. 200 CE), the Jerusalem Talmud (ca. 400 CE), and the Babylonian Talmud (ca. 600 CE).

Belief in resurrection was not exclusively Pharisaic, but its acceptance by Pharisaism made its world view helpful for a defeated people needing hope. It is possible that many Pharisees still hoped for a messiah. If so, then Pharisaic belief also gave the people a this-worldly hope that may have contributed to the second revolt against Rome. However, after the second devastating defeat messianic hopes were treated cautiously. Most apocalyptic texts of Second Temple Judaism were preserved not by Jews, but by Christians, for whom apocalypticism furnished a world view through which to interpret Christ.

4 EZRA

The apocalypse called 4 Ezra was written in response to the destruction of Jerusalem by the Romans.[6] It attempts to reconcile that disaster with divine justice. It was probably written in Palestine sometime around 100 CE. The aftermath of the Jewish-Roman war is the real historical setting for the writing of the apocalypse, but the fictional setting of the book is the destruction and exile under the Babylonians in the sixth century BCE. The first destruction became paradigmatic for the second. In typically apocalyptic fashion, the destruction of the Second Temple is put into perspective by seeing it as the playing out of a pattern that goes beyond the particular event. The perspective supplied by this analogy allows the readers (Jews who were distressed over the events of 70 CE) to see their own time in light of the broad sweep of history and God's plans for the cosmos. The book is analyzed in detail here to provide an example of how apocalypticism supplied solutions for the problem raised by Jerusalem's fall.[7]

The book falls into seven sections. The first three are dialogues between Ezra (the priest-scribe who brought the Torah from Persia to Judah around the turn of the fourth century BCE) and the angel Uriel in which Ezra voices pessimistic and bitter complaints against God's ways. Sections 4–6 are a series of visions. In section 4 Ezra undergoes a conversion in which he comes to accept God's ways. The movement of Ezra from desolation to consolation is a key element in the apocalypse, and is probably intended to effect the same transformation in 4 Ezra's readers. The remaining visions interpret Israel's present and reveal the future. Section 7 is an epilogue in which Ezra's position as pastor, scribe, and revealer is reinterpreted.

Section 1 (3:1–5:19)

The book begins,

> In the thirtieth year after the destruction of the city, I was in Babylon—I, Salathiel, who am also called Ezra. I was troubled as I lay on my bed, and my thoughts welled up in my heart, because I saw the desolation of Zion and the wealth of those who lived in Babylon. (3:1-2)

The problem 4 Ezra seeks to address is the desolation of Zion (meaning the Temple built on Mount Zion in Jerusalem) and the distress of the Jewish people. The desolation contrasts with Rome's prosperity.

Ezra launches into a review of history starting with creation. The review is pessimistic, stressing the failure of almost everyone to obey God's will. The cause of the failure is the evil inclination in human hearts.

> Yet you did not take away their evil heart from them, so that your law might produce fruit in them. For the first Adam, burdened with an evil heart, transgressed and was overcome, as were also all who were descended from him. Thus the disease became permanent; the law was in the hearts of the people along with the evil root; but what was good departed, and the evil remained. (3:20-22)

This is a criticism of God. God could have made humans different, but left the evil inclination in place. God thus left humanity powerless to obey Torah.

Israel's sinfulness might make its punishment understandable, but Ezra's experience of Babylon (Rome) throws God's justice into question: "Then I said in my heart, Are the deeds of those who inhabit Babylon any better? Is that why it has gained dominion over Zion?" (3:28). The obvious answer is, No. Ezra challenges God to find any nation on earth that is righteous, and says, "You may indeed find individuals who have kept your commandments, but nations you will not find" (3:36).

The angel Uriel confronts Ezra and says that he will answer Ezra's questions if Ezra can solve three problems: "Go, weigh for me the weight of fire, or measure for me a blast of wind, or call back for me the day that is past" (4:5). Of course Ezra cannot solve the problems. Uriel responds, "You cannot understand the things with which you have grown up; how then can your mind comprehend the way of the Most High?" (4:10). Ezra is not satisfied with this answer, and says bitterly, "It would have been better for us not to be here than to come here and live in ungodliness, and to suffer and not understand why" (4:12). Using the analogy that the trees cannot conquer the sea, nor the sea conquer the forest, Uriel says, "So also those who inhabit the earth can understand only what is on the earth, and he who is above the heavens can understand what is above the height of the heavens" (4:21).[8] The events into which Ezra inquires cannot be comprehended without knowledge of what happens above the heavens, where God is. This is typically apocalyptic.

Ezra is unwilling to admit that the answers to his questions require esoteric knowledge.

> I implore you, my lord, why have I been endowed with the power of understanding? For I did not wish to inquire about the ways above, but about those things that we daily experience: why Israel has been given over to the Gentiles in disgrace; why the people whom you loved has been given over to godless tribes, and the law of our ancestors has been brought to destruction and the written covenants no longer exist. We pass from the world like locusts, and our life is like a mist, and we are not worthy to obtain mercy. But what will he do for his name that is invoked over us? It is about these things that I have asked. (4:22-25)

Ezra does not understand how the world works. In the apocalyptic outlook, apparently not shared by Ezra, direct revelation of God's plans is the only way to grasp what happens on earth.

The rest of the vision consists of revelations of the future. At the end of time the good will receive their reward and the evil their punishment. Chapter 5 enumerates the traditional apocalyptic signs of the end, among which are cosmic disturbances: "The sun shall suddenly begin to shine at night, and the moon during the day. Blood shall drip from wood, and the stone shall utter its voice; the peoples shall be troubled, and the stars shall fall" (5:4-5).[9]

Section 2 (5:20–6:34)

The second section begins with a prayer of Ezra reminding God that Israel is the chosen people, yet it has been brought lower than any other nation. In the ensuing dialogue, the angel reminds Ezra that he cannot understand God's ways. The rest of the section stresses that God has a plan older than creation, and that God's imminent intervention will affect the whole universe. The judgment will be preceded with the usual apocalyptic signs.

Section 3 (6:35–9:25)

The third section begins with a prayer of Ezra recalling the six days of creation and reminding God that all was created for the sake of Israel. The angel agrees that God made the world of Israel, but says that Israel must pass through dangers in order to inherit the world. He uses the analogies of a river that must go through narrow passages to reach the wide sea, and of a city that can be reached only through a narrow and difficult entrance.[10] Ezra's reaction is to pity sinners, who compose the vast majority of humanity. Uriel reproaches Ezra for questioning God's judgment and says, "Let many perish who are now living, rather than that the law of God that is set before them be disregarded!" (7:20).

Next comes an eschatological timetable.

359

For my son the Messiah shall be revealed with those who are with him, and those who remain shall rejoice four hundred years. After those years my son the Messiah shall die, and all who draw human breath. Then the world shall be turned back to primeval silence for seven days, as it was at the first beginnings, so that no one shall be left. After seven days the world that is not yet awake shall be roused, and that which is corruptible shall perish. (7:28-31)

After this come resurrection, judgment, rewards, and punishments. The messiah is human, since he is mortal. He is called God's son, as is the Davidic king in 2 Samuel 7 and Psalm 2. This passage represents the integration of the hope for the establishment of an earthly messiah with the expectation that this world will pass away and a new one take its place. There will be a messianic kingdom of 400 years, followed by the reduction of all to the silence that reigned before creation. Then there will be a new beginning and a new world.

This does not comfort Ezra. News of a future world comforts only those who will enjoy it. They are such a tiny minority that Ezra is left with his grief. Uriel says, "For this reason the Most High has made not one world but two" (7:50). Ezra should look to the future world and not fasten on this one. Using the images of precious stones and metals, the angel says that what is good is always scarce. So it is with human beings. Uriel has no pity for sinners who get what they deserve. Ezra despairs because he is convinced that almost all humanity is sinful. He even goes farther and claims that *everyone* is unrighteous: "For all who have been born are entangled in iniquities, and are full of sins and burdened with transgressions" (7:68). In response to an appeal to God's mercy the angel says,

The Most High made this world for the sake of many, but the world to come for the sake of only a few. But I tell you a parable, Ezra. Just as, when you ask the earth, it will tell you that it provides a large amount of clay from which earthenware is made, but only a little dust from which gold comes, so is the course of the present world. Many have been created, but only a few shall be saved. (8:1-3)[11]

Uriel discloses that Ezra is among the righteous. He ends his revelation with the words, "Therefore my judgment is now drawing near; I have not shown this to all people, but only to you and a few like you" (8:61-62).

Section 4 (9:26–10:59a)

This section is the turning point of the book because it is where Ezra turns from despair to acceptance of the angel's message. Ezra begins by praying about Israel's situation. Then he spies a woman in deep mourning over the death of her son. Ezra reproaches her.

You most foolish of women, do you not see our mourning, and what has happened to us? For Zion, the mother of us all, is in deep grief and great distress. . . . For if you acknowledge the decree of God to be just, you will receive your son back in due time, and will be praised among women. (10:6-7, 16)

The woman refuses to be diverted from her grief. Ezra continues,

Let yourself be persuaded—for how many are the adversities of Zion?—and be consoled because of the sorrow of Jerusalem. For you see how our sanctuary has been laid waste, our altar thrown down, our temple destroyed; our harp has been laid low, our song has been silenced, and our rejoicing has been ended; the light of our lampstand has been put out, the ark of our covenant has been plundered, our holy things have been polluted, and the name by which we are called has been almost profaned; our children have suffered abuse, our priests have been burned to death, our Levites have gone into exile, our virgins have been defiled, and our wives have been ravished; our righteous men have been carried off, our little ones have been cast out, our young men have been enslaved and our strong men made powerless. And, worst of all, the seal of Zion has been deprived of its glory, and given over into the hands of those that hate us. (10:20-23)

Ezra utters a litany of Israel's losses. It is an expression of the desolation the Jews suffered because of the revolt. Suddenly the woman is transformed into a large city with "huge foundations." Uriel appears and supplies an allegorical explanation of the vision of the woman and the city, the key element of which is the identification of the woman as Zion, mourning over the destruction. The woman's transformation into a city symbolizes the restoration of Jerusalem.

After this vision and interpretation, Ezra no longer challenges God's judgments. Somehow his experience has reconciled him to God's ways. Precisely how this takes place is disputed. Perhaps in the act of consoling the woman who turns out to be Zion, Ezra sees his own sorrow in a new light. Perhaps in seeing the future restored city, Ezra can take comfort in it. The result is that he himself takes the advice he offers the woman, acknowledging the decree of God to be just. By no longer fixating on the distressful results of God's decree on sinners, Ezra can do what the angel has encouraged him to do all along, turn his attention to the future. Ezra now becomes the recipient and the conveyer of revelation.

Section 5 (10:59b–12:50)

This section is a vision and its interpretation. It involves the kind of strange imagery seen in the book of Daniel. Its central figure is an eagle, the symbol of Rome. The eagle has three heads, representing the three Flavian emperors—Vespasian, Titus, and Domitian—and twelve wings, probably standing for the emperors preceding the Flavians. After a description of the interactions of the wings and the heads, reflecting the succession of emperors, their oppositions and alliances, a lion appears. The lion makes a speech to the eagle which begins,

> Listen and I will speak to you. The Most High says to you, ''Are you not the one that remains of the four beasts that I had made to reign in my world, so that the end of my times might come through them? You, the fourth that has come, have conquered all the beasts that have gone before; and you have held sway over the world with great terror, and over all the earth with grievous oppression; and for so long you have lived on the earth with deceit. You have judged the earth, but not with truth, for you have oppressed the meek and injured the peaceable; you have hated those who tell the truth, and have loved liars; you have destroyed the homes of those who brought forth fruit, and have laid low the walls of those who did you no harm. (11:38-42)

Rome's hegemony is portrayed in brutal terms. Its social injustice is detailed here for the first time in 4 Ezra. Its rule is interpreted within four kingdoms, a pattern known from Daniel 2, 7, and other Hellenistic documents. The four-kingdom scheme is used to put the reign of the present kingdom into historical perspective. After the succession of kingdoms comes liberation through God. By appealing to this pattern with its deep roots in Israel and the ancient Near East, the message of hope is made powerful. The lion announces to the eagle that the Most High has noticed its injustices, and will soon destroy its kingdom.

In the interpretation of the vision (12:10-35), the identity of the eagle's heads and wings as kings is specified. Then comes the interpretation of the lion as the messiah, son of David. The role of the Davidic Messiah here is that of judge. Those who are liberated are a ''remnant.'' The idea that God preserves a remnant of the people is an old one in Jewish literature. Those who are saved are within God's borders, indicating that the holy land is the locus of salvation.

Section 6 (12:51–13:58)

> And lo, a wind arose from the sea and stirred up all its waves. As I kept looking the wind made something like the figure of a man come up out of the heart of the sea. And I saw that this man flew with the clouds of heaven; and wherever he turned his face to look, everything under his gaze trembled, and whenever his voice issued from his mouth, all who heard his voice melted as wax melts when it feels the fire. After this I looked and saw that an innumerable multitude of people were gathered together from the four winds of heaven to make war against the man who came up out of the sea. And I looked and saw that he carved out for himself a great mountain, and flew up on to it. (13:2-6)

The passage depends on Daniel 7. It draws on the images of the Son of Man accompanied by clouds, and the mystery and power of the sea. The might of the figure like a man is graphically portrayed in the reaction of people and of nature to his presence. A crowd of humans from all over the earth gathers to fight him. In the next verses the man causes a stream of fire to destroy his enemies, so that only ashes are left. Then the man descends from the mountain and gathers to himself a peaceable crowd. Although Ezra is frightened by the vision he says, ''It is better to come into these things, though incurring peril, than to pass from the world like a cloud, and not to see what will happen in the last days'' (13:20). This is a reversal of his position in the earlier dialogues where he would rather die than understand such terrible mysteries.

Uriel interprets the man from the sea as the messiah, God's son, whom God has hidden until the last days. At the eschaton, the messiah ascends Mount Zion and judges the wicked and liberates Israel. The wicked are the assembled nations, and the peaceable crowd is the lost tribes of Israel, exiled in 722 BCE (13:35-40). When asked why the man arose from the sea, Uriel explains, ''Just as no one can explore or know what is in the depths of the sea, so no one on earth can see my Son or those who are with him, except in the time of his day'' (13:52). Only Ezra is given the secret, because he has been loyal to Torah and loves wisdom (13:53-56).

Section 7 (14:1-48)

In this section, God speaks to Ezra directly for the first time. ''On the third day, while I was sitting under an oak, suddenly a voice came out of a bush opposite me and said, 'Ezra, Ezra!' And I answered, 'Here I am, Lord,' and I rose to my feet. Then he said to me, 'I revealed myself in a bush and spoke to Moses when my people were in bondage in Egypt''' (14:1-3). There is a clear parallel drawn here between Ezra and Moses. The apocalypse reaches back to Israel's sacred traditions for paradigms for God's action. God says concerning Moses, ''I told him many wondrous things, and showed him the secrets of the times and declared to him the end of the times. Then I commanded him, saying, 'These words you shall publish openly, and these you shall keep secret''' (14:5-6). Moses received precisely the kind of eschatological knowledge granted to Ezra. Moses is told that he must publish some of the revelation, presumably the Torah, and that he must keep the esoteric knowledge hidden.

Ezra points out that the Torah and the secret revelations to Moses no longer exist, having been burned in the destruction of Jerusalem. He says, ''Send the holy spirit into me, and I will write everything that has happened in the world from the beginning, the things that were written in your law'' (14:22). God agrees. He tells Ezra to instruct the people not to seek him for forty days (the length of time Moses spent on Sinai receiving the Torah), to gather five skilled scribes, and to bring them to God. God will dictate things to be published (Torah), and things to be kept secret (esoteric knowledge).

A voice called me, saying, ''Ezra, open your mouth and drink what I give you to drink.'' So I opened my mouth, and a full cup was offered to me; it was full of something like water, but its color was like fire. I took it and drank; and when I had drunk it, my heart poured forth understanding, and wisdom increased in my breast, for my spirit retained its memory, and my mouth was opened and was no longer closed. Moreover, the Most High gave understanding to the five men, and by turns they wrote what was dictated, using characters that they did not know. They sat forty days; they wrote during the daytime, and ate their bread at night. But as for me, I spoke in the daytime and was not silent at night. So during the forty days, ninety-four books were written. And when the forty days were ended, the Most High spoke to me, saying, "Make public the twenty-four books that you wrote first, and let the worthy and the unworthy read them; but keep the seventy that were written last, in order to give them to the wise among your people. For in them is the spring of understanding, the fountain of wisdom, and the river of knowledge. And I did so. (14:38-48)

So ends 4 Ezra. Ezra, under the power of the Holy Spirit, dictates the complete body of divine revelation conveyed to Moses but lost in the destruction of Jerusalem. The passage emphasizes the miraculous nature of the undertaking, and the tremendous volume of knowledge involved. The twenty-four published books are the Hebrew Bible. It is the seventy unpublished books that are the most important here. It is they that truly contain the spring of understanding. Torah is the word of God, but the esoteric knowledge obtained by the seer is also direct revelation, and it is the secret wisdom that is necessary for grasping God's plans.

This book offers an apocalyptic solution to the problem of the destruction of Jerusalem, the distress of the Jews, and the success of the Romans. Uriel constantly tells Ezra to stop concentrating on the woes of the present and look to the brilliant but hidden future. Ezra voices the concerns and complaints that many Jews of the postwar era must have felt, but he is finally persuaded to accept God's will joyfully when he tours the future city of God. From them on he becomes a willing recipient of apocalyptic knowledge. Like other apocalyptic works, 4 Ezra accomplishes its purpose of consolation and exhortation to hope by putting things into historical and cosmological perspective. To restrict oneself to looking at worldly events leads to despair. Knowledge of heavenly secrets yields hope and understanding.

2 BARUCH

This work is another apocalyptic response to the destruction of Jerusalem. It was written around the same time as 4 Ezra. Baruch was the secretary of the prophet Jeremiah, who lived before and during the destruction of Jerusalem in the sixth century BCE. The earlier destruction is the paradigm for interpreting the second, as in 4 Ezra. There are many points of contact between 4 Ezra and 2 Baruch that make some sort of direct relationship between them likely, but its precise nature is disputed. No attempt will be made to offer a solution to that problem here. This section will not analyze 2 Baruch in detail, as was done with 4 Ezra. Rather, it will examine several key passages that deal directly with the fall of Jerusalem and with the issue of Israel's situation after the fall.

The basic solution of *2 Baruch* to Jewish distress over the loss of Jerusalem and the Temple is apocalyptic. Another world is coming that rewards the good and punishes the evil. The destruction of Jerusalem is punishment for Israel's sins, but it also helps to hasten the eschaton. The movement from distress to comfort that the book seeks to effect in its readers is embodied in Baruch himself. In the first sections he is at the point of despair over the destruction of Zion, but over the course of the work he learns to accept God's will and to encourage his fellow Jews. As in 4 Ezra, the seer voices thoughts that are corrected by an angel or God.

The book opens with God telling Baruch that Jerusalem is about to fall because of the people's sins. Baruch's response embodies Zion theology.

O Lord, my Lord, have I come into the world for this purpose that I might see the evils of my mother? Not so, my Lord. If I have found grace in Thy sight, first take my spirit, that I may go to my fathers and not behold the destruction of my mother. For two things vehemently constrain me: for I cannot resist Thee, and my soul, moreover, cannot behold the evils of my mother. But one thing I will say in Thy presence, O Lord. What, therefore, will there be after these things? for if Thou destroyest Thy city, and deliverest up Thy land to those that hate us, how shall the name of Israel be again remembered? Or how shall one speak of Thy praises? or to whom shall that which is in Thy law be explained? Or shall the world return to its nature of aforetime, and the age revert to primeval silence? And shall the multitude of souls be taken away, and the nature of man not again be named? And where is all that which Thou didst say to Moses regarding us? (3:1-9)

For Baruch, the loss of the Temple has dire implications. It means the destruction of Israel and the cessation of God's worship and praises. There will be no one to listen to Torah, the world may pass out of existence, humanity will perish, and the promises to Moses will be nullified.

God says that the destruction of Jerusalem is temporary, as is the exile to come, and that the world will not pass out of existence. At the same time, God says that the downfall of Jerusalem does not entail the consequences Baruch expects. God goes on to say,

Dost thou think that this is that city of which I said: "On the palms of My hands have I graven thee"? This building now built in your midst is not that which is revealed with Me, that which was prepared beforehand here from the time when I took counsel to make Paradise, and showed it to Adam before he sinned, but when he transgressed the commandment it was removed from him, as also Paradise. And after these things I showed it to My servant Abraham by night among the portions of the victims. And again also I showed it to Moses on Mount Sinai when I showed to him the likeness of the tabernacle and all its vessels. And how, behold, it is preserved with Me, as also Paradise. (4:2-6)

365

God quotes from Isaiah 49:16 in which God's complete devotion to Jerusalem is expressed vividly. Yet Baruch hears that God is about to destroy Zion. God's words reconcile Zion theology with Jerusalem's ruin. The divine oracle in Isaiah never applied to the earthly Zion in the first place. There is a heavenly sanctuary that God meant. This draws on the ancient near eastern idea that earthly temples have heavenly counterparts. In *2 Baruch*, it is the heavenly Temple that matters. Unlike some other uses of the heavenly Temple in Judaism and Christianity, *2 Baruch* never says that the heavenly Temple will descend to earth. Throughout *2 Baruch* the importance of the earthly Temple is downplayed in favor of the heavenly world. Although there is an earthly messianic kingdom anticipated (chaps. 72–74), it is but a prelude to the next world. In chapter 51 the faithful go to heaven and live with the stars.

Baruch objects that if the Gentiles conquer Jerusalem and pollute the sanctuary, it will reflect badly on God's name. God replies that the divine name, which is eternal, is unaffected by such events. God adds that divine judgment will descend on the destroyers in due time. In the meanwhile, Baruch is assured that the Gentiles will not destroy Zion. Angels are instructed to destroy Jerusalem lest the enemy take the credit. Then "A voice was heard from the interior of the temple, after the wall had fallen, saying: 'Enter, ye enemies, And come, ye adversaries; For he who kept the house has forsaken it'" (8:1-2). As Ezekiel says that God left the Temple before its fall in 587 BCE, and as Josephus says the same thing about the destruction of 70 CE, *2 Baruch* says that God left the Temple before it fell. If God leaves, the Temple falls.

In chapter 44 Baruch addresses the people. At its beginning Baruch says that he is about to die. He exhorts the people to obey the Law, adducing the destruction of Zion as an example of the consequences of disobedience. The rest of the speech contrasts the present world, corruptible, passing, full of sorrows, and the future world, eternal and full of hope. "Because whatever is now is nothing, but that which shall be is very great" (44:8). The people react fearfully to the news of Baruch's impending death: "For where again shall we seek the law, or who will distinguish for us between death and life?" (46:3). As Moses says in Deuteronomy 30:15-20, the choice of whether or not to obey Torah is a choice between life and death.

> There shall not be wanting to Israel a wise man nor a son of the law to the race of Jacob. But only prepare ye your hearts, that ye may obey the law, and be subject to those who in fear are wise and understanding; and prepare your souls that ye may not depart from them. For if ye do these things, good tidings shall come unto you.
>
> (46:4-6)

The chief trait of the wise man is that he knows Torah. The presence of the wise in Israel is crucial because it makes obedience to the Law possible.

In chapter 77, Baruch addresses the people, urging them to obey Torah. They promise to do so, but utter another lament over their loss.

> For the shepherds of Israel have perished,
> And the lamps which gave light are extinguished,
> And the fountains have withheld their stream whence we used to drink.
> And we are left in the darkness,
> And amid the trees of the forest,
> And the thirst of the wilderness. (77:13-14)

Baruch answers them.

> Shepherds and lamps and fountains come from the law:
> And though we depart, yet the law abideth.
> If therefore ye have respect to the law,
> And are intent upon wisdom,
> A lamp will not be wanting,
> And a shepherd will not fail,
> And a fountain will not dry up. (77:15-16)

Chapters 78–86 are a letter of Baruch to the exiled northern tribes. He recalls that formerly Israel had righteous men and prophets. "But now the righteous have been gathered, and the prophets have fallen asleep, and we also have gone forth from the land, and Zion has been taken from us, and we have nothing now save the Mighty One and His law" (85:3). This verse is an apt description of Israel after 70 CE. The rest of the epistle exhorts the people to prepare their souls by submission to God, and thereby to escape this corruptible world and inherit the future glorious world.

CONCLUSION

The destruction of Jerusalem and its Temple by the Romans in 70 CE was a watershed in Jewish history. Before that disaster, Jews had a land of their own, even if under foreign domination, and a physical Temple staffed by priests and Levites in which a sacrificial cult was performed. But even prior to 70 CE, various Jewish groups were evolving ways of living out being Jewish that could potentially exist apart from land, Temple, and sacrifices. In particular, the Torah-centeredness of the varieties of Judaism both inside and outside Palestine made possible the reconstitution of Judaism around the written and oral Torahs after the destruction of Jerusalem. The Pharisees were best equipped to remold Judaism according to their own world view, and the postwar teachers, now called rabbis, were particularly influenced by Pharisaic teaching and practices.

Apocalypticism afforded comfort to some Jews after Jerusalem's fall.

367

Apocalyptic solutions to Israel's situation are found in 4 Ezra, *2 Baruch,* and the *Apocalypse of Abraham.* Hopes for a restoration of Israel in this world were kept alive between 70 and 132 CE, and probably played a role in the second Jewish uprising of 132 to 135 CE. After that time, apocalyptic expectations were discouraged by the rabbis for the most part. Judaism was now to concentrate on the sanctification of everyday life, and on the maintenance of a Jewish identity in the midst of a foreign and often hostile world.

SELECT BIBLIOGRAPHY

Most of the secondary works in the select bibliography of the preceding chapter are relevant for this chapter as well.

Breech, E. "These Fragments I Have Shored Against My Ruins: The Form and Function of 4 Ezra," *JBL* 92 (1973): 267-74.

Cohen, Shaye J. D. "The Significance of Yavneh: Pharisees, Rabbis, and the End of the Jewish Sectarianism," *HUCA* 55 (1984): 36-41.

Horsley, Richard A., and John S. Hanson. *Bandits, Prophets, and Messiahs: Popular Movements at the Time of Jesus.* Minneapolis: Winston, 1985.

Murphy, Frederick J. *The Structure and Meaning of Second Baruch,* SBLDS 78. Atlanta: Scholars Press, 1985.

Neusner, Jacob. *First Century Judaism in Crisis: Yohanan ben Zaakai and the Renaissance of Torah.* New York: Ktav, 1982.

_____. "The Formation of Rabbinic Judaism: Yavneh (Jamnia) from A.D. 70 to 100," *ANRW* II, 19/2, 3-42.

Rhoads, David M. *Israel in Revolution: A Political History Based on the Writings of Josephus.* Philadelphia: Fortress Press, 1976.

Saldarini, Anthony J. "Reconstructions of Rabbinic Judaism," in *EJMI,* 437-77.

Sayler, Gwendolyn. *Have the Promises Failed?: A Literary Analysis of 2 Baruch.* SBLDS 72, Chico, Calif.: Scholars Press, 1984.

Schürer, Emil. *The Jewish People in the Age of Jesus Christ,* 3 vols., rev. Geza Vermes, Fergus Millar, Matthew Black. Edinburgh: T. & T. Clark, Ltd., 1973–87.

Stone, Michael. *Features of the Eschatology of IV Ezra.* Atlanta: Scholars Press, 1990.

_____. *Fourth Ezra.* Minneapolis: Fortress Press, 1990.

_____. "Reactions to Destructions of the Second Temple: Theology, Perception, and Conversion," *JSJ* 12 (1981): 195-204.

Thompson, A. L. *Responsibility for Evil in the Theodicy of IV Ezra,* SBLDS 29, Missoula, Mont.: Scholars Press, 1977.

Yadin, Yigael. *Bar Kochba.* New York: Random House, 1971.

PART III

Christian Interpretations,
Jewish Roots

CHAPTER THIRTEEN

Early Christian Interpretations of Jesus

Primary Readings: Matthew, Hebrews, Revelation

This chapter investigates three New Testament interpretations of Jesus. The purpose is simply to indicate how Jewish elements are central to these interpretations, so this chapter is not a full treatment of the three books. The books were chosen because they each offer clear instances of early Christian use of Jewish elements to understand Jesus, yet each one uses different aspects of Jewish thought for that purpose.

THE GOSPEL OF MATTHEW: JESUS AS TEACHER OF TORAH

Matthew, written around 85 CE, represents Jesus as the ultimate Torah teacher whose mission is only to Israel. Jesus teaches his disciples the true interpretation of Torah, and they bring that interpretation to all nations. The author was probably a Jewish Christian who did not conceive of Christianity as a new religion, but saw it as Israel following the Torah interpretation of the teacher sent by God. Several of the passages discussed below were examined in chapter 11 under the heading, "Jesus and the Torah."

Fulfillment of Scripture

Matthew 1 and 2 is an infancy narrative. It opens with the verse, "An account of the genealogy of Jesus the Messiah, the son of David, the son of Abraham" (1:1). Here Matthew presents two of Jesus' main credentials. Jesus is a true Jew, descended from Abraham, and can be the Davidic messiah because he is of the line of David. The title "son of David" receives more attention in this gospel than in the other three gospels. The word translated "genealogy" here is the Greek word *genesis,* "beginning" or "origin." Matthew may be alluding to the first book of Torah. There follows a genealogy of Jesus illustrating that he is truly son of Abraham and son of David. A genealogy is a chronological list of one's ancestors. Genealogies were especially important in postexilic Judaism, where it was crucial to define the community. They played a central role in the work of the Chronicler.

The rest of the infancy narrative is structured around "formula quotations," a

371

frequent form in Matthew. Formula quotations are citations of the Hebrew Bible, accompanied by a formulaic statement that Jesus fulfills the biblical passage. That Jesus was born of a virgin, was born in Bethlehem, went to Egypt, that the innocent children were slaughtered by Herod, and that Jesus grew up in Nazareth, all happened because God planned it beforehand and predicted it in the Hebrew Bible. The theological point is that Jesus' ministry was predicted in detail by God, and that Jesus' ministry is indeed the work of God. Jesus is the goal of Israel's history. Such use of Israel's Scripture recalls Qumran's mode of interpretation, and shows that Christian use of the Hebrew Bible was rooted in Jewish soil.

Matthew 1 and 2 contradict Luke's infancy narrative in various ways. (Mark and John do not have infancy narratives.) Whereas in Matthew Jesus' family must flee to Egypt for fear of Herod the Great, in Luke they appear publicly in the Temple shortly after Jesus' birth. Luke does not mention Jesus's flight to Egypt. In Luke, Jesus' family lives in Nazareth, goes to Bethlehem because of the census in the time of Quirinius (6 CE), and then returns to Nazareth. In Matthew, Jesus' family apparently lives in Bethlehem and is forced to flee to Egypt by Herod. When Herod's son Archelaus assumes the administration of Judea in 4 BCE, the family goes to Nazareth of Galilee, ruled by Herod Antipas, to escape the rule of Archelaus (Matt 2:22). Both gospels manage to have Jesus born in Bethlehem and grow up in Nazareth, but they do so in very different ways.

Given the discrepancies between Matthew and Luke, and the fact that Matthew's narrative is structured around formula quotations, it appears likely that at least some of the details in the stories of Jesus' infancy were generated by early Christian reflection on Hebrew Scripture. Matthew was not interested in historical writing as such. He wanted to show how Jesus fulfilled the words of the prophets. A brief examination of the first formula quotation in Matthew will help to show how Matthew's use of Scripture resembles that of Judaism.

Matthew connects Christian belief in Jesus' miraculous conception and birth with a prophecy from Isaiah: "All this took place to fulfill what had been spoken by the Lord through the prophet: 'Look, the virgin shall conceive and bear a son, and they shall name him Emmanuel,' which means, 'God is with us'" (Matt 1:22-23; quoting Isa 7:14). Isaiah uttered his prophecy in Jerusalem in the eighth century BCE when Ahaz was king of Judah. At that time Assyria was threatening the kingdoms of Syria, Israel, and Judah. Syria and Israel were pressuring Ahaz to join them in an anti-Assyrian alliance. In Isaiah 7:3-9, God tells Ahaz through Isaiah not to worry about Syria and Israel, because they are both about to fall. Then Isaiah describes a sign that God will give to show that the prophecy is true.

Look, the young woman is with child and shall bear a son, and shall name him Immanuel. He shall eat curds and honey by the time he knows how to refuse the evil and choose the good. For before the child knows how to refuse the evil and choose the good, the land before whose two kings you are in dread will be deserted. (7:14-16)

The NRSV translation presented here says that Isaiah spoke of a "young woman." The Hebrew word is 'almāh, and its basic meaning is indeed "young woman." A different Hebrew word, bĕtûlāh, is the technical term for "virgin." There is no indication in the Hebrew text that Isaiah refers to a virgin. When the Hebrew Bible was translated into Greek, 'almāh was translated by the Greek term parthenos meaning "maiden" or "virgin." Some early Christians, reading the Greek text, took parthenos to mean "virgin," and associated it with what they believed was a miraculous birth of Jesus. However, Isaiah spoke of a child to be born while the crisis under Ahaz was still in effect. The point of the sign, the birth of a child with a special name, was that Syria and Israel would fall before the child reached the age of reason, the ability to distinguish between good and evil. In fact, the two kingdoms did fall shortly after the prophecy. The name of the child, Emmanuel, is correctly translated by Matthew as "God with us." For Isaiah, the name does not define the nature of the child, that is, that the child would be divine. It is a symbolic name, indicating that God is with Judah and will act soon. Such symbolic names are common in Israelite and Jewish history. The prophet Isaiah gives his own child a symbolic name in 8:1-4.

Matthew was not interested in historical criticism, any more than his fellow Jews were. For them, Scripture was the word of God, literally inspired, and so verses could be lifted from their context and seen as referring directly to a much later time. Further, like Qumran, the early Christians did not only comment on history by means of Scripture, they read history through Scripture. Their view of what happened was colored by their reading of what Scripture said must have happened. Matthew's interpretation could not be expected to convince the rabbis of Jamnia who were his contemporaries, any more than similar interpretations of biblical prophecies by the Qumran community convinced the Jerusalem establishment.

Jesus as Teacher of Torah

Matthew's emphasis on Jesus' teaching is striking when compared with how little Jesus teaches in Mark. As was observed in chapter 8, Matthew collects the sayings of Jesus in five main sermons. The first is the "Sermon on the Mount" (Matthew 5–7). Matthew makes this sermon Jesus' principal statement of his message. As Moses received the Torah on Mount Sinai, Jesus goes up onto a mountain to deliver the definitive interpretation of Mosaic Torah. Toward the beginning of the sermon, Jesus makes an emphatic statement that his ministry should not be interpreted as the abrogation of Torah, but the confirmation of it (5:17). Torah lasts till the end of the world (5:18). Torah is to be obeyed in all of its details (5:19). The problem with the scribes and Pharisees is only that they do not go far enough in observing their own stringent interpretations (5:20; 23:2-3). The Sermon on the Mount continues with a series of six antitheses in which Jesus quotes Torah saying, "You have heard that it was said, ..." In each case Jesus authoritatively interprets Torah. Toward the end of the sermon, Jesus makes the following general statement: "In everything do to others as you would have them do to you; for this is the law and the prophets" (7:12). The verse is also found in Luke 6:31, but without the words about the Law and prophets.

Matthew's view of Jesus as Torah teacher influences the gospel in many of its details. For example, in all three synoptic gospels, Jesus is asked what is the greatest commandment (Mark 12:28-33; Matt 22:34-40; Luke 10:25-28). Each of the gospels has him answer by quoting Deuteronomy 6:5 concerning love of God, and Leviticus 19:18, which enjoins love of neighbor. Only Matthew ends the story with the words, "On these two commandments hang all the law and the prophets" (22:40).

In chapter 11, the conflict between Jesus and the Pharisees and scribes in Mark 7 and Matthew 15 was examined. It was noted that Mark's version makes the issue one of kosher foods. Mark states that Jesus "declared all foods clean" (7:19). Matthew drops that line. There is no indication in his gospel that he agrees with Mark's statement. Matthew emphasizes that the issue between Jesus and the Pharisees in this instance was the washing of hands, a purity rule peculiar to the Pharisees (15:20). For Matthew, Jesus upheld Torah, and did not annul the dietary rules. A similar case was made for Matthew's concern about the sabbath in chapter 11, where Matthew 12:1-8 was compared to Mark 2:23-28. There it was seen that Matthew is more concerned than Mark to prove that Jesus' activity on the sabbath was fully sanctioned by Torah.

Matthew probably wrote his gospel partly in reaction to the rabbinic reformulation of Judaism at Jamnia after the destruction of Jerusalem, which may account for his long harsh attack on the scribes and Pharisees in chapter 23. However, although Matthew attacks the Pharisees, he shares their presuppositions. In 23:2-3, Jesus even recognizes their authority: "The scribes and the Pharisees sit on Moses' seat; therefore, do whatever they teach you and follow it; but do not do as they do, for they do not practice what they teach." These verses do not picture Jesus as undermining Pharisaic interpretation of Torah, but as upholding it.

In the final scene of the gospel, the eleven apostles (minus Judas Iscariot, the betrayer) meet Jesus on a mountain in Galilee. Jesus says to them,

> All authority in heaven and on earth has been given to me. Go therefore and make disciples of all nations, baptizing them in the name of the Father and of the Son and of the Holy Spirit, and teaching them to obey everything that I have commanded you. And remember, I am with you always, to the end of the age. (28:18-20)

Torah language permeates these verses. "Disciple" comes from the word "to teach," and denotes students. The disciples are to make learners of all nations *teaching* them to *observe* Jesus' *commandments*. This echoes Jewish tradition, where the teaching of people to observe God's commandments is central. Matthew's idea of what Jesus has done, and what the church does, is modeled on Judaism. This passage is the only place in the gospel where the disciples are said to teach. Until this point, the verb ''teach'' had only Jesus as its subject. Now that Jesus' earthly ministry is completed, the disciples have ''graduated'' from their own school of discipleship, and can teach others. Jesus remains with the church as the one who authorizes the teaching of the disciples. The disciples' teaching consists of the commands they have been taught by Jesus.

Matthew adds an eschatological touch characteristic of his gospel when he has Jesus remind the disciples of the end of the age. Throughout the gospel, there are frequent reminders that the eschaton is coming in which people will be judged according to their reaction to the message of Jesus and his disciples.

Jesus and the Gentiles

In Matthew 28:18, Jesus tells the disciples to go to all nations. But the mission of Jesus, and of the disciples during his life, was limited to Israel. In Matthew 10:5-6, when Jesus sends the disciples out on a mission, he warns them, ''Go nowhere among the Gentiles, and enter no town of the Samaritans, but go rather to the lost sheep of the house of Israel.'' In 15:21-28, Jesus is disinclined to heal the daughter of a Gentile woman. He says, ''I was sent only to the lost sheep of the house of Israel'' (15:24). Matthew reconciled the church's Gentile mission with the fact that Jesus did not pursue a ministry to the Gentiles by saying that during the life of Jesus, he and his disciples ministered only to Israel, whereas after the resurrection, the mission was broadened to include all nations.

THE LETTER TO THE HEBREWS: JESUS AS HIGH PRIEST

Jesus and High Priesthood

The Letter to the Hebrews uses the Hebrew Bible to interpret Jesus. Every step of the way its argument depends upon interpretation of the Hebrew Bible. Hebrews is especially interested in using priestly concepts and images to explain Jesus and his function. The chief category of analysis is that of high priest. All high priests are mediators between God and the people. Their function is to remove any obstacles, particularly sin and impurity, between God and the congregation. That is precisely the function of Jesus.

Hebrews 1–3 establishes that Jesus is greater than the prophets, the angels, and Moses. The book begins,

Long ago God spoke to our ancestors in many and various ways by the prophets, but in these last days he has spoken to us by a Son, whom he appointed heir of all

375

things, through whom he also created the worlds. He is the reflection of God's glory and the exact imprint of God's very being, and he sustains all things by his powerful word. When he had made purification for sins, he sat down at the right hand of the Majesty on high, having become as much superior to angels as the name he has inherited is more excellent than theirs. (1:1-4)

Jesus is spoken of in terms that recall the personification of wisdom seen in Proverbs 8–9, Sirach 24, *1 Enoch 42,* Wisdom 7, and elsewhere. In the Jewish wisdom tradition of the Hellenistic period, Jewish speculation stopped just short of considering wisdom a goddess. She was present at the creation, and God created the world through her. In Wisdom 7 she is the perfect representation of God, and the one who holds the universe together. Ideas about wisdom are used in Hebrews 1:1-4 to interpret Jesus. Jesus becomes more than human. He becomes the one through whom the universe was created and the perfect reflection of God. In Hebrews 1:4, Jesus' work is conceived of as purification, the task proper for priests.

At the end of chapter 4, the high priesthood of Jesus begins to receive detailed treatment. Jesus was fully human and suffered as do all humans, and so he can represent humans before God. At the same time, he has passed through the heavens and is present with God, and so can represent God to humans. He is the perfect mediator. Hebrews 5 elaborates on Jesus' participation in humanity, his suffering, and his choice by God to be high priest. Two passages from Scripture are introduced that are taken to refer to God's choice of Jesus as high priest. The first is Psalm 2:7: "You are my Son; today I have begotten you" (Heb 5:5). The second establishes the possibility of being a priest outside of the tribe of Levi: "You are a priest forever, according to the order of Melchizedek" (Heb 5:6; quoting Ps 110:4).

Jesus and Melchizedek

Chapter 7 takes up the idea of Melchizedek's priesthood again. Melchizedek is a "type" of Jesus. That means that Melchizedek was a figure who lived before Jesus and foreshadowed him. Melchizedek is an obscure figure who appears in Genesis 14:17-20. He is king of Salem (probably Jerusalem) who brings out bread and wine to Abraham who is returning from war. Melchizedek is said to be "priest of God Most High." Abraham gives him tithes from the spoils from his battles. Since Melchizedek's parents are not mentioned in Genesis, Hebrews argues from silence and concludes that he has none, and therefore has no beginning and so is eternal, as is his priesthood. In this he resembles the "Son of God," Jesus, who also has no beginning and possesses an eternal priesthood. Because Abraham gives tithes to him, Hebrews concludes that Melchizedek is superior to Abraham, and since Levi is in the loins of Abraham when he pays tithes, Melchizedek is superior to Levi and to the priestly tribe descended from him. Strange though this reasoning may seem, it is the same sort of analysis used by Stoics of the Hellenistic and Roman period on their own texts, and employed by Jewish analysts on the Jewish Scriptures. The analysis assumes that the biblical text is literally inspired, and that the smallest details of the Bible contain secrets that can be discovered by allegorical methods.

Now Hebrews introduces Jesus into the argument.

> Now if perfection had been attainable through the levitical priesthood—for the people received the law under this priesthood—what further need would there have been to speak of another priest arising according to the order of Melchizedek, rather than one according to the order of Aaron? For when there is a change in the priesthood, there is necessarily a change in the law as well. Now the one of whom these things are spoken belonged to another tribe, from which no one has ever served at the altar. For it is evident that our Lord [Jesus] was descended from Judah, and in connection with that tribe Moses said nothing about priests.
> (7:11-14)

A Jewish priest must be a member of the tribe of Levi. But God chose Jesus to be high priest, and Jesus was of the tribe of Judah. Scripture does speak of another priest, outside the tribe of Levi, namely Melchizedek (Gen 14:18; Ps 110:4). So Jesus must be of the order of Melchizedek. The parallels between Jesus and Melchizedek confirm that. That a priest arises (Jesus) who is outside the Levitical priesthood proves that the Levitical priesthood was inadequate, for God does not do unnecessary things. The text goes farther and claims that since the priesthood and the Law are so closely associated (the people receive the Law through the priests and the priests are governed by the Law), the change in the priesthood implied by Jesus' appointment must entail a change in the Law itself. For Hebrews, Christianity leaves the Jewish Torah behind.

The author brings the argument together in the next verses.

> It is even more obvious when another priest arises, resembling Melchizedek, one who has become a priest, not through a legal requirement concerning physical descent, but through the power of an indestructible life. For it is attested of him, "You are a priest forever, according to the order of Melchizedek" [Ps 110:4]. There is, on the one hand, the abrogation of an earlier commandment because it was weak and ineffectual (for the law made nothing perfect); there is, on the other hand, the introduction of a better hope, through which we approach God. (7:15-19)

Having an "indestructible life" connects Jesus with Melchizedek, and becomes the credential that qualifies each for priesthood. The Torah and its Levitical priesthood are "useless" since they cannot really bring people near God, the aim of priestly activity. The permanence of Jesus, who has no beginning or end, demonstrates the superiority of his priesthood.

The former priests were many in number, because they were prevented by death from continuing in office; but he holds his priesthood permanently, because he continues forever. Consequently he is able for all time to save those who approach God through him, since he always lives to make intercession for them. For it was fitting that we should have such a high priest, holy, blameless, undefiled, separated from sinners, and exalted above the heavens. Unlike the other high priests, he has no need to offer sacrifices day after day, first for his own sins, and then for those of the people; this he did once for all when he offered himself. For the law appoints as high priests those who are subject to weakness, but the word of the oath, which came later than the law, appoints a Son who has been made perfect forever.

(7:23-28)

"Perfect" is a word common in Hellenistic religions and philosophies, and denotes an advanced state of being. In some cases, it means to have left the limitations of this world behind. Hebrews characteristically combines Hellenistic philosophical notions with biblical concepts and images. In a priestly sense, to be "perfect" means to be able to be in the presence of God. It is equivalent to being ritually pure. Because Jesus is perfect for ever, he is for ever in the presence of God, and therefore is capable of making constant intercession for his followers. All high priests need sacrifices in order to enter the sanctuary, and Jesus sacrifices himself.

Jesus' Sacrifice

Hebrews 8 argues that the new covenant, predicted by Jeremiah 31, is superior to the old. Everything having to do with Mosaic religion was but a shadow of what was to come through Jesus. Hebrews 9 describes the earthly Temple in Jerusalem. The climax of the description comes in 9:6-7: "The priests go continually into the first tent to carry out their ritual duties; but only the high priest goes into the second, and he but once a year, and not without taking the blood that he offers for himself and for the sins committed unintentionally by the people." There follows an allegorical interpretation of the Temple, making the outer tent symbolic for the present age, which must be passed through in order to reach the sanctuary, where God is (9:8-10). But 9:11-28 supplies an alternative allegorical interpretation, in which the sanctuary is heaven, abode of God, and the outer tent stands for this world. In this second interpretation Jesus as high priest enters the sanctuary, heaven, once and for all.

Once a year, on the Day of Atonement, the high priest goes into the sanctuary. He brings the blood of animals to cleanse the sanctuary, thereby atoning for the sins of priests and people (Leviticus 16). Jesus' activity is analogous to that of the high priest. When Jesus enters the heavenly sanctuary, of which the earthly is but a shadow, he also must bring blood. The general priestly principle is stated in 9:22: "Under the law almost everything is purified with blood, and without the shedding of blood there is no forgiveness of sins.'' Here the bloody death of Jesus is interpreted as a sacrifice, analogous to the Temple sacrifices.

> Thus it was necessary for the sketches of the heavenly things to be purified with these rites, but the heavenly things themselves need better sacrifices than these. For Christ did not enter a sanctuary made by human hands, a mere copy of the true one, but he entered into heaven itself, now to appear in the presence of God on our behalf. Nor was it to offer himself again and again, as the high priest enters the Holy Place year after year with blood that is not his own; for then he would have had to suffer again and again since the foundation of the world. But as it is, he has appeared once for all at the end of the age to remove sin by the sacrifice of himself.
> (9:23-26)

The phrase ''Holy Place'' here denotes the innermost room of the Temple, as is clear from the fact that the high priest enters it only once a year. The terminology thus differs from the more usual usage of ''Holy Place'' for the outer room of the Temple, and ''Holy of Holies'' for the inner room. Jesus has attained access to God, and he has done this by sacrificing himself. Jesus is both priest and sacrificial victim. His death purifies not only himself, but all Christians.

Fleshly and Heavenly

Throughout Hebrews, there is a contrast between the Jewish and the Christian cults in which the Jewish cult is seen as fleshly and the Christian is seen as heavenly. This contrast is informed by a Platonic view of the universe as divided between the physical and the spiritual. In Hebrews 12 the contrast is extended to Mount Sinai, Mount Zion, and Jerusalem.

> You have not come to something that can be touched, a blazing fire, and darkness, and gloom, and a tempest, and the sound of a trumpet, and a voice whose words made the hearers beg that not another word be spoken to them. (For they could not endure the order that was given, ''If even an animal touches the mountain, it shall be stoned to death.'' Indeed, so terrifying was the sight that Moses said, ''I tremble with fear.'') But you have come to Mount Zion and to the city of the living God, the heavenly Jerusalem, and to innumerable angels in festal gathering, and to the assembly of the firstborn who are enrolled in heaven, and to God the judge of all, and to the spirits of the righteous made perfect, and to Jesus, the mediator of a new covenant, and to the sprinkled blood that speaks a better word than the blood of Abel. (12:18-24)

Fire, darkness, and tempest refer to the theophany (divine appearance) at Sinai. As terrifying as that was, its holiness was but a shadow of the true access to heaven that Christians now enjoy through Christ. Similarly, Jerusalem is but a shadow of the heavenly Jerusalem.

Hebrews 13 draws the conclusion to which all of Hebrews has been leading. Since Judaism possesses only the shadows of the reality Christians have attained in Christ, Christians should make a clear break with Judaism. In 13:13, this is put in biblical terms. Christians are exhorted, "Let us then go to him [Jesus] outside the camp." "Camp" is a biblical term for Israel. It is taken from a military situation, where Israel is encamped and ready for holy war.

The Letter to the Hebrews depends heavily on Jewish cultic terms and concepts, as well as on other elements drawn from the Hebrew Bible, to interpret Jesus, his work, and the Christian church. What the Jewish cult symbolizes, the Christian cult possesses in reality. The high priest's job is to remove the obstacles between Israel and God. In reality, he cannot do so. Jesus establishes permanent access to the heavenly sanctuary for Christians. The result is a negation of Judaism in view of the fact that Christianity has surpassed it. This is quite a different solution to the problem of the relation between Judaism and Christianity from that adopted by Matthew.

THE BOOK OF REVELATION: JESUS AS ESCHATOLOGICAL WARRIOR

Historical Setting

Although the New Testament is full of apocalyptic imagery, symbols, and concepts, the book of Revelation is its only apocalypse. The Greek word translated "revelation" in the title of the work is *apocalypsis*. Some versions of the Bible leave the title of the book untranslated, and call it the Apocalypse. It was from the title of this book that scholars adapted the word "apocalypse" as the name of the genre to which this and similar books belong. Like all apocalypses, Revelation tells the story of a revelation given to a seer (John) concerning the heavenly world and the eschaton. The historical situation within which the book was written was the persecution of Christians and Jews under the Roman emperor Domitian in 96 CE. Unlike most of his predecessors, Domitian insisted on emperor worship, and punishment was threatened against those who refused. Although the persecution was not widespread and few lost their lives, Revelation was written when Christians thought the full powers of the Roman Empire were being mobilized against them.

Satan and the Roman Empire

The Christians who wrote and read this book faced the greatest power the world had ever known: Rome. It was obvious to them that the power behind the Roman Empire was more than human. Such tremendous might must have a supernatural source. Since Roman might was aimed at the heart of Christianity, the worship of God and Christ, the supernatural force behind the empire had to be evil. Revelation 12 and 13 explain the evil force. Chapter 12 opens with the vision of a woman in heaven, probably representing the heavenly Israel. Then

380

another figure appears: "A great red dragon, with seven heads and ten horns, and seven diadems on his heads. His tail swept down a third of the stars of heaven" (12:3-4). As is revealed farther on, the dragon is Satan. His portrayal as a red dragon with horns and a long tail is the source of modern depictions of the devil. The dragon causes havoc in heaven. Since the stars are heavenly beings (angels, in Judaism), the dragon wages war directly on them.

The heavenly war is described more explicitly in the next verses.

> War broke out in heaven; Michael and his angels fought against the dragon. The dragon and his angels fought back, but they were defeated, and there was no longer any place for them in heaven. The great dragon was thrown down, that ancient serpent, who is called the Devil and Satan, the deceiver of the whole world—he was thrown down to the earth, and his angels were thrown down with him. (12:7-9)

The description of Satan derives from his identification with the "ancient serpent" that deceived Adam and Eve, and through them the whole world (Genesis 3). Satan was originally an angel in heaven. In Job 2 and Zechariah 3 he is the heavenly prosecuting attorney. Eventually Satan was associated with the angels who left their place in heaven and thus disobeyed God (Genesis 6; *Book of the Watchers*). Revelation 12 draws on a tradition that sees the departure of the disobedient angels from heaven as the result of a war with angels loyal to God. The rest of Revelation 12 hails Satan's defeat as a victory for God and those faithful to God. Having been thrown down to earth from heaven, the dragon tries to pursue the woman, who now also is on earth. He fails. "Then the dragon was angry with the woman, and went off to make war on the rest of her children, those who keep the commandments of God and hold the testimony of Jesus. Then the dragon took his stand on the sand of the seashore" (12:17-18). The rest of the woman's children are those whom Revelation considers faithful Christians. Satan's anger at Christians explains their present suffering. The sea symbolizes supernatural forces against God.

Chapter 13 opens with a strange and terrifying beast rising out of the sea. The scene recalls Daniel 7, in which four beasts from the sea represent kingdoms. In Revelation 13 the beast is the Roman Empire. "And the dragon gave it his power and his throne and great authority. . . . They worshiped the dragon, for he had given his authority to the beast, and they worshiped the beast, saying, 'Who is like the beast, and who can fight against it?'" (13:2, 4). The might of the Roman Empire is explained. Satan gave it his authority and power. Subsequent verses detail Satan's campaign against God and against those who are loyal to God.

The Apocalyptic Jesus

Chapters 12 and 13 furnish a framework within which to view Domitian's persecution. The rest of Revelation gives hope to those exposed to Satan's wrath.

381

Satan's defeat in heaven is but a prelude to his final defeat at the end of time at the hands of Jesus the eschatological warrior. But Jesus has already defeated Satan, because when Jesus walked the earth he resisted Satan, even to death. Christian martyrs are assured that by their deaths they too overcome Satan and gain entry into the heavenly sanctuary. In Revelation 5 Christ appears in heaven as a slain lamb. A sealed scroll containing God's plans for the final battles against evil can be opened only by Jesus. When he does so, the plan is set in motion, and the battle between good and evil begins. Christians participate in that battle as they resist Satan's onslaughts on earth by means of the Roman Empire.

Jesus is first introduced in Revelation with the following words: "Jesus Christ, the faithful witness, the firstborn of the dead, and the ruler of the kings of the earth" (1:5). Jesus' "witness" is his testimony to God even in the midst of persecution. His resurrection vindicates him, and is but the first of many resurrections. All faithful to God will rise in the end. Jesus' power is expressed in that he is ruler of all kings. Christians have nothing to fear from the Roman Emperor, who is but a king of the earth.

The seer, John, is granted a vision of Christ in all his supernatural glory and strength. He sees

> One like the Son of Man, clothed with a long robe and with a golden sash across his chest. His head and his hair were white as white wool, white as snow; his eyes were like a flame of fire, his feet were like burnished bronze, refined as in a furnace, and his voice was like the sound of many waters. In his right hand he held seven stars, and from his mouth came a sharp, two-edged sword, and his face was like the sun shining with full force. (1:13-16)

Jesus portrayed in these terms would be a comfort to Christians who thought that they were opposed by Satan himself. A Christ of such supernatural and terrifying magnitude could be a match for the prince of demons.

Chapter 14 contains an image of Jesus as the Son of Man who reaps the earth. Harvest is a common apocalyptic image for the final judgment in which good and bad are finally separated.

> Then I looked, and there was a white cloud, and seated on the cloud was one like the Son of Man, with a golden crown on his head, and a sharp sickle in his hand! Another angel came out of the temple, calling with a loud voice to the one who sat on the cloud, "Use your sickle and reap, for the hour to reap has come, because the harvest of the earth is fully ripe." So the one who sat on the cloud swung his sickle over the earth, and the earth was reaped. (14:14-16)

Warlike imagery is employed in chapter 19 to depict Jesus' going out to the final battle with Satan.

Then I saw heaven opened, and there was a white horse! Its rider is called Faithful and True, and in righteousness he judges and makes war. His eyes are like a flame of fire, and on his head are many diadems; and he has a name inscribed that no one knows but himself. He is clothed in a robe dipped in blood, and his name is called The Word of God. And the armies of heaven, wearing fine linen, white and pure, were following him on white horses. From his mouth comes a sharp sword with which to strike down the nations, and he will rule them with a rod of iron; he will tread the winepress of the fury of the wrath of God the Almighty. On his robe and on his thigh he has a name inscribed, "King of kings and Lord of lords."

(19:11-16)

It is this eschatological warrior who conquers Satan.

Revelation is roughly contemporary with 4 Ezra and *2 Baruch*. The latter two works envision an earthly messianic kingdom that has an end, followed by a more complete fulfillment of eschatological hopes. Revelation follows this same pattern. In 20:1-6, Satan is bound in the abyss, and the martyrs rise to rule the earth with Christ for one thousand years. Then Satan is released, a final battle is fought in which he is defeated, and all the forces of evil are thrown into a lake of fire to be tormented forever.

The New Jerusalem

Chapter 21 describes the descent onto earth of a new Jerusalem. In the new Jerusalem the faithful live without suffering or sorrow. God's blessings are showered on it.

I saw no temple in the city, for its temple is the Lord God the Almighty and the Lamb. And the city has no need of sun or moon to shine on it, for the glory of God is its light, and its lamp is the Lamb. The nations will walk by its light, and the kings of the earth will bring their glory into it. Its gates will never be shut by day—and there will be no night there. People will bring into it the glory and the honor of the nations. But nothing unclean will enter it, nor anyone who practices abomination or falsehood, but only those who are written in the Lamb's book of life. (21:22-27)

Revelation's symbols and concepts are rooted in Judaism. It is the new Jerusalem that is the goal of history. Zion ideology supplies the images for the description of God's eschatological city. Priestly terminology is used to speak of the holiness of the city. But entry into the new Jerusalem is determined by one's name being written in the "Lamb's book of life." The idea of heavenly books containing judgments on humans and angels is common in apocalypticism. Here it is the adherents of Christianity, followers of "the Lamb," who are saved. The absence of a temple in the new Jerusalem may be a claim to superiority over the Jewish cult.

CONCLUSION

Jesus and his first followers were Jews; of that there is no doubt. To understand the historical Jesus one must see him in the light of first-century Jewish Palestine. The same is true of the earliest Christian movement. This final chapter goes farther and demonstrates that an appreciation of late Second Temple Judaism also contributes much to the interpretations of Jesus that were devised after his death. The Jewishness of Jesus was taken seriously not only by the first Jewish Christians who struggled to grasp who Jesus was and what God had done through him. His Jewishness was also taken as an axiom of later interpretations of Jesus. If Jesus was a Jewish messiah foretold by the Hebrew Bible, then it is in Jewish terms that one must understand him. The texts analyzed in this chapter show three different ways of understanding Jesus in Jewish terms. For Matthew, Jesus is Torah teacher. For Hebrews he is high priest. For Revelation, Jesus is eschatological warrior. These are but three examples of how Judaism was integral not only to Jesus himself, but to early Christian interpretations of him.

SELECT BIBLIOGRAPHY

Attridge, Harold W. *Hebrews*. Philadelphia: Fortress Press, 1989.

Bornkamm, G., G. Barth, and H. J. Held. *Tradition and Interpretation in Matthew*, Philadelphia: Westminster Press, 1963.

Bourke, Myles M. "The Epistle to the Hebrews," in *NJBC*, 920-41.

Caird, G. B. *A Commentary on the Revelation of St. John the Divine*. London: Adam and Charles Black, 1966.

Charles R. H. *A Critical and Exegetical Commentary on the Revelation of St. John*, 2 vols. New York: Scribner's, 1920.

Collins, Adela Yarbro. "The Apocalypse (Revelation)," in *NJBC*, 996-1016.

―――. *The Combat Myth in the Book of Revelation*. Missoula, Mont.: Scholars Press, 1976.

―――. *Crisis and Catharsis: The Power of the Apocalypse*, Philadelphia: Westminster Press, 1984.

Davies, W. D. *The Sermon on the Mount*. Cambridge: Cambridge University Press, 1966.

Fiorenza, Elisabeth Schüssler. *Invitation to the Apocalypse*. Garden City, N.Y.: Doubleday & Co., 1981.

Kingsbury, Jack Dean. *Matthew: Structure, Christology, Kingdom*. Philadelphia: Fortress Press, 1975.

Meier, John. *The Vision of Matthew*. New York: Paulist Press, 1979.

Overman, J. Andrew. *Matthew's Gospel and Formative Judaism: The Social World of the Matthean Community*. Minneapolis: Fortress Press, 1990.

Tilborg, S. van. *The Jewish Leaders in Matthew*. Leiden: Brill, 1972.

PART IV

Notes, Glossary, Index

NOTES

INTRODUCTION

1. This book uses the term "Hebrew Bible" rather than "Old Testament." The latter term implies that there is a *new* testament or covenant, and so contains a Christian bias. "Hebrew Bible" is a descriptive term for the texts written mostly in Hebrew and held sacred by both Jews and Christians.

2. "BCE" stands for "before the common era," and "CE" for "common era." The common era is the time shared by Jews and Christians. Christians are accustomed to use "BC," standing for "before Christ" and "AD" standing for "Anno Domini," the Latin for "year of the Lord." Since not everyone is Christian, "BCE" and "CE" are preferable.

1. PREEXILIC ISRAEL

1. "Reed Sea" is the correct translation of the Hebrew phrase *Yam Sûph*. The popular idea that Moses led the people through the midst of the *Red Sea* has no foundation in the text.

2. The section on ancient Jewish society depends on Saldarini, following Lenski, Eisenstadt, Sjoberg, et al.

3. Saldarini, 5.

4. Sjoberg, 109, as quoted in Saldarini, 25.

5. Saldarini, 39-45, following Lenski, 214-96.

6. This section depends on Malina.

3. THE EXILE

1. "Chaldeans" is the name of the people who ruled in Babylonia at this period.

2. The Hebrew text has "The Lord Yahweh." It cannot be translated "The Lord LORD," so the problem is solved by translating "Yahweh" as "GOD." *See also* the explanation of "LORD" in chapter 1.

3. Menstruation was thought to make women impure. It is used as a paradigm of impurity here and elsewhere.

4. By this is meant the attitude that certain acts, like offering an animal to God or cleansing the sanctuary with blood, will automatically bring about an effect like God's forgiveness. Ezekiel holds no such view.

5. Note the similarity of this chapter to the good shepherd imagery of John 10 and the last judgment scene of Matthew 25.

6. The mountain to the east is the Mount of Olives. This passage may have inspired Luke's version of the ascension of Jesus from the Mount of Olives. *See* Klaus Baltzer, "The Meaning of the Temple in the Lukan Writings," *HTR* 58 (1965): 263-77.

4. THE RESTORATION

1. Not all material in Ezra 3–6 is from this period; 4:7-23 is from the next century.

2. Zechariah 9–14 is a later addition to the book.

3. Genesis does not say that the serpent who deceived Adam and Eve was Satan. Later tradition makes the identification, but there is no indication that the Yahwist had any such figure in mind.

4. *See* Hanson.

5. "To draw near" means to go to God's Temple to participate in the cult. There "judgments" can be obtained through the priests.

5. HELLENISM AND THE MACCABEES

1. "Ben" means "son" in Hebrew. Jews did not have surnames, so they used fathers' names to distinguish persons with the same first names. The book of Sirach is also called Ecclesiasticus.

6. APOCALYPTICISM

1. Collins, *AI,* 4.

2. Collins, *AI,* 10, following Koch, 28-33.

3. Compare Jesus' beatitudes (Matt 5:3-12; Luke 6:20-23).

4. Nickelsburg, "Apocalyptic and Myth."

5. *See* Suter.

6. Collins, AI, 39.

7. Passages in this section noted RSV follow the Revised Standard Version. The NRSV obscures the Aramaic bar 'ĕnāš (literally "son of man") by translating it as "human being." The more literal translation makes the following discussion intelligible, and it suggests a connection between Daniel 7 and the term "Son of Man" in the gospels.

8. Knibb shows that in "intertestamental literature" the idea is common that the Babylonian Exile did not really end under the Persians.

7. QUMRAN: A PRIESTLY, APOCALYPTIC COMMUNITY

1. References to documents are according to the following convention. The first number is the number of the cave in which the scroll was found. The "Q" stands for "Qumran." What follows "Q" is usually an abbreviation of the name of the document but sometimes this is replaced by the number of the fragment on which the text is found. In the case of the *Community Rule,* the scroll was found in cave one, and it is called *Serek* meaning "Rule" in Hebrew.

2. The *Damascus Document* does not follow the convention mentioned in the note above because two medieval copies of it were originally discovered at a synagogue in Cairo at the end of the last century. Extensive fragments of the work were found at Qumran.

3. Translation of the Qumran texts are from Vermes, *DSSE.* Passages in the scrolls are referred to by column number only, since it is assumed that readers will be using *DSSE,* without line numbers. Within quotations from the scrolls, parentheses indicate "glosses necessary for fluency," and brackets "likely reconstructions" (*DSSE,* 58).

4. The text actually reads "Belial."

5. The reference to exile in Damascus is why this text is called the *Damascus Document.* Most scholars doubt that the geographical indication is to be taken literally. It may refer to the Qumran settlement itself as an exile, or purely figuratively to the fact that the sect is not in control of Judaism, as it should be.

NOTES

6. Many of the scrolls, including the *Damascus Document,* are to some degree fragmentary. We do not possess the entire *Damascus Document.* Vermes has rearranged the document, putting columns 15–16 after 9, because that seems to have been the original order of the text.

7. The practice of swearing by holy objects such as the Temple is attested in the Gospel of Matthew, where Jesus forbids swearing by heaven which is God's throne, earth which is God's footstool, the Temple, or one's head (Matt 5:33-37).

8. *See* Jesus' question about saving a life on the sabbath (Mark 3:4).

9. What follows is similar to Josephus' report on requirements for admission to the sect.

10. "Jerusalem" is supplied by Vermes, and is supported by 1QM 7, discussed below.

11. In the citations of the commentaries, "p" indicates that the document is a pesher, and it is followed by an abbreviation of the biblical book to be explained.

12. According to Vermes' numbering, those are 1, 2, and 7-11.

13. This echoes Psalm 41:9: "Even my bosom friend in whom I trusted, who ate of my bread, has lifted the heel against me." John 13:18 uses the same verse to characterize Judas' betrayal of Jesus.

8. SCRIBES, PHARISEES, AND SADDUCEES

1. This section depends on Saldarini. To fill in some of the gaps in the evidence, he uses comparative material from Egyptian, Mesopotamian, Greek, and Greco-Roman sources.

2. Saldarini, 312.

3. 3rd rev. ed. Oxford: Clarendon Press, 1955. Quoted in Neusner, *Politics,* 5.

4. *Politics,* 81.

5. Neusner, *Politics,* 83.

6. Saldarini, 280.

9. TRANSITION TO ROMAN RULE

1. "Caesar" was originally the proper name of a Roman family. After the death of Julius Caesar it became one of the titles of the Roman emperor. The Caesar referred to here is Augustus, formerly Octavian, adopted son of Julius.

2. In the gospels the "Herodians" are mentioned several times. They were probably people associated with one of the Herodian courts in some capacity (Saldarini, 149, n. 15. *See* bibliographical information there.).

3. The nickname means "little boots" and was a name from his childhood.

4. Acts 12 says that Agrippa I killed the apostle James and arrested Peter. Agrippa's death is considered punishment for blasphemy in Acts 12.

5. *See* the *Damascus Document,* where the exile did not end with Cyrus but continued up to the time of the Qumran community. *See also 1 Enoch 89:73* and Knibb (in bibliography of chap. 6).

6. This section depends on Collins.

7. *JLBBM,* 214, 227 n. 10.

8. This is similar to the view of the Gospel of John. There the only way to be in touch with God is through the only one who has ever descended from heaven, the Son of Man. The influence of wisdom theology on the christology of John has long been recognized.

9. Charles (*APOT,* 237) was so surprised by the identification of Enoch with the Son of Man that he changed the text to *"This* is the Son of Man."

10. JEWISH PALESTINE UNDER ROME

1. Much of this chapter, particularly the analysis of social groups, depends on Horsley and Hanson.

2. "Revolutionaries" as used here means those who would overthrow the power structure through violent means.

3. The translation of the Greek here retains the Greek form of the bandit's name. "Hezekiah" is the Hebrew form. Similarly, "Judas" is the Greek form of "Judah."

4. In addition to the passages discussed here, *see Ant.* 20.5.2 § 102; *War* 2.17.8 § 433; 7.8.1 § 253.

5. *See* Mark 7:11.

6. Mark 6:17-29 and parallels.

7. At Qumran baptism also had eschatological significance. In 1QS 3, it is made clear that baptism depends on one's inner disposition, so that passage furnishes a further parallel to Josephus' description of John's baptism.

11. JESUS, A JEW OF FIRST-CENTURY PALESTINE

1. It is called "Q," after the German word *Quelle*, "source."

2. Different scholars explain these somewhat differently. What follows combines Perrin ("The Presupposition"), Fuller, and Meier.

3. 11.

4. *Jesus the Jew*, 69-80.

5. Horsley, *Spiral*, 203-7.

6. Sanders, chap. 1.

7. Horsley, *Spiral*, chap. 10.

8. This section depends largely on Perrin and Duling, 412-25.

9. *See* Tannehill.

10. *See* 4 Ezra 7:3-9.

11. *Jesus and the Language*, 28.

12. *See* Hollenbach, "Liberating."

13. This section draws on Sanders, chap. 9.

14. Matt 8:11; Mark 14:25 and parallels; Matt 22:1-14 and Luke 14:16-24; etc.

15. Mark 6:4 and parallels; Luke 4:24; 13:33; Luke 13:34-35 and parallels; John 4:44.

12. THE REVOLT AGAINST THE ROMANS

1. This section follows the discussion of Goodman.

2. This section depends on Horsley, Rhoads, and Schürer.

3. The word translated "fanatics" here is the Greek *zēlōtas*, which could be translated "zealots." This reference does not seem to denote the later Zealots, and Josephus makes no such connection. (*See* Horsley, *Bandits*, 214.)

4. That stricture was so odious to the Jews that it caused yet another uprising under the next emperor, Antoninus Pius, who rescinded the order.

5. This section depends primarily on Neusner.

6. 4 Ezra consists of chaps. 3-14 of 2 *Esdras*, which is part of the Apocrypha. Chaps. 1-2 and 15-16 are later Christian additions.

7. Two other apocalyptic responses are 2 *Baruch*, to be discussed below, and the *Apocalypse of Abraham*, not treated in this work.

8. The entire discussion here is similar to that in John 3 between Jesus and Nicodemus. *See* esp. John 3:11-13.

9. Similar images are ascribed to Jesus in Mark 13.

10. Compare Jesus' words, "Enter through the narrow gate; for the gate is wide and the road is easy that leads to destruction, and there are many who take it. For the gate is narrow and the road is hard that leads to life, and there are few who find it." (Matt 7:13-14).

11. Jesus says, "Many are called, but few are chosen" (Matt 22:14).

GLOSSARY

Anointed. Smear with oil as a sign of designation for a special task. "Messiah" is from the Hebrew and "Christ" is from the Greek for "anointed."

Apocalypse. "A genre of revelatory literature with a narrative framework, in which a revelation is mediated by an otherworldly being to a human recipient, disclosing a transcendent reality which is both temporal, insofar as it envisages eschatological salvation, and spatial insofar as it involves another, supernatural world" (*AI*, 4).

Apocalyptic. Typical of apocalypses.

Apocalypticism. The world view typical of apocalypses.

Apocrypha. Books contained in the Septuagint, but not in the Hebrew Bible. Most are accepted by Catholics as canonical (and so are called "Deuterocanonical"), but not by Protestants or Jews.

Apostasy. Abandonment of one's religious faith or loyalty to God.

Ark of the Covenant. Box that served as a traveling shrine for the Israelites, in which were the tablets of the covenant. It was deposited in the Holy of Holies in Solomon's Temple, but apparently did not survive the destruction of the Temple by the Babylonians.

Asia Minor. Ancient name for what is now Asian Turkey.

Babylonian Exile. The deportation of the leading citizens of the kingdom of Judah to Babylonia in 587 BCE. Cyrus allowed them to return in 538 BCE.

Bandits. Members of groups (bands) who lived on the fringes of society by raiding.

Běrîth. Hebrew word for "covenant."

Canon. Sacred books considered normative. Books considered to be part of the Bible.

Christ. "Anointed," from the Greek *christos*.

Circumcision. A cutting off of the foreskin of Jewish males as a sign of the covenant.

Cosmology. A system of knowledge dealing with the nature of the universe.

Cosmos. From the Greek *kosmos* meaning "ordered universe."

391

GLOSSARY

Covenant. An agreement or pact between two parties. Hittite suzerainty covenants (treaties) were the model for Israel's relation with God.

Cult. Practices centering on the Temple, its sacrifices, and its liturgy.

Day of Atonement. An important feast day in the fall when atonement was made for the people and priests, and the Temple was cleansed.

Dead Sea Scrolls. Scrolls discovered in 1947 and in following years which are thought to be connected to the nearby settlement of Qumran.

Determinism. The belief that everything is preordained, including human history.

Deuteronomistic. Characteristic of the Deuteronomistic History (Deuteronomy through 2 Kings).

Diaspora. A general name for the Jewish communities outside Palestine.

Dispersion. English translation of "Diaspora."

Elder. A group within the ruling classes of ancient Israel. Elders were prominent citizens, probably the leading members of the leading families.

Epicureans. Hellenistic philosophical school that denied divine providence.

Eschatology. Teaching concerning the end of things. Apocalyptic eschatology refers to the end of the world and society as presently constituted.

Eschaton. From the Greek, meaning "end." In apocalypticism it refers to the end of the world as presently constituted.

Essenes. A Jewish sect believed to be responsible for the Qumran library.

Ex eventu prophecy. Prophecy after the event, typical of apocalypses.

Exile. See Babylonian Exile.

Genealogy. A list of one's ancestors.

Gentiles. Non-Jews.

Gerizim. The sacred mountain of the Samaritans, located near ancient Shechem.

Halakah. Jewish law.

Ḥănnukāh. A feast celebrating the Maccabean victory over the Seleucids.

Ḥăsîdîm. A group devoted to Torah that supported the Maccabees in the early stages of the revolution.

Hasmoneans. Name used for the Jewish dynasty established by the priest Mattathias and his five sons who revolted against the Seleucids.

Hellenism. Multifaceted culture created through the interaction of Greek culture and local cultures beginning with the conquests of Alexander the Great.

Hellenistic reform. An attempt, begun in 175 BCE by some members of the upper classes of Jerusalem, to make the city and its institutions Hellenistic.

Ḥerem. Spoils of war belonging to God, and meant to be offered to God in holocaust.

Ḥesed. God's lovingkindness for Israel, expressed in God's deeds on behalf of Israel.

Holy of Holies. Innermost and most sacred room of the Temple.

GLOSSARY

Holy Place. The nave of the Temple. The second holiest room of the Temple, where most of the activity within the building took place.

Holy War. War in which God fights on behalf of Israel.

Horeb. Name given to Mount Sinai by the northern Israelite tribes.

Idumeans. Natives of the territory south of Judah. They were forcibly circumcised by John Hyrcanus. Herod the Great was an Idumean.

Israel. Name adopted by the northern kingdom after the split with the Davidic dynasty. The name is applied more broadly to the southern kingdom after the fall of the north, as well as to all worshipers of Yahweh descended from them.

Jamnia. Roman name for the town called Yavneh on the Mediterranean coast of Palestine where Yohanan ben Zakkai went during the Jewish revolt. It became the first center of rabbinic Judaism after 70 CE.

Jews. All who are descended from the natives of the ancient kingdom of Judah.

Judea. Name given by the Romans to the area controlled by the city of Jerusalem.

Kingdom of God. God's rule, expressed through mighty deeds. Precisely how the kingdom works itself out in history (or at the eschaton) changes with different authors and contexts.

Levites. Israel's lower clergy, of the tribe of Levi.

Maccabeus. Name meaning "hammer," applied to Judas son of Mattathias, probably for his military feats against the Seleucids. Applied by extension to his brothers.

Masada. Fortress northwest of the Dead Sea where the Sicarii held the Romans off until 74 CE.

Messiah. From the Hebrew word for "anointed." One who is set aside and anointed to perform a special task for God.

Mishnah. Written collection of rabbinic legal rulings, written ca. 200 CE.

Monotheism. Belief in one God.

Mystery. A technical term in apocalypticism, denoting God's plans kept secret from the beginning of the world, and now revealed to a human seer through a heavenly intermediary.

Nabateans. Arab people from east of the Jordan.

Oral Torah. The name applied to the oral traditions of the Pharisees and then the rabbis. The traditions were collected and written down in rabbinic literature, and were thought to have been given to Moses on Sinai with the written Torah, and then passed down through the generations orally.

Parable. In its broad meaning, any sort of figurative speech, from similes and analogies to prophetic oracles to extended narrative metaphors. In a more restricted sense, used of short stories told by Jesus.

Parthians. Rulers of the empire east of the Roman Empire until the third century CE.

Passover. A feast celebrated in the spring that remembers God's liberation of Israel from Egypt.

GLOSSARY

Peasants. Members of the lower classes who made their living by cultivating the land. Usually the basic unit of production and consumption was the family, but local and imperial authorities supported themselves by heavily taxing the peasants.

Pentateuch. The first five books of the Hebrew Bible.

Pericope. A short unit of text.

Persia. The empire that ruled most of the eastern Mediterranean from the middle of the sixth century BCE until the conquests of Alexander the Great.

Pharaoh. The name for the ancient Egyptian kings.

Pharisees. Political interest and table fellowship group that existed from the second century BCE through the first century CE.

Priest. One of a hereditary class that had traditional rights to serve God in the sanctuary.

Prophet. One who speaks for God.

Pseudepigrapha. Books written in the name of others, usually figures from the distant past. The name is applied to a large body of literature falling outside the limits of the canon.

Pseudonymity. False or fictional attribution of a literary work.

Ptolemies. Hellenistic dynasty that ruled Egypt from the late fourth to the latter half of the first centuries BCE.

Purify. To put things back in their proper category. To remove that which defiles so that someone or something is restored to its proper state.

Purity rules. Rules safeguarding the distinction between sacred and profane.

Qumran. A settlement among the cliffs at the northwest shore of the Dead Sea. The settlement is associated with the library called the Dead Sea Scrolls found in neighboring caves.

Rabbi. A term meaning "my great one" in Hebrew and applied to teachers of Torah after the destruction of the Temple in 70 CE.

Rabbinic literature. Literature created by the rabbis. The parts mentioned in this book are the Mishnah (ca. 200 CE), Tosephta (ca. 250 CE), the Palestinian Talmud (ca. 400–450 CE), and the Babylonian Talmud (ca. 500–600 CE).

Restoration. The period of rebuilding Jerusalem, the Temple, and Jewish society after the Babylonian Exile (from 520 BCE onward).

Retainer. One, such as a scribe or a soldier, whose occupation was to serve the ruling class.

Sabbath. The seventh day, sacred to the Lord, on which no work was to be done.

Sacrifice. Something offered to God. In the case of an animal, it involved ritually slaughtering, burning some (or all) of it on the altar, and dividing the rest between the priests and offerers, or in some cases, giving it entirely to the priests.

Sadducees. A political interest group, probably composed of some of the leading priests and landowners, which existed from the latter half of the second century BCE to the destruction of Jerusalem in 70 CE.

394

GLOSSARY

Salvation. Rescue; liberation. In most of the Hebrew Bible the term refers to rescue from enemies, oppression, natural disasters, and so on. Later the term can refer to being brought to heaven to live.

Samaritans. Inhabitants of Samaria, the land between Judea and Galilee. Most Judean traditions portray the Samaritans negatively.

Sanctification. Making something or someone holy, pure, able to approach God.

Sanctuary. From the Latin *sanctus* meaning "holy." A sanctuary is a holy place. "The sanctuary" often means the Temple, or the Holy of Holies.

Sanhedrin. Governing council in Jerusalem, composed of leading priests, elders, and scribes. The Sadducees and Pharisees had members on it.

Sapiential. Having to do with wisdom.

Satan. From the Hebrew *śāṭān* meaning "accuser." Originally the angelic prosecuting attorney in God's court; later one of the names for the leader of demons.

Scribe. One whose occupation involved reading and writing.

Scroll. Roll of papyrus or treated leather used for writing.

Sect. Minority group that sees itself as separate from and opposed to the dominant society and is very conscious of its social boundaries.

Seer. One who sees visions or receives special revelations in apocalypses.

Seleucids. Dynasty that ruled Syria and other lands after the breakup of Alexander's empire.

Septuagint. An important Greek translation of the Hebrew Bible along with some other books. It was the principal version used by the early Christians. Books in the Septuagint but not in the Hebrew Bible are the Apocrypha.

Sicarii. A Jewish group that emerged in the fifties CE that used terrorist tactics against the ruling class of Judea.

Sinai. The mountain on which God gave Moses the Torah.

Society. A broad term encompassing the religious, cultural, political, economic, and kinship aspects of a group of people.

Son of God. Term applied in Jewish tradition to a Davidic king, Israel as a whole, a righteous Jew, an angel, and others. Applied by Christians to Jesus.

Son of Man. Often means simply "human being." The term can be applied to angels, in which case it is usually said that they are *like* a son of man. It is applied to the angelic representative of Israel in Daniel 7, and by the early Christians to refer to Jesus as eschatological judge, a use that parallels that found in the *Similitudes of Enoch*.

Stoics. An influential Hellenistic philosophical school to whom Josephus compares the Pharisees.

Suzerainty treaty. Treaty between a vassal and his lord. Hittite suzerainty treaties served as models for Israel's relation with God.

Synagogue. Jewish institution whose origins are obscure. It is the place where Jews meet weekly for prayer, and Torah reading and exposition.

GLOSSARY

Syncretism. Interaction of cultural elements from diverse cultures to form a new cultural entity.

Synoptic gospels. Matthew, Mark, and Luke, so called because owing to their similarities they can be placed side-by-side and compared in detail.

Tabernacles. Autumnal festival, timed to coincide with the harvest of fruits.

Talmud. Two bodies of rabbinic commentary on Mishnah, one from Babylon and the other from Palestine. They form part of the Oral Torah.

Tanak. Jewish name for the Hebrew Bible. It is an acronym for the three parts of Scripture, Torah (*Tôrāh*), Prophets (*Nĕbî'îm*), and Writings (*Kĕtûbîm*).

Tent. In the Bible "tent" often refers to the desert sanctuary.

Testament. A literary genre comprising a narrative of the last hours of an important figure, and his or her last words. In "New Testament" and "Old Testament," the term means "covenant."

Theodicy. A defense of the righteousness of God.

Theophany. A divine appearance.

Tithes. An offering to God, given to the priests, consisting of a tenth of agricultural produce.

Tôrāh. The term's earliest use meant "instruction," applied to priestly rulings or instructions. It came to be applied to the first five books of the Hebrew Bible. Later it could be used of all of Scripture, and later still of the entire Jewish way of life.

Watcher. An angelic figure who "watches," or guards.

Weeks. Feast celebrating the wheat harvest, falling fifty days after Passover.

Wisdom. Knowledge of how the universe, including human life, works. In the wisdom tradition, wisdom is available to those with the time to study wisdom handed on orally and in writing, to observe human life, and to reflect on their observations. Apocalyptic wisdom is esoteric wisdom given to an elite.

Yavneh. Town on the Mediterranean coast of Palestine to which Yohanan ben Zakkai was allowed to go by Vespasian during the seige of Jerusalem. It became the center for the rabbinic reformulation of Judaism after the war of 66–70 CE.

Zadokites. Priests descended from Solomon's high priest Zadok.

Zealots. Group of Jews from the countryside who fled to Jerusalem before the Roman advance in 67–68 CE. "Zealots" was their self-designation, alluding to their zeal for the Torah.

Zion. Name of the mountain on which the Temple was built. The word could be used more broadly to speak of all of Jerusalem.

INDEX

F

Famine, 100, 116, 127, 281, 300, 302

Fasting, 87, 124, 195, 211, 234, 334-35, 356

Fate, 138, 222-23, 241

Feasts, 77, 87-89, 100, 104, 132, 152, 173, 182, 194-99, 205, 212, 215, 289, 296, 301-3, 309, 316, 354

Felix, 302-6, 309

Festus, 306, 309

1 Enoch, 168-77, 182, 185, 188, 262-72, 336, 376

1 Maccabees, 142-43, 150-55, 242, 260

Flood, 43-44, 85

Florus, 307-9, 346-47

Forgiveness, 86, 194-95, 325-29, 335

G

Gaius (Caligula), 251, 298-99, 308-9, 345-46

Galilee, 68, 227-28, 233-34, 237, 250-51, 277-78, 282, 286, 288, 291, 298-99, 302, 308, 314-18, 321, 331, 348-49

Gamaliel, 235, 243

Garden of Eden, 44, 50, 100, 165, 172

Gentiles, 85, 97-103, 106-8, 115-18, 121-31, 147-48, 151-52, 177, 199, 211, 251-58, 261, 278, 286-87, 289, 292, 298-99, 301, 306-7, 319, 323, 328, 330, 333, 346-47, 359, 366, 375, 383

Gerizim, 279-80, 295

Greece, 59, 135-38, 140, 177, 179, 183, 197, 206, 213, 227

Greek, 138, 142, 156, 168, 251

Gymnasium, 137, 145-46

H

Harvest, 87-89, 100, 116-18

Hasmoneans, 135-62, 176, 178, 184, 188, 193, 211-13, 220, 229, 237, 243, 247-51, 255, 258-60, 273-74, 277, 288

Healing, 234, 314, 317, 319, 332, 339

Heaven, 166-74, 179-83, 206, 208, 214, 232, 252, 261-68, 290, 315, 325, 328, 331, 358, 362, 366, 376-83

Heavenly books, 174, 180, 183-84, 268, 383

Hebrew, 129, 142, 251, 273, 373

Hellenism, 135-62, 166, 179, 222-23, 240, 243-44, 249, 316, 362, 376-78

Hellenistic reform, 145-48, 156, 176, 183, 192, 197, 237, 259, 339

Herod Antipas, 234, 250-51, 273, 296, 314, 316, 347, 372

Herod the Great, 69, 76, 82, 225-28, 235, 237, 243-50, 258-59, 262, 273-74, 277, 282-99, 307-8, 316, 346, 351, 372

Herodians, 68, 220, 234, 250-51, 282, 285, 288-90, 299, 316, 346

High priest, 118-20, 126, 129, 133, 143-45, 150-56, 159, 181, 183, 189, 191, 204, 211, 226-28, 243, 247-48, 264, 284, 290, 296, 302-6, 321-22, 348-52, 375-80

Hillel, 236

History, 34-37, 50, 53, 87, 113, 137, 142-43, 149, 163-67, 173-76, 180, 183, 185, 188, 191-95, 209, 223-24, 229, 234-36, 248, 257-58, 261-62, 274, 278, 280,

R

S

T

NOTES